Sanguinomicon

THE PATH OF
VAMPYRE
MAGICK

COMPLETE 5TH EDITION
"THE STRIGOI VII CODEX"

FATHER SEBASTIAAN

BAST
BOOKS

This copy of *Sanguinomicon: The Path of Vampyre Magick* was formally consecrated on_____*(date)* and is the property of_____*(Sobriquet)*.

Fifth English Edition

Sanguinomcon, The Path of Vampyre Magick Complete Fifth Edition of The Strigioi Vii Codex

Foreword by Konstantinos

Original Vampyre Ankh Design: PN D'Drennan

Original Dragon Ouroboros Design: Mavenlore

Contributions from and special thanks to Victor Magnus, Meijin, Kaedrich Olsen, Azrael Hex, Darieum, Khassa, Rose Sinister & May Leigh

Printed in the United States of America.

Bast Books
7119 W. Sunset Blvd
Los Angeles, CA 90046

V

PRAISE

"Vampire fads come and go, emerging each decade in some new form. But for those for whom the Vampyric mystique is a calling, the choices inspired become a life path. The Sanguinomicon offers a compelling and elegant presentation of the history, rituals, and customs of a specific spiritual movement. It has the quality of permanence, and it will likely make an enduring contribution to sanguinary lore."

—Dr. Katherine Ramsland, author of
The Science of Vampires and Piercing the Darkness

"To the uninitiated, the practice of Vampyrism may seem a hidden practice which is bent on antisocial behavior and self-destructive tendencies. What The Sanguinomicon has made clear is that Vampyrism is a practice which is defined by self-preservation, enlightenment, and social interaction with those 'of the blood' who seek both spiritual and material excellence. Father Sebastiaan has gathered a striking collection of vampiric perspectives that will define a foundational consideration of Vampyrism as a living and breathing tradition. The Strigoi Vii Codex & Sanguinomicon is a suitable tome for all who seek to study or discover their potential as individuals."

—Michael W. Ford, Akhtya Nachttoter,
The Black Order of the Dragon

"The Sanguinomicon provides a unique and valid look at one of the oldest Vampyre traditions in the modern living vampire subculture. Full of rich descriptions and details of the past, it delves deep into the many aspects long whispered about in the shadows. Highly recommended."

—Corvis Nocturnum, author of *Allure of the Vampire: Our Sexual Attraction to the Undead.*

"A clearly and concisely written tome! It offers easily accessible information on the ethical and well-established ways of the Strigoi Vii. Heed well these words of wisdom and they will guide you to the gate of eternity. What you do, then, depends on you."

—Kaedrich Olsen, author of *Runes for Transformation*

"An exquisite compilation containing the mysteries of Strigoi Vii. This must-have tome encourages expansion through in-depth self-exploration upon the path of the Vampyre Magick for the beginner and the adept. I have gained great personal insight from *The Sanguinomicon* challenges you to delve into the most comprehensive and honest approach to Vampyrism available. You won't be disappointed!"

—Lucien von Wolfe, founder of *Tantric Vampires*

"A must-have for any student—or creature—of the night, whether you're interested in vampires and vampirism from a cultural and historical perspective or you want to take your magical practice to the next level. For vampires and the people who love them, this book takes a deeper, spiritual, and utterly glamorous approach to the truth in becoming a Living Vampyre. Read it to unlock secret knowledge within yourself and find the Vampyre within."

— Varla Ventura, author of *Varla Ventura's Paranormal Parlor* and *Banshees, Werewolves, Vampires, and Other Creatures of the Night*

WARNING & DISCLAIMER

The books of the *The Strigoi Vii Codex & Sanguinomicon* are written for serious individuals who wish to unlock their own hidden potential. The rituals and Mysteries within these pages require the Seeker to be of sound mind and body. If you suffer from mental disorders, such as bipolar disorder or schizophrenia or serious physical ailments, such as heart disease, epilepsy, or other chronic illnesses, please, for your own safety, refrain from exploring the Strigoi Vii Mysteries. The authors, the OSV, and the publisher will not accept responsibility for the misuse of the material contained within. Nor do they condone or endorse underage sexual behavior or illegal or criminal activities of any sort.

CONTENTS

Book 0: Liber ZHEP'R
"The ELORATHIAN / STRIGOI VII PROSPECTUS" | 1

Book I: Liber JAHIRA
"Coming forth by Day" | 77

Book II: Liber CALMAE
"Coming forth by NIGHT" | 155

Book III: Liber Morrah
"Coming forth by TWILIGHT" | 257

VAMPYRE MAGICK | 321

INTRODUCTION TO VAMPYRE MAGICK BY MICHAEL W. FORD 323

5TH EDITION SANGUINOMICON

Sanguinomicon: The Path of Vampyre Magick AKA The Strigoi Vii Codex: is the updated and revised 5th edition of Father Sebastiaan's legendary book *Vampyre Sanguinomicon: Lexicon of the Living Vampire* Weiser Books, September 2010 and *Vampyre Magick: Grimoire of the Living Vampire.* Weiser Books, February 2012.

This new edition released on Friday May 13th 2022 in hardcover and followed by a Kindle and Softcover editions. This book is the more advanced edition of the BLACK VEILS: Master Vampyre Edition 888 released in 2020. This details the initiatory teachings of the Strigoi Vii path & magickal tradition.

NOTE FROM AUTHOR

Like many esoteric systems, and as chaos magicians, Strigoi Vii is inspired by and draws upon other traditions of Magick, Vampyrism, and Vampirism. Many of our founding members started off in other traditions and brought these teachings with them making Elorathian Vampyrism / Strigoi Vii a meta-paradigm of Vampyrism / vampirism. For the sake of clarity, honor, and transparency, here are some of our revealed sources. Give credit where credit is due. Please enjoy exploring these other traditions and may you find they further your Zhep'r.

Dayside, Nightside, Twilight and *Communion* originate with the Temple of the Vampire (TOV). Please refer to the *Vampire Bible* by the TOV for more information.

The Sanguine Mass is inspired by the rituals *Calling of the Undead Gods* of the TOV and the *Gnostic Mass* by the Ordo Templis Orientis (O.T.O.).

The concept of *Aeonic Words* and *Xeper* (Zhep'r) is inspired by the Temple of Set / Order of the Vampyre. Check out the book *Energy Work of the Vampyre* by Don Webb for more source information.

Kitra (lovers), *Mradu* (warriors) and *Ramkht* (magicians) draw inspiration from the castes of Councilor, Warrior and Priest which were first introduced to the Vampire Community by the Kheprian Order. They evolved into Aeonic Words and Pulses of the Vampyre Current of Elorath over time and have their origins in the Jungian archetypes of lovers, warriors, and magicians.

OTHER WORKS BY FATHER SEBASTIAAN

Vampyre Sanguinomicon: Lexicon of the Living Vampire
Weiser Books, September 2010

Vampyre Magick: Grimoire of the Living Vampire
Weiser Books, February 2012

Black Veils: Master Vampyre Edition 888
Bast Books, October 2020

Mysteries of Paris: The Darkside of the City of Lights
Bast Books, July 2021

The Vampyre Sebastiaan, part 1: The 1990s
Bast Books, Forthcoming 2023

This book born of Love and Loyalty is dedicated to all who have heard the Calling—those yet to awaken, the Awakened, and the

Ascended. I raise my chalice to honor you, my Family.

So we begin…

Remember these words…

THE TRADITION

THE MAGICK

THE QUEST

THE ORDER

THE CURRENT

The Practice

The Culture

The Community

THE STRIGOI VII CHARGE

I AM Strigoi Vii.
In Love and Loyalty.
I am the Ruler of My Dream and seek never to die.
When in My Dayside, I am rational and materialistic. Yet, by My own Will,
I can enter the world mystic
And move to My Nightside, beyond the Veil.
I realize all things are possible and by My will I prevail.
Within the equilibrium I find My Twilight.
I move closer to Zhep'r with every Flight.
I understand the difference between knowledge and belief.
Death is My only true enemy—it shall never conquer Me.
I am Immortal, and Life I embrace.
I lead, explore, and feed to My taste.
I create, I love, and I celebrate,
For I know Life's pleasures all surely await!
I shall always embrace The Black Veils & Strigoi Vii Principles,
My Covenant, The basis of Our Mysteries and beginning of My imprint.
Though I sit atop the food chain, I respect all other living things, For they have
their place due to the Energy they bring.
Thus, I honor those who give Me the most precious gift.
Strigoi Vii is My spiritual Family, My sacred Heritage.
None shall keep Me from Zhep'r, for I am My own God!
I rejoice in My nature, Myself I applaud!
With Love & Loyalty.
I AM Strigoi Vii.
HAIL ELORATH!

Mortal-minded— "There are many beliefs and perspectives"

*Immortal-minded— "I know no beliefs or faith that
lead to gnosis. Only results equal knowledge"*

ELORATHIAN /STRIGOI VII SACRAMEMNTS

Vampyre Mass (Sanguine Mass the SV Codex, Red Mass in Black Veils)
Communion (Group Energy Exchange & Amplification)
Blood & Roses (Vampyre Hand-Fasting)
    First Rings
    Second Rings
    Third Rings *
Requiem Rising (Vampyre Funeral)
Consecration Rites
    Sacred Space
    Tools / Weapons / Ankhs
    Cleansing
    Banishment
    Phylactery Creation
    Halo Consecration *
Seasonal Rites
    Crimson Festival (Valentine's Day)
    Dragon Festival (Walpurgis / Beltane)
    Dayside Festival (Summer Solstice)
    Bast Festival (Lammas)
    Samhain Festival (Halloween)
    Nightside Festival (Yule)
    Dark Moon
Ascension Rites
    Prospectii (Dedication / Baptism)
    Jahira (Coming forth by Day)
    Calmae (Coming forth by Night)
    MorRoii (Coming forth by Twilight) *
    Kharrus (Ordination) *

Secrets of these rites only known to select members of the Priesthood & Magisters.

CARPATHIAN VAMPIRES BY J.M. DIXON

Excerpted from J.M. Dixon's *The Weiser Field Guide to Vampires* (Weiser Books, 2009) 16–22.

The real Dracula was not the first of the vampires, nor was he the origin of vampire myths. In fact, Vlad Dracula grew up in a beautiful land rich with vampiric folklore, and he likely used that folklore intentionally to encourage the myths that surrounded him. The peoples of the region of eastern Europe near the Carpathian Mountains are known for their folktales, the most famous of which are about vampires—creatures that they call the *Strigoi.*

The *Strigoi Morte* are the vampiric spirits who roam and hunt without bodies, feeding on the energies of living humans, sometimes when the humans are sleeping or dreaming, and sometimes while they are wide awake and simply in the wrong place at the wrong time. Unlike the vampires of modern legends, the Strigoi Morte are not considered demons or the angry spirits of those who were murdered or not buried properly. The people of this region, even today, simply believe that the Strigoi Morte are the spirits of *Strigoi Vii*—living vampires—and are no longer in possession of a physical body.

The Strigoi Vii, sometimes also called *Morrah*, are thought to be a race similar to humanity but different in their need to feed on human energy or human blood. Although there are thought to be other types of vampires in the region, they are the most well-known, particularly among the Roma who live there.

The *Roma*, remain an often nomadic people, spread through many countries, but with a long history in Romania in particular. They have a great love of fantastical stories and scary tales, but behind each of their fictions is a backbone of facts—even their stories of vampires. According to them, the Strigoi Vii were a tall, beautiful, pale, strong, intelligent, well-mannered, regal, and often wealthy people—usually landowners, businessmen, and, historically, even royalty and nobility.

Like the Strigoi Morte, the Strigoi Vii primarily fed upon the life energies of humanity, picking a single volunteer to feed from for a length of time. According to the Roma, the Strigoi Vii could also feed on human blood, but it was only the young and inexperienced who chose to do so. Much as was suggested in Bram Stoker's novel *Dracula*, the Roma and vampires in the region, especially in Romania, have a long history of working together amicably. The wealthy, landowning Strigoi Vii could provide the Roma caravans with fair pay for manual labor or entertainment, as well as safe passage through their land, in particular protecting the Roma people from discrimination and potential attackers. The Roma would also provide one valuable service that the discreet vampires of the region could not do without: food.

The Roma and vampires of the region practiced a tradition they referred to as *lording*, whereby one Gypsy, usually a female volunteer, would be chosen to go live with the Strigoi for the time her family was on the land. The vampire was generally allowed to feed upon her at his leisure, and her family was protected in return. And though it was not an actual part of the bargain, the vampire would always treat the guest with the utmost respect and often bring gifts to the family as a show of traditional vampiric gratitude. According to members of the Carbone de Travois Gypsy family, this arrangement was still in common practice not even eighty years ago in Romanian lands. One member of that family professes that her great-aunt Piranda was lorded out to a wealthy vampire in the 1910s and '20s.

Piranda's younger sister Nia described the vampire as very tall with light brown hair, always immaculately dressed and perfectly clean shaven, with a lithe, masculine physique. Nia added that he smelled "pretty." In 1918, when Piranda spent the summer with him, he had the first car Nia had ever seen. Among other things, he gave the family oxen and cows, blankets, clothes of all kinds, and permission to cut his trees and hunt the wild game on his land. Nia said he seemed to genuinely care about Piranda, inviting her back to his home every summer when the family passed through, going so far as to keep a special campground cleared for them, with a well that only they were allowed to use. Nia said her sister returned to the family at the end of each summer looking "fit and fine like old wine."

Piranda's vampire, whose name has been lost to time, is far from the only Strigoi Vii to have been reported in the area. Most everyone has heard of Prince Vlad Dracula, "the Impaler." Born in Transylvania in 1431, he ruled Romania during a difficult time. The Turks were attacking in waves, and with his forces completely outnumbered, he used his intelligence to wage psychological warfare on his enemies, which also served to keep his own people in line and instilled confidence that they would prevail. As long as he lived, he kept peace in his land and kept the enemies on the run. However, not so many people know about this famous vampire's brethren, or even about his master.

Prince Vlad Dracula was the son of Vlad Dracul, "the Dragon," and his name literally meant "Vlad, son of the Dragon." Both he and his father were members of the Ordo Dracul, the Order of the Dragon— an organization made up of eastern European royalty. Surviving Gypsy families claim that, throughout the history of this region, most of the nobility were Strigoi Vii, which lends some credence to the claims some make that the membership of the order was exclusive to vampires, the term *dragon* being used as a code word for *vampire*. Oddly, this fact was most likely well known at the time, since Christians of the period, particularly in that region, would often refer to vampires as devils, demons, or dragons. And in the case of the Romanian language, one word, *dracul,* meant all three of those things at the same time. A case in point: the incubi and succubi of medieval folktales are interchangeably called both "vampires" and "demons."

Prince Vlad not only had underlings among the other vampires; he also had a master. Few stories mention Dracula's lord and master, the king of the region in that day, and it is doubtful that many even wonder about his existence. His name was Matthias Corvinus. Likely a Strigoi Vii himself, King Matthais was far from intimidated by the Impaler. In fact, he once had the prince imprisoned for three years, or possibly longer, due to various political motivations and his need to have a less independent prince in Vlad's position. A wise and peaceful man, Corvinus was far from the warlord he is claimed to have been in the popular cinematic depictions of the underworld, finally committing his armies to the defense of Romania only after Vlad had fallen in love with and requested the hand of a relative of his, likely the sister of the king— Vlad's request, incidentally, having been made during his captivity in the king's castle.

The Strigoi Vii type of vampire certainly has a deep history in the region of the Carpathian Mountains, documented by writers such as the monk Montague Summers and recounted in the stories of Gypsy families like the Carbone de Travois band. It is probably because of this history that modern vampires often use the term *Strigoi Vii* when describing themselves, especially when trying to avoid the stigma that often accompanies the term *vampire*.

THE AEON OF ELORATH BY MAGISTRA MEIJIN

A Vampyre's Calling

Nineteen ninety-five was a landmark year for Vampyres. As trends go, the vampire had once again mesmerized both subculture and the general population at large. It's influence shapeshifted and blended into the energy of the times and there wasn't a human alive who hadn't been touched in one way or another by the presence of the vampire. Nearly everyone knew at least something about vampires. What was known commonly in the '90s was noble, elegant, powerfully immortal, and romantic. By this time the assortment of cultural offerings, as well as two prodigious initiatory Vampyre groups, had made their presence well known. The Temple of Set had some 10 years prior established the Order of the Vampyre as a subgroup in its organization. The Temple of the Vampire, a legally recognized religious organization in the United States, had been quietly gaining strength and members for the prior eight years, under the direction of the Undead Gods. To this day, these organizations continue onward in doing their work.

Both groups share an important connection. The founders of the Temple of the Vampire and the Order of the Vampyre claim to have had definitive and transformative contact with what they described as a primal, conscious, and self-aware Vampyric force that directed and guided their actions. This was no simple "spirit, being, or god" but something older, deeper, and uniquely interested in guiding those who would hear its words to Immortality and beyond. Such a force manifest in the physical world cannot be described as anything but an almost alien seeming presence. It took the form of both Vampire and Dragon and directed the founding initiates to make its teachings and words known. These Vampyric organizations have served and continue to serve the will of the Dragon. The time of their founding was however one that was heavily influenced by the previous secrecy and this, among other things, affected their mode of transmitting their teachings. The world was not yet ready for an Open Rule.

By 1995 things had begun to change.

Mysterious and unpredictable in its ways and direction, the Dragon would manifest again. This time to an impressionable young man calling himself by the name of Father Sebastiaan. He was a young, personable, and flamboyant individual and like many of that time period, under the sway of the prevalent cultural vampire glamour. While he was not alone in his interest in the widespread cultural appeal of the vampire, Sebastiaan had something about him that was different from the masses. He was more than simply enthralled by the glamour of the media vampire. It was almost as if he had been directed to the vampire movement by an unseen hand.

In hindsight, it can be easily seen that his unique interests and focuses were no accident. Unknown to him at the time, his life purpose was already under the direction of the Dragon. His special talents made him uniquely well suited for what was to come. Sebastiaan was already an occult practitioner and immersed in the serious Vampyric teachings of those who had preceded him. He was also an avid role player and gamer and had an intrinsic awareness of the older myths that had influenced both the development of the games and the creators of them.

Having begun a career as a dental technician, by 1995 he had already redirected that skill into making vampire fangs for friends and individuals, offering them a physical connection to Vampyric glamour and power. He enjoyed the company of vibrant and influential people within the New York club scene and held the respect (and envy) of many in the city who were themselves Vampyres or belonged to various Vampyre traditions and groups. His natural talent for organizing events was noticed and fostered by some of the most world-renowned club owners and promoters of the time. To some, those types of interests and unique focuses would be labelled a passing phase, to be left behind as a hobby upon growing up. However, there was much more to it than that. Those talents and interests had formed Sebastiaan into being perfectly suited for what was to come.

On a hot August night in 1995, Sebastiaan received a life-changing message. In very much the same manner as the founders of the two previous vampire organizations had experienced, the message came intensely and unexpectedly.

In those early days of the '90s, Sebastiaan ran an ongoing Vampire the Masquerade live-action game group at the hugely popular and well-known Limelight club in New York City. The building itself was a gothic revival style Episcopal church built in 1844 that had been deconsecrated and transformed into a nightclub. Little known to most of his masquerade group, Sebastiaan had been incorporating some of the rituals of the Temple of the Vampire into the role play. In effect, Sebastiaan had himself been doing a Communion in that old church and calling the Undead Gods. Groups of thousands of people partied nightly in the Limelight. The Lifeforce they produced was immense and it should come as no surprise that Sebastiaan's work was rewarded, and his call to the Ancients was heard.

And so, on that August night, Sebastiaan was working in the Limelight helping a promoter run one of the many theme nights. He had gone off alone into one of its back rooms to get supplies. The intensity of what happened next is something that ultimately can only be known to him. My words can never give the fullest description of that moment.

Sebastiaan saw and heard a Force. A dark shadow of movement and energy appeared and connected, and communicated, with him. What Sebastiaan heard was at once both telepathic and audible. Much of what was conveyed will remain private for only Sebastiaan to know. Of import here, both a Name and a Word were conveyed to him: *ELORATH.* He was also given a task: to further extend the reach of the Dragon He was to bring the real Vampyric teachings to the public in a manner accessible and useful to all. In alignment with this, he would serve to reignite the way for the Open Rule of the Vampyres once again. Open Rule is a term that refers to a period when Vampyres are publicly known and have the respect and admiration of all those they encounter, both within and without the Vampyre Community. Under Open Rule, Vampyres act as trusted leaders and guides. Open Rule existed in ancient times and was foretold to occur again.

I have never asked Sebastiaan if he was given a choice as to whether or not he would accept the task put to him. I suspect he was not. I also suspect that on that night in the Limelight he could not have had the understanding of the difficult but rewarding road ahead of him. Sebastiaan was destined to be known as the Vampyre Magus of a new Aeon.

On that August night, Sebastiaan emerged from the encounter changed. His gaming days abruptly ended, and he became devoted to the vision he received, and to fulfilling his part in it. It was not even a week later that he would face the first tests of what would become near lifelong questions on his character and other personal judgments. Along with the first of those challenges, he also met a trusted and now lifelong friend: Victor Magnus.

Despite the difficulties and strange turns Sebastiaan's quest has led him to, he has never once faltered in following the path, nor failed in his service to the Dragon. It is now three decades in the future from that fated night. The glory that was the Limelight is now a shopping mall. Like many places of magic, the passage of time transforms them. The true nature of such places goes hidden and the magic can only be sensed by those attuned to it. For others, the magic lives on, existing in pictures and invoked memories preceded by the words "remember when?"

What I have written here by its nature might invite skepticism or ridicule. The forces of the world do not go easily into allowing new forms. There may be those who will seek to undo the good done with hate and misinformation. The proof of what I have written is already known. To see the positive effects, one need only look to the worldwide influence Sebastiaan has had in his work for and with Elorath. Thousands of individuals now call themselves Vampyres and have been transformed by his teachings into noble, vibrant, and wise Vampyres, passionately driven to Zeph'r. There are, of course, those who have by their failings misunderstood or misrepresented what was given to them by Sebastiaan. Even so, his positive influence on the world, the individual, and the culture cannot be denied. A new Magus and a new Aeon have come forth fully revealed.

It is not surprising that as we stand here in 2022, after another apocalyptic year of illness, death, and cultural upheaval, that this should happen. Aeons are known to build until the energy and the time is ripe. The ways of the old world have now been replaced. Things as we knew them before that day in 2020, when we were told to close our homes and stay inside while a worldwide pandemic spread and killed, will never be the same.

For years, the Internet has enhanced connectivity and the ability to be heard. At the beginning of the influence of the Internet there was a great revealing of formerly unknown Vampyric groups and ideas. The pandemic has forced us all to find ways to communicate and connect with others that we had never previously considered. For many, there has been more time alone for reflection, combined with a forced awareness of the fragility of life and the harsh realities of death. It has paved the way for the new Aeon.

It is a prime time for the message of Elorath to be delivered, touching individuals in ways it had not previously. It should be no surprise that a Magus of this new Aeon has also appeared. There has also been a mystery played out. Seemingly unrelated pieces of a long-played puzzle have come together to reveal more of the picture. Some of you out there will by now know how your piece of this puzzle fits. The Aeon will have its way. In symbolic form, the message of the Aeon was illustrated in a scene from the movie *Queen of the Damned*. Lestat, when speaking to a group of reporters, chose to be broadcast on a large screen from a remote location. He knew this type of projection would be far-reaching. Illustratively, because he dwelt in the Nightside and Twilight his message was not able to be given in the Dayside. He revealed himself by a flickering computer connection. His face, larger than life onscreen, only served to project the message even more powerfully. The words he had for the Vampires who would hear him were spoken as both an invitation and a challenge:

"Come out, come out, wherever you are!"

Father Sebastiaan has issued this same message, both prior to and during the pandemic. These words, and his message, are a call to embrace the noble nature of the Vampyre and to come out of the shadows. The message of the Aeon of Elorath is clear.

What Is an Aeon?

To avoid misunderstanding, a good definition of an Aeon is in order. In Gnosticism, an Aeon is a type of energetic manifestation in time and space that comes forth from the Supreme Being as a force or power.

This specific type of energetic force is sent to bring about certain changes that are needed to maintain the continuation and evolution of the universe. Aeons are most often associated with a time, but this is not an entirely correct view. Aeons can exist alongside each other; in that they are a type of energetic force that solidifies a mindset or idea.

In regard to time, an Aeon can typically be the point most associated with the zenith of the Aeons intensity. Location, or space, also has its importance. Much like the Summer of Love and the location of Woodstock defined an age, an Aeon tends to be defined by a specific time and its events, as well as in the place or places where the most noticed manifestation of energy occurred. Aeons are not beings or Gods. An Aeon can be most simply described as a type of divinely manifested energy that affects the mind and actions of a large number of individuals in a way that is both unprecedented and previously unknown in the world. This effect often has its smallest beginnings in seemingly unrelated ways.

There is a point in the birth of an Aeon wherein a certain individual will be chosen to act as its main conduit. At the same time, there is an unfolding of the energy throughout the world that seemingly comes from nowhere. Certain events, fads, and themes begin to form. Specific ideas grab hold, and there is a large-scale change in understanding and thought.

For the individual chosen to act as the direct intermediary and perpetrator of the Aeon, it is hard to know for certain if they are born to the role or if a combination of experiences, inclination and talents form them. My thought is that it is a bit of both. The genetic and personality traits, as well as life experiences, early on attract the attention of the Aeonic force.

Although it may seem that such divine attention would be enviable, the chosen individual has an extraordinarily difficult role to play. He or she is tasked beyond all others, and the tasks and trials encountered are unending. Our level of existence in the world and the laws that govern it do not easily make way for large scale change without resistance. This very resistance equals the greatest challenge for the one who has been chose for this path. Yet, no matter the difficulty, the Aeonic force will prevail.

Despite this, there are great rewards. The chosen of the Aeon receives a form of immortality and ongoing energy—for as long as the Aeon maintains force. There is also the reward of evolution and the benefits of universal progression.

Aeons are not something that happen in neat sequential order, where one Aeon ends and the next begins. In a very simple sense, an Aeon can be viewed as a mindset. Those who hold the views of older Aeons are those who have found agreement with the mindset representative of that Aeon. They serve as a vital part of the living force that maintains and shapes the energy of the Aeon upon the world.

The Magus and the Word, a Brief History

There is a title given to the individual who is chosen by the force of the Aeon as its representative and direct intermediary. As titles go, it seems a lofty one. But as I stated, being chosen to aid the divine is only seen as enviable by the misinformed. Being a Magus is not all a bed of gilded roses.

Working directly with the will of the divine on Earth is not an easy task. In many ways this gift is also a curse. One of the Magi of the Temple of Set summed up that curse by stating that "It is the curse of the Magus to be misunderstood." There is nearly always some difficulty in accurately illustrating and representing the meaning of the message given by the divine. There are also promptings from the divine that lead the Magus to act in strange and unpredictable ways.

The title of Magus is an old title first used in ancient Persia as the name of its priests. Interestingly, in the Bible, the term magi, the plural of magus, has been translated from Latin to mean wise men and kings. In more modern times it was used as one of the grades in the Golden Dawn. This initiatory grade system was based on the Kabbalistic Tree of Life as first illustrated by a Jesuit scholar by the name of Athanasius Kircher. Inspired by earlier teachings, his book *Oedipus Aegyptiacus* was published in 1682. In his book, the descriptions of the Sephiroth on the Tree of Life and their associated mystical principles as a divine path of spiritual ascension was laid out. The Golden Dawn took this inspiration and formulated a ten-level system that corresponds each grade directly with one of the levels.

Aleister Crowley, who was a member of the Golden Dawn, later went on to form his initiatory order after hearing an Aeonic word of his own. His word was Thelema, and his Aeon was the Aeon of Horus. In the founding of his own initiatory order Crowley changed and altered some of the original grades of the Golden Dawn. Mainly, this was done in a manner that lined things up with the initiatory concepts Crowley's own *The Book of the Law*. In doing so, he also took away some of the more direct Kabbalistic associations of the grades previously used.

Most initiatory groups from Crowley's time forward have used the grade structure of the Golden Dawn in one manner or another. Anton LaVey, the Magus of the Age of Satan, was well aware of Crowley's grade structure when he formed the Church of Satan. He further modified the grades to suit his purposes into a five-grade system. Magus became the 5 ° and the highest degree of the Church of Satan. LaVey, in recognition of his direct pact and personal work with the Prince of Darkness, achieved this degree as well. His Word was Indulgence, and his Aeon was called the Age of Satan. The degree of Magus was also bestowed onto Micheal Aquino after his encounter with the divine in the form of the Egyptian Neter Set leading to his founding of the Temple of Set in 1975. Its Word was Xeper and the Aeon was called the Aeon of Set. The Temple of Set in its initiatory structure changed and refined the grading system significantly once again in a reflection of its understanding and initiatory purpose. They added an aspect to the designation of Magus in that an "Aeon enhancing Word" could also be put forth. As it stands, currently each of the Aeon enhancing Words of the Temple of Set have held their place as powerful, evolutionary, and divinely given in their own right. The concept of a Word, in its most simplistic sense, was inspired by the ancient Greeks and is used to describe and symbolize a singular concept that best defines an Aeon. Aeon enhancing Words are much the same but are instead used descriptively and symbolically for concepts that enhance the Aeon and its main Aeonic word. The validity of the Word and the attainment of the degree of Magus is most obviously shown by a marked spiritual evolution of the individual who attains it as well as the effects of that evolution on their actions. The transformative effect this individual has on the world or large masses of individuals is also easily seen.

Elorath and the Aeon

By now, if you have not encountered it before, you may be asking. "What is Elorath?" Perhaps, the simplest beginning is to understand Elorath as a manifestation emanating from the great Dragon. That Dragon has been known by many names throughout history. Elorath is a force that emanates from the Dragon and is directed into the world. It has its own individual consciousness and will. It chose the name Elorath as a way of communicating itself understandably within the human world. The name Elorath can also be seen as a Word as it is descriptive of a divinely inspired concept. Since Elorath is a type of force that emanates from the Dragon, an understanding of the Dragon is needed to fully understand Elorath.

In a sense, the Dragon can be seen as a type of First Form. It is the force of life and immortality, and it exists not only as itself but also as its individuated manifestations within humans as consciousness and Lifeforce within them. Typically, the Dragon lies sleeping within humans operating only their base functions of being alive and breathing and their drive to continue the species. For others, the fire of the Dragon burns brighter, either naturally or by contact with another who has the Radiance and then becoming Awakened to a deeper understanding of it. This understanding can eventually lead to the attainment of immortality and a mastery of life on levels far beyond just the physical. The Dragon is unending. Its symbol is the ouroboros.

Elorath is not a god. The most easily understood descriptive for it is the Force of a Form. It exists subtly yet powerfully within each individual and has also been described in the teaching of the Ordo Strigoi Vii as a Current. This Current flows through each individual and those who are aware and awakened to it maintain a shared agreement and mindset in the understanding of its ways. At times Elorath has been seen and felt like a chaotic force. This is an important aspect of Elorath and the Dragon from which It emanates because chaos, as a mathematical rule, is needed for the building and propagation of life. It is the emergence of complexity from something simple. Beyond that chaos allows for deviation in all things and assures they will not merely remain on a path of fixed finality and end. Chaos as a principle not only allows for infinite growth but can also be seen to have as a First Form brought about the ability of creation itself. Change and the deviation of the chaos principle are necessary. Life itself could not have come into being without the breaking of eternal sameness.

The basic Form of immortality and Lifeforce has prominence for those who have identified with the Vampyre and Awakened the Dragon within. It has been known, since its first Awakening in those it touched, to agree with being described as Vampyric. All must feed to live, and this concept plays out on a universal scale from the lowest to the highest levels of existence. For the Vampyre, knowledge of the Dragon and partaking in Lifeforce gathering and usage assures not only individuated immortality and Life but also at its highest levels of understanding and use, aligns the Vampyre with an ascension that is precedent in the universal order itself.

As we stand looking out upon the revealing of a new Aeon there is the joy of what is yet to be. There will be further adventures as the Aeon of Elorath unfolds. It is an exciting time. A time when Vampyres can be known for what they truly are. It is a time when those of the Blood can once again walk the earth proudly.

The work that the Magus Sebastiaan began two and a half decades ago moves onward. His combination of Vampyric teachings inspired by what came before him as well as what has been developed independently within the Ordo Strigoi Vii by an assortment of initiates continues. For those who are Vampyre and who take the time to carefully experience and test the Vampyric mysteries, great advancements of understanding will occur. For those who apply these things to their lives on a personal level, a transformation unlike anything the individual would have thought possible awaits.

In Eternal Service to the Dragon,
Hail Elorath
Magistra Meijin
Strigoi Vii V° Magistra Templi

THE ORDER OF STRIGOI VII
BY MAGISTRA MAELLE

The Order of the Living Vampire, or formally the Ordo Strigoi Vii (OSV), was officially established early in the twenty-first century by the direction of the Ancestors. With its beginnings in meetings before this, members of the Sabretooth Clan realized there was a calling to form an esoteric fraternal and initiatory order to further the preservation and prosperity of the more evolved Strigoi Vii Vampyre Mysteries. The OSV is very separate and at the same time in equilibrium with Father Sebastiaan's Sabretooth Clan which consists mostly of Dayside Philosophical Vampyres. Over the years it has evolved, developed, and fostered traditions, philosophies, and magickal experiments, which have been copied and modified by countless other groups.

Even though the OSV is an elite, sovereign, highly selective invitation-only order, it has worked with, befriended, inspired, guided, and honored many other traditions of Vampyrism and vampirism. Nevertheless, the OSV remains neutral, independent, and completely free of any formal affiliations. This flexibility has allowed an inward focus on the collective Zhep'r of the Strigoi Vii Mysteries and has allowed it to influence and be influenced on terms which benefit the collective membership at the time.

When I met Father over the Internet in the late 1990s, I was a member of the Temple of the Vampire and the Church of Satan, both of which greatly inspired me and drew me to their teachings and philosophies, but I could not fully come into agreement with using the image of Satan as my sole definition of inspiration and focus. This led me to the Temple of Set and eventually led me to become a cofounder of the Ordo Strigoi Vii.

In contrast to Father, I am a highly secretive and private individual, a description which represents a vast majority of the other Strigoi Vii I have met. Many would find it unusual that I am a mother of four, yet I hold perspectives that are hard, no-nonsense, Darwinistic, predatory, and opinionated. I hold no public image, have no desire for fame, and only wish to inspire the select few who pass through the gates of the OSV's sanctums. Settling to this reality, none shall cross me or my Nightside or Dayside Families, for both are separate, yet equal, in my heart.

On my request, in 2010 the OSV officially adopted the sigilium of the Ouroboros surrounding the Vampyre Legacy Ankh, which is representative of the new direction and which, as of this writing, remains secret. However, through the books of the *Strigoi Vii Codex* we share our mysteries. Father Sebastiaan has graciously offered to compose and direct these projects as a contribution to the Family. We strive to select the best-quality candidates and seekers for our order through sponsorship and application. This screening process lets us select the most sincere and dedicated individuals who will stand out as role models of the Strigoi Vii Mysteries. To this date this formula remains a discreet secret and only known to the Synod, the Spiritual and administrative body of the OSV.

Ronin are those who practice the Strigoi Vii Mysteries in whole or in part and are not members of the Order; these solitary individuals who, either by choice or by not having been accepted to the Order, represent the vast majority of those who practice Strigoi Vii. Some Ronin will eventually be accepted to the Order, whilst others choose to remain solitary. One major misconception is that Ronin are looked down upon by the order; actually, they represent the two extremes of diversity amongst those who imbue Vampyric Current.

Black Swans are Dayside Vampyres and have adopted, inspired, or been touched by the Vampyre Current. They represent those close to the Vampyre Current, be they lovers, friends, fang clients of Father, performers at events, or people who simply enjoy our company. Many Black Swans embrace the Dayside Mysteries as a philosophical path on their own terms through the outer teachings known as the Black Veils.

Whatever the relationship with the mysteries, be it initiate, Black Swan, or Ronin, everyone is on what the Freemasons have called "The Scale," each on an equal level, although on different portions of the path, exploring each in their own way.

Let this book serve your own interests; we share our knowledge, ceremonies, and mysteries with the world through this text. Let it inspire, challenge, and set you free; whatever the case, what you benefit is yours. However, within the Order we continue to experiment and prosper as flexible yet defined spiritual philosophers of the Vampyre Community.

Eternally, Magistra Maelle
Strigoi Vii VII° Ipissimus
Past Grande Magistra of the O.S.V. (2002-2013)

FOREWORD BY KONSTANTINOS

Imet Sebastiaan what feels like an immortal lifetime ago. It was 1996, and we were both at a taping of *The Ricki Lake Show*. The topic? You guessed it. Instead of his now-trademark folded cowboy hat, Sebastiaan wore a more period-popular top hat, à la Gary Oldman in *Bram Stoker's Dracula*. At first glance, I thought he had to be another of the role-players—the audience and panel were filled with young "kids in capes." But Sebastiaan was different. His enthusiasm was almost infectious, and I didn't have to talk to him long to notice that, for him, this wasn't mere roleplaying. Even at a young age, he "got" what the real power behind this whole scene was, even if he didn't know the word for it yet.

That word? *Psychodrama.* I've made it pretty clear in *Vampires: The Occult Truth* that the evidence supporting the existence of movie-caliber immortal blood drinkers is sketchy at best. The case for psychic vampires is much stronger. Was blood a metaphor for beings that can take the energy of the living? More bizarrely, could these beings be either living or in a state that can only be called undead? The evidence sure seems to suggest this possibility.

What does this mean for those who pine for immortality of the Lestat or Edward type? (Okay, just the Lestat type—who really wants to shimmer and eat deer?) While some beautiful immortal may not carry you out the window and give you a dark kiss in an ancient tower or leaf-covered graveyard, it doesn't mean the power behind the vampire realm is forever closed off to you.

Again, that delicious word. *Psychodrama.*

All magic is psychodrama. Without extravagant rituals that speak to something deep in our subconscious, our minds simply can't reach the altered states necessary for accessing the unseen world. We live in a world that is dominated by daytime consciousness requirements. Few bosses ask how many spiritual planes you can travel through per minute or how many spells by Microsoft you've mastered. Mystical altered states are as repressed as can be, with drained mobile phone batteries representing the only true down time for many.

I've seen psychodrama do eerie and wonderful things. It has healed me of a malformed vein that was threatening my brain and life, and MRIs don't lie. Psychodrama, when mastered, can result in more than just an altered state. With the right ritual structure, an altered state can result in powerful, real change in the physical world. Even quantum experiments in which individuals try to affect random number generators have proven that test groups with some kind of meditative preparation always do better. Amazing to see science "discovering" what occultists have always known and tabulating the results under controlled lab setups.

You hold in your hands a unique kind of book. Rather than claiming that vampires are born to some exotic bloodline or going on and on about why the author is special in some way that conveniently matches fictional vampires, this book gives you techniques for working with pure psychodrama. No ego or delusions required. The change you get out of it is directly proportionate to how deeply you let its structure affect you.

Since that day years ago, Sebastiaan and I have always stayed in reasonable contact. We've done a couple of Endless Night events in New Orleans together and plan to do more. We've had enough Jack Daniels and absinthe to facilitate the necessary quick catching up each time we get together. Over a couple of glasses recently, Sebastiaan reminded me of the first time he saw the term *Strigoi Vii*—literally "living vampire"—in my book. While the beings it described likely never existed, they do now, don't they? I'm delighted that Sebastiaan did what all occultists should do: he used psychodrama to bring something forth into reality.

As I type these last words, the last drops of water have erased the sugar cube in the absinthe glass in preparation nearby. With a swirl of the cloudy glass, and the promise of altered states it too can help provide, I raise my glass to the best example of a sane living vampire I know.

Konstantinos

Author of Vampires: the Occult Truth and Nocturnal Witchcraft and Nocturnal Witchcraft: Magick After Dark

BOOK 0

LIBER ZHEP'R "THE ELORATHIAN PROSPECTUS"

CHAPTER 1

SO WE BEGIN

"Some are born to sweet delight; some are born to endless night."

—William Blake, "Auguries of Innocence"

Since the dawn of civilization, the vampire has danced through the dreams and nightmares of every culture. These whispers have been expressed over the past four eons through our Glamour, evident in folklore, literature, art, and the media, as well as many other spheres. Each new generation recognizes and embraces some new masque of the Immortal vampire archetype.

Why is this so? Is there not truth in every myth? There truly is, but it is most often hidden beneath metaphor and thus not immediately recognized. Therefore, your first task is to put aside what you already believe or think you know about "vampires" and listen carefully. What lies within these pages may initially seem for many readers to be sheer nonsense. However, for some rare few it will ring of familiarity. These blessed individuals have the unique potential to experience the world in a manner quite unknown to the rest of humanity. It is for those with this Dark Flame that this book has been written.

"Liber Elorath" is the cornerstone and the first of a series of core syllabus texts of the Strigoi Vii written from the perspective of the Ordo Strigoi Vii (OSV). Each tome of the is Codex is organized into a regimented system that disseminates the core mysteries, traditions, philosophies, and teachings of the Strigoi Vii. Thus, each book is intended to be a spark that ignites the Awakening of a Dark Flame, or the hidden potential, that may lie within you. That Awakening is the first step on the journey into the magickal, spiritual, and philosophical system we call Strigoi Vii. Whether you are a Seeker exploring the possibility of SV Initiation or a curious scholar of the esoteric, this book is the foremost authority and resource on the Mysteries of the Living Vampyre.

This manifesto will set you on the first steps of understanding Zhep'r or the metamorphosis and evolution from a mortal's perspective to that of the Immortal. When beginning on this Great Work, you must first look within yourself as you would into a mirror, reading beyond the myths perpetuated in the mortal mind throughout history, and truly understand your own soul. Many splendid gems of truth are buried in the dull earth of history and legend. Consider the film The Matrix. Morpheus offers his student Neo a choice. He could explore the world beyond his ken by swallowing a red pill or instead take a blue pill and return to the mundane world. The original advertising campaign for The Matrix asked: "What is the Matrix? You will have to see it to understand!" Strigoi Vii is no different. At this very moment, you are faced with the choice between living a complacent, "normal" life or rising above the world to transcend ordinary experience and gain a profound and extraordinary perspective.

In order to achieve success, you must test and experiment with these Vampyre Mysteries. You shall begin to see through and beyond the mirror, a Quest which can only be embarked on in solitude. Only a few can possibly see past the enthralling Glamour that has seduced the mortal-minded for centuries. As one of our mortal patrons has said, "This reality is beyond fiction. " You must forget all you think you know about the vampire in order to comprehend the world known to the Family of the Strigoi Vii.

When reading and exploring the books of the Strigoi Vii Codex, you may not agree with or feel drawn to some of the Mysteries that lie within. This is only natural, and skeptical questioning is the first step to unlocking this knowledge and comprehending how you may best apply it for yourself. We are catalysts of transformation for our Family as well as others Awakened to the subtle world. Those pursuing the Mysteries must be willing to study, analyze, and test the material presented in these texts. If you read the Strigoi Vii Codex and do not experiment with or attempt to solve the Mysteries yourself, it will be as if you took the trouble to perfectly learn all the rules of chess yet never played a single game. You will be just another bibliophile who adds this Codex to their collection. Results are inarguable. They are the only way you will ever know the truth of the Mysteries and determine if you are of the Family. This is the first step toward experiencing Awakening and Initiation. Achieving these results will take time, patience, and effort. Yet without validation, you will never know the potential power of the knowledge that lies within your hands at this very moment.

> *"The one glimpse he had had of the title was enough to send him into transports, and some of the diagrams set in the vague Latin text excited the tensest and most disquieting recollections in his brain. He felt it was highly necessary to get the ponderous thing home and begin deciphering it, and bore it out of the shop with such precipitate haste."*

H. P. Lovecraft, "The Descendant" (describing the Necronomicon)

This Strigoi Vii Codex refers to the collection of texts containing the written Outer Circle teachings of the spiritual and philosophical meta-paradigms of our Tradition, as defined by the O.S.V. Strigoi Vii are engaged with and dedicated to spiritual and material mastery of their own mortal coil and beyond. They are willing to tread the path necessary to guarantee the Immortality of the Self and serve the Greater Vampyre Current.

This Codex is essentially the modern equivalent of earlier works on the same subject, including the Book of Coming Forth by Day, better known today as the Egyptian Book of the Dead. It may also be likened to other sacred texts such as the Tibetan Book of the Dead and the Buddhist Sutras. The Outer Strigoi Vii Mysteries focus on achieving the equilibrium of the Dayside (Physical, Materialistic, Rational, and Skeptical), Nightside (Ethereal, Lifeforce, Chakras), and Twilight (Astral, Equilibrium, Flight & Shapeshifting). Book 0: Liber Zhep'r "The Strigoi Vii Prospectus" is the foundation for an introduction to this Codex. Each subsequent book explores deeper and deeper Mysteries through exercises and lessons. The Book I: Liber Jahira, "Coming Forth by Day," explores the Corporeal Dayside Mysteries of Strigoi Vii. Book II: Liber Calmae, "Coming Forth by Night," explores the Ethereal Nightside. Finally, Book III: Liber Morrah "Coming Forth by Twilight," completes the Outer Mysteries of the Living Vampyre. Upon completing these Mysteries, the Strigoi Vii establishes a solid foundation and is Adept from which to secure their Quest for personal immortality of the Self. This is a transformative journey from the mentality of the mortal-minded to that of the Immortal. We Strigoi Vii call this journey of transformation Zhep'r.

The Strigoi Vii Codex is also known as the Sanguinomicon and in the first printing and is indeed inspired by the Necronomicon, a fictional and nonexistent magickal grimoire created by American horror writer and fantasist H. P. Lovecraft (1891–1937) and often mentioned in his stories. The etymology of the word sanguinomicon is based in Greek and Latin. The word sanguine in Latin means "of blood"; the word nom means "law" in Greek. Thus, one approximate English translation of Sanguinomicon would be *"Book of the Laws of Blood."* For the Strigoi Vii, it is the core sacred text.

> *"The Revelations of the Devout and Learn'd*
> *Who rose before us, and as Prophets burn'd,*
> *Are all but Stories, which, awoke from Sleep,*
> *They told their comrades, and to Sleep return'd."*
>
> —Edward Fitzgerald, *Rubiyat of Omar Khayyam*

Path of Strigoi Vii

Strigoi Vii is the plural for Strigoi Viu, the Romanian word meaning, approximately, "living vampire" and/or "vampire witch." This is the word from which we take our name. In Romanian mythology the word strig (strega in Italian) translates to mean "witch." One source of this word is the ancient Roman mythological shrieking vampire bird known as the strix. We feel this name is best suited to describe our family and iits traditions, magickal systems, Mysteries, and philosophies. Strigoi Vii is a distinct form of Vampyre witchcraft. It shares many elements with modern neopaganism and other esoteric systems, yet still remains completely unique.

Strigoi Vii is focused on esoteric and spiritual truths which find the roots in the outer teachings of Black Veils Vampyrism. They are sovereign individuals who are self-initiated and energetically sensitive beings that are part **Shaman**, part **Alchemist**, part **Sorcerer**, part **Necromancer**, part **Witch** and part **Magician**. Strigoi Vii are Lifeforce Vampires and distinct from *psychic vampires* (energy deficient beings) and *sanguinarians* (blood drinkers).

Strigoi Vii learns to **Gather Lifeforce** by interacting with the excess residual living environment around them. They then refine the gathered energy into a higher form known as **Ambrosia** through a highly sacred alchemical act, known to Strigoi Vii as Communion. Once this act is completed the Vampyre can then, as an individual or a group, direct the Ambrosia toward a goal or intention through Strigoi Vii Magick and Sorcery.

Many great thinkers such as Aristotle, William Blake, Carl Jung, Friedrich Nietzsche, Albert Einstein, Ayn Rand with her philosophy of Objectivism, and Ragnar Redbeard (author of Might Is Right) have expressed elements of our Corporeal Dayside perspectives in various ways. However, it must be noted that the Dayside philosophy is only partially revealed by these viewpoints or thinkers. Moreover, many of these personages unfortunately incorporate objectionable sentiments (such as racism and sexism) into their more excellent philosophies. You can also see elements of our Ethereal Nightside perspectives reflected throughout history in the esoteric realms, including the Chaos Magick of Peter J. Carroll, Sumerian and Egyptian magic, Hinduism, Buddhism, the Thelema of Magus Aleister Crowley, Gnostic teachings, Judeo-Christian mysticism, and Hermetic Magick from ancient times.

We define the process of syncretism as reading between the lines and seeing the elements of the Mysteries in disparate myths, stories, and thoughts, and then putting these fragments back together into greater and more practical truths. As Strigoi Vii, that is what we do, seeking truth and reason through our own insight as well as that of other awakened beings.

For the last millennium, and even during the days of Sumer and Khem (better known as today as Ancient Egypt), the forefathers of the Family have been in the shadows, working in secrecy with our Ancestors. However, all of this is changing now. With the guidance of our Ancestors, a new generation of the Family is finally deliberately revealing Our collective heritage. We are gathering together and slowly coming out of the shadows in order to take part in the future and embrace our past as One.

Vampyre or Vampire?

As members of a tradition rooted in diverse historical narratives and folk-lore, we Strigoi Vii make a distinction between the words 'Vampyre' and 'vampire'. This subtle spelling difference may seem confusing; however, our traditional spelling denotes a profound difference between fantasy and reality. Typically, Strigoi Vii spell 'Vampyre' with a capital 'V' and a 'y' to designate the term representing our existence and our Mysteries.

For example, when referring to the practice of Lifeforce energy gathering from the Strigoi Vii perspective, one would say "Vampyrism". When we spell vampire with an 'i' and lowercase 'y', it refers to the mythological, literary, or popular concept of the vampire. Then again, some members of the Family feel the words Vampyre and vampire are both somewhat cliché and simply prefer to refer to themselves as Strigoi Vii. We Strigoi Vii are proud of and honor our heritage and traditions, and understand that there isn't universal consensus in regards to how one chooses to identify.

Many of the original Vampyre covens of Angel Halo (Los Angeles) and Gotham Halo (New York City) employed the spelling of Vampyre with a y, influenced but the 1984 book "The Order of the Vampyre" apart by the Temple of Set, and the infamous New York City nightclub, "Club Vampyre," which closed in 1993.

At the time, it was a commonly held belief in our community that 'Vampyre' was the more classic spelling, popularly used in the nineteenth century. But the etymology and history of the word "vampire," however it is spelled, is much more nuanced than that.

The word traces its roots from Eastern European and Turkish words such as *upior*, upyr, and *vapir*. The spelling "vampire" was recorded in French publications as early as 1692, long before the spelling "vampyre" showed up in the English language. Both spellings, 'vampire,' and 'vampyre,' are well established in the written record.

John William Polidori is often given credit for the first English depiction of a modern-day Vampyre in his classic short story "The Vampyre," written in 1819, but it is really the English poet John Stag who must be credited, as his poem, also known as "The Vampyre," was published in 1810, nine years before the publication of Polidori's work, and there is ample evidence to show that Polidori was familiar with the poem. Nevertheless, it is from Polidori's novel, and not John Stag's poem, that the creature known today in popular culture as the vampire first became popular with the public, after the production of an 1820 opera based on the novel, this time called "Le Vampire" was wildly successful.

Lord Byron, the infamous 19th century rake who was certainly an inspiration for Polidori's original tale, was erroneously given credit for "The Vampyre," much to the frustration of both men. Polidori was incensed to be overshadowed by a man with whom he had a complicated personal history (the villainously vampiric Lord Ruthven of Polidori's novel is an obvious barb at Byron's darkly romantic reputation), and for his part, Byron made it clear that he did not wish to be associated with vampire stories at all, stating, *"I have, besides, a personal dislike of vampires, and the little acquaintance I have with them would by no means indulge me to divulge their secrets".*

At the end of Victorian era, Jack the Ripper terrorized the Whitechapel district of London, causing a media sensation and a frenzy of rumors about the supernatural. While the murders themselves occurred in 1888, the official investigation didn't take place until 1894, just as Bram Stoker completed the draft of his famous novel, *Dracula*.

During the editing process, Stoker's publisher decided it would be best to change all mentions of the word 'Vampyre' in his novel to 'vampire'. Vampyre seemed too ethnic, given the politics of the time— especially given that the main suspects in the Whitechapel murders were two Eastern European men, Seweryn Kłosowski and Aaron Kosminski. In 1895 a race riot occurred in London's East End over Scotland Yard's inability to convict a suspect and infamously, the case has never been formally considered solved.

The removal of some of the overt ethnic overtones from *Dracula* reflected socially acceptable standards in the Victorian world prevalent amongst members of high and society at the time. After that, the word was popularly spelled with an 'i.'

Nevertheless, it was the power imbued in John Polidori's creative decision to spell Vampyre with a 'y' in 1819 which initiated a chain of events that established the archetype which remains so iconic to this day, and as such, Vampyre with a 'y' was used by many in the old school subculture to differentiate between fantasy and lifestyle, and the Strigoi Vii, Sabretooth Clan and Black Veils continues to be further this tradition today.

CHAPTER 2

ELORATHIAN / STRIGOI VII PRINCIPLES

"[T]here are two types of laws; just and unjust. I would be the first to advocate obeying just laws. One has not only a legal but a moral responsibility to obey just laws… a just law is a code that squares with the moral law… rooted in eternal law and natural law."

—Dr. Martin Luther King, Jr.,
"Letter from Birmingham City Jail"

The Five Elorathian / Strigoi Vii Principles:

1. Law; Strigoi Vii are abide by the laws of the Mundane World.
2. Responsibility; all Strigoi Vii are adults.
3. Blood; the Strigoi Vii see blood as a metaphor for something far more subtle·
4. Quest; the Strigoi Vii have a unified cause—the current and the quest.
5. Secrecy; the Strigoi Vii are an open secret, hidden in plain sight.

These Principles lie at the foundation of the Mysteries and contain our most sacred values. In fact, they have greatly influenced the original Black Veils in the many incarnations. They have been created in order to ensure us the freedom of a solid, real-world, Dayside foundation. The edition presented here pertains exclusively to the Strigoi Vii and the Ordo Strigoi Vii.

The Strigoi Vii Principles have been the source of our ethics and power and is our staff and our shield. It exists for the preservation and prosperity of our Mysteries, Family, and the Order and is endorsed by the Synod. Those who are not Strigoi Vii or outside the tradition and OSV are not expected to uphold these Principles, as they are not bound to them. Of course, we of the Strigoi Vii encourage even those who are not of the Family to recognize and respect the common sense inherent in our Principles. These simple guidelines provide Us with the freedom to maneuver unhindered through the mundane world.

From the perspective of the Strigoi Vii, other codes of conduct have high merit; however, they have not fully captured or expressed in words how to avoid potential liabilities faced in the tangible Dayside realities of the everyday world. Contemporary Dayside reality must be addressed in order to ensure the security and prosperity of the Family in the Nightside. It is unwise and self-defeating for a Strigoi Vii or Black Swan to betray themself by violating the common sense of these Principles. These simple guidelines should not be seen as restricting, but instead as empowering, as they offer us the means to exist and thrive responsibly and judiciously within muggle society.

If a Strigoi Vii violates these Principles, they will suffer not only obvious consequences within the Vampyre Community and amongst the Family, but, most importantly, a condition of negative Zhep'r known as khaskt, which means "loss of opportunity." In effect, those who violate the Veil are robbing themselves of their own Zhep'r and actually reversing their opportunity for Immortality of the Self. Khaskt can be seen as the Strigoi Vii equivalent of negative karma. Yet it is much more potent for those attuned to the Vampyre Current through Initiation, or by employing the Mysteries on any level.

Strigoi Vii promote social responsibility and recognizes that the consequences of our actions may have various, often negative, real world as we become more visible to the mundane world through Open Rule. Those who proudly bear the Legacy Ankh and or Legacy Ouroboros close to their hearts, be they Strigoi Vii, Black Veils Vampyre or Black Swan, make the statement that they are in agreement with the Principles of the Strigoi Vii and have read the Black Veils. These Principles are innate common sense for the responsible members of our Family. These Principles give us the freedom and foundation to live and thrive within mundane society without offending or placing fear into our Source.

1st Principle: Law ~ *Strigoi Vii are abide by the laws of the Mundane World.*

Adherence to the laws of our local governments, even if we disagree with them, is essential to provide Us with the freedom to explore our Nightside nature. Criminal or illegal behavior is greatly condemned within Strigoi Vii culture. By this, we do not refer to minor legal infractions such as parking violations. We are referring to serious crimes such as fraud, drug dealing, murder, rape, assault, and theft. Remember innocent until proven guilty is essential. Strigoi Vii are free spirited and individualistic. However, all Strigoi Vii are expected to act with common sense and practice social responsibility. It is the duty of every Strigoi Vii to conduct themselves in a manner that will not bring negative consequences upon the Family.

2nd Principle: Responsibility ~ *Strigoi Vii are adults.*

We must honor the need for minors to establish a skeptical, objective, and rational Dayside foundation before exploring and embracing the Nightside. Those who have not reached the age of majority (eighteen in the United States) must not be encouraged or permitted to explore our Mysteries, participate in Vampyre ritual, or enter our Sanctums under any conditions. Thus, no child shall ever be formally Initiated into the Mysteries of Strigoi Vii, either privately or publicly.

Those children curious about our Mysteries should explore the basics of yoga, quantum physics, theology, paganism, magick, Reiki, martial arts, and the works of philosophers such as Charles Darwin, Frederick Nietzsche, and Ayn Rand. This way, they build a solid foundation that shall better prepare them to pursue Zhep'r upon coming of age.

3rd Principle: Blood ~ *Strigoi Vii see Blood as a metaphor for something far more subtle.*

From the perspective of the Strigoi Vii, the Art of Gathering Energy occurs purely on a subtle Lifeforce energetic level, and thus Living Vampyres do not need to drink of Corporeal, physical blood for gathering energies. The word Blood with a capital B is merely a metaphorical term for the subtle vital Lifeforce better known as *Lifeforce* in Sanskrit, *Chi* in Chinese medicine, or *Ki* in Japanese martial arts. On the Nightside perspective, We practice other, more subtle forms of absorbing and obtaining energy, which We find much more efficient and pertinent to our Mysteries. On a Dayside level, the decision not to drink blood leads to a clear avoidance of legal liabilities and health risks such as blood-borne diseases, including hepatitis, syphilis, HIV/AIDS, and many more.

4th Principle: Quest ~ *Strigoi Vii have a unified cause—the Current and the Quest.*

The Current is the signature of our Family. The collective duty of all Strigoi Vii is the Quest of Family. We must search out those with potential to Awaken, yet who are not aware of their potential. However, We never force a potential to follow our way, as Vampyres are not mindless followers. Potentials must be allowed to come to the Family in their own way and in their own time. The Strigoi Vii should always use one of the proven tools for supporting the Quest of Family, as to not degrade our Mysteries. Give the Seeker a hint, let them feel the Calling, and come when and if they are ready. Never support or join an organization or individual that actively opposes the Family or our Quest. Never enter into debates with the mortal-minded or try to convert them to our ways, as such behavior is in conflict with the Glamour and a waste of time and energy. Betraying the Quest of Family is not only betraying the Family, but also yourself.

5th Principle: Secrets ~ *Strigoi Vii is an open secret, hidden in plain sight.*

Secrets protect and bind us. Our Mysteries are our own, and those who wish to explore them should seek them out alone, through personal initiative and action. As a sleight of hand magician employs the Principle of "hidden in plain sight," so does the Living Vampyre.

Here follow three examples of the Principle of Secrets. Firstly, take example from the Adeptus and Magisters. Honor your Sorors' and Fraters' right of privacy, such as in respect to their mundane identity. Never disclose their personal information to anyone, especially to the mortal-minded, but even to other Family members, without their explicit permission. The only circumstance under which the Synod would disclose the given name and identity of any Strigoi Vii is if such information was required under the legal jurisdiction of the proper authorities.

Secondly, public discussion of Strigoi Vii and the Mysteries outside of the Sanctums, such as with the media, on social networking websites, in public, or with those not of the Blood, is an obvious violation of this Principle. At all times speak only for yourself and never represent the greater Family or OSV outside of the guidelines of the Quest of Family. Leave that to those select members of the OSV who are properly trained in public relations. Supporting this Principle furthers the Glamour and protects our Mysteries.

Finally, one of the most important aspects of these Principles is avoiding discussion of the Mysteries with someone who has not had the opportunity to read the Black Veils and Strigoi Vii Codex and reflect on the contents. Respect free will and let Seekers gain a first impression of the Mysteries and formulate an opinion on their own. When an individual has the opportunity to read a text, they shall draw their own conclusions, whilst if you tell them about it, they will more likely only be able to see it from your perspective.

Summation

The Strigoi Vii Principles is our code and applies only to the Strigoi Vii or those involved with the OSV. Employ these proven Principles, and you will have a solid foundation for Zhep'r. Do not debate with others who disagree or cannot see the common sense outlined here. As they are not in agreement, simply smile and say, *"We must agree to disagree, for free will is the whole of the law."*

CHAPTER 3
PHILOSOPHY

"There are more things in heaven and earth, Horatio, Than are dreamt of in your philosophy."

— William Shakespeare, *Hamlet*

Elorathian / Strigoi Vii philosophy is difficult to explain in a few or even many words. First and foremost, Living Vampyres are passionate about life and seek its continuance. Strigoi Vii philosophy has at its core Immortality and preservation of the Self, whilst being in touch with our core primal and animalistic nature and simultaneously finding empowerment in modern society.

We employ a philosophical stance called that of the "Immortal-minded," centered on our Quest for Immortality of the Self. This ethos is in direct contrast to the common "mortal-minded" perspective on life. This is why you see references to "mortals" in Strigoi Vii literature. Additionally, in our daily life We seek an equilibrium between our Dayside and our Nightside philosophies. We call this equilibrium the Twilight. Without the Twilight, it is impossible to fully achieve Zhep'r.

The Dayside is the beginning of the journey of Zhep'r and deals with the

Mortal Coil of reality as perceived and experienced through the five senses. Here the Strigoi Vii seeks individual mastery of the Self and achievement of a strong-willed, autonomous, objective, and rational foundation. Yet mastering the Dayside also involves a strong awareness of an instinctive, primal inner nature of every human and Living Vampyre. This is the cornerstone of mastery of the Self and the Dayside. The Strigoi Vii takes a responsible approach to the material world and associated indulgences. They are aware and in control of the duality of their primal animalistic urges and their civilized, refined nature. The Strigoi Vii is mindful of their similarities to, as well as their distinct differences from, the mortal minded. The Strigoi Vii also seeks dominion over the mortal coils, such as happiness, a long and healthy corporeal life, accumulation of life experience and knowledge, and material mastery in prosperous living circumstances (including financial freedom and a high standard of living). The Living Vampyres look to the future with ambition and excitement, yet do not deign to mortgage their present for future hopes.

By nature, Strigoi Vii are very independent and individualistic. However, they may also be highly social beings when they so choose or when the mood strikes them. For the Strigoi Vii, the personal, inwardly empowered ego, which focuses on preservation and evolution of the Self, always comes before all else. In essence, their knowledge of who they are comes from within. The Living Vampyre draws a clear distinction between this inwardly empowered ego and the insecure, externally gratified ego. Individuals with an externally gratified ego have no intrinsic sense of Self. Instead, their Self is shaped and changed by their personal interactions, material circumstances, and how they are perceived by others. In a vain attempt to fill the void within them, they set about controlling and manipulating others for a burst of temporary, hollow ego satisfaction. Such an approach to life has nothing to do with personal evolution. Living Vampyre's philosophy encourages the personal self-mastery of knowing and controlling oneself first, not controlling others. Free will is amongst the highest of all virtues to the Strigoi Vii, and thus We respect the free will of all sentient beings.

In order to truly live life, you must fully experience it with all your senses. However, before this can be achieved, you must first break free of subjugation to mortal slave bonds such as destructive drugs, unhealthy relationships, mind-numbing television shows, escapism through video game or Internet addictions, and constant indulgence in unhealthy fast foods, to mention just a few. Such things are merely distractions which, when practiced to excess, only dull the senses, harm the body, and thus prevent you from truly living. A true Strigoi Vii know how to amuse themself in a nondestructive manner and control their possessions, finances, and pastimes instead of being controlled by them.

In true postmodern fashion, the Strigoi Vii see constructed boundaries and social roles for what they are and seek to live life as they choose without being bound by artificial conventions. Strigoi Vii are very sensual, romantic, and passionate and may often have a taste for the ways of the libertine. An important element of Strigoi Vii is carnal pleasure and worship of the flesh and seeing one's body as a temple of flesh. Many Strigoi Vii deliberately subvert or deny the gender and sexual roles and class strictures found in mundane society. Living Vampyres love the finest pleasures of life, such as conversation and debate, art, music, gourmet food, dance, and literature. They will never force others to adopt their views or actions, always respecting others' free will above all else. However, they will also try to inspire and encourage others to live a more unfettered and fulfilling life.

Strigoi Vii do not prescribe to blind faith, and thus strive to break the conditioning of mortal-minded beliefs and dogma, seeking knowledge only through results. In this sense, the Strigoi Vii is very similar to the scientist who constantly investigates and tests the world around him before drawing conclusions or fashioning laws of nature.

Money and monetary gains are not seen as evil by the Strigoi Vii unless they control and warp the Self through avarice and greed. The Strigoi Vii view money and capital as a form of material energy that is neither beneficial nor harmful. Thus, they call such currencies "monetary energy." The Strigoi Vii are very careful to never allow themselves to be controlled by their material possessions.

Common amongst the Strigoi Vii is the modern application of historical and long-lost forms of customs and chivalry. These can range from holding elegant masquerade balls or Victorian tea parties to the study of dead languages. Taking inspiration from the code of chivalry of medieval knights, many masculine Strigoi Vii embrace gentlemanly codes of conduct, strive for individual nobility, and treat all others with courtesy. It is also common to find feminine Strigoi Vii embracing the role of truly elegant ladies and sincere witches. They draw directly upon the feminine aspect of the word Kitra and the Vampyre Witch and their Queen Within as a source of their empowerment and mastery. However, it is worth noting that Strigoi Vii recognize and respect alternative lifestyles and "abnormal" conceptions of individual gender roles. Even though the yin and yang of masculine and feminine may be seen as distinct yet balanced opposites, many Living Vampyres have varied understandings and applications of masculinity and femininity.

The above examples and behaviors reflect only a portion of the Dayside perspectives found within the Family. As always, Strigoi Vii encourages individuals to define their own attitudes and paths in life.

The Nightside is the equal opposite of the Dayside in Strigoi Vii philosophy. In the Nightside, the Strigoi Vii moves beyond the Mysteries of rational reality such as science and the laws of physics. The Living Vampyre must have an absolute grounding in the Dayside to effectively explore the Mysteries of the Nightside. In the Nightside, the Strigoi Vii can investigate the many subtle worlds that intersect with our material world. The Nightside encompasses the Ethereal, the domain of Lifeforce (vital life energy) and many forms of energy sensitivity and manipulation. The mortal-minded view our Nightside as occultism and mysticism. The beginnings of Strigoi Vii theology lie in the Nightside. Our theology is not a trendy new-age blind acceptance of crude belief and faith, but rather a scientific approach to exploration of the subtle worlds. In the Nightside, the Strigoi Vii deeply explores quantum physics, meditation, energy work such as Reiki, Tantra, and yoga, and sacred geometry. Individual experience and achieved results form the foundation of Strigoi Vii theology, not antique articles of accepted dogma.

The Twilight represents a higher level of the Vampyre Mysteries and is detailed in the tome "Coming Forth by Twilight. "The Twilight is the contrasting balance between the Dayside and Nightside, allowing the Strigoi Vii who becomes adept in Twilight to fully enjoy the pleasures and benefits of both. With such mastery, the Strigoi Vii can rise to fully embrace the experiences of the Astral, dream walking, and higher planes of existence.

Gnosis is the personal experience of divinity, spirituality, and the

Self. A most important part of Gnosis for the Strigoi Vii is the Quest for Immortality. The Strigoi Vii strives for personal survival and preservation of the Self beyond the First Death of the Corporeal body. To this end, the Strigoi Vii always seek to increase their own Zhep'r and master an evolved state that may be described as timeless, nonlinear, and transcending ordinary reality. Yet the Strigoi Vii must first ignite the Quest of Immortality of the Self through a deeply rooted foundation in the Dayside perspective. Through mastery of the Dayside and the Nightside, as well as the equilibrium between them, known as Twilight, the Strigoi Vii may truly discover personal Immortality of the Self.

> *An adoration of Osiris, Un-nefer, god great within Abydos, king of eternity, lord of everlasting, traversing millions of years in the duration of his life, son eldest of the womb of Nut, engendered by Seb the chief, lord of ureret crown, lofty of the white crown, prince of gods and of men, he hath received the crook [and] flail and the dignity of his fathers...*
> *Eternity it is and Everlastingness, Eternity is the day, Everlastingness is the night.*
>
> —*The Papyrus of Ani,* or *The Egyptian Book of the Dead,*
> E. A. Wallis Budge (trans.)

Zhep'r is the Strigoi Vii word for metamorphosis, evolution, transformation of the Self, and the Quest of Immortality. This term is formed from two words: the Egyptian *Kheperi* (transform) and the Greek *Zephyr* (the god of the West Wind.) The word Kheper is also related to the terms *Kheperi* and the Egyptian transformation of Kheperu and can be translated as "to come into being," "to become," and "transformation." Another source of the word is *Khepera,* the name for the morning incarnation of the Sun god in Egyptian mythology. The associated Egyptian symbol or hieroglyph is a scarab beetle. The scarab beetle lays its eggs in carrion, which gave the Ancient Egyptians the impression that these insects were born from death. Thus, the scarab came to represent rebirth. Although our term Zhep'r has a different phonetic value than the original Egyptian word (the Egyptian word is pronounced khef-fer, and our term is pronounced zef-hur), it carries a similar definition and meaning. There is another earlier form of this Aeonic word, *Xeper*, which is employed by the Temple of Set, a left-hand path esoteric order founded in 1975 by Michael Aquino.

Strigoi Vii are agents of change, beings of evolution and transformation. Zhep'r is this process of change. Nothing in the universe is absolutely fixed and eternal. Strigoi Vii revel in evolution. To the Strigoi Vii, Chaos is freedom!

From the Dayside perspective, Zhep'r is self-mastery and improvement. Dayside Zhep'r focuses on furthering the material coils such as financial freedom, improving one's personal Glamour, and living a prosperous, healthy, and long and vital life. From the Nightside perspective, Zhep'r is the Awakening and mastery of the Strigoi Vii's psychic abilities, connection to the subtle worlds and the achievement of spiritual Immortality of the Self. The core of the Strigoi Vii Quest is conquering the Second Death, which is the dissolution of the consciousness that occurs sometime after the physical body has ceased to function. Strigoi Vii call this the Oblivescence, or the process of forgetting, as the soul is washed in a spiritual amnesia or is fully energetically dispersed, depending on your perspective. Zhep'r is further expressed in the process of self-deification. This involves solving the Mysteries on a personal level, Awakening the Dragon (higher Self), and Coming Forth by Twilight.

For the Strigoi Vii, Zhep'r is not a goal but a constant journey. There is no end to the Quest of Zhep'r except Second Death. Thus the Second Death is the only true enemy of the Living Vampyre.

"Belief is a Tool."

—Peter J. Carroll, author of *Liber Null & Psychonaut*

Is Strigoi Vii a religion? Yes and no! Vampyric Gathering of Energy is not a religion but an action performed by the Strigoi Vii. Strigoi Vii our philosophy and traditions, as well as our Art of Gathering Energy, are a group of tested concepts and applications, not a belief system. Thus, Strigoi Vii is not a religion in the common sense of the word. Its reality is far more complex.

The Strigoi Vii Mysteries are a spiritual and philosophical metaparadigm or meta-belief system, which is based on the ability to paradigm shift (utilize various belief systems and methods, based on applicability, to achieve a specific purpose). For the Strigoi Vii, belief is a tool that can be applied at will. Thus, the Living Vampyre may adopt and discard different epistemological systems and philosophies as it suits their needs, rather than acting unconsciously on inescapably ingrained belief.

One of the characteristics of those attuned to our nature is that they cannot truly be of another "religion." So, it is incorrect for an Awakened Strigoi Vii to say, "I am a pagan," or "I am a Satanist." The awakened Strigoi Vii has come to the collective agreement that religion is a system of arbitrary belief used by humans to attempt to understand the reality around them as well as to control others' behavior. Our use of religion is different. Strigoi Vii employ belief systems, known as paradigms or ideologies, to adopt a temporary view that will aid them in Zhep'r or employment of the Glamour. They then discard the system when it is no longer useful. This viewpoint is very similar to the mechanics of Chaos Magick.

To make an analogy, Strigoi Vii is like the core operating system of a computer, whilst each paradigm is like a separate program or application. The program you employ depends on your need. To navigate the Internet, you choose a web browser. A word processing program is useful only if you wish to create a text document. For example, a Strigoi Vii may love the practices and traditions of Asatru, or Norse paganism. Thus, they may employ the rituals and magick of that particular paradigm to further their sense of Self and increase their Zhep'r. However, this does not make that Strigoi Vii truly an Asatru; they are simply employing or "wearing" Asatru beliefs and traditions as one would wear an article of clothing. Many of the feminine Strigoi Vii appreciate the goddess-centered elements found within many traditions of neopaganism. Thus, they can make use of the beliefs of myriad pagan religions and enjoy the pleasures of feminine goddess-oriented empowerment. Many members of our Family may have a preferred paradigm as a mortal might prefer a specific type of cuisine or genre of literature.

Today, We are seeing a new movement sometimes known as "Traditionalist Strigoi Vii" developing within the Family and Vampyre Current. These pioneers find existing without beliefs or paradigms and recognizing their true

Self is most beneficial to them. To these traditionalists, any belief, even a temporarily adopted one, can be seen as a crutch. However, Strigoi Vii are nothing if not mutable and flexible. They may wear many masks, not only in their spiritual existence, but in their everyday lives as well. Strigoi Vii are Sunday school teachers, politicians, university professors, doctors, artists, religious leaders, and police officers. There are even Strigoi Vii within the ministry of the Catholic Church!

Such seeming paradoxes are possible because, whilst personal paradigms have strong meanings for these individuals, they clearly realize they are Strigoi Vii first and foremost. How else do you think so many members of the Family have walked through the history of mankind so easily and gracefully?

> *A monster then, a dream,*
> *A discord. Dragons of the prime,*
> *That tare each other in their slime,*
> *Were mellow music match'd with him...*
> *What hope of answer, or redress?*
> *Behind the veil, behind the veil.*
>
> —Alfred, Lord Tennyson, "In Memoriam"

The Dragon has long been associated with mystery, magick, power, nobility, and divinity. The Dragon is a powerful symbol that is as deeply ingrained in the world's mythology and legends as the vampire mythos. Within each Strigoi Vii, the Dragon exists as a higher consciousness of the Self. This Divine Spark breathes forth the Dark Flame for each member of the Family and is the Throne from which all perception is experienced. Within Strigoi Vii theology, the Dragon represents our pacts with ancient divinities, the spiral helix of the divine potential existing in our subtle bodies, our higher Self, and our animalistic primal nature. Thus, word Elorath, our spiritual Blood, is seen as a "Dance of Dragons" by many within the Family.

The concept of the higher Self has been recently popularized by contemporary new-age and occult movements. However, it was recognized long before. Aleister Crowley spoke of the higher Self as the "Holy Guardian

Angel" within each person, or the manifestation of true will. Other cultures have called the higher Self or similar concepts by various names. The Hermetic Order of the Golden Dawn called it the Genius, and it was named the Daemon in Greek mythology. An early appearance of the term occurs in the fifteenth-century grimoire entitled The Book of the Sacred Magic of Abramelin the Mage.

The Corporeal manifestation of the Dragon is the reptilian brain, which is the portion of the brain first identified by Dr. Paul D. MacLean. It is also known as the brain stem, or the lower part of the brain. The reptilian brain controls essential involuntary functions such as the cardiovascular and respiratory system. We share the structure of the brain stem with reptiles, and it is also believed to be responsible for primitive rage and flight-or-fight responses. In the mammalian brain, the brain stem represents the most ancient and unchanged part of the brain structure. Other, more highly evolved, portions of the brain exist in their present form due to the process of mammalian evolution. The reptilian brain may be seen as the seat of primitive and animalistic functions.

For the Strigoi Vii, achieving Communion with the Dragon is to see the world through the Dragon's emerald eyes: to see beyond our set conceptions and engage in pure perception, unhindered by ingrained mortal-minded ideas of what is and what is not. Such Communion may be achieved through meditation, development of the Self, and the furthering of Zhep'r. For the Strigoi Vii, experiencing and maintaining this Communion is a foundational point in personal evolution and self-knowledge. Awakening the Dragon of the Self is a core Principle of the Strigoi Vii Mysteries.

CHAPTER 4

ART OF GATHERING ENERGY

*Energy is the only life and is from the Body; and Reason is the bound
or outward circumference of Energy.
Energy is Eternal Delight.*

—William Blake,
"The Marriage of Heaven and Hell"

E very living being transfers energy. This transfer occurs in every interaction, be it as simple as two people trading glances across a room,
a conversation between a mother and child, or even one animal
devouring another. As Albert Einstein explained in his theory of relativity, matter and energy are incontrovertible (E = mc2). Everything in the
physical world contains energy and can be transformed into energy, from
the lightning in the sky during a thunderstorm to the chair you are sitting
in as you read this book. Moreover, as Newton stated, energy can never be
created or destroyed, only transformed. When you eat, the food does not
"disappear." Instead, part of it is transformed into energy that powers your

physical body, and part of it remains as waste products. The transformation and transmission of energy is an endless cycle. The Gathering of Energy is a core practice of Living Vampyrism.

Every person who has been in a large group of people knows the experience of collective energy. The "energy of the crowd" can be sensed in various circumstances, such as a concert, political rally, sporting event, or university lecture. When a group of people gather for one focused purpose, a huge amount of collective emotional and corporeal energy is produced. Many people will report feeling "psyched up" or "energized" after taking part in such a gathering. Humans are amazing beings! When a large number of humans come together and share a thrilling or emotionally charged experience, they release huge amounts of energy. We, as Strigoi Vii, can sense and gather this ambient energy. We call collective energy generated by large crowds Ambient Energy and learning how to gather and absorb this Lifeforce energy is the most elementary form of the Strigoi Vii Nightside practices.

Anyone working in a performance-oriented profession, such as a musician, DJ, tour guide, public speaker, motivational coach, professor, or politician, experiences a flow of energy between themselves and their audience. Many who choose such professions or even become celebrities do so because they have a deep hunger for this experience. They feel charged and exhilarated in front of an audience. The emotions of the audience, whether approval or disdain, provide a "flavor" of the Lifeforce energy during such a performance. That is why so many of these individuals are drawn to Strigoi Vii.

You may ask if this applies on a subtle level for divine entities. Absolutely! The gods and goddesses of mortal religions absorb Ambient energy on a grand scale from their worshippers. For example, the godform Allah receives energy from the daily prayers of millions of Muslims. More than 1.1 billion people send immense amounts of energy toward the godform Jesus every Sunday morning. Could it be that when humans worship their deities with such loving free will they are really giving life to and feeding the most successful Vampyres in history?

The Art of Gathering Energy, at its core, is an exchange of energies. As practiced by the Strigoi Vii and defined by the Strigoi Vii Codex, the Art of Gathering Energy is a series of methods for ethically and honorably gathering the surplus subtle life energies radiated by the human body. The Art of Gathering Energy is an integral part of the nature and existence of the Strigoi Vii. All Strigoi Vii who move toward the Nightside practice this sacred Art, usually instinctively at first, then consciously as an Initiate, and finally without effort once they have Ascended to a high level of mastery. Please note that the purpose and intent of our Art of Gathering Energy is completely distinct from that practiced by traditional psychic vampires. One of the biggest misconceptions is that all vampires drink blood. This is simply not true. The Strigoi Vii of Romanian myths as well as the modern day Strigoi Vii are typically not blood drinkers. Our energy gathering is most effective on a subtle level and spiritual. From the Dayside perspective, there are the obvious health risks like contracting HIV, hepatitis, or infection and the fact that in many cultures drinking blood is not only taboo—it is considered an act of cannibalism and assault as well. From the Nightside perspective, blood drinking is not an efficient technique to provide the large amounts of energy required to fuel transformation. For the Living Vampire, all references to blood are strictly metaphorical and symbolic. The purpose of our Vampyrism is, first and foremost, to fuel direct Offerings of Lifeforce in Communion with the Vampyre Current, and thus our Ancestors.. Communion is the main catalyst to ignite Zhep'r and the most sacred and private act within all the Strigoi Vii Mysteries. Communion is the gateway to Immortality of the Self. On a more advanced level, the Lifeforce procured is used for the application of Clavicula Sangraal Vampyre Sorcery, a multidimensional vibrational system that is at the core of the Inner Mysteries. However, at the most basic level, Vampyrism takes place in order to fuel Zhep'r and to raise the metabolism of the subtle body, which aids in the process of furthering Zhep'r.

The human body is the most evolved Corporeal entity, and thus creates a specific, high-intensity frequency of Lifeforce (the Sanskrit word for vital Lifeforce), which is the most suited to the energetic system of the Strigoi Vii subtle body. Lifeforce is thus the source and fuel of life, that is why we consider Ourselves Living Vampires. Other frequencies of Lifeforce, such as that from animals, plants, or objects, have their uses. However, they are simply not compatible with and cannot be of use in fueling Zhep'r. Nor are they suitable for the Offering in Communion. Many un-Awakened Living

Vampyres practice Gathering unconsciously, as their subtle bodies vibrate on a higher frequency than the average human and create an instinctual thirst for Lifeforce. Through the disciplines of the Art of Gathering Energy— will, intent, and training— the un-Awakened Vampyre can learn to master Gathering Lifeforce as an art. This "need" for subtle energy is akin to the "thirst" or "hunger" in vampire literature and media. As Zhep'r increases, so does the Need for more energy.

The Art of Gathering Energy can be seen by the uninformed as a maliciously predatory act. However, we are not without a deep-rooted system of ethics. Although the Art of Gathering Energy is an action that intentionally and consciously draws Lifeforce energy from the subtle bodies of humans, it is not a parasitic act, as is the case with traditional psychic vampirism which is feeding on negative emotions. Through our Art of Gathering Energy, as in the transfer of energies within the web of life, the flow of energy is actually healthy, advantageous, and very pleasurable for the human. This is a highly symbiotic relationship and has truly evolved beyond what most would consider true predation. Within the Strigoi Vii Mysteries, the gathering of energies from Lifeforce energies never involves the drinking of physical blood, ending the life of any living being, or causing physical harm of any kind. If done with respect and care, the Art of Gathering Energy is not physically, emotionally, or spiritually harmful to the human subtle body in any way. The Art of Gathering Energy is beneficial and affirming for the Strigoi Vii and the mundane alike.

As a rough analogy, one might consider the pilot fish that attaches itself to a shark. The pilot fish consumes parasites and bits of undigested food that would otherwise potentially cause harm to the shark. Despite the fact that sharks are often seen as consummate predators, it is extremely rare for a shark to consume a pilot fish, even when it swims into the shark's mouth to remove pieces of food from its teeth (thus preserving them from decay.) Both the pilot fish and the shark benefit from and mutually thrive due to their symbiotic relationship. So is it with the mortal-minded and the Vampyre.

Throughout history, many subtle energetic techniques such as Reiki, Tantric workings, and yoga have utilized similar processes as the Art of Gathering Energy. Gathering Lifeforce, in our view, is an exchange of energies

Performers such as actors or musicians exchange energy with their audience every time they perform. The only difference is that the Strigoi Vii has a specific intent and purpose in collecting this excess energy. One can also witness this relationship and exchange of energies reflected in the symbiotic relationship between deities and their worshipful followers, or celebrities and their starstruck admiring fans. Such acts are, in our worldview, unconscious applications of our basic Arts of Gathering.

In effect, gathering lifeforce can, from our view, be considered a healing act. It may be seen as beneficial to the mortal world, for We remove and unblock stagnant energies and inspire the flow of radiant energies through the subtle world and humanity's collective consciousness. This is why so many are unconsciously seduced by Vampyres. However,, Strigoi Vii do not slaughter or torture for pleasure or any other purpose! Any such act is always reprehensible within the ethical system of the Strigoi Vii. We respectfully take what We need due to a pure love of life. Our clear intent is that our sources live happy, fulfilled, and content lives.

All we have to go upon are traditions and superstitions. These do not at the first appear much…Yet must we be satisfied, in the first place because we have to be, no other means is at our control, and secondly, because, after all these things, tradition and superstition, are everything. Does not the belief in vampires rest… on them?

—Bram Stoker, ***Dracula***

For it is the life of all flesh; the blood of it is the life thereof…Ye shall eat the blood of no manner of flesh; for the life of all flesh is the blood thereof: whosoever eateth it shall be cut off.

—Leviticus 17:14

CHAPTER 5
FAMILY

"Blood is thicker than water."

—Proverb

Frater, We are of the same Current of Blood, the same frequency of spirit. We are those with the drive, courage, love of life, will, and desire to embrace the opportunity for Immortality of the Self. Never forget this is the agreement which bonds us as Family. As you experience Zhep'r, you will come to understand this.

—Magister Dimitri, August 1997

Strigoi Vii, as a collective of individuals and a Family, are bound by an unbreakable spiritual and metaphysical bond. To reflect this bond, we metaphorically refer to those of the Strigoi Vii Family as "of the Blood," or simply by the Latin word for blood, Sanguine. The Family of Strigoi Vii does not exactly correspond to a biological mortal family. We experience a far stronger bond with other Strigoi Vii that is difficult to explain to those who are not of the Blood. We call this our Nightside Family.

When encountering another of our tradition, we often immediately recognize them through the *Radiance*, or a subtle intuition of who and what they are. The strength of the Radiance depends on several factors. A Strigoi Vii who has reached a high level of Initiation, is strongly in tune with the Current of Elorath, or has recently been sated with Lifeforce or made Communion may emit a Radiance that burns like a flame. Un-Awakened individuals will often exhibit a dim glimmer of the Radiance, whilst for some it will shine like a lighthouse in the darkness. Some Strigoi Vii have described the experience of sensing the Radiance as being strongly and seemingly inexplicably drawn to another or feeling a deep-rooted and unexplainable sympathy with or liking for someone. Many Strigoi Vii have also reported that others of the Family emanate a sort of subtle "glow," hence the term Radiance.

The Currents that surge within our souls are deep rooted and, from a certain perspective, quite ancient. Our sense of pride in our Family and our connection with others of our Family is a reflection of this agreement. We do not know the origins of the Current, nor do We dwell on this. We look toward the here and now as well as the future yet recognize our commonality as Family.

Awakening as a process comes to members of the Family in three different forms: Latent Vampyres, Born Vampyres, and Made Vampyres. Such experiences affect each Vampyre differently, as not everyone is at a point of self-awareness when they realize the Vampyre Current is present within them.

Latent Vampyres are formally known as *Klavasi*. This is the most common type of awakening within the Current—when a Strigoi Vii realizes their Radiance. It occurs at some point after puberty. One theory on the origins of Latent Vampyres is that during or shortly after the conception of their Corporeal bodies, an Ancestor implanted the seed of the Current within them while they were in their mother's womb. Another possibility is that one or both of their parents carry a spiritual gene of the Current in their subtle bodies and passed it on to their child, thus giving them the potential to Awaken as a Latent Vampyre. The awakening is usually triggered by experiences like trauma, being fed on deeply by another Vampyre, being in the vicinity of a large Communion rite, being exposed to one of the many avenues of the Quest, having a sexual encounter with another Vampyre, or a series of bizarre events that seem akin to fate. Most Seekers are Latent Vampyres and many describe the awakening as akin to the realization one is gay or that they have a calling. Latent Vampyres may always feel drawn to the others of the Family. The Strigoi Vii Codex primarily caters to Latent Vampyres and the Initiation structure aids them in their awakening and furthers their Zhep'r.

Born Vampyres are formally known as *Quissain* and are very rare. Such individuals were virtually born Awakened and instinctively are aware of what they are. As children, the Quissain are usually very eccentric and will most often have multitudes of symptoms such as dyslexia, antisocial disorders, hyperactivity, and more. Born Vampyres will almost always display psychic abilities and excel in energy work such as yoga and Reiki. What is most interesting is that Quissain make up the most Ronin and rarely Initiate. Amongst the Family they manifest mostly as pure Ramkht in frequency and behavior, with a strong sense of confidence and natural talents at the Art of Gathering Energy.

Turned Vampyres are formally known as *Ardetha* and undergo a series of rites and conscious Initiations—or they have been touched on such a deep level that they Awaken. The ritual for made Vampyres is only known to select Magisters and is rarely used. Sometimes this is known as the Kiss of Elorath. There are many controversies regarding Ardetha amongst members of the Strigoi Vii Family, some believing that we can only be born to what we are (purebloods), whilst others feel that in this time and age it is important to allow mortals (or "half-breeds") the opportunity to become. Whatever the story, the individual must demonstrate potential and a sincere interest in joining the Family. Such an Awakening is usually very traumatic and cannot occur without the agreement and involvement of a Strigoi Morte who is willing to become the Patron of the individual who is to receive the Kiss.

Paths constitute the variety of ways people interact with the Strigoi Vii Mysteries. There are three paths within the Strigoi Vii Mysteries: Black Swans, Ronin, and Initiates.

Black Swans are those who do not consider themselves a Strigoi Vii, yet are drawn to the Mysteries and our Current. Black Swans can be involved in the OSV and often benefit from elements of the Mysteries. Most often Black Swans are friends, lovers, companions, or mundane family members of a Strigoi Vii Ronin or Initiate. Many Black Swans have read the the Black Veils and Strigoi Vii Codex and are in at least partial agreement with our Outer Mysteries. It is very common for Black Swans to offer themselves as consensual energy donors in order to benefit from the Awakening and healing powers of the Art of Gathering Energy or to experience energy transfer on a sensual level. Black Swans who feel the Calling and Awaken to the Mysteries may choose to embrace the Mysteries on their own terms as Ronin or through formally Initiating at a later point.

Ronin are individuals who do not follow the standard Initiatory formulae of Strigoi Vii yet are in agreement with our Mysteries. They are solitary practitioners and loners. The word Ronin originates from the Japanese samurai of the Tokugawa era and means "to be without a lord." The term thus befits the solitary Strigoi Vii. Ronin are the equivalent of solitaries in other esoteric systems, and they often do not involve themselves directly in the Strigoi Vii movement. Being solitary and independent, yet still "of the Current," Ronin consider themselves Strigoi Vii but have not formally Initiated. Ronin most often focus solely on the Outer Mysteries and may have their own personal system of achieving Zhep'r. It is not uncommon for a Ronin to eventually become a formal Initiate of the Mysteries.

Initiates are the most common type of Strigoi Vii and closely work within the standard formulae of Ordeals as detailed within the Strigoi Vii Codex. They find the sequential system of Initiation greatly complements their own Zhep'r and use the Mysteries as a powerful personal tool. However, based on their own personal predilections, Initiates still pursue individual approaches to building Zhep'r and empowering their will. Being an Initiate of Strigoi Vii by no means limits individuality or the pursuit of Zhep'r. The Initiate's commitment to the Mysteries allows them to easily interact with and relate to others of the Family through the common perspectives of personal validation and organization. Initiates are the members of the Family most often Initiated into the Ordo Strigoi Vii or who sit on the Synod, due to their clearly stated qualifications and intent. One can compare Initiates to those who have gone through a university system and earned a formal degree, whilst Ronin are most often self-taught. To extend the analogy, Seekers would be prospective students who have expressed an interest in attending a particular university or starting a course of study but have not yet committed themselves.

> *We know each other*
> *by secret symbols,*
> *there is subtle appraisement;*
> *even if we [speak] a brief greeting*
> *or do not speak at all, we know our Name*
> *we nameless initiates, born of one mother,*
> *companions of the flame.*

> —H.D., "The Walls Do Not Fall"

A Sobriquet is a "Vampyre Name," and Strigoi Vii tradition encourages that, upon the Prospectii validation, the Initiate adopt this fresh, new name for exclusive use amongst other Strigoi Vii. This is quite similar to the magickal motto used within the Hermetic Order of the Golden Dawn. Sobriquets should reflect a piece of the Initiate's personality and are used within ritual and magickal workings. Such names can reflect the individual's current, vision of themselves, or identification with an ancient or obscure god or goddess. Examples include Mael ("prince" or "king" in Gaelic), Irhandi ("sorcerer" in Sumerian), and Lilith (Hebrew/Sumerian goddess).

When a Magister is Initiated, they take a second Sobriquet as their Magister name, which is their "true name" and never revealed to anyone outside the Family. The Sobriquet is to be used for correspondence with other Strigoi Vii and as a working tool in ritual and meditation. Sobriquets are similar to magickal names in mortal-minded esoteric traditions or a "handle" on the Internet. The Vampyre Sobriquet also provides additional security and privacy, as addressing a Strigoi Vii by their legal or given name is rude and disrespectful, unless they specifically request it in an open forum, or you have a personal friendship with them and are interacting in the mundane world. In addition, the Sobriquet allows the Strigoi Vii to enter a new state of mind where they are free to express themselves amongst other members of the Family.

A Sobriquet is different from an assumed "scene name," which is used for social purposes, or a "given name," which is a legal name used in the Dayside and the mundane world. The Sobriquet should be un- related to any previous aliases, magickal names, or other names the Strigoi Vii has used. Thus, when the Strigoi Vii make the Rite of Dedication, they should from that point on use a completely new and fresh name amongst the community. It should reflect a point of personal empowerment and a new beginning.

This name is chosen in StrigoiVii.org virtual sanctums as a username and maintains privacy and focus on Zhep'r.

> *And I have felt*
> *A presence that disturbs me with the joy Of elevated thoughts; a sense sublime*
> *Of something far more deeply interfused,*
> *A motion and a spirit, that impels*
> *All thinking things, all objects of all thought, And rolls through all things...*
>
> —William Wordsworth, "Lines Composed
> a Few Miles above Tintern Abbey"

The Vampyre Current of Elorath, or simply the "Current" as seen by Strigoi Vii Mysteries, flows through each member of the Family and is symbolized by the number XXIII (23). The Current emanates from the Aeonic word Elorath and generates an egregore. The reason for this numerical linkage is revealed in the Inner Mysteries. The Current is the Blood that attunes and unites the Family by the word Elorath. Egregores, in occult parlance, are group spirits comprised of the collective will, purpose, and group mind and soul of a collection of individuals. The Egregore of Elorath represents the lineage and collective "Current" of the Strigoi Vii and its various projects.

Being of the Current, or metaphorically "of the Blood," implies the possession of a subtle gene that cannot be found in the DNA of the cor- poreal body. It is something far more subtle and complex and can only be understood by solving the Mysteries. The Current is a spiritual frequency and is the collective soul that manifests through advancing collective Zhep'r. Being a word of power, Elorath is the result and Current of the collective will, soul, and dharma of the Family.

Others who are Awakened or knowledgeable about the occult can identify the egregore of Elorath. Yet only those of the Blood can fully understand and experience the intimacy of Awakening to the Current of Elorath. Those who are Awakened to the Current or accept the Calling are aware of their True Nature. Many will ignore the Current, often thinking themselves to be misled or merely harboring fantasies and are thus unable to accept what lies within them. In religions such as Santeria, the postulant seeks to find their "head," or their attunement to an Orisha (one of the divinities of that religion). In Christianity, one may relate to a specific patron saint. This is the same as hearing the Calling and discovering one's attunement to the Current of Elorath. However, all Strigoi Vii are free and encouraged to attune to other Currents and paradigms; this is within the nature of the Strigoi Vii culture.

Once a Strigoi Vii has recognized the Current within themselves, they proceed to higher levels of attunement, such as recognizing their Patron guides, which can be any god form or Ascended Master, whether known to humankind or not. Awakened and un-Awakened Strigoi Vii alike can recognize the Radiance or Calling of the Current within others of their kin. The Radiance draws those of the Family to each other. This mysterious attraction cannot be explained, yet it creates a deep bond of love and loyalty that runs deeper than mortal perceptions and alliances.

The full origins of Elorath are unknown. Suffice to say that Elorath has a discrete subtle conscious behind It. Many who cannot understand Elorath create fabricated stories to explain Its origin or nature and may even deny Its existence. However, Elorath cannot be weakened by such petty disbelief, and through the many who employ Our traditions or Mysteries, it becomes stronger and more Awakened.

There are various sub-Currents and aspects of Elorath known as Pulses. The singularity is Elorath Itself. The foundation of these Pulses is known as the Trinity Pulses, containing three different words of power and aspects: *Kitra* (weavers/lovers), *Mradu* (guardian/warrior), and *Ramkht* (magician/inspirators). The archetypes behind the Trinity Pulses in their modern conception were first introduced to the Vampyre Culture by the Kheprians; however, Strigoi Vii employ them in our own vision. They actually based on Carl Jung's interpretation of archetypes of the warrior, lover and magician.

Whilst there are many who carry the true Nature, and, of those, even fewer will "take the red pill" and pursue the steps to fulfill their Awakening.

The Trinity lies at the foundation of the Current of Elorath and consists of the subcurrents or "Pulses" who use the words of Kitra, the lovers, weavers, and councilors; Ramkht, the magicians and inspirators; and Mradu, the warriors and guardians. Each Strigoi Vii contains within themself elements of all three of these Currents. However, a few select Strigoi Vii are drawn to and identify with a specific one, which they discover through their journey of Zhep'r. These rare individuals are known as the Chorus of Elorath, or Kharrus. Each Priest/ess's attunement to a pulse determines how an individual Strigoi Vii interacts with and processes energy. The Chorus of Elorath maintains equilibrium within the Family and the Current of Elorath. Only these Priest/esses can are ordained into these Pulses, yet all Strigoi Vii can easily engage with the characteristics of these Pulses of the Current in order to experiment with processing energy and to test their talents.

Please note that those who hear the Calling to the Kharrus represent only a very small portion of the Awakened Family. Since the vast majority of the Family are solitary and work on an individual basis, they have no need for initiation into one of these Pulses, as the essential function of the Chorus is within group ritual. In contrast, however, there are also those who are formally ordained into two or more Pulses of the Current. However, some Strigoi Vii who attempt to fully master more than one Pulse sometimes experience a lack of focus in their ritual experience and journey of Zhep'r.

KITRA ~ *Councilors of Elorath*, who know and vibrate with the word ***Kitra***, are by nature catalysts of energy flow and cycling. They represent the Jungian archetype of the lovers. Energetically, their techniques focus on weaving, cycling, healing, flowing, and sensuality. They are often drawn to and talented in dance, music, poetry, lovemaking, performance, and healing. They are by nature highly sensual and are often physically attractive or possess a strong physical presence. Kitra have an essential need to be loved. Weaver energies are often very feminine in nature, yet it is not uncommon to meet male Kitra. The regalia of the Kitra is the crown and chalice, and they will usually wear their ritual cord over the hips. Kitra formal garb, such as ritual and temple robes, will often be very flirtatious and erotic, like that of a belly dancer.

MRADU ~ *Warriors of Elorath,* who know and vibrate with the word ***Mradu***, are charged with protecting the Family within and without. They represent the Jungian archetype of the warrior. Mradu are loyal, grounded, protective, often manifest a fondness for strategy of many kinds, and are drawn to the energetic techniques of defense, grounding, shielding, filtering, and defending the Family. They are also excellent at mediating disputes and have a strong need to provide love, thus complimenting the Kitra. Their energies are very masculine in nature and their Corporeal bodies are often large in size so as to facilitate the process of grounding energy. Many Mradu are male; however, it is not uncommon to encounter female Mradu. The regalia of the Mradu is a weapon such as a sword or spear. Mradu often wear their cord from shoulder to waist, like a nineteenth-century military sash. Mradu ritual and temple robes may incorporate military-like design or vestiges of medieval armor.

RAMKHT ~ *Magicians of Elorath*, who know and vibrate with the word ***Ramkht***, fuel the intent of the Current. They represent the Jungian archetype of the *magician*. Their energies partake of the duality of masculine and feminine, so both men and women are equally drawn to this Pulse. Of all the Currents, the inspirators focus on the energy techniques of dreaming, inspiration, manifestation, guiding, and leading the Family. The Ramkht are often seen as the most intellectual and scholarly of all the Trinity Pulases, yet this is an over-generalization. Individuals associating with the Ramkht Current are frequently natural teachers and leaders and drawn to literary and philosophical matters. The regalia of the Ramkht includes a consecrated and attuned wand or rod. In ritual Ramkht often wear a ritual cord around their shoulders like a priestly vestment. Ramkht ritual and temple garb is often long and flowing, almost androgynous in appearance.

It was meet that we should make merry, and be glad: for this thy brother was dead, and is alive again; and was lost, and is found.

—"The Parable of the Prodigal Son," Luke 15:32

The Quest of Family, or the Family Quest, is the duty of each and every Strigoi Vii initiate. The dual purpose of the Quest is to advance the individual and the collective of the Family through mutual inspiration and support. The Quest of Family involves finding others of the Blood and introducing them to their heritage subtly, without force or the "conversion" techniques practiced within mortal religions.

The central element within the Family Quest is respect for the free will of all sentient beings. The Family Quest should be executed only through subtle hints and inspiration. Thus, no Strigoi Vii should ever shame the Family by proselytizing like a member of a desperate religious cult. This is against the nature of the Quest. Power comes only from free will and independent thought.

THE LEGACY ANKH is the sigil that represents the Black Veils whilst the Dragon Ouroboros represents the Strigoi Vii path. These precious artifacts are proudly worn, discreetly in public and openly in ritual, by both Strigoi Vii and Black Swans to symbolize their support and dedication to the Strigoi Vii Mysteries, and the Family.

The ankh, or, in Latin, the crux ansata (cross with a handle), was originally the Egyptian hieroglyph meaning "life." Many Ancient Egyptian artworks, especially funerary art, depict gods and pharaohs bearing this symbol. The ankh was also associated with Osiris, the god of death and rebirth, and mummies were often adorned with ankhs to symbolically convey the gift of life after death. Over time, the ankh came to symbolize Immortality and can even be seen as a key to unlocking the gates of death. The Rosicrucian's and members of Hermetic orders often use this symbol in their rituals. The Coptic Christians, as well, employed it as a symbol of life beyond death. Ankhs incorporating mirrors into their design have sometimes been used to symbolize perception of the subtle reality.

The bladed ankh first surfaced in popular culture in the 1983 film The

Hunger, directed by Tony Scott and based on the novel by Whitley Strieber, who also, significantly, wrote the novel Communion. With its historical symbolism, cultural significance, and esoteric nature, the ankh was the obvious symbol for the Strigoi Vii. In 1996, Master Metal Manipulator D'Drennan was commissioned by Father Sebastiaan to make an exclusive version of a bladed ankh to represent the Mysteries and our Family. Thus was born the Legacy Ankh, the most commonly recognized international symbol of the Vampyre movement and the Family. Since there are so many imitators of our sigil, the Legacy Ankh is legally copyrighted and trademarked by the Ordo Strigoi Vii in order to protect it and to avoid any misuse of the symbol. We wish to make it clear that this scimitar-bladed ankh is the exclusive symbol of Black Veils as defined by the Ordo Strigoi Vii and is to be recognized and respected as such.

The Mundane refers to the mortal world outside the gates of the order. This is the "normal" world whose inhabitants are not aware of who and what we are or of the meta-physical realities to which we are Awakened. Other Awakened tribes, such as various vampire/Vampyre Legacies and Initiates of other esoteric systems, are not counted within the mundane. They are simply "Others," and may be seen as spiritual cousins of the Strigoi Vii. Terms such as dane, mortal-minded, or hyle (the Gnostic term for an un-Awakened individual) are used to refer to members of the mundane world.

The Dayside aspect of the Strigoi Vii Mysteries is the main tool we use to master our corporeal self and achieve a strong interaction with the mundane world. We employ Dayside philosophies in our everyday mundane lives to improve and further develop our Self. This grounding in the Dayside is known as the Dayside Principles and is studied in the Jahira Mystery.

Strigoi Vii refer to their "mundane" or "mortal" families as their "dayside family." Many Strigoi Vii's dayside families cannot understand or accept their nature, so the Strigoi Vii can only interact with their birth family on a strictly Dayside level. However, some fortunate Strigoi Vii have understanding birth families who accord them the luxury of openly expressing their nature. The process of disclosing one's Vampyre nature to birth family or friends is sometimes rather humorously called "Coming out of the Coffin." This term originated from the Long Black Veil events in NYC in the 1990s, which were held on Thursdays in a gay club called MOTHER. To evolve in

Zhep'r, the Strigoi Vii must learn to accept and balance their Dayside birth families as well as their Strigoi Vii Family.

> *See worlds on worlds compose one universe,*
> *Observe how system into system runs,*
> *What other planets circle other suns,*
> *What varied beings people every star...*

—Alexander Pope, *Essay on Man*

Other Tribes, or Others, comprise those who are not directly of our Current. They include Awakened or un-Awakened individuals, traditions, or groups that are drawn to the vampire archetype, yet are not Strigoi Vii. It is not uncommon for Strigoi Vii to be confused with these "Others." While there are similarities between the Strigoi Vii and other tribes, we are still very distinctly different from them.

The Others and associated tribes and organizations have manifested mostly on the internet since about 1996 or 1997. Many of these online groups spell vampire with an i and lowercase v. These groups are often known collectively as the "online vampire community" (or OVC), as most community interactions take place online, or simply as the "vampire community" (VC). The OVC rarely represents the old-school, in-person, real vampire community that has existed in fellowship for decades, mostly in large cities such as London, New York, and Los Angeles. The following discussion and definition of some tribes of Others takes place from the Strigoi Vii perspective and is as objective as possible.

Traditions is the Strigoi Vii term for other occult and pagan systems and specifically referring to the different paths of Vampyrism / vampirism. Each tradition comprises a specific paradigm of rituals, philosophies, and practices. Increasingly more Traditions are emerging in recent years. The first tradition to be established was *Setian* (Order of the Vampyre from the Temple of Set) in 1984, followed by *Tiamantis* (Temple of the Vampire, or TOV) in 1989, the *Sahjaza* in 1996, the *Kheprians* in 1998 and the *Aset Ka* in 1997.

Kheprians and the Kherete represent a special case as a Tradition amongst ethical psychic vampires. Kheprianism is a tradition of vampirism that has brought many of its members great success, and individual Kheprians have frequently maintained good relations with individual Strigoi Vii and many other Traditions. Kheprians believe that their founder modified their chakras during their previous lives, allowing them a better footing in the subtle reality. Thus, they believe they have a stronger control over the ability to avoid the Second Death and reincarnate with their subtle bodies intact from incarnation to incarnation. They believe this modification in their subtle bodies has caused symptoms of psychic vampirism. The Kheprians should also be recognized as an influential Legacy, as their groupings of warrior, priest, and councilor helped further define and develop the Strigoi Vii Currents of Mradu, Ramkht, and Kitra. The Kherete Path is a new term reflecting groups and individuals who follow the Kheprian traditions yet are not members of House Kheperu or the Kheprian Order.

Tiamantis is the name we Strigoi Vii call the tradition of living vampires known as the *Temple of the Vampire*, or TOV. The TOV has similarities in their Dayside ideologies to LaVeyan Satanism, yet consider themselves followers of a primordial Vampire religion. Publicly, the Church of Satan is a completely separate entity from the TOV, yet they do have many members in common. Members of the TOV spell vampire with a capital V. These individuals share many of the philosophical perspectives of the Strigoi Vii, and thus may be similar to us in certain ways. Magister Dimitri claimed to be a TOV member, and His presence introduced some of the teachings to the Strigoi Vii community, such as Communion, Twilight, the Dragon, Dayside, and Nightside.

Others types of people in the VC;

Traditional psychic vampires are termed *asarai* by the Strigoi Vii and found within and without the Vampyre Culture. Traditional psychic vampirism is clearly defined in Dion Fortune's book *Psychic Self-Defense* and Anton LaVey's 1969 magnum opus *The Satanic Bible*. Asarai are also discussed in Konstantinos's contemporary book *Vampires: The Occult Truth*. Traditional psychic vampires are parasites who primarily drain others of their emotional energy, and there is nothing positive about them. Asarai are individuals who intentionally or unintentionally create psychological drama and harmfully siphon energy from others. They can Awaken and become ethical psychic vampires, but most asarai are un-awakened, unable or unwilling to confront and manage their nature. Many of the ethical psychic vampires consider asarai to be un-awakened to their nature and thus not able to manage their condition.

Asarai fulfill the traditional archetype of the psychic vampire. Their vampirism may take many forms, including emotional or even sexual predation. Most asarai are found in everyday life in many guises. They rarely identify with the Glamour or are even aware of the Vampyre Culture. Some examples of asarai include a lover or friend who is emotionally damaged and continually creates psychodrama in the lives of others. Such individuals will leech on to people around them, playing on their sympathies, and drain them of their resources. A classic asarai may manifest as a patient in a nursing home who is horribly bitter and negative about her life. Nurses and caregivers will often feel literally drained as they care for these individuals and find these asarai occupying all their resources and attention. A particular student who intimidates the other members of the class and monopolizes the teacher's attention may very well be an asarai. Cancer patients or people suffering from terminal illnesses often manifest very powerful symptoms of traditional psychic vampirism, though generally without knowledge or malicious intent. People who claim to be "sex addicts" are often actually asarai as well.

However, there are some asarai who identify with the vampire image or lifestyle, so be cautious and aware of these individuals! They will sometimes flock to the contemporary gothic subculture or assume the new-age persona of an individual with a "damaged aura" or "leaky chakras," often leading others to confuse them with responsible and ethical psychic vampires who wish to manage their condition. Many asarai who have attempted to enter the sphere of our Family are truly craven, negative, and energy-deficient beings. These traditional psychic vampires are also attracted to self help groups as portrayed in the movie Fight Club (1999). It should be noted that the Strigoi Vii do not agree with redefining terms such as psychic vampire to accommodate contemporary social trends created by people who do not remember or wish to respect the old ways as properly defined by notable logicians such as Dion Fortune and Aleister Crowley. Therefore we recognize the differences between traditional psychic vampires (asarai) and their ethical counterparts.

The best defense against asarai is to completely avoid them! However, this may not be possible when you have an asarai as a colleague, supervisor, or member of your immediate mundane family or social circle. When interaction with an asarai is unavoidable, you must not cater to their games. Becoming involved in their machinations only feeds their parasitism and causes them to want more. Endless circling arguments, unhealthy attempts at gaining attention, "guilt trips," or unnaturally intense emotional reactions are all tactics of traditional psychic vampires. Energy filtering and shielding may also offer some defense, but it is best to simply avoid them altogether. Both Dion Fortune and Anton LaVey outline excellent and time-tested defensive techniques against these traditional psychic vampires in their respective books.

Ethical psychic vampires are the most common and numerous tribe of Others. These oft-Awakened energy sensitives have an energy deficiency or damage to their subtle energy bodies. They must feed from the Lifeforce of other humans in order to maintain their physical, emotional, and mental well-being. The abbreviations psi or psy for ethical psychic vampires are very common in the OVC, and these individuals have formed their own support networks and organizations. They share a great deal of terminology with the Strigoi Vii and employ similar energy-work techniques. The vast majority of individuals who are aware of their condition as psychic vampires (the process of which they also refer to as Awakening) have formed their own ethical codes, including versions of the Black Veils, and strive to find solutions for and a balance within their condition. To them, Vampyrism is a condition brought about by a damaged or inefficient subtle body that cannot generate enough vital energy on its own. In contrast, the Strigoi Vii are not ethical psychic vampires. While we have some superficial similarities to this tribe, our intent and motivation for gathering Lifeforce is completely different. Strigoi Vii seek to harvest the excess Lifeforce of humans to evolve in Zhep'r and to increase the frequency and metabolism of our subtle bodies.

Gaja are "wannabe vampires" who have always been present around the Vampire Community, often as victims of their own Glamour. Strigoi Vii are often amused by these irresponsible posers who lurk on the periphery of our Sanctums or in the general vamp community. Many gaja wear gauche Dracula capes, cheap store- bought plastic fangs, and spend their nights moping about the local darkwave nightclub claiming to be hundreds of years old. It is not rare to find a traditional psychic vampire who is also gaja. Very often gaja will either attach themselves to Strigoi Vii, begging to be "turned" into a vampire, or, conversely, childishly and comically insult Strigoi Vii , claiming we are not "real vampires." Gaja often manifest as "dark gurus," claiming nonexistent powers, and deluded role-players who take their hobby too seriously. Far too commonly, they adopt our terminology and claim to be Awakened, when in fact they have only learned a few elements of Strigoi Vii and have no actual understanding of our Mysteries. Do not confuse gaja with "fashion vampires," who simply enjoy the dramatic, aesthetic, and romantic trappings of the vampire archetype. Such individuals are merely enjoying themselves and are not truly gaja. The true Strigoi Vii can identify gaja with little effort.

Sanguinarians, or sanguine vampires, are individuals who feel they need to consume physical human blood to maintain their spiritual, physical, and mental health. Sanguinarians are one of the most controversial groups within the online vampire subculture. From the perspective of the OSV and the Synod, the consumption of blood contains extreme risks (such as blood-borne diseases) and is an inefficient form of obtaining Lifeforce. At the time of this writing, the Synod and the OSV have only encountered a few rare individuals who truly practice sanguinarianism as more than a sexual fetish or as a consequence of Renfield's syndrome (a pseudo-psychological disorder in which the individual believes they must consume blood). Claiming status as a sanguinarian vampire is sometimes done solely for social shock value or as a misguided attempt to relate to the vamp community. However, a fair number of Sanguinarians are blood fetishists who enjoy the vampire archetype for the purpose of enhancing their sexual fantasies. Please refer to the Veil on Sanguine Feeding, Black Veils Master Vampyre Edition 888, Chapter 5 for the Strigoi Vii position on this practice.

Fangdom are not just one tribe but many different groups of fans who are attracted to specific writers or cinematic works. They are mostly not spiritual in any way. Two examples of well-organized and outstanding groups of literary vampires include the fans of *The Vampire Chronicles* by Anne Rice and the *Twilight* novels (known as Twilighters) by Stephanie Meyer. Some members of these tribes may even be potentials and introduced to the Family through research into the vampire culture. They do provide an excellent source of willing donors and prepare mortals for Awakenings as Black Swans. Fans can also be considered any organized or unorganized tribe who enjoys series such as *Dark Shadows, True Blood*, and others.

Other tribes include the many Others out there who are awakened to the Current but identify as being part of other traditions and do not claim their kinship to our Blood. They may be similar to us, Awakened to the same subtle worlds and perceptions that We are privileged to know. There cannot be an absolute list or measure of the characteristics of our Blood, so there are many of the Family who are on paths that bear different names but are truly the same. When you encounter them, you will know them by their Radiance and spiritual signature of the Dark Flame. Always seek to know the individual beyond the group to which they may belong. our real Sorors and Fraters will speak through wisdom, humbleness, results, and achievement. Those truly of the Blood will not try to control others before they can control themselves.

However, bear this caution in mind! Those who speak of themselves in grandiose or self-glorifying terms are not of the Blood or worthy of your attention, as they are obviously insecure and claiming powers they do not have. Wisdom dictates that you avoid unwittingly falling into the orbit of such pretenders. Just keep your astral eyes open and your Fellows will be revealed.

CHAPTER 6
THE SANGUINARIUM

"Let me not to the marriage of true minds
Admit impediments…"

—William Shakespeare, Sonnet 116

The Sanguinarium is the word for the elements of Vampyre Culture which is drawn from the Legacy of the Strigoi Vii and the adhere to Black Veils. The etymology of the word Sanguinarium roughly translates from Latin to mean "guild of the blood." It is the international covenant network, and tribe of Family individuals, businesses, and gatherings, which are focused on Vampyrism. At the core of this movement is the Ordo Strigoi Vii (OSV), which is the Inner Circle of the Family and the spiritual leadership and administrative authority, the Synod. The Sanguinarium began in the early 1990s and is now an international movement, which in some respects is very separate from and in contrast to the majority of the online vampire community.

The Sanguinarium represents the social aspect of the Family. Ronin, as solitary individuals, practice Strigoi Vii and potentially Initiate into the Mysteries on a private basis. Many will enter the Sanguinarium for various periods of activity and then leave, only to return at a later time to network with and discover others of the Family.

Those coming to the Sanguinarium are treated as individuals above and beyond any organizations to which they belong or affiliations they hold. The Sanguinarium no longer focuses on initiatory groups such as clans, covens, or households, as they distract from the unity of the Family and the focus on the individual. The core of the Sanguinarium is the Strigoi Vii Principles. Initiates of Strigoi Vii who violate the basic Vampyres principles are deemed destructive to themselves and the Family and will most likely call down the khaskt upon themselves. This is a self-imposed curse that can be best equated to the mortal concept of negative karma. Other consequences may include excommunication for serious crimes, such as using one's status in the Family to manipulate minors or take part in major criminal activities such as drug dealing, rape, abusing animals or humans, or murder.

The Ordo Strigoi Vii (OSV) began as a small collective of individuals from a mix of spiritual traditions who Sabretooth obtained fangs from Gotham Halo (New York City). The ritual of making fangs allowed personal interactions with and connections to each individual. At this time, fangs were one of the primary symbols employed by like-minded individuals involved in Vampyrism when networking with each other. What made those who would eventually be the seeds of the OSV stand out amongst these fang clients is that they were unified in having a more spiritual approach to Vampyrism. One of these clients, who offered the initial influence and guidance, was the late and now ascended Dimitri. His Vampyre-pagan coven, known as Haven, all obtained fangs and became the nucleus of the origins of the Strigoi Vii movement, which inspired Father Sebastiaan to found the coven of Sahjaza. In fact, the very term Strigoi Vii was brought to the attention of the Family by Magister Dimitri, who claimed Slavic lineage from the Balkans in Eastern Europe.

Eventually, a convergence of individuals from diverse traditions and perspectives came together to painstakingly test and experiment with various philosophies and esoteric systems. Over time, individuals in this group each verified the reality of Communion and the Strigoi Morte, as well as many other aspects of the Corporeal and subtle realities. This movement formed the foundations of what is now the system of Strigoi Vii as outlined within this book.

Today, membership to the OSV is strictly by invitation only and of such secrecy that some claim the OSV and the Synod may not even exist. Every invitee must have a personal invitation from the Synod, a Adeptus, Priest/ess or a Magister. Invitations are presented discretely and secretly, and it is considered a great honor amongst the Strigoi Vii to be invited into this exclusive order of the Family. Such invitations are reserved only for the most dedicated and exceptional role models, who are generally Traditionalist Strigoi Vii. The vast majority of members are anonymous and very private about their affiliation, as the OSV is a secret society.

The Synod is spiritual leadership of the Current and the OSV, and its members are the architects of the Black Veils & the Sanguinarium. The Synod's primary focus is the preservation and prosperity of the Family & Current of Elorath. They are tirelessly further the Quest of Family and act as examples for upholding the Strigoi Vii Principles and the Black Veils.

The members of the Synod are responsible for moderating and organizing virtual forumss at StrigoiVii.org, dealing with public relations and media representation, approving and updating publications and the Strigoi Vii websites. Many members of the Synod offer their services as ministers, advisors, or teachers of the Mysteries. They may preside over ceremonies such as Initiations, weddings, and consecrations for the Strigoi Vii community.

But if ye sholde youre trouthe kepe and save.
Trouthe is the hyeste thing that man may kepe…

—Geoffrey Chaucer, *The Canterbury Tales*,
"The Franklin's Tale"

Traditions and etiquette are at the heart of Strigoi Vii culture. The Strigoi Vii have their own traditions of etiquette. The old-school traditions of formality and chivalry are highly respected by the sincere members of the Family. There are no absolute or steadfast laws of etiquette, but these traditions are tools of communication and charming demonstrations that show one is of the Current. However, as so many Strigoi Vii are solitary, only a few employ this etiquette frequently. Yet it is still helpful to know in case of an eventual meeting between members of the Family.

As a sign of respect, those present who hold the most junior level of initiation should show their respect and dedication by making the first action in any application of etiquette.

First and foremost, when in Sanctums, never address a Vampyre or any of their guests by their given name unless they present it first. Only use their Sobriquet or whichever name they prefer.

Hand written correspondence is greatly valued amongst the Strigoi Vii, and a handwritten letter carries much more weight than electronic correspondence. Spending time and energy on the presentation as well as the content is a sign of patience and regard. Of course, this is not always possible. When written correspondence takes place between two Strigoi Vii, whether it be online or through letters, it is traditional to begin with the Latin Ave, which means "greetings," and close with "Eternally," "Forever," "I Remain," or whichever formal salutation the Strigoi Vii prefers.

The Vampyre Greeting, conceived of by one of the Founding Fathers of Gotham Halo, Lord D'Drennan, may take slightly different forms in varying locations. However, all forms of this greeting should begin with each Vampyre steadily looking into the Throne behind the other's eyes, and thus facing each other's Dragon within. Then, once the gaze has been broken, the greeter, usually the individual who has attained Initiation junior to the other, takes the hand of the senior Vampyre and kisses the back. This is then repeated by the other party.

When entering a Halo, it is customary to announce oneself to the active members of the Family if one has the intention of entering Sanctums or Noir Havens. If the Vampyre is present on mundane business related to their Dayside or merely taking a personal holiday, this is not necessary. However, many Strigoi Vii consider it good manners to announce oneself in all cases.

In the case of a personal invitation to a private event or domicile, many Strigoi Vii deem it proper etiquette to bring a bottle of absinthe or fine red wine. Absinthe is highly regarded by the Strigoi Vii and was an important part of the vampire/Vampyre culture long before it became popular in Europe and amongst poets and artists. Absinthe was often brewed by individuals sometimes referred to as "alchemasters" or "alchemistresses." The Black Veils absinthe ritual is a wonderful and secretive ceremony used to celebrate important events such as birthdays. Today, due to modifications in U.S. laws, true absinthe is available for purchase in America. The Bloodbath, a drink created by Soror Ambrosia at the Long Black Veil (LBV) Noir Haven in Gotham, is also a wonderful toasting drink and a tradition amongst the Strigoi Vii. The LBV recipe for the Bloodbath is one-third Chambord or other raspberry liquor, one-third red wine, and one-third cranberry juice. Both drinks are wonderful for Moots and as after-ritual cocktails. Many Strigoi Vii also enjoy the aptly named Romanian Vampire wine, available in many large cities. However, if the personal tastes of the Strigoi Vii do not include alcohol, flowers or gourmet food or candy also make excellent "hostess" gifts.

As in vampire folklore, a Strigoi Vii should never enter another's home without first being invited. However, the reason for this is merely simple courtesy and not an unholy curse! It is considered a serious breach of etiquette for a Strigoi Vii to attend a gathering to which they have not received an invitation, especially if the gathering takes place within a Sanctum. Similarly, an invited Strigoi Vii should never bring guests, whether mortal or of the Family, to any gathering without first consulting the Host. However, Strigoi Vii should also be hospitable to other members of the Family and include them in group activities if possible. It is not at all uncommon for a Strigoi Vii to generously offer their resources and services to a Soror or Frater if they are needed.

Quabals are face-to-face, private gatherings of Strigoi Vii for the purposes of ritual, feasting, Initiation, discussion of the Mysteries, socialization, and the pursuit of special interests. Members of the Family are charged with taking the initiative to organize such gatherings on a regional and international level. Quabal may occur with varying frequencies, such as one-time only, weekly, monthly, bimonthly, or annually. The most secure place to network and announce Quabal is on the Synod-endorsed message boards at StrigoiVii.org.

Quabals are different from organizations such as covens or lodges because they are discrete cabals, which are fluid instead of fixed, organized groups into which individuals Initiate. Quabal are intended to promote individualism, action, and flexibility rather than solid structures. The elasticity of the Quabal system allows for a high level of freedom and comfort among the participants, as opposed to the many obligations that may be associated with covens or lodges. The Sanguinarium remains fixed as an international movement; Quabals occur as necessary.

The organizer of a Quabal is simply known as the Host, and it is the Host's duty to coordinate the location and date, distribute invitations, and choose the purpose of the Quabal, such as a discussion circle (sometimes known as a Kull), social meet-up, or full ritual. Proper tradition and etiquette requires all attendees to assume responsibility for their own expenses such as food, ritual supplies, or transportation. For example, if a space such as a hotel room or dance studio must be rented for a ritual, the cost should be shared amongst the attendees.

Quabals are best held in private, away from the mortal-minded, in order to further a sense of secrecy and privacy. In Quorum, members of the Family must be able to speak freely and openly without violating the Strigoi Vii's Principle of Secrets. Open Quabal is welcome all those who are Initiated into the Family as long as they RSVP with the Host, whilst Closed Quabal are open only to specifically invited individuals. The Host of any Quabal must be at least Initiated as a Adeptus to organize or "call forth" the Quabal, whilst a group ritual may only be led by an Adeptus, Priest/ess or Magister.

Group rituals should only take place in Quabal, and those in attendance must have at least read the Strigoi Vii Codex and secured the approval of the Host. It is in the best interests of everyone that the un-Initiated and those unfamiliar with our Mysteries do not attend Quabal. They will not be able to take part in the discussion or activities, and thus will feel out of place. Not only may this make them uncomfortable, but it will also act as a distraction from the intended focus of the Quorum.

Moots differ from Quabal in that they function as social events. Examples of Moots include preplanned meet and greets, discussions over dinner or coffee, or after parties following a formal Quabal. Gatherings such as these are perfect places to make in-person contact with others of the Family. Moots may also function as a way to screen others in a public place for potential inclusion in a Quabal. This is the only occasion when Black Swans may be in attendance, but, even so, their presence is discouraged and should always be announced to the Host in advance. Moots can be held in more exposed public places such as restaurants, taverns, cocktail lounges, coffee shops, or parks. Proper Moots should not be held in loud bars or during nightclub events, as a sense of intimacy is essential to the meeting.

Remember that Moots are different from a Quabal. It is possible to hold a Moot before or after a gathering to make the gathering more flexible. However, Quabal where Communion ritual and deeper discussion of the Mysteries take place must be limited only to initiated members of the Family. Neither Quabal nor Moots are for those who are simply curious, looking for a social network, or wishing to "sightsee." It is essential to preserve the sanctity, integrity, and seriousness of any gathering.

Sanctums are sacred places to the Vampyre, be they physical locations temporarily created in a ritual, or virtual, such as forums as StrigoiVii. org. They are often used for Quabal and Moots when they can be secured from the mundane world. Some legendary Some sanctums cannot be fully secured, so secrecy and discretion is necessary when assembling in these places. Outer Sanctums may include restaurants, parks, nightclubs, coffee shops, and art galleries. Moots and discreet rituals can be held in Outer Sanctums, if the mundane world is not alerted. Secret, or Inner, Sanctums are spaces away from the eyes of the mundane, such as private temples, back rooms of Noir Havens, private message boards, places created in ritual, or personal domiciles that have been consecrated. An Inner Sanctum must be a location where intimate conversations and group ritual between members of the Family may freely take place without distractions. When a Quabals involving ritual is in session, the space is considered an Inner Sanctum where only Initiated Vampyres and, depending on the circumstances, invited Black Swans may be present. In any Inner Sanctum, guardians are best posted to protect the sacred space. The moment an interruption or disruption by occurs, the Sanctum is compromised.

Steads are sanctums specific sacred places and historical sites such as the Pyramid of Giza in Egypt, the Temple of Ur in southern Iraq, the Mayan pyramids on the Yucatan peninsula in Mexico, and the Minoan temple on the Greek island of Santorini.

Noir Havens are semipublic, Outer Sanctum social events for celebration and pleasure and are most often held in lounges, nightclubs, or bars. These gatherings were originally organized specifically by Strigoi Vii and welcome members of other Awakened traditions, Traditions, tribes, and alternative/underground subcultures.

Noir Havens originally started in venues such as gay, gothic, or fetish nightclubs, but they are more commonly secret parties in the back room of a "mainstream" club. Salon Noirs (also called Courts) are a variation on Noir Havens and are essentially cocktail parties and a lounge of dark pleasures. The concept originated in the Belle Époque period in Paris, beginning in the 1880s through the onset of World War I. Often, Noir Havens will include the word black (in various translations) in their name. Some examples include the original Noir Haven, Long Black Veil of New York City; Black Trillium of Toronto; Black Xion of Amsterdam; and Lutetia Noir of Paris.

Noir Havens may be as small as a Monday club night at a local gothic club or dark lounge, or as large as an elaborate masquerade ball. It all depends on the desired audience and the determination of the organizers and promoters. However, Noir Havens are best held in exclusive venues as to avoid contact with mundane settings. Most often, such events will have an invite-only or restricted door policy and enforce a specific dress code such as costume, gothic, or fetish attire. Such regulations screen out those who are not serious or sympathetic attendees. More intimate gatherings such as Moots and Quabal should take place separately from Noir Havens. Havens are places for dancing, art shows, performance rituals, music, drinking, and celebration, not the sacred, intimate, and private Family gatherings.

The Vampire Ball events began at the BANK nightclub in NYC in January 1996 and have since spread across the world. They have inspired a style that mixes masquerade ball, pagan/esoteric gathering, and fetish ball. These events often have firebreathers; bands; DJs; ballroom, tango/salsa, Victorian, burlesque, and belly dancing; vendors selling unique wares and performance art with a strict masqued dress code. Vampire Balls are ceremonies, and no self-respecting vampire / Vampyre would go without proper attire, nor would the producers tolerate those out of dress code. The most famous of the Vampire Ball events include the New York Vampyre Ball and the Endless Night Vampire Ball in New Orleans over Halloween weekend.

Halos are sacred to the Strigoi Vii. Those initiated into the Outer Mysteries are often attracted to cities due to the large fluxes of energy in these places. Areas with large populations contain immense reservoirs of energy that are constantly radiated outward, and thus are a perfect source of excess life-force for the Vampyre. Strigoi Vii call such areas Halos. Specific cities have always been considered Halos and contain large populations of Strigoi Vii. The most notable Halos are Gotham (New York City), Angel

(Los Angeles), Wyvern (Seattle), Crescent (New Orleans), Albion (London), and Lutetia (Paris). Other Halos exist and continue to grow in energy as more and more Awakenings take place. The activity of Strigoi Vii in these areas usually results in a spontaneous naming beyond the mundane name of the city and which often comes from a historical title or characteristic of the city.

In the late twentieth and the early twenty-first centuries, Halos hosted large communities of Vampyres who organized Courts, Quabal, Moots, banquets, and other such events. Seekers still often travel long distances to Halos to meet other Strigoi Vii in person. The communities of Strigoi Vii and other Awakened ones within Halos evolve, grow, or diminish according to the collective social interests of the Family.

Gotham Halo, once called the "Rome of Vampyres," is the largest and most famous of the Halos. It is not restricted by geographic or civic boundaries, and so includes the five boroughs of New York City, northeastern New Jersey, Westchester County, and Long Island, or what is often called the New York metropolitan area. What makes the Gotham Halo so intense and powerful is that, after Tokyo and Mexico City, New York is one of the largest metropolitan areas in the world. Gotham also has been the seat of an incredible amount of history for the Vampyre/vampire subculture. Almost every tradition or tribe in the vamp community has had members within the Gotham Halo.

CHAPTER 7

VAMPYRE SABBATHS & THE WHEEL OF THE YEAR

Vampyre Sabbaths or "Festivals" are the annual sacred holidays of the Strigoi Vii and celebrated widely in the Vampyre Culture. Inspired partially by the Pagan Wheel of the Year and the dates are used to mark the founding of the Aeon of Elorath. Traditionally this calendar is lunar (sundown to sundown), beginning with 3-day Samhain Festival or (Halloween). This calendar was formally adopted on the founding day of the Aeon of Elorath on August 17th, 1995. Each year has a specific name given S.Y. is the abbreviation for Sanguine Year of this new Vampyric Age.

The Dark Moon is a sacred time for the Strigoi Vii. During this period, no moon appears in the sky, as sunlight does not reflect from it in a manner that is visible on Earth. The Dark Moon phase lasts approximately three days and occurs between the last visible sign of the waning moon and first appearance of the new crescent moon. This period of absolute dark is highly suitable for many Nightside applications.

During the Dark Moon phase, Ethereal and Astral energies can be more easily harnessed and manipulated. This is excellent time for Communion with the Strigoi Morte and with the Dragon.

For many, the Dark Moon represents a period between life and death, a time of solitude, darkness, and self-contemplation. In Khem, or Ancient Egypt, periods such as this were known as the Hours of Tuat, when the sun god would enter the underworld and make his passage alone and in darkness before emerging with life once again.

The Dark Moon also represents the darkest aspects of the goddesses Lilith, Hecate, and Kali, dark goddesses of the vampire mythology. From the perspective of the Outer Mysteries, this is a time of personal contemplation, soul searching, and solitude from the mundane.

Many Strigoi Vii prefer to spend the time of the Dark Moon in absolute solitude and restful quiet, and they pause to reflect before resuming their regular plans and activities.

Beyond the Dark Moon, the major festivals are the Nightside Festival, the Dayside Festival, the Samhain Festival, and the Dragon Festival.

The Nightside Festival (December 21 in the Northern Hemisphere and June 21 in the Southern Hemisphere) is the longest night of the year, which is recognized as the holiday of European pagans, or Yule. During this festival We delve deeply into our Nightside, celebrating freedom and distance from the metaphorical symbol of the light of the sun. The Nightside Festival is a celebration of our Nightside Family and a time for exploration of our magickal and primal natures before many of us celebrates mundane holidays such as Christmas with our birth families.

The Dayside Festival (June 21 in the Northern Hemisphere and December 21 in the Southern Hemisphere) is the shortest night of the year, the summer solstice, and the time when Sol (the sun) is dominant. This is a time for deep reflection and application of the Seven Dayside Pillars. We focus on our Dayside natures and celebration of our mortal families, materialistic achievements, and the Corporeal world. On this day, We should also reflect on our personal Dayside weaknesses. Through contemplation, we understand how we may see these as challenges to be turned into tools to further increase our Zhep'r. We revel in what the materialistic and Dayside life has to offer us and plan our Dayside goals for the coming year, such as a career change or major purchase such as that of a car or home.

The Samhain Festival falls on October 30 (Halloween Eve), October 31 (Halloween / Samhain proper), and the following day of November 1 (All Saints' Day). This three-day festival is often considered the Great Sabbath by many Vampyres and remains one of the most popularly celebrated festivals. These are the nights of balance and metamorphosis, as well as the Vampyre New Year, inspired by the Celtic/pagan New Year. It is the gateway leading to the longer nights of the year and encompasses many diverse holidays such as All Hallows Eve, Halloween, the Day of the Dead, and All Saints' Day. The Samhain Festival is most commonly celebrated on October 31. As of this writing New Orleans is where the Vampyre Community and many other vampire tribes gather.

During this festival, We often enjoy expressing our Glamour in full force and walking openly amongst the mundane. It is one of the most popular of all celebrations, since so many Vampyres enjoy the theatrics of Halloween, or Samhain. On this night, the Veiled Shroud Between Worlds is most easily crossed. This is the time for the Strigoi Vii to celebrate the most important holiday of the Family. Many do so by attending carnival-style masques with a funereal theme and by saying farewell to the previous year.

In late September and throughout the preceding months, all the Family begin to prepare costumes and masks for this night. During the Great Festival, we celebrate Aeon of Elorath as a whole.

The Dragon Festival (May 1st Walpurgisnacht / Beltane). This celebration began as a pre-Christian European holiday and was later co-opted by the Christians. Traditionally this night, Walpurgisnacht, is the night when demons, faeries, banshees, and other such legendary creatures are said to hold their dark celebrations. To the Strigoi Vii, the Dragon Festival represents our higher Selves and our Dragons. This festival is also a major celebration of the Family when the Dragon Mass is held on a worldwide level.

There are also several minor Strigoi Vii festivals, including the Crimson Festival, the Bast Festival, and an individual's Ascension Festival.

The Crimson Festival takes place on February 14, St. Valentine's Day, and has become very popular within the Vampyre Community. From the Immortal's perspective, this the time when We celebrate Our deepest passions and romances, as well as past and present loves. Here We recognize the partnerships and marriages that helped Us in our personal evolutions. The Crimson Festival is also a festival of the Hunt, celebrating its seductive, civilized, and glamorous aspects. The symbolism of crimson is related to the concept embodied in the words For the Blood is the Life, which is a metaphor for sustaining Ourselves by feasting on Lifeforce energy.

The Bast Festival takes place near the mundane pagan holiday Lammas and celebrates the deadly predators of the animal kingdom, especially felines, as a tool to attune ourselves to our primal natures. It is usually celebrated on August 1. This festival is about life and death, feeding and hunting. It is the primal twin to the Crimson Festival. The Bast Festival is often held far away from civilization, such as deep within a forest or in the desert around large bonfires. During these celebrations, one group takes on the roles of predators (hawks, cats, bears, eagles, lions, etc.) whilst another takes on the roles of prey (rabbits, mice, deer, etc.) and a simulated hunt is enacted.

Additional holidays celebrated by the Strigoi Vii are one's Dayside birthday and one's Awakening Day, which is their Nightside Birthday

CHAPTER 8

GLAMOUR

*Vampires, they say, blow an unearthly beauty, Their bodies are all
suffused with a soft witch-fire,*
Their flesh like an opal... their hair like the float of night.
Why do we muse upon them, what secret's in them?
*It is because, at last, we love the darkness, Love all things in it, tired
of too much light?*

—Conrad Aiken, *The Jig of Forslin*

Glamour represents the powers of mesmerism, seduction, and control which legends and literature assign to the vampire. This is the third of the Seven Dayside Principles learned in the Jahira Ordeal. A "Glamour" may be described as a magic spell, or, most commonly, an alluring or fascinating attraction. The moth that immolates itself within a candle flame is irresistibly drawn to the burning glamour of the fire. In such a manner do the mundane flock to Us when We apply our Vampyre Glamour. There are two levels of our Glamour: the Outer Glamour and the Inner Glamour.

The Outer Glamour is often used by the newer Initiates or those embroiled in the aesthetics of gothic vampire imagery, such as fangs and dramatic attire. Mortals love such trappings, as they are eternally seduced by the fantasy of the vampire. A Strigoi Vii may use the Outer Glamour by attending a gathering dressed in a gothic or otherwise striking costume that is likely to fascinate people, thus drawing them and their associated energies to the Strigoi Vii.

Then, when the Strigoi Vii grows in Zhep'r, they begin to manifest the Inner Glamour, which is mastered only through experience, talent, and skill. This level of Glamour involves techniques such as neuro-linguistic programming (NLP), voice control, the art of seduction, deliberate body language, aromatherapy, and the application of psychological and subliminal cues. Many of the techniques of the Inner Glamour are used by public speakers, successful corporate executives, and sleight-of-hand magicians. Since the days of prehistoric humans, those who have fully mastered these techniques have been often elevated by mortals to the place of gurus, heroes, or gods. Even now, those who have this special "charisma" often find a place as politicians or celebrities. Beginning to be less dependent on the Outer Glamour, yet still being able to recognize and reflect on it and occasionally employ it when necessary, is a strong trait of a potential Magister.

Today, the Living Vampyre can master this art of seduction and control of their personal presence to further their Zhep'r. All humans are instinctually disposed toward fascination and seduction. This can be seen in their courtship and mating rituals. Each Strigoi Vii must embrace their personal Glamour to fully be loved, desired, and revered. It is through proper application of the different levels of the Glamour that we maintain our position as the rulers of our own personal worlds.

We can employ and take advantage of the Glamour that appears in folklore, mythology, art, and literature. There are few archetypes more compelling and enduring than that of the vampire. Every culture has stories and legends of some sort of vampire. Through the Glamour, this archetype has been branded into the human collective unconsciousness. Mortals instinctively fear, love, and worship the vampire archetype. Our Family and Mysteries directly benefit from this fascination, which we tap with little effort.

Today, we begin a new open Glamour. Despite the legends, for centuries the majority of mortals did not believe We actually, physically, existed. Many of the mortal-minded today worship not only the Ascended Masters as their deities, but also the icon of the vampire. Our image pervades every aspect of mundane society, from bestselling novels to hit television shows and movies. Every Halloween party has at least a few "fashion vampires" in attendance. We represent everything for which most people long: romance, power, mystery, freedom, and, most importantly, Immortality.

Also, the recent "metaphysical" and new-age fads have created an ethos in which the mundane are ready to accept Our existence with enthusiasm and passion. Every major bookstore contains a section on magick and the occult. Many write books describing their encounters with vampires. People claiming to be vampires today openly go on talk shows, write books, and are the subjects of documentaries. It is as if the world has been awaiting Us.

Be proud of your heritage, for the vampire archetype is truly Immortal, like our personal Quest of Immortality. Employ the Glamour with skill and wisdom, and your own individual nobility will be realized.

Fangs aided me in my Awakening. Wearing fangs was something I always wanted to experience, and for me it was an incredibly profound event. When I first looked into the mirror with them, something just clicked, and a primal and empowering urge came over me! Of course, the fangs themselves were merely a placebo, but I embraced it! For me, like many other Strigoi Vii to whom I spoke, getting my fangs was a true rite of passage. Fangs cannot make a Vampyre, but they can sure add your psychodrama and glamour!

—Adrien Black Moon, Strigoi Vii Initiate and fang
client of Father Sebastiaan, London, England

Fangs, a classic symbol of the Vampyre Glamour, can be a powerful tool and a rite of passage. They are also a long-standing Vampyre tradition. Many may find fangs cliché, yet this is not necessarily the case. Within the vampire mythos, fangs are a constant and important symbol. As with many aspects of the Glamour, this conditioning is intentional.

Fangsmiths (those who make custom fangs) have consistently noticed that when an individual gets their fangs and looks in the mirror for the first time, there is a subtle shift or transformation as they begin to view themselves differently. Thus, for many, going through the ritual of having a pair of fangs made by a Fangsmith is an Initiation into the subculture or Family. There is nothing metaphysical about this. It is a psychological metamorphosis that may ignite Zhep'r and be the first step to Awakening.

You should procure quality fangs made by a Fangsmith, not the ones made by Hollywood SFX artists or dentists. Special-effects fangs are usually made overlarge to create the proper camera image, and most dentists are not trained or skilled in fangsmithing. Your fangs should be caps, small and subtle, made without a bridge (so you can speak easily), and prepared from the highest-quality dental acrylics.

The best part is that, unlike the cheap, boxed fangs available in most Halloween shops, good fangs will be customized to your face and tooth color. This means they will be fitted for you, so you may feel that the fangs are a part of yourself. Many Vampyres wear their fangs often and feel incomplete without them, as fangs are a symbol of our nature. This symbol can do many things. Fangs act as a tool of the Outer Glamour. They can be a tool of seduction, as everyone is attracted to vampires. Also, they are a symbol of the Blood and our primal nature.

That is why so many Initiates consider that getting a pair of custom fangs from a proper Fangsmith or "Family Dentist" is an essential part of the Glamour and of Jahira - Coming Forth by Day.

CHAPTER 9
INITIATION

"Then took the tree of Mystery root in the World of Los
Its topmost boughs shooting a fibre beneath Enitharmons couch The
double rooted Labyrinth soon wav'd around their heads."

—William Blake, *The Four Zoas*

Ordeals are formalized rites of passage into the Mysteries, teachings, and traditions of Strigoi Vii for Initiates that resonate with the word Elorath. Each of these psychological and spiritual equations is solved by the individual on a solitary basis or with the guidance of other Initiates. The Ordeals are a roadmap and regimented, sequential system of learning and Ascension that directs a Strigoi Vii through the Gates of Zhep'r towards the ultimate goal of being an Adeptus. They may be likened to grades and degrees in a scholastic institution or within occult groups such as the Hermetic Order of the Golden Dawn or Freemasonry. The Seeker achieves Initiation by bringing the Strigoi Vii Mysteries into their sphere of understanding. Verification of this understanding occurs through the achievement of specific results.

Mastery of the Strigoi Vii Mysteries is an individual and personal process, not a Family endeavor. It is the achievement of a spiritual Ascension, not of a social label or title that implies one individual's superiority over another. Each Mystery is a form of agreement and attunement within the Current and should only be done at the individual's own pace.

The Outer Ordeals are most often undertaken on a solitary basis, as only the Vampyre Current and our Ancestors, may truly judge an Initiate's worth. Some Strigoi Vii choose to formalize their Initiation through a ceremonial ritual witnessed by a Priest/ess of Strigoi Vii.

The Outer Mysteries are the elementary foundations of Strigoi Vii Initiation. They are preferably done as points of self-Initiation. Each should be done sequentially. It is traditional to take about six months before moving on to the next Ascension, and to do otherwise is generally considered hasty. It marks someone as being without the patience or maturity for Immortality.

PROSPECTII 0° Strigoi Vii Dedicants understand the word Prospectii and are those who have shown a vested interest in the Mysteries and potential for Zhep'r. Seekers are individuals who have Awakened to a curiosity about their True Nature. They are drawn to the Black Veils and have shown a sincere dedication and understanding of the Strigoi Vii Mysteries. Traditionally, these dedicates of Strigoi Vii are known as Bellah, or the beautiful ones. Prospectii first begins by building a personal foundation of experience and knowledge that may lead them to pursue formal initiation. They may also choose to formally dedicate and validate their Initiation on a solitary basis or perform it before a Priest/ess through the Prospectii *Rite of Dedication* found at the end of this chapter. Some Strigoi Vii initiates wish to mark their Ascension by meeting with a fangsmith and having a pair of custom fangs made as a personal symbol of transformation and often will obtain and consecrate a personal Legacy Ankh. What is most important to note is that becoming a Strigoi Vii dedicant is not considered a formal Initiation; it is considered an experimental stage of Zhep'r, where the dedicant is expected to maintain a skeptical and rational exploration of the Mysteries and personal validation is key.

JAHIRA I° *(Initiates)* - Through understanding the mysteries of the word JAHIRA are those who have Come forth by Day. This level of Initiation is for those who have sincerely dedicated themselves to mastery of the Dayside foundations of Strigoi Vii philosophy in the objective, profane and corporeal world. The Jahira focuses on the Seven Dayside Pillars: I. *Cult of One*, II. *Creativity*, III. *Glamour* (Social Dynamics), IV. *Wellness*, V. *Solvency* (material mastery), VI. *Preservation* and VII. *Perpetuity* (Immortality). They are expected to test the rational and pragmatic Dayside foundation before moving on to the Higher Mysteries and have seriously chosen to shift from a state of the mortal mind to that of an Immortal-minded perspective. The ritual of Ascension for marking this initiation is known as the Rite of Day or the Jahira Ascension.

CALMAE II° *(Sorors/Frater)* - Through understanding the mysteries of the word CALMAE are those who have Come forth by Night. They have moved beyond the Corporeal foundations of the five senses and touched on the deeper Mysteries of the subtle realms.. The Calmae has been introduced to the Ethereal level of reality and is familiar with Lifeforce. Those who are Coming forth by Night further work toward mastering the Immortal-minded perspective, energy work, understanding the Anatomy of Death, and the Art of Gathering Energy and work with the Sanguine Mass Communion ritual. Traditionally, Calmae were addressed "Sir," "Madame," or "Lady" to reflect their level of Initiation, however; Soror or Frater is now more common. The ritual of ascension for marking this initiation is known as the Rite of Night or the Calmae Ascension.

Morrah III° *(Adeptus)* - Through understanding the mysteries of the word Morrah are those who have Come forth by Twilight and have validated the existence of the Vampyre Current within themselves. The Morrah Adeptus initiation is the goal of most Strigoi Vii practitioners, and they are considered fully mature Vampyres. They have achieved true Flight (out-of-body experiences, or OBE) and mastered outer forms of the Art of Gathering Energy, whilst demonstrating perceptual control and Awakening of their Dragon exercises. To formally initiate to Morrah, one must balance the Dayside and Nightside perspectives into a strong equilibrium of Twilight, living in all three perspectives. Those who have Come forth by Twilight may act, if they choose, as "acolytes" and lead group Communion rituals, as at this point, they should have enough mastery to handle larger amounts of Lifeforce directed in the offerings. The ritual of ascension for marking this initiation is known as the Rite of Twilight, or the Morrah Ascension.

R° K° M° a Strigoi Priest/ess understanding the word KHARRUS (Chorus of Elorath). Some Morrah Adeptus choose to accept the duties of Priest/ess as formal minister of the Strigoi Vii and the Vampyre Current. They are charged with presiding the Strigoi Vii Sacraments such as presiding over *Ascension Rites, Blood & Roses* (Vampyre handfastings), *Requiems* (Vampyre funerals) consecrating temples and Sanctums and leading group Communion. Kharrus formally choose a Pulse of Kitra, Mradu or Ramkht to initiate into. Initiation as a Priest/ess of Elorath is entirely optional and is not required, open only to the most dedicated Strigoi Vii.

MAGISTERS are individuals who have formally mastered the Midian Mysteries and are taught the Inner Mysteries. These teachings are only administered to the most sincere and dedicated Adeptus Initiates who have Come forth by Twilight and almost exclusively within the providence of the OSV. Magisters are the Inner Circle of the Strigoi Vii movement and are taught the secrets of vibrational sorcery, or *Clavicula Sangraal* and the *Labythrine of Kaladra* and maintain their own private structures, teachings, and Initiations. Since details of the levels of Initiation within the Magister Ordeals are kept from the mundane and Outer Mysteries, as they cannot be described and are oral traditions; it is simply put that those who are not Initiated will not understand.

In Latin, Magister means "master" or "teacher." It was a title of respect given to highly educated individuals in the classical era, the Middle Ages, and the Renaissance. The female equivalent of this title is Magistra. They have made great progress in Zhep'r, as they have achieved full Communion with the Current and dedicated themselves fully to their own personal Quest for Immortality. Magisters have experienced a full equilibrium of Twilight. Magisters have testified to possess the necessary skills to defeat the Second Death. Magisters are shining examples of the Mysteries, traditions, and philosophies of Strigoi Vii.

Every Magister, by accepting the secrets, is to know the Black Veils and the Mysteries of Strigoi Vii and many support the Quest of Family. Magisters are dedicated to the evolution, preservation, and prosperity of the Strigoi Vii Mysteries, Current and Family. Traditionally, Magister Initiations are held in private with only other Inner Circle members present and on a secret time of the year during a private conclave. However, they can be done elsewhere, if necessary. The Magister Ascension ritual is a private ceremony in which the Strigoi Vii seeking Ascension performs a personal initiation rite before at least 3 other Magisters.

A genuine Magister has no need to advertise their level of Initiation. The true Magister has achieved an inwardly empowered ego and focuses exclusively on their own Zhep'r. Magisters, of course, may be at different levels of evolution based on their personal interests and dedication to their journey of Zhep'r.

Ascending to Magisterhood is not the end of the evolution of Zhep'r for the Strigoi Vii. In reality, it is only the beginning of one's exploration of the Inner Mysteries and deeper secrets of the Vampyre.

Rite of Dedication

This simple ritual of self-Initiation is the most basic of all formal Initiations within the Strigoi Vii Mysteries. Ritual is a powerful tool of personal reflection and empowerment, as well as a rite of passage showing dedication to the Mysteries of the Living Vampyre.

The only tools needed are a completely private, darkened room, a mirror, a black candle, and a Dragon Ouroboros and Legacy Ankh pendants. The room should be as dark as possible and must be locked or otherwise secured so that you will not be interrupted during the ceremony. This ritual, if possible, should be performed at midnight during the New Moon. Hang the mirror on the wall or place it on a table or shelf so that it is at eye level and light the black candle to represent your journey into the darkness. Then, with sincerity, look directly and deeply into your own eyes in the mirror and speak the Strigoi Vii Charge after making a declaration of your chosen Sobriquet. To further enhance the ritual experience, it may be empowering to wear your fangs (for the purposes of psychodrama) and a Legacy Ankh pendant whilst Nightklad (clothed only by the darkness to allow energies to flow) or while wearing a mask and black robe. Some Initiates may also choose to utilize music and incense to help set the mood. You should employ whatever tools will aid in making your Initiation a singular and profound experience.

This simple act of dedication is the first step on your journey of Zhep'r. It should be performed alone unless you have the luxury of knowing ordained Strigoi Vii Magisters. However, it is permissible to perform the Prospectii Validation Rite in the presence of an Initiated lover or partner who is already of a higher level of Initiation. In both cases, however, the entire Initiation must be performed by the individual. Be aware that any witnesses act as observers only and not "examiners" or "benefactors." It is your free will that must be exercised first and foremost. Thus, you should preside over your own Initiation. You, and only you, are qualified to say if you are ready to advance to the next step in your journey of Zhep'r.

Summation

Strigoi Vii is not a path for the masses, for mortals lack the dark flame of the Current of Elorath, the essence of our Family. Many will come to challenge the Mysteries and fail, out of frustration, lack of potential, or lack of sincerity. Those who are dedicated to deciphering the Mysteries should advance carefully and without undue haste. Be sure that you are absolutely ready for each step of Zhep'r. Strigoi Vii titles are reflections of what the individual practices and stating what Vampyre Mysteries they understand. They are not invented titles in the hierarchy of a fantasy social club or role-playing game! Earning a title, be it an Initiate or Magister, denotes a serious and personal experience of Ascension and journey through Zhep'r.

Many will initially come to our Mysteries eagerly, be an active presence in the OSV for a short time, perhaps even express a desire to Initiate, and then abruptly or gradually drift away from our Current. These half-hearted ones, known to us as *Phyle*, choose to remain bound to their limited, mortal-minded perspective. Phyle will never truly revel in the pleasures of Ascension through Zhep'r and thus cannot experience the Immortal's perspective of personal godhood. The journey of Zhep'r is arduous and, at times, frustrating. However, it is a journey the likes of which you have never even imagined before, with incomparable rewards to be gained through perseverance and application.

In conclusion, honestly evaluate your personal reaction to the Strigoi Vii Codex. If what you have just read seems intimately familiar, if you can truly say, "I feel as if I somehow knew this already," and you possess a strong curiosity to know more, you are then indeed a true Seeker. The next step is up to you. Simply test and experiment with the Mysteries within. If you find your personal exploration results in enlightenment, then you are experiencing Zhep'r. To those few who are of our Blood, welcome to the honor of our Family.

PROSPECTII TESTIMONIAL

These are confidential and private questionnaires that are used within the OSV to evaluate the completion of an ordeal. This will only be seen by the Synod officers who will reply with notes and reflections will be sent back if one does not pass the evaluation. Please keep answers reasonably short and concise at most 300 words. If you do not understand something there is a lesson waiting to happen. These testimonials are based on the honor system and be truthful there is no rush for true Zhep'r. Submit these questionnaires with a freewill donation to synod@strigoivii.org.

1. What is your dayside name and approximate physical location?
2. How long have you been seeking to pursue Strigoi Vii initiation?
3. What is your Vampyre Name (sobriquet) and why did you choose it?
4. Have you consecrated your sigils and how?
5. What are your experiences with the Vampyre Current?
6. What other "real vampire" books have you read any preferences?
7. Have you read Black Veils: Master Vampyre Edition what are your reflections?
8. Have you completed the entire suggested reading in the appendix of this Strigoi Vii Codex?
9. Who is your Adra (mentor) and why did you choose them?

BOOK I:

LIBER JAHIRA
"COMING FORTH BY DAY"

The beginning of the chapters of coming forth by day, and of praising and glorifications, of coming forth from and going into the underworld glorious in Amentet beautiful; to be said [on] the day of the burial going in after coming forth.

—The Papyrus of Ani, or The Egyptian Book of the Dead,
E. A. Wallis Budge (trans.)

Welcome to the syllabus of the aspiring Jahira, "Coming Forth by Day," entitled "Liber Jahira." "Liber Jahira" differs significantly from "Liber Elorath: The Strigoi Vii Prospectus," which is a two-dimensional introduction that serves as a basic set of concepts regarding Strigoi Vii. "Coming Forth by Day" is a three-dimensional text, as it contains not only instruction but applicable and tangible examples, as well as exercises the prospective initiates can test for themselves through the word Jahira. Thus, with this book, the Jahira will explore and validate the

Dayside Mysteries and that are established in the Book of Day section of The Black Veils.

To explain Vampyrism from the perspective of the Strigoi Vii, We begin with the basic Hollywood concept of the vampire as introduced in "The Strigoi Vii Prospectus." While the Strigoi Vii Vampyre is rational and real and the Hollywood vampire fantastical, our reality has much in common with its namesake archetype. Society is in love with the fictional vampire for a reason. The vampire possesses what humans recognize they do not: power, control, seduction, sorcery, and, perhaps most notably, Immortality.

Of all these traits, Immortality (in the sense that We understand it) is the most unattainable for the average human. Perhaps this is why they idolize the vampire archetype and attempt to become like it. However, as far-fetched as it may seem, the journey of the Strigoi Vii is as much about Immortality as its Hollywood counterpart, albeit from a very different perspective.

We all believe we understand death. Death, we are told from an early age, is the only certainty in life. So, aware of the restrictions of our bodies and the inevitability of their decay, we set our thinking to a timescale of one hundred years or less. This manner of thinking is called the mortal mindset. However, what if there were no such restriction? How would our lives change? How would we view our existence if we stopped racing against the inevitable clock? Would we rush less and perhaps accomplish more? Would we perceive our experiences and actions differently? What would our priorities be if there were no "deadline?"

To adopt the Immortal mindset is to break free of the limitations we place on our own minds and selves. To be Immortal-minded is to be timeless, to live in the moment (from the perspective of The Throne). While thinking of the past and planning for the future have their place, often we fail to live at all because we constantly obsess over how to cram too much into the continually dwindling days of our lives. We find ourselves defaulting to the habit and routine that makes up many mortal-minded people's perception of a "normal life"—a cycle of sleeping, working, eating, and repeating. We measure out our lives with the spoonful of school, family, career, retirement, all rushing us to the inevitability of death. We rarely stop to consider our actions. Are they fulfilling? Fruitful? We seem to know what is expected of us by a mortal-minded world, but what do we really want?

To be mortal-minded is to live according to acceptable standards of the so-called norm, or as the great French philosopher Michel Foucault put it, to "normalize" oneself to the mass mindset.

To be Immortal-minded is live to the fullest and as one chooses, recognizing limitless possibilities.

To be mortal-minded is to expect and accept death as prescribed by the myriad belief systems known to the mundane.

To be Immortal-minded is to be open to the idea that death does not have to be inevitable.

The Strigoi Vii Codex series is aimed at helping you achieve Zhep'r, a transformative process that extends to every facet of your being. The first step of Zhep'r is the evolution from a mortal-minded perspective to one that is Immortally-minded.

Let Us begin....

CHAPTER 10
DAYSIDE INITIATION

The Argument: As the true method of knowledge is experiment the true faculty of knowing must be the faculty which experiences.

—William Blake, *All Religions Are One*

Within "The Strigoi Vii Prospectus," we learned about the elementary concepts of Strigoi Vii through a general outline of the Strigoi Vii Mysteries. Here in "Coming Forth by Day," We will begin to directly apply those foundations. We shall do so by forging, through the Seven Dayside Principles that are found in The Black Veils, an applicable functionality in the Dayside corporeal world of the five senses. These Principles, their applications, and testimonials are detailed in this text. By testing and embracing these concepts, you will establish yourself firmly in the rational, material world we call the Dayside or through the word Jahira. Many occult systems absolutely ignore this concept and jump directly into the esoteric mysteries. Such an approach caters to individuals looking for quick fixes and, in practice, yields few or no results. Just as a student seeking to become a surgeon must first learn basic human anatomy and physiology, so must you build a strong Corporeal foundation before moving on to higher Strigoi Vii Mysteries.

With these practical foundations, you will have the platform from which to firmly launch yourself into the Higher Mysteries from a Strigoi Vii perspective. You should always be mindful of the basic foundations you will learn here. Even if you have mastered these Principles already, it is empowering to review them on a consistent basis and re-experience them from your advancing perspective. Return to these Dayside principles during times when you find the Nightside overwhelms your perceptions. Doing so will root and ground you, and then you may resume your Nightside activities with balance and renewed vigor. Without this balance, there is no duality; thus you cannot live within the Twilight of reality.

The following is an overview of the basic concepts of the Dayside Principles as found in The Black Veils: Master Vampyre 888 Edition. Also you will find a detailed description and practical applications in the following chapters of this book.

The Dayside Pillars (as defined in The Black Veils):

First Pillar: The Cult of One involves establishing an Immortal- minded perspective and an inwardly empowered ego. Embrace your essentially self-sufficient and solitary nature. Understand and empower your will. Embrace a love of life and take steps to realize your dreams as attainable realities. Be able to forgive yourself for past trespasses and look toward a future where you fulfill all possibilities and dreams. Black Veils: The Optimum Self, Meditation, Eternal Present, Ego, Confidence, Conquering Negativity, Conscious and Unconscious.

Second Pillar: Creativity know your purpose (dharma), set goals, meditation techniques, how to learn more efficiently, how to flow in life and be in the zone. Black Veils: Dharma & Purpose, Flow, Goals, Distractions.

Third Pillar: Glamour is to become socially empowered. Master your body language, physical appearance, presence, expressions, and the way you subtly communicate. The result will be immensely rewarding relationships with lovers, business associates, friends, mortal family, and Strigoi Vii Family. Black Veils: Context, VIBE, Body Language, Calibration, Gratitude, Kino – Touch, Listening, Voice Tone and Win-Win.

Fourth Pillar: Wellness is to make your personal Corporeal vessel, the Temple of the Self, a healthy and vibrant foundation. Strive for both personal vitality and longevity. Be always mindful of your own self-preservation and avoid threats to your Corporeal well-being. Black Veils: The Vessel, Diet, Movement, Rest, Sports.

Fifth Pillar: Solvency is a lifestyle in which you are the master of your material world. Money is not the goal but a useful tool—use it to your advantage. Achieve individual material independence, regardless of if you are in a committed relationship or not. Forge a strong sense of self-reliance regarding financial matters. Black Veils: Solvency, Materialism, Enterprising.

Sixth Pillar: Preservation are survival skills ranging from bushcraft (wilderness), street smarts, CPR/First Aid and risk reduction. Black Veils: Group Survival, Martial Arts, Prepping, Street Smarts, Bushcraft

Seventh Pillar: Perpetuity (Survival): Establish a personal legacy that will continue to live on and provide you with energy beyond your physical existence. Create works such as music, art, dance, and literature that will help build and contribute to mundane and Vampyre Cultures. Black Veils: Apotheosis, Children.

Empowering the Quest (the Eighth Pillar) begins with supporting the Family Quest to reach out to other members of the Family. Discover creative ways in which you can further enhance the experience of the Strigoi Vii Mysteries amongst the Vampyre Culture. The goal of this Pillar is to simply introduce an individual to Strigoi Vii without mentioning anything other than suggesting discretely that they read Strigoi Vii Codex or refer them to the StrigoiVii.og website. Remember, answering questions defeats the purpose of the Quest and violates the individual's own ability to make his own educated opinion. Any other steps are in violation of the Strigoi Vii Principles of the Quest and Secrets.

On a personal level, this principle begins with a tradition known as Gifting. Gifting refers to giving a copy of The Black Veils and or Strigoi Vii Codex to a likely Seeker. You may choose to present your personal copy to a Seeker with whom you are close or obtain them a new copy. Gifting is a tool of unity, energy flow, and exchange amongst Strigoi Vii. This generosity offers an individual the ability to fuel their own gratitude, enhances the Quest, and maintains a positive flow of energy. Gifting is only one example of empowering the Quest of Family and is elaborated on, along with many others, in Chapter 16, "The Quest of Family."

In your exploration of the Jahira Mysteries, begin to learn from the archetypal primal examples in this world. Consider the perspective of the noble and majestic rulers of the wild, such as the lion, shark, wolf, hawk, and eagle. As the Jahira formally embraces and Awakens to their Nature, their worldview shifts from mortal to Immortalist, from human to Vampyre. This can be called "Predatory Spirituality." This is a choice and requires consistent reflection, effort, and action on the part of the Strigoi Vii.

Realize that only results matter in your journey of Zhep'r. Personally confirmed knowledge, or Gnosis, as discussed in the Prospectus, is achieved through actions, effort, and results—not empty words, belief, or faith. As a Jahira, begin to loosen your grasp on the mortal-minded slave bonds of poverty, mental suppression, and depression. No Vampyre should ever be a member of the downtrodden proletariat! Be an objective skeptic. Always test and confirm all experiences in life for yourself.

Never force another to acquiesce to your perspectives. Invite them to open, respectful discussion, and, if they are Family and ready, they will come to their own understanding. If you speak with reason and demonstrate results, they may choose to agree. Always respect everyone else's right to have free will and to hold their own opinions.

Let logic and reason rule and guide you in your journey through the Strigoi Vii Mysteries. Take nothing on faith or blind belief! Tangible results of your experiments in Vampyrism can manifest as if you experienced them through the five senses.

Observe your actions and how they affect the mortal minded. Learn to act to your advantage around them. Walk proudly upright, speak in slow clear tones, and gently or sternly look others directly in the eye when talking to them. You will command their respect through simple techniques because it is the nature of most people to be followers. Thus, always present yourself as a leader and embrace your own noble nature. In turn, always treat all sentient beings with respect and regard. Appreciate the power of a long and healthy life, happiness, pleasure, and personal power. Be confident in your ability to secure all these things.

Uphold and abide by the common sense and logic of the Strigoi Vii Principles at all times, without exception. When you feel you have come to agreement with the Mysteries of the word Jahira, make the Jahira Ascension Rite, and proudly walk through the Gates of the Dayside of your own free will.

Seek out other members of the Family through the Quest if you need guidance and encouragement. However, do not drain them by imposing mental slave bonds on them. This journey is your own—no one else can tread your path or tell you exactly how to proceed. Embrace your Blood and realize your potential. It is a solitary journey through Zhep'r, and only you can take the initiative. Yet it is the most important journey you will ever take. In the book *The Teachings of Don Juan: A Yaqui Way of Knowledge*, Carlos Castaneda writes that any true path must have a heart. The path of Zhep'r is the heart of the Strigoi Vii.

Zhep'r is the metamorphosis of the Ascended Self, combined with the foundation of a spiritual Awakening to and awareness of the perspective of the Strigoi Vii. It is necessary to understand and realize the many truths which come with Vampyric transformation. Once the Seeker achieves and maintains a high state of Zhep'r through initiative and action, the individual Living Vampyre can be prepared to defeat the Second Death of the Self. The Mysteries and Words of Elorath are both the keys and the map—a system to facilitate this transformation.

Take your time and only proceed when you are ready. However, realize that there is a limit to the mortal coil. The opportunity is before you at this very moment! Carpe noctem and carpe diem! Do not lose Zhep'r by endless procrastination, for you only have one opportunity for success in this short mortal life. This is your chance to seize what is rightfully in our Blood. These things should be established firmly before taking on the challenges within the Second Ordeal of Calmae.

> *"A good book is the precious life-blood of a master spirit, embalmed and treasured up on purpose to a life beyond life."*
>
> —John Milton, *Aeropagitica*

The Grimoire: A Strigoi Vii's Book of Shadows

The Grimoire is the core tool of the Jahira. The term is often associated with ancient (sometimes diabolical) books of magick. The Strigoi Vii grimoire is a journal of personal practices and a spiritual diary of Zhep'r. Any notebook or journal can serve as a grimoire. However, many Strigoi Vii like to recognize the importance of their grimoire by customizing their book with leather covers, decorations, magickal signs, or similar embellishments. Each grimoire should be customized and attuned to the individual. Some even wish to keep their grimoire online in a secure server for ease of access and security purposes. However, a physical book is always more personal and intimate.

> *that way of inspiration is always open,*
> *and open to everyone;*
> *it acts as go-between, interpreter,*
> *it explains symbols of the past in to-day's imagery,*
> *it merges the distant future with most distant antiquity,*
> *states economically*
> *in a simple dream-equation*
> *the most profound philosophy... .*
>
> —H. D., "The Walls Do Not Fall"

THE RITE OF JAHIRA

The Dayside Initiation, also known as the Rite of Jahira Ascension, comes to an individual once they have Come forth by Day to their own personal satisfaction. Only perform this rite if you are in agreement with and have tested and validated the Strigoi Vii Dayside Mysteries. At the core of this ritual is validation of knowledge and application of the Seven Dayside Pillars as found in The Black Veils. If you are willing to abide by these pillars and critically examine the Mysteries, you will be ready to perform the Rite of Jahira. The ritual is simple. It is preferably performed during a Dark Moon phase when the moon is not visible in the night sky. Find a private place, such as a secluded spot in the wilderness or a personal room, free from intrusion and interruption. Place a mirror at eye level on the western wall, on the ground, or in some other convenient place. If indoors, light some candles, close the curtains to block out all outside light, and turn off phones and other electronic devices. You may wish to play some music and light your favorite incense for ambience. When your space is prepared, spend some time in meditation and self-reflection and focus strongly on your intention in performing this ritual. At the stroke of midnight look directly into your own eyes in the mirror and recite the following Oath:

The Jahira Oath

I speak beyond the Gates of this World.

Ancestors, I come before You in pure love and sincerity.

I, [Sobriquet], come into this sacred Sanctum of my own free will, to stand before my Nightside Family, in love and loyalty, with the full intent of Initiating myself into the Mysteries of the Dayside. I seek entrance through the Gates of Day into the Word of Jahira.

I vow to test and explore the Strigoi Vii Mysteries from an objective perspective.

I vow to uphold the Strigoi Vii Principles and the Seven Dayside Pillars as my foundation, sword, and shield.

(Take your Legacy Ankh and Dragon Ouroboros in your hand and place it over your heart.)

I place these symbols of Our Family and Mysteries above my heart to formally (re)consecrate it. I vow to honor and keep the Secrets of Our Family.

Thus, I now declare I have Come forth by Day as the Vampyre (insert sobriquet here) of the Strigoi Vii.

If you wish to have this Ascension further validated, you may request to perform it during a Sanguine Mass before a Adeptus, Priest, or Magister. You can also perform the rite with a Strigoi Vii or Black Swan partner present. If you would like your Ascension formally recognized by the Family and the Order, you may submit a written testimonial to the Synod.

CHAPTER 11

THE EVOLVING HUMAN

"What a piece of work is a man! how noble in reason! how infinite in faculty! in form and moving, how express and admirable! in action, how like an angel! in apprehension, how like a god! the beauty of the world! the paragon of animals!"

—William Shakespeare, *Hamlet*

The Strigoi Vii practitioner is a transhumanist, or one who seeks to transcend the current human state. Advancing technologies and medical science have provided many new Corporeal opportunities for life extension. Yet this is just one aspect of several levels of advancement toward Immortality. Since the Mysteries and Words of Elorath are a series of keys to unlock potential for Zhep'r, one must begin to think like the Immortals and move beyond the limiting conditionings of the mundane.

On the Corporeal level, the Strigoi Vii is absolutely physically and genetically identical to any other human being. The difference begins in the subtle world, or the Ethereal and Astral bodies, where Our "Blood" truly exists. This Blood only gives one the potential for Zhep'r. It is not a promise or guarantee! Initiative, will, and discipline are required to realize your potential and ignite this Dark Flame.

First and foremost, the Living Vampyre is a lover of life, finding opportunity for Zhep'r in all of life's beautiful facets. We are far from the eternally damned and spiritually agonized creatures of darkness that many mortals believe us to be. Continue to disregard the Hollywood conception of the vampire! The Immortal looks beyond mortal-minded society and to the laws of nature for the truest lessons.

Even within the established structure of civilization, survival of the fittest still persists. Those with the greatest talents and aptitude generally prosper, while the weak and ignorant often despair and die. Modern philosophers call this social Darwinism. Complete and indiscriminating equality is a mortal-minded construct. Darwin's theory of evolution states that those living beings with particular advantages will prosper and pass their strengths on to their offspring. So is it in the human world and civilization, no matter how altruistic and inclusive one wishes to be. While the Strigoi Vii would never condone discrimination or prejudice, we also refuse to blindly claim that all people are "the same" and shut our eyes to the talents and strengths of exceptional individuals. If everything were created equal, how could anything be extraordinary? We recognize that we have the potential to evolve from a mortal-minded to an Immortal-minded state and celebrate our nature. We are the true kings and queens of our own individual and personal realities! This is how we truly Live life.

The Immortal-minded individual, realizing the responsibility of their Blood, reduces risk and distractions that interfere with their Zhep'r. The Immortal-minded strive to surround themselves with others who inspire Zhep'r, choosing their associates from both the Family and the outstanding mortal-minded. As all actions are ex- changes of energy, you will receive personal energies from all those with whom you interact. If you wish to be inspired as an artist, as- sociate with other gifted artists. If you want to become a successful business owner, open a business in a location where your product is in demand. As part of overcoming a drug habit, end your associations with people who abuse drugs. Avoid those who sustain their own bad luck and unhappiness, as they will only transmit their misery to you. This process may be difficult if such people are friends or members of your social circle, yet you must end these destructive relationships if you truly wish to increase your Zhep'r. Moreover, you will discover that association with positive, like-minded individuals will have significant constructive results in the corporeal realm.

This is not to say that you must disassociate with all but other Family members, as many cultlike religions and spiritual paths mandate. Strigoi Vii is not a cult and does not encourage you to discard important interpersonal relationships! However, We are encouraging you to surround yourself with people who bring vibrancy and joy to your life, who augment your talents, provide perspective, and edify you. Do not waste your time with the terminally miserable or depressed. Surround yourself with those who love you and love life.

Energy is the currency of Immortals. We see that the whole world is ripe for enjoyment. There is life and love in everything, ranging from a quiet dinner at home with a loved one to participation in an exciting mountain-climbing expedition to the success of earning a university degree. Above all, the Immortal-minded path is one of conservation. We celebrate life in all its many aspects and do not waste energies or physical resources. Those of the Blood are not destroyers! Life is about creation and the rising flow of energies.

The Immortal subscribes to the rules of courtesy and chivalry. We always strive to be ladies and gentlemen! Whenever possible, we show respect and consideration to all those around us, including the mortal- minded, as well as Family members. Even if we dislike an individual, We will be civil in their presence and politely avoid future contact unless they serve a positive purpose in our lives. Being Strigoi Vii brings with it a significant responsibility. If we are to be the rulers of our own worlds, we must recognize the obligations associated with that role. Just as any reputable head of state would seek to always be above reproach in their behavior, so must we. The Strigoi Vii does not get angry at those who are not in agreement with their perspective, for those who are not of the Family will never completely understand our ways. Also, the Strigoi Vii never argues with those who do not agree with the truth, nor will we sermonize. Doing so is simply a waste of energy.

The Living Vampyre honors their history and has a deep appreciation of their spiritual heritage; holding their Nightside Family in utmost esteem, yet respecting other obligations. Corporeal commitments, including those to the mortal-minded, are not to be disregarded. Our Blood does not constitute a carte blanche to be disrespectful or irresponsible. Since we seek to embrace the next steps in human evolution, we must embrace the associated accountability. We must never disregard or hold in contempt those who are not capable of Zhep'r. The Strigoi Vii is not haughty.

The Immortal-minded seeks self-deification and self-divinity. Thus, we worship no beings save ourselves. We revere and honor the Strigoi Morte as the mortal minded in the Chinese or Native American traditions would revere an ancestor. However, we do not worship or pander to them. We approach them with an attitude of mutual respect and reverence. We choose to recognize our own potential godhood and personal divinity! For example, a member of a Christian church may live in fear of committing "sins" against the code of their religion and timidly bow their head before their god, praying for favors and deliverance. We as Strigoi Vii proudly celebrate ourselves and our Strigoi Morte Ancestors and draw strength and dignity from our Blood.

The Immortal develops a strong sense of patience and seeks to maintain a long-term perspective rather than an impulsive short- term perspective. We embrace the immediacy of each day yet recognize the importance of future planning. We accept the ancient Roman poet Horace's dictum carpe diem, or "seize the day," as a core philosophy. However, we do not seize the day due to a fear of imminent death! The Strigoi Vii knows they have the opportunity for Immortality, yet simultaneously recognizes the unique importance of each single moment.

The Immortal-minded Vampyre rejects new-age superstitions and blind faith in favor of occult knowledge that produces tangible results. The rest of the world now calls some of these revealed magickal secrets "science." Unfortunately, much of new-age doctrine is no more than pop psychology for people seeking a quick fix. The Strigoi Vii critically examines all modes of thought and chooses to ascribe only to those which further Zhep'r.

The Vessel of the Vampyre

The Strigoi Vii knows the Corporeal body is their temple and physical center known as the Vessel. The health and maintenance of the Vessel affects all other layers of the Self. The Strigoi Vii seeks to maintain their physical health and pursues Corporeal Immortality and evolution through technology and other means. We never disregard the tangible world and our place in it. We would never seek to mortify our flesh if it costs us a sacred flow of energy! This is why, for example, so many Strigoi Vii avoid extreme body modification like cuttings and implants. This is because such modifications change the flow of energy within the body, and a Vampyre is sensitive to these changes. However, Strigoi Vii are individualistic and unique, each on their own path. Some Strigoi Vii do embrace body modification and related practices in order to further their own personal expression or for specific focuses of energy. However, from a Dayside perspective, extreme modification of one's physical body can potentially serve as a detriment when entering certain professions or forming particular relationships. As pragmatists, Strigoi Vii seek to maintain Our Selves in a way that does not limit Us on any level.

"I am of a sect by myself…"
—Thomas Jefferson

"My mind is my church."
—Thomas Paine

The First Dayside Principle: The Cult of One

The Cult of One is the first Dayside Pillar at the core of the Evolving Human. For Zhep'r to truly take root, one begins inwardly with Mastery of the Self. The Strigoi Vii must embrace their Vampyre nature as a Cult of One. The Strigoi Vii realizes that the Self must be the center of their individual world, and they prioritize above all else what matters most to the Self. Becoming a Cult of One does not mean focusing on an egotistical, self-centered perspective. Instead, it involves embracing individuality, self-sufficiency, and absolute mastery of the Self.

The concept of "selfhood" appears in many world religions, philosophies, and sciences. In his famous "Allegory of the Cave," Plato spoke of the discovery of Self and truth as similar to a chained prisoner being released from a miserable, dreamlike cave into the pragmatic light of the sun. The Western Cartesian Self is organized around rationality and the intellect. Eastern practices such as Buddhism sometimes speak of seemingly "losing" the Self in union with those of others or with the energies of the universe. Psychologically speaking, both Freud and Jung discussed the psyche and the components of the personality. In contemporary postmodern thought, there is a trend toward dismissing the "essential" Cartesian Self and perceiving one's self as being no more than a collection of experiences and memories. These comprise only a very few examples of historical and contemporary conceptions of the Self. A fundamentally important part of the Strigoi Vii evolution of Zhep'r is to come to a personal and validated understanding of your own Vampyric Self.

So many members of mortal-minded cults and some traditions become yes-men to their leaders, both mundane and spiritual. Strigoi Vii validate their own experiences individually. They approach life, spirituality, and philosophy as a scientist would approach a promising yet untested theory. In effect, the Strigoi Vii are in agreement with any group that shares our perspective and not in agreement with any organization, no matter their name or claims, that is not interested in questioning and validating its own teachings.

This individualism is at the core of our nature. We of the Family are by nature very convivial yet coincidently independent. The vast majority of Strigoi Vii are solitary and have no interest in using the Family as a social clique. Even fewer participate in Quabal and Moots. Many prefer to walk this path alone as solitary individuals, finding agreement with the Mysteries that they have validated themselves. Realizing this element of our nature is one of the many steps in Coming forth by Day.

One of the most intriguing characteristics that differentiates the Immortal-minded from the average mundane is the capacity for independent thought and action. The mortal-minded generally operate on a metaphorical frequency of zero, unable to connect or operate, essentially set to "off." Like those trapped in the Matrix or the world of Fight Club, the vast majority of those who embrace the mundane perspective are virtually incapable of independent thought on a consistent basis. They shut off their brains by watching television, immersing themselves in useless and time-consuming activities, or succumbing to peer pressure and the constraints of the "normal." They are essentially playing an endless game of follow-the-leader. As stated in the philosophy of Ayn Rand, most people worship the principle of "we," where the greater good is always more important than the individual. They are thus locked into a current of needless self-sacrifice. Pop culture refers to this as the "cubicle" or "lemming" mentality.

The Strigoi Vii thinks differently from the profane. They operate on a frequency of one, where the individual comes first. They revel in their individuality and find power in solitude. However, Strigoi Vii do not cause harm to others due to blind egotism. They reverse this thought and, instead of being brainwashed followers, realize that there is power in numbers as well as solitude. To the Vampyre, 1 and the sacred I are one and the same thing! Unlike the mortal-minded, the Living Vampyre acknowledges that all sentient actions are selfish and serve the I, be it volunteering for a community service project or helping someone in need. These are certainly worthwhile and laudable actions, but it is completely unrealistic to claim the good Samaritan or volunteer worker does not benefit the I in some manner by their charitable actions. There is no purely selfless act!

The Results of the Age of Aquarius

We have witnessed the end of the Piscean Age, the which some say is the fourth age of the humanity's current evolution. The Piscean era of "self-sacrifice" and "virgin purity" dawns from the non-Gnostic Judeo-Christian mindset. However, throughout history, a select few have come into agreement with or have achieved similar perspectives to our Current. They have kept the Dark Flame alight in the blackness of the Piscean Age. The coming age, the era that our Family eagerly anticipates, is dawning. Some call it the Age of Aquarius. Magus Aleister Crowley called it the Age of Horus. It will be an Age of the Self, where individual divinity and secular rationalism will be celebrated.

In the Age of Horus, the love between the mundane world and Vampyres will deepen. As of this printing, the Strigoi Vii see this love epitomized by the mass popularity of vampire-themed books, films such as *Twilight* and *Underworld*, and television programs such as *True Blood*. Bram Stoker's *Dracula* and Anne Rice's more contemporary vampires have seduced countless readers. The world has moved from fearing us to embracing us in all levels of their culture. Just compare the archaic, grisly, Eastern European vampire legends to the current popularity of media images like the Vampire Lestat. Our Glamour has never seen such great success! This is the perceived results of Aeon of Elorath and Open Rule.

You might think that joining or coming into agreement with a movement like the OSV, or labeling yourself Strigoi Vii, is subscribing to the herd mentality. Actually, it is quite the opposite. Unlike a cult, the OSV is truly a "think tank" where you, as a member of an international network of likeminded individuals, can utilize our resources and find inspiration to further your Zhep'r and Self. The Mysteries and the OSV are simply tools to unlock what is in your Blood. They are not cult dogma designed for the purpose of control. Strigoi Vii are independent, critically minded, inquisitive individuals. When we choose to associate with each other in a group setting, we do so on a footing of respect and equality.

In conclusion, what do you get if you add zero a thousand times? You get zero. What do you get when you add one a thousand times? A spiritual nation of a thousand independently thinking individuals who share a common agreement and an individual pride in their collective heritage.

You might have been a sparkle of clear sand. You, who remember for a twinkling instant
All things, or what you think all things to be, Whose cries consume you, or whose joys
Hoist you to heaven, such a heaven as you will: You might have been a dream dreamed in a dream By some one dreaming of God and dreamed by God.
You might indeed have been a God, a star, A world of stars and Gods, a web of time;
You might have been the word that breathed the world.

—Conrad Aiken, "Preludes for Memnon"

To be a ruler of the Self is the Strigoi Vii will. In the process of Awakening, we admit our differences from others. Indeed, many Strigoi Vii may even realize this before their Awakening. Before We have the ability to ignite the Dark Flame of the Vampyric transformation of Zhep'r, We must first begin to adopt the perspective of rulers of our own lives from an Immortal-minded perspective. In order to achieve this, you must embrace the reason and logic within your Blood. Look deep into the mirror, meet your Dragon, and explore the labyrinth of the Mysteries in order to discover those hidden truths. The Strigoi Vii Mysteries are simply a reminder of what you already know. All you must do is remember and embrace it!

The cornerstone of Strigoi Vii philosophy begins with thinking like a majestic and noble ruler of the Self. This ideology is forged by developing a no-nonsense perspective and building a solid foundation in the material world. The Corporeal world is composed of matter and energy, and only through mastery of this layer of reality can the Strigoi Vii truly be prepared to explore the more subtle realms that lie beyond the mirror.

The philosophy of the Living Vampyre is an active mastery of one's own life, not the passive victim mentality lying within the hearts of most people who blindly stumble through life. The Strigoi Vii is in love with life and sees the beauty in all things. The only true enemy of the Strigoi Vii is the absolute death of the Self, or one's own personality. The "ruler of the Self" mentality ignites the Strigoi Vii's love and passion for life. Strigoi Vii seek only the best in personal mastery of their finances, mental and physical health, pleasure, and success in any of their interests and endeavors. The Strigoi Vii will not waste energy with frivolous and wasteful behavior or individuals. They place their own physical and mental well-being as the top Corporeal priority in their life.

All Strigoi Vii naturally exhibit a strong sense of individuality and independence. However, at the same time, the Living Vampyre can be social by nature, exhibiting a strong love for pleasure and all that gives life flavor. The interests of the Strigoi Vii may include soirées, literature, cinema, theater, travel, sports, bon-faire, music, and dance, to name just a few. Even with this inherent love for such indulgences, the Strigoi Vii realizes the most rewarding experience remains personal Zhep'r. The Vampyre never sees failure as anything more than a lesson and challenge about how to reapproach an issue and then obtain success. The Strigoi Vii embraces all different facets of life, both positive and negative, and does not seek to be placated by false and simpleminded notions. Life is the ultimate experience, and, being grounded in reality, the Strigoi Vii is fully aware that the heaven or hell the mortal-minded population perceives is simply self-created. As long as the Strigoi Vii is still alive, they will stop at nothing to get the most out of each and every moment. The final Second Death is truly the only destroyer of the Self.

The Vampyre dances through life, never taking slights and offences personally, and is adaptable in their ways. Strigoi Vii often strive to be neutral and noncommittal so they have many options to be flexible in their actions.

The Sensible Hedonist

The Vampyre is a model and symbol of chivalry. They often employ, in their personal Glamour, forms of etiquette that are not common to the era in which they live. They are thus masters of seduction and elegance and are sensible hedonists, never belittling themselves with base or unrefined behaviors. By employing the Glamour, the Vampyre always seeks to be thoughtful to others and rejects senseless and indiscriminate behavior, whilst still gratifying their own desires.

The Strigoi Vii is extremely proud and graceful and displays deep love and pride in their heritage, ancestry, and Family. They show an absolute level of respect, helpfulness, and courtesy when it comes to interacting with other members of the Family, both Awakened and un-Awakened. Additionally, a Strigoi Vii extends this courtesy to other deserving persons, whom We call Black Swans. Strigoi Vii always employ good manners and respect in all social dealings, Immortal and mundane. Our bond with others of our Blood does not mean we are rude to those not of our Family.

Many mortals possess an externally gratified ego, always seeking approval and attention from others of their kind. The Strigoi Vii naturally embraces an inwardly empowered ego. Self-satisfaction without the necessity of others' approval is a strong character trait of Strigoi Vii. For the Strigoi Vii, performing, or what the mortal-minded would consider "getting attention," is simply a means of stimulating an audience to freely send precious life energy toward them. Unlike the mortal-minded, the Strigoi Vii do not seek to inflate their own ego and importance through such actions. The Strigoi

Vii moves forward in a world where they are their own god. Only they, and no one else, can truly judge and satisfy themselves.

The spirit of the Living Vampyre is strong. Strigoi Vii are beings of pure life and love. They walk through each and every moment strong and revitalized once they come to this Awakening. Right before them there is energy for the taking, both physical and subtle. This is the living testament of the Strigoi Vii embracing the Self.

> *"With great power there must also come—great responsibility!"*
>
> —Stan Lee, *Amazing Fantasy, No. 15*

Vampyre Virtues

Immortal morality is different from the mundane perceptions of the mortal-minded. It is a path only for a few, and the unprepared and unthoughtful who attempt it will often be disappointed in their failures.

The average, spiritually un-Awakened mortal-minded, who are known to Us by their Gnostic name of hyle, often harbor the strong misconception that they are ultimately superior to all else. Most people only see the life of their own species as of any value and will slaughter and torture animals for food, sport, pleasure, and unnecessary scientific and medical experiments. The Strigoi Vii do not lower themselves to such views and actions, preferring that such horrid acts be on the bloody hands of others. We only end life when necessary for survival or defense, not for pleasure. Thus a Strigoi Vii would never physically harm a person or animal needlessly. In fact, quite a number of Strigoi Vii adopt this philosophy in their personal lives as vegetarians or even vegans.

The Strigoi Vii realizes that the transfer of energies is a reality of life. However, the Vampyre, who is ever more civilized, never seeks to torture their "prey." The Vampyre gathers and harvests life as expressed in their passion for all living things, never being destructive or wasteful. We perceive all living creatures with the knowledge that they are there for our survival, and thereby deserve our respect.

ARKTE

"Arkte has therefore come to mean much more than just sympathy for animals. It mandates respect for them, a need to understand them on their own terms, not ours..."

The Aeonic word of Lilith Aquino, VI° Ipsissimus, Temple of Set, Founding Grand Master of the Order of the Vampyre, Maga of the word ARKTE

However, the Strigoi Vii does not sacrifice their well-being or Self for others without extreme need. The concept of martyrdom is deeply rooted in mortal-minded morality. Most mortals ultimately believe that sacrificing oneself is the highest and greatest possible act. Just consider the story of Jesus from the Christian perspective, who "died for the sins" of all other humans, or suicide bombers who are willing to die for their religious beliefs. To the Strigoi Vii, the sacred I supersedes an abstract and fallible religious faith, as well as the anonymous and unappreciative masses. If Jesus' sacrifice had truly worked under the terms of Christian dogma, there would be much less sin and suffering in the world. Despite the terrorist attacks of suicide bombers, the beliefs and ideologies of their sponsoring groups or nations are not widely established. Even contemporary popular culture, such as the books and movies in the Harry Potter series, pass along the mortal-minded message that self- sacrifice is necessary for the greater good.

We, as Strigoi Vii, understand that ultimately most self-sacrifice potentially can limit or destroy the Self, and rarely, if ever, actually benefits some theoretical "greater good." As we worship only the Self, so do we refuse to destroy that Self, no matter what mortal-minded morality might prescribe. It is certainly worthy to help others, but much mortal-minded behavior of this sort stems not from altruism or true love of others, but from conditioning and selfishness. Mortal-minded sacrifice truly fosters an empty sense of false superiority, for the "martyr" can consider themselves better than others on account of their sacrifice. However, would not true superiority consist of taking pride in oneself? Instead of throwing one's life or livelihood away in a dramatic gesture, would it not be much better and wiser to live thoughtfully, respectfully, completely, and in a manner that benefits the Self? Thus does one show respect to others as well as love of the Self.

CHAPTER 12

AWAKENING YOUR DRAGON

"Now the serpent was more subtle than any beast of the field..."

—Genesis 3:1

To Awaken the Dragon means to rise up and make Communion (communication) with the Strigoi Morte and your higher self (Dragon). This is the most essential action of Zhep'r, save only the Arts of Gathering Lifeforce and the circuit of Communion with the Strigoi Morte. This chapter will delve into several simple exercises and philosophies geared toward beginning this Communion with the Divine Self known as the Kia or Dragon. Put aside your fear, acknowledge your desire, strengthen your will, and embrace the Journey!

"The only thing we have to fear is fear itself."

—Franklin D. Roosevelt

Fear is the most limiting barrier for most mortals. Mortal fears are nearly endless: fear of death, poverty, solitude, career failure—every hyle suffers from at least one such debilitating dread. For the majority of the mortal-minded, mastering fear is nearly impossible. However, those of the Current are evolved humans who must overcome this most basic of obstacles. We do not mean, however, that the Strigoi Vii should recklessly and dangerously "face" or overcome their fears.

Often the mortal-minded seek to ignore very real problems by bluntly denying their phobias (often coarsely called "being a man"), which usually means embracing an even more closed-minded ideology. This is a patriarchal, mortal-minded route that most often leads to failure. As seen through the **Dragon's Gaze**, overcoming fear involves rejecting the concept of linear Immortality (the mortal-minded perspective) and embracing the perception of timelessness (the Immortal-minded perspective).

Space and time as experienced from the Corporeal perspective are illusions. In his theory of special relativity, Albert Einstein showed that our perceptions of space and time depend on our position as an observer. An observer moving with great speed will perceive time differently from a stationary observer. A clock moving at accelerated speed runs "slow" compared to a nonmoving clock. Quantum physics shows that the results of an experiment depend on who is watching— the presence of an observer affects the outcome. From the Corporeal perspective, reality is relative. Begin to disassociate from the mortal- minded perspective and embrace that of an Immortal. You need to realize that you an observer, sitting on the **Dragon's Throne**. Thus, your experience is personal to you. Your body, home, belongings, pets, job, writings, and so on are not you; they are only Corporeal possessions. They are not the true Self and are separate and distinct. To be Immortal-minded, you must begin from the perspective of the Dragon. Here is the very first step of true disassociation from the mortal minded mentality and Zhep'r.

Once you can taste the experience of timelessness, fear becomes another extension of the Corporeal world, which, being relative, can be viewed from different perspectives. Begin with the exercise known as Throning. This powerful tool of Awakening Your Dragon allows you to sit on the Throne of Your Self. The Dragon does not truly exist in the ordinary reality, even with a Corporeal counterpart of your Dragon's Throne. We cannot invoke, evoke, or talk to it, because it is Us; that from which all experience is observed.

Your Dragon is essentially your perceptive Self, the observer, the part of your consciousness that is and sees. We cannot observe it because who then would be making the observation? That would be like asking your eyeball to look at itself. We also cannot contemplate it, because once again, who would be doing the contemplation? To further understand this concept, we employ the tool and exercise of *The Dragons' Throne*.

Where is your consciousness? As a very simple exercise, close your eyes for a moment and think of something important to you, such as a favorite book or a treasured memento. Visualize it as clearly as you can. Where does this "thinking" take place, and where do you "see" the image? Do you visualize with your arm or your stomach? Obviously not—you visualize with your mind, and the mental image is "located" in the forehead, right behind the eyes and between the temples. This is where your Throne is situated.

Applying Dragons' Throne:

Stand or sit about a meter away from a mirror hanging at eye level. Your back should be straight, and you should be comfortable but in no danger of falling asleep. we suggest sitting in a wooden straight-backed chair, if possible. Once ready, stare directly into your own eyes in the mirror. Many find this exercise disconcerting after a few moments but try not to break contact. Attempt to gaze into the Throne behind your eyes by looking through your pupils and through the mirror. Try doing this for five minutes to begin, and then add another five when you are ready. As you master this discipline, all sounds, lights, and experiences around you will begin to fade away. You will be sitting on your personal Throne. Your sense of time and space will also be lost. You will be the only being in existence, for your Throne is timeless. Your sense of time and space will merge with this expansion of your awareness, as your sense of Self surpasses the limitations of ordinary awareness. While looking from the Dragons' Throne, all may be possible.

Throning is the first of many techniques Strigoi Vii use to disassociate from the mortal-minded viewpoint and embrace an Immortal-minded perspective. With this basic exercise, you will be able to realize that your fears are illusions and merely barriers of suppression placed on your consciousness. With this realization, you will then be able to release your Self to explore existence on a profound level. Future exercises in the Strigoi Vii

Codex will add to your personal empowerment. Therefore, it is highly recommended that you practice Throning frequently. It is an excellent exercise to perform before retiring for bed.

More advanced Vampyre exercises include the Vampyres' Presence, The Vampyres' Gaze and the Vampyres' Voice.

"Most people want things like a candle-flame, flickering, shifting. You, on the other hand, want like a forest fire."

—spoken by Desire in
The Sandman: Endless Nights by Neil Gaiman

Desire is one of the most basic emotions, the deep-rooted feeling of want and need. In order to fuel your will, you must consciously reach into your Self and evoke the desire for the specific goal or action you would like to achieve. Desire is the tinder that lights the fire of motivation. For the mortal-minded masses, desire is a weak thing that centers on the need for basic survival and distractions. Most of the mortal-minded desire unearned wealth, complete job security, a cutting-edge home entertainment center, the newest video game console, and other such prosaic and often unattainable goals. Magus Aleister Crowley said that magick is *"the art and science of causing change in accordance with the will."* The majority of the mortal-minded eschew magick because their will is not forged to produce change. Their desire is mundane and lukewarm. Desire is the directed fire that fuels intent and will. Thus, the Strigoi Vii has the desire and will to achieve their birthright as magickians and sculptors of change.

I am. I think. I will... What must I say be- sides? These are the words. This is the answer.

—Ayn Rand, *Anthem*

The Dragons' Will

The Will is an essential companion to the Self for a Vampyre. Without will, no deed is accomplished, no end is achieved, no desire is fulfilled, and no idea sees realization. Will is the motive force necessary to change states from being to doing. When will is absent, we have only the dormant, inactive state of being—not the actualized, active, progressive state of achieving. Enter will, and the observer becomes the performer. Its will enables us to bridge the gap between the intangible and the Corporeal, to bring thoughts into action and plans to fulfillment.

We hear this word will spoken often: the will to survive, great strength of will, lack of willpower. But what does it mean?

Will is not to be confused with desire. Desire can be an immobile thing. If left to its own devices, a desire will never fulfill itself. It is but an idea, a thought. A car without gasoline will not run on its own, and without a given direction it cannot reach any destination.

WILL = DESIRE + ENERGY + GOAL

Contrary to many people's assumptions, the will is not a set force, something one is born with that can never be changed. It would be a convenient excuse to say one was simply not born with willpower, but such is untrue and an excuse for laziness. The will can grow and become more potent and, inversely, diminish with disuse. The will can be strengthened by a variety of methods.

The training of professional athletes is a notable example of techniques that strengthen the will. The athlete in training does not seek to become what they are told they must be, but rather strives to overcome their limitations and turn their own potential ability into real ability. An athlete may receive guidance and advice from coaches, training programs, and other athletes, but ultimately their evolution is a personal one.

It is the same for the Vampyre. While there are proven methods that will help you achieve Zhep'r, you can only be shown the door to the Vampyre Mysteries. Only your own effort will lead you to accomplishment. Desire is essential, but it is not enough. For every goal desired there is some price to be paid to achieve it, and you must be willing to follow through on your intentions! Dissociate your Vampyres'

Will from the imposed will of others. Frequently partake of actions that allow you to ride your Dragon's will and strengthen the reigns of that will. Use the Dragon's will, and any goal can be achieved as long as you fuel it with enough desire and life.

Practical Application: Strengthening the Dragons' Will

One of the greatest indicators of a weakened will is an inclination toward procrastination and stagnation. One of the greatest methods to strengthen the will is to overcome procrastination. Begin with small tasks. These small tasks, like pebbles, are easy to overlook, but if left alone will gradually accumulate into a mountain of unproductivity. Here is a very simple exercise to increase productivity and strengthen your will.

Take a few index cards or sticky notes and write on them the following words, in very large, readable handwriting: DO IT NOW. (And yes, do this exercise right now!) Take these cards and put them in visible places around your house or office: in the kitchen, by the computer screen, next to doors, in proximity to tasks and projects that you frequently shirk—perhaps by the garbage can or laundry basket. Also place a few next to the television, if you have one, or in any area of the house or office to which you might "escape." Now, follow the advice you have given yourself. Whenever there is a small task to be done, do it immediately, whether it is something you avoid or not. Even though they are not large endeavors, timely performance of these small tasks can greatly strengthen the will. Any bodybuilder will tell you it is not the weight on the bar that builds strong muscles; it is the repetition of exercises. Such is the same with will. Repetition of small exercises of your will builds its character and ensures its strength.

It is rarely lack of ability that hinders one from successful achievement. It is a lack of will.

There she sees a damsel bright,
Dressed in a silken robe of white,
That shadowy in the moonlight shone:
The neck that made that white robe wan,
Her stately neck, and arms were bare;

Her blue-veined feet unsandaled were
And wildly glittered here and there
The gems entangled in her hair.

—Samuel Taylor Coleridge, "Christabel"

Psychodrama is like the symbol of the Dragon. We use the vampire as our overall archetype in the Dayside—powerful, primal, beastly yet civilized, romantic and beautiful, Immortal, a lover of life, more than human, and, most of all, a magician and a true sorcerer.

We use this archetype not only as a role model but as part of a powerful tool called psychodrama. We can pick the elements of this Im- mortal persona we find most empowering and place them into our vision. We then use that for empowerment.

This is why we relate to the concept of the vampire mythology in the modern incarnation. Many of us have embraced this archetype and identified with it for our entire lives. We love the power, romance, sensuality, strength, and Immortality it represents. This is our tool, our role model. When we put on a pair of fangs, it empowers us. That is why so many, including our cousins from other traditions, come to a Fangsmith. The Glamour at its most basic levels is an example of this psychodrama. We then further it with symbolism in ritual and our personal lifestyles. We Rise to the occasion with this power.

Ritual of Applying Psychodrama: The Primal Howl

Find a secure room where you will not be observed or interrupted. Stand before a mirror, put your fangs on, begin to Throne, and then growl and tap into your primal nature. Envision being the wolf, great cat, or hawk on the hunt. Physically growl and make animal sounds. As in the previous exercise, you may initially find this awkward. However, even if you feel embarrassed, persist! Your discomfort is a product of childish conditioning. You will eventually begin to feel your connection with these empowering totems.

When the opportunity arises, run through the woods naked, enacting the personalities of these animals. Paint yourself and wear a mask, as theatrics are powerful tools of the psychodrama! Do this alone at first, and then, if possible, join others of the Family. Leap through the air like a wolf, throw your arms up like a bear, break free of your mortal bonds, and you will begin to Awaken Your inner inner Beast!

One common ritual in the Gotham Halo, created by the late D'Drennan, is the Gotham Howl. This is a basic ritual embraced by the Family and members of the community. It releases Our primal nature and honors the psychodrama which sets Us free and unites the Family. During this ritual, all participants throw back their heads and howl like wolves. We suggest you experiment with this ritual, whether it be in solitude or at a Quabal. As you howl, you will feel the fire of the Dragon surging within you.

CHAPTER 13

EMPOWERING YOUR
PERSONAL GLAMOUR

"For every two minutes of glamour, there are eight hours of hard work."

—Jessica Savitch

O nce you have a concept of the nature of the Glamour from The Black Veil, you can use the provided exercises to experience it firsthand. We now move beyond the basics. It is essential to realize that the Glamour is not as simple as watching a vampire movie, wearing black clothes, and speaking with a cliché faux Romanian accent. It is much more than this. Within this chapter, you will discover several practical exercises and examples of applying psychology and neuro-linguistic programming (NLP). For the Adeptus Vampyre, Glamour is a seduction of those around you that will help you get the results you desire in life.

The Glamour is not intended for just simple ego gratification, for this is a waste of time and energy. The Glamour should be used to further your Self and control your life. Such powers must be employed with the specific and greater intent of empowering your Self. It is below the Strigoi Vii to mock or abuse the weak-minded. This is considered unacceptable abuse, like a young boy torturing a helpless puppy. Strigoi Vii are above such games! Those who use such power for the wrong purpose will lose the attentions of the Strigoi Morte and Vampyre Current. Such individuals are not worthy of Zhep'r.

The Glamour is a set of applied skills and, like Zhep'r, must always be rehearsed and practiced, even when one has reached a level of Mastery. There is no end to the study of the Glamour—like Zhep'r, it is an ongoing path.

Before you employ the Glamour, begin by visualizing your intentions and proposed applications. The Glamour is used for noble personal causes. Some examples include making subtle connections for the Art of Gathering Energy, securing a raise or better position at your job, courtship through seduction and attraction of a mate, sealing a long sought-after business deal, improving one's stage presence, furthering relationships with friends and family, and so on. As you can see, there are endless applications of this advanced Glamour in all spheres of life, from business, entertainment, and performance to personal relationships and more. Mastering the Glamour can make one's life more enjoyable. It can be a fuel for Zhep'r at its finest!

First and foremost, you should study and read. Peruse books on body language, seduction, hypnotism, self-improvement, and psychology. Look to historical examples of applications of the Glamour. Robert Greene, the author of *The Art of Seduction*, *The 48 Laws of Power*, and *The 33 Strategies of War*, provides countless historical examples and ap- plications of the Glamour. His books are extremely popular amongst those of the Family. Machiavelli's *The Prince* is also a classic text on how to employ the Glamour to gain power.

The Glamour can be as overt and communicates itself subconsciously through behavior and subtle cues and does not always always scream "I am a Vampyre!" through visual aspects of clothing and action. Rather, employing the more advanced Glamour techniques sends others the direct message that you are a powerful and evolved being, drawing them strongly to you.

Fledglings will often express their Awakening by rebelling against the masses. They may assume traditional punk or gothic garb, get several piercings, and employ dramatic and extreme makeup and hair colors. This is an easy way to get attention and stand out from others. Many of those with the Dark Flame come from the underground subcultures and communities, due to their Promethean creative and curious nature. However, the outré appearances often adopted by members of these cultures can be limiting, as they inhibit the individual's ability to "code shift" within the Corporeal world. Those of us who are innovators in subcultures often choose to present ourselves in a manner so that we can blend in with the mundane world, such as by choosing tattoos that can be covered if necessary.

It is true that the more "dramatic" professions such as rock musician, body modification artist (tattooist or piercer), or entertainer can be extremely seductive to many of the mundane world. Strigoi Vii who follow such lifestyles have the associated freedom to consistently assume extreme appearances. However, even such individuals often find it challenging to employ all of the aspects of the Greater Glamour on a complete level. For example, if you have extensive piercings and tattoos, as well as outlandishly colored hair and all-black attire, you will most likely find it somewhat difficult to successfully apply for a large bank loan or an upscale apartment rental. The Vampyre must be able to be a chameleon and relate to those within the mundane world in many different spheres.

As part of mastering the Glamour, look in the mirror and practice your expressions as if you were a public speaker. Be mindful of your physical appearance: exercise to maintain a healthy and attractive physical body, dress with care, and smile and speak with a powerful and controlled voice. Practice every day! Some of us are already talented in these areas, whilst others must practice more. Such rehearsals are employed by the most successful businessmen and leaders.

The Glamour is about achieving desired reactions from others. Test and experiment; observe and learn what works best for you. Keep notes in your grimoire and trade applications of the Glamour with other Strigoi Vii. The most important goal is to improve your experiences in life. Remember, your personal Glamour is your own! Employ it, and you can increase the power of your personal relationships and have a much more fulfilling life. Try the following exercises and applications. There is no better time to begin than now.

The Dragons' Presence

This is a simple exercise to influence the minds of others to your will. It combines several techniques of psychology and presence. Like most techniques of the Glamour, it will take time to master; however, it is a simple combination of methods, and it will certainly gain the desired results if employed properly.

Begin with personal physical awareness. When interacting with others, make sure your posture is perfect and your back straight. Look directly into their eyes and speak slowly, subtly mimicking their blinking patterns. Speak in a calming voice and focus on the use of true statements such as "It is Friday morning" or "The library will close in an hour so we need to be there soon." Study the individual's physical gestures and discreetly mimic them; for example, if the person to whom you are speaking often rubs their chin, do the same. They will unconsciously acknowledge the similarity and become more comfortable and open in your Presence.

The Vampyre Presence combines several NLP techniques called "pacing." Watch as a calming and agreeable effect comes over the individual with whom you are interacting. Practice the entire exercise or break it up into individual applications. Do not be discouraged if you do not get results at first. It may take repeated practice for some, and it will be completely natural for others.

The Vampyre chameleon is distinct from the fledgling Vampyre who often comes to the Mysteries with the image of the cape-wearing, fanged, gothic Hollywood vampire in their mind. They are often very surprised to discover that the reality of Strigoi Vii can be much more than this stereotyped image. This image is fun for the fledgling, for Halloween, or even as a fetish or at special events, but in reality it has limited application for the Glamour. The Adeptus of Strigoi Vii is a true chameleon. They can "codeshift," or meld, into the communities in which they function, ready to employ the Glamour to obtain Lifeforce and further their own needs and goals.

With the opening of one's *"Dragons' Eyes,"* the fledglings will find there are members of the Family in almost every possible position in society, from bus drivers to professional athletes to lawyers and professors and doctors. We are everywhere! For the Magister this is no surprise, as we assume many different roles throughout mundane society.

As the Strigoi Vii grows in Zhep'r, they will find themselves less conditioned by the Glamour and have more understanding of their own Self. Thus they shall gain the freedom to explore their own unique self-expression balanced with the Glamour. We are not shallow individuals who claim to "transcend" ordinary society yet ultimately conform to the rules of a sub-culture just as codified as any mainstream clique. We are an evolved and unique individuals.

It is true that Strigoi Vii are often eccentric, with many, but not all, possessing a love of body arts and unique accoutrements such as Victorian fashions or antique jewelry. Such accessories can be a form of subtle communication between Strigoi Vii. Know where you are and what works for you, depending on the situation. For example, Freemasons in the United States wear "badges" such as rings or pins. However, the Freemasons of the United Kingdom only communicate through body language and preexisting knowledge of their brothers. There are no hard and fast rules, only techniques of personal empowerment!

Vampyres should be able to express themselves on an aesthetic level but not intimidate the outside world or appear foolish.

Rather, we should communicate who we are through subtlety, self-control, and power—elements of the our Glamour.

Vampyre Aesthetics: Three Basic Motifs of Strigoi Vii Dress (Garb)

Vampyre aesthetics use motifs that are defined by the Merriam-Webster dictionary to refer to a *single or repeated design or color*. Within the VC (Vampyre Culture) motifs refers to a style of dress or look, of which the basics include *Salon Noir*, *Majestic*, and *Ceremonial*.

Motifs should be elegant, mysterious and compliment the Vampyre in their Glamour techniques in both the profane and the ethereal with subtle hints of Vampyric symbolism. With this as a foundation, the Adeptus Vampyre should employ their motifs to aid in the techniques advised in *William Mortensen's book The Command to Look: A Master Photographer's Method for Controlling the Human Gaze*. Every Adeptus is an ambassador for our Culture and inspiration for fledglings, so setting an example and making an effort only amplifies the Vampyre Current for the individual and community. The key here is to achieve a timeless look that echo's through the ages.

Salon Noir Motif

The most basic default style for the Vampyre aesthetic which can be used in any situation is that of the Salon Noir Motif which can be used within and outside salons and empower the Vampyre in a multitude of scenarios. This is style is inspired by a Victorian funeral, a formal dark business affair, Long Black Veil events, dumb supper, a séance for Houdini, or a dinner party hosted by Vanessa Ives from Penny Dreadful.

Couture should be tailored suits, ties, cravats, capes, corsets, vests, smoking jackets, evening attire, and cocktail dresses. The salon noir style should be elegant and mysterious while amplifying confidence and clothing should be flattering yet comfortable.

The *colors* of the fabric should be black on black with limited patterns and occasional accents of dark emeralds, sapphires, scarlets, or deep reds which compliment but do not distract the black background. Absolutely no visible commercial logos or symbolism, especially which resembles fascism or any political stance.

Nails for the ladies and eccentric gents should be stilettos to resemble claws, or simply clean and well-manicured. *Makeup* should not be extravagant and have a natural or subtle feline or wolfen look or resembling ancient cultures such as Egyptian or Phoenician. *Fragrances* should not be overbearing and best to include pheromones to create seductive sent.

Footwear is most empowering when it is leather for faux without colored laces, best primarily black and no sneakers, sandals, or canvas materials. Heels and boots are welcomed, but make sure comfort for dancing and walking is taken into consideration.

Jewelry should be subtle and pronounced and is most often silver is preferred, with complementary esoteric symbolic rings, Legacy Ankh or occult sigillum pendants, silver chain necklaces, and lapel pins with occult symbols to show order, halo, or coven.

Accessories beyond jewelry should be subtle and elegant can including leather walking canes, cowboy hats, witchy hats, cardigans, scarves, gloves, top hats, faux or vintage fur accents, old spectacles, pocket watches, etc.

Fangs should be custom-made by a talented fangsmith and subtle whereas the wearer should be able to speak clearly and drink cocktails with them on. Contact lenses should be artistic, visible, look subtle and or striking to the soul with a slight glance.

Majestic Motif

This motif applies when a formal, regency, aristocratic or highly theatrical aesthetic is in order. This can be a highly formal salon noir style but is usually more as one is presenting yourself at an Endless Night Vampire Ball, Anne Rice Coven Ball, Babylonian Grande Vampyre Salon, Monarch's court, royal coronation, Venetian masquerade, or courtly affair. Depending on the affair the default color is black, yet darker colors may be permitted by the host or theme that can include more prevalent whites, purples, yellows, and reds.

Example sub-motifs include: Dark baroque (Versaii French 18th century style), Venetian Carnival, Aristocratic Victorian and Regency. All suitable for a grande Vampyre affair.

Ceremonial Motif (*see Ritual Attire Black Veil*)

The ceremonial motif is best suited for rituals, ceremonies, working magick, attending or presiding an initiation, Blood and Roses (Vampyre Wedding), Requiem (Vampyre funeral) or a seasonal rite. Different traditions of Vampyrim use different symbolisms inspired by different paradigms including Khemetic (ancient Egyptian), Celtic, Tiamantis, Sumerian, Babylonian.

There are three sub-motifs of Formal, Robes or Nightklad. Black or dark colored robes, masks, and body jewelry coming as one would envision a witch, warlock, wizard or dark acolyte or priest/ess. Tradition holds that the officiants presiding of the ritual should carry blades. *Formal attire* is basically Salon Noir in all black suits or cocktail dresses, often with Venetian masks. *Black robes* without prominent color contrasts. Limited jewelry such as a Legacy Ankh or Dragon Ouroboros. Masks emphasize putting one's ego behind the actual, higher purpose of the ritual. Finally, Nightklad means clothed only in darkness and its best to see the *NightKlad Black Veil*. Mradu should wear armor or warriors vestments, Kitra in seductive sensual costumes akin to a belly dancer and Ramkht in priestly or wizard like vestments. Rather simple and straightforward, but quite sublime elegance. The focus is on the ritual, and not on the participants.

The Vampyre Warlock (*see Vampyre Gent & The King Within Black Veils*). Aesthetic empowerment of the Vampyre Brother, or Frater, involves truly embracing the Black Veils of the Vampyre Gentleman or the Vampyre King Within, the embodiment of the masculine element of divine nature. Aesthetics can be a powerful psychodramatic tool for the Vampyre Frater. Gents in general, have a more compact set of options than the Vampyre Witch when employing the aesthetic elements of the Glamour, especially through the Salon Noir Motif or the Majestic Motifs. One of the most effective presentations for the male Vampyre is a black-on-black or dark-colored suit and tie, which speaks of sophistication and dominance and thus commands respect.

CEOs and politicians wear suits of basic colors in order to project dominance in public meetings and business affairs. Politicians will often wear simple accessories such as lapel pins in the shape of their national flag to show their patriotism. Similarly, the Vampyre Gentleman may bear the Legacy Ankh or Ouroboros lapel pin or cufflinks with dashing black leather gloves or other striking accessories from contemporary and past ages. These accessories will act as *zymys*, or masculine-empowered lures, to draw the curiosity of others and communicate one's position within the Family.

Fraters, see how the mundane will perceive you when you are dressed in a well-pressed, all-black suit. It is quite a powerful statement, and people will see and respond to you differently. From this foundation, go and explore what works for you, the individual. There are a hundred other applications that can further the Self.

The Vampyre Witch (*see Vampyre Witch & The Queen Within Black Veil*) is truly the embodiment of the feminine element of the Strigoi Vii nature. She should present Herself as a powerful Dragon Goddess. Her feminine power can and should be used to great advantage. Women, historically, have often been considered weaker and gentler than men. This is a myth! the Vampyre Witch is beautiful and powerful! She can use such patriarchal stereotypes to ensnare men with Her Glamour, as Circe ensnared Odysseus.

The Vampyre Witch may employ contemporary sexual stimuli in a natural yet empowered way, without appearing crude or coarse. When one thinks of a courtesan or geisha, they may think of a refined, educated, and powerful goddess whom mundane men worship and women fantasize about resembling. The Vampyre Witch can manipulate and seduce both genders through simply triggering instinctual responses, then further empower herself with more advanced techniques based on this foundation. The Vampyre Witch will sometimes sabotage Herself and make the mistake of trying to cater to an ideal (often unrealistic and unattainable) self-image, rather than paying attention to the responses of others. She will then end up intimidating Her targets and will become frustrated as to why She cannot provoke the intended reaction. If the Vampyre Witch wishes to seduce an individual who has specific tastes, she should determine what pleases them, either through asking questions or observation, and respond accordingly. No matter what her physical appearance, the Vampyre Witch should embrace her natural charms and talents—then strike! Consider, for example, Cleopatra or Marilyn Monroe, who were physically not exceptionally attractive. Cleopatra was small in stature and plain of face, and Marilyn Monroe would wear approximately a size 12 or 14 dress today! However, both women learned to use the powers of seduction, body language, fantasy, and imagery to gain the responses they desired. Cleopatra seduced and controlled two of the most powerful men in history, and Marilyn Monroe became an international sex symbol. These results speak for themselves. Today these powerful women are worshipped as goddesses, and nearly everyone in the world knows their names.

Re-examining traditional gender roles and markers can be very powerful for both the Vampyre Gentleman and the Vampyre Witch. We live in a society comprised of many different sexual orientations and predilections. A good example is a dandy, or someone who takes on the characteristics and mannerisms commonly associated with the opposite gender. This can, as well, be a powerful tool of manipulation or seduction. For example, the contemporary movie star Johnny Depp presented a feminine appearance in the *Pirates of the Caribbean* movies. He wore eyeliner and jewelry and behaved in a sexually ambiguous manner. Consequently, both men and women consider him a sex symbol. The great actress Marlene Dietrich sometimes wore men's tuxedos to parties, and people of both genders were enamored of her. Many, but not all, drag queens employ the feminine aesthetic in a glamorous way, and much of women's corporate power attire takes its keys from formal male suits. Vampyre Gentleman and Vampyre Witch should never forget the power of each other's aesthetics and adopt them themselves when appropriate.

For the purposes of Strigoi Vii workings, we pull energy toward ourselves. This is why Vampyres often wear black more than any other color, sometimes complementing it with crimson, purple, or silver. On a purely Corporeal level, black clothing is quite often seen by the mundane as striking, slimming and distinguished.

Summation

Whether Vampyre Gent or Witch, embrace your self and your personal tools of empowerment. The so-called mating game exists at the foundation of society. For animals, "sexual selection" is simple—the strongest members of any species strive to mate with the strongest of the opposite sex in order to ensure superior offspring and the survival of the species. For humans, it is much more complicated. Although inherent genetically programmed responses still exist, "strongest" means something very different for wolves, for example, from what it means for humans. Human beings are attracted to each other based on appearance, intelligence, charisma, wealth, and numerous other factors. From the Strigoi Vii perspective, the Vampyric Witch's feminine power often comes through aesthetic seduction and control, while dominance and authority may be effective for the male Living Vampyre. However, with the many complexities of modern society, the Vampyre Witch and Vampyre Gentleman should carefully examine and dance within the many available gender and sexual roles when employing the Glamour to their greatest advantage. Watch and experiment, verify and learn, find out what works for you, and then enjoy the results!

CHAPTER 14

MASTERY OF THE SOLVENCY PILLAR

"Rich and poor are states of mind and conditioning. The Strigoi Vii thinks rich and masters their own material world instead of being its victim. When a Strigoi Vii is monetarily broke, that is not the same as being poor. It is only a temporary state."

—Father Sebastiaan,
inspired by the book *Rich Dad, Poor Dad*

For the Strigoi Vii, money is a vessel of energy and a tool of power. From the Dayside perspective, we seek mastery of our material world and avoid being a slave to it as so many are. To the Strigoi Vii, money is simply a tool, just as a paintbrush is the tool an artist uses to create a great dayside masterpiece.

We are not talking about senselessly amassing wealth for decadence only, but sensible savings and the ability to indulge in sensible he-donistic pleasures like gourmet food and drink, fine and quality clothing, freedom to travel, adventure and a good place to live (see Vampyre Lair Black Veil) that suits their desires and personality. The Strigoi Vii sees money as just another tool and will not be blindly seduced by such symbols of slavery! Instead, the Strigoi Vii thinks as a master of their money, which they see only as an instrument for personal evolution.

The individual nobility of the Vampyre Current of Elorath can be most easily witnessed through this Principle. Those of the Family do not see money as "the root of all evil." So many mortal-minded work their entire lives for a faceless corporate Egregore, world government, or an impersonal university hoping for a high salary, basic health benefits, and investment package. Most of these people will one day find a pink slip in their mailbox or be "let go" in some corporate downsizing plan. Even if they avoid these near inevitabilities, they will be slaves to "assets" such as a home or to credit card debts. The combination of contemporary corporate globalization and rampant consumerism means that most mortal-minded find themselves in a never-ending cycle of debt and dissatisfaction. They make choices based on what they are brainwashed into believing they want, not what actually fulfills them.

The Strigoi Vii applies money practically to increase their experiences and satisfy their curiosity about life. Why should the Strigoi Vii Vampyre spend $100,000 to purchase a fast sports car when they can rent it for an afternoon for $1,000 and enjoy it just as much? They appreciate the experience to its fullest, and then spend the other $99,000 on a lasting and more important investment, such as traveling the world or obtaining a university education. In the end, which is more permanent?

For those truly of our Current, experience and knowledge are valued above money or any material item. Cars, fancy clothing, houses, computers, and all physical items will expire. The Strigoi Vii see the value in these items, yet do not become slaves to them. They seek to make an investment in themselves, enriching their own lives through travel, education, developing their musical and artistic skills, or any other discipline that focuses on creation, not consumption!

Of course, material items, such as the security and comfort of a private personal lair or investment in a practical car for transport or a piece of real estate that will eventually make more profit, are within the concept of the Vampyre's material mastery.

Physical items are not you! They must contribute to your experi-ence in life. Spend your money and wealth on your Self and invest not in external obsessions that are simply going to decompose or be destroyed. Yet treat yourself well as there is reasonable decadence which can be sensible. Would you not rather have those things that are of true value to an Immortal such as knowledge, experience or Legacy?

CHAPTER 15

REINFORCING IMMORTALITY

"And the will therein lieth, which dieth not. Who knoweth the mysteries of the will, with its vigor? For [it] is but a great will pervading all things by nature of its intentness. Man doth not yield himself to the angels, nor unto death utterly, save only through the weakness of [a] feeble will."

—Joseph Glanville,
quoted in *Ligeia* by Edgar Allan Poe

According to the Merriam-Webster Dictionary, the word *immortality* is defined as a state of unyielding existence. Achievement of this state is at the core of Strigoi Vii Zhep'r. From the mortal-minded perspective, this may seem to be completely impossible. However, certain forms of potential Corporeal Immortality will be explored here. The Higher Mysteries explore the realities of Nightside Immortality, which cannot be understood without first mastering the Dayside perspective.

Immortality has been the dream of humanity ever since their first contemplation of the mortality of the soul. For the most part, it is completely out of their grasp. The vast majority of religions claim to grant Immortality and everlasting life if their followers adhere to a particular set of principles. However, these are not solid guarantees, as there is no way to actually prove religious faith and bring it into the realm of knowledge. Faith and belief, the cornerstones of human religion, still imply the lack of tangible or verifiable evidence, the opposite of Gnosis. Listed here are three basic possibilities of Corporeal Immortality: posterity, production of offspring, and science.

Posterity consists of branding yourself into the collective societal consciousness so that you are never forgotten. Your actions, image, words, or creations continue on and survive for many future generations. Examples of those who have achieved posterity include writers, artists, musicians, actors, war heroes, religious leaders, politicians, and inventors whose deeds and names live on today.

Even the wealthy who do not have such talents or skills to define themselves can "buy" their way into Corporeal but not spiritual Nightside Immortality by donating huge sums of money to museums, universities, or commercial ventures that then bear their name. Rockefeller Center in New York City, named after the millionaire Nelson Rockefeller, is an example of this sort of legacy Immortality.

If you just mention and remember names such as Jesus, Queen Elizabeth, Confucius, Alexander the Great, Sappho, George Washington, Leonardo Da Vinci, and so on, you will be contributing to their Corporeal Immortality and posterity. The drive for power and desire to leave a mark is inherited by a select few of the teeming masses of humanity. This is identical to the true spark of our Current. Many try and few truly Ascend to Immortality.

In nature, there may be as many as eleven to twenty unborn sharks in their amniotic sac. The fledgling sharks will follow Darwin's law of survival of the fittest, turning on one another for sustenance, until only one is born. It is not unknown for a human fetus to absorb or "devour" its twin in the womb. Both the god of Abraham and Mother Nature are indiscriminate and oftentimes cruel for the sake of survival. The mortal-minded worship anyone who shows dominance and power to survive. Even if they cannot achieve it themselves, they will follow and attach themselves, like groupies, to that legacy.

Their main motivation is survival of the Self. Why else would Virginia Woolf have written so many great works of literature, including her own memoirs? Or would Elvis have sought after fame so desperately?

For example, Rembrandt, who has become a common name in textbooks and art classes, has been dead for hundreds of years. Yet through his numerous self-portraits, we continue to know his face and image.

No matter what your accomplishments, your branding in the public memory creates an indelible "cult of personality." However, this imprint becomes its own entity. Is it still you? Does the legacy of Sylvia Plath, the so-called suicide poet, for example, represent her actual life and body of work?

Offspring is another path to Corporeal Immortality and is why humans have such a strong desire to mate and reproduce. The production of offspring is about survival of one's genes. The sexual drive of courtship and reproduction is one of the most dominant of all human instincts. Having children guarantees that one's genes will continue from one generation to the next. For example, many modern parents wish for their children to surpass their own achievements and have better lives than they had. Socially, the dominant parents have left their mark on the next generation, often in ways they never expected. This is a natural trait amongst all species. The bottom line is first, personal survival, and then, survival of the species. This is expressed in the mundane world as well, as many cultures revere their ancestors, such as the Chinese and Native Americans and practitioners of African syncretistic religions, such as Santeria, Yoruba, Candomblé, and Voudoun.

Many different cultures even practice rituals to honor their ancestors. However, by honoring and venerating their ancestors, they are essentially worshipping themselves as members of such an exalted family line. Moreover, these people think that perhaps if they keep the memory of their ancestors alive, their children will do the same for them after they are dead! Visit any large cemetery, and you will see the massive, elaborate monuments designed to show the glory of both the deceased and the family that raised such mausoleums.

Science today, unlike any other time in known history, is showing signs of the possibility of extended life or even Immortality. The mapping of the human genome, the potential of cryonics, and the discovery that aging is indeed a genetically programmed process are some examples of ground-breaking science in the area of life extension.

You may ask, *"What can I do right now?"*

The first and most obvious thing is to do your best to reach a point of good health and physical wellness. Use common sense. If you are an addicted smoker, simply quit immediately, for obvious reasons. Avoid drinking alcohol to excess. Drink a great deal of water (at least eight to ten eight-ounce glasses per day) in order to remain hydrated. Exercise daily. Other suggestions include reducing your consumption of, or completely eliminating, refined sugars and processed foods. Avoid fast foods! Move to more organic items and eschew food that is filled with steroids and chemicals. Eat a balanced amount of protein and green vegetables. Of course, if you live in a country such as the United States that does not have socialized health care, and you do not have health insurance, obtain it as soon as possible. Critically examine the popular diets of today, as many are fads that may actually be harmful to your health. This is primarily not about your appearance. It is about your personal health and keeping your body intact and strong for a long life. Healthy weight and body type for one person might not be the same as for another.

Consider the preservation of your physical body or DNA. The most affordable process is to take a cotton swab, wipe it inside your mouth, and put it in a well-sealed, heavy-duty plastic bag in the freezer. This will preserve your DNA. You can also purchase DNA preservation kits. More advanced techniques include making arrangements with a cryonics or mummification facility. Some examples include the Cryonics Institute in Clinton Township, Michigan, and the Alcor Life Extension Foundation in Scottsdale, Arizona; or Summum in Salt Lake City, Utah, for mummification. These can be easily found on the web through your favorite search engine. When contacting these organizations, do not mention that you are a Vampyre, for these ways of burial are often unpopular amongst mortal-minded society, and a public connection between Vampyres and cryonics or mummification would not serve our Glamour or their business relations. (Please always be respectful of the interests of others, especially when involved in business relations with them.)

Even though science does not offer a solution to the puzzle of mortality at the present time, the speed at which new thresholds are broken show us that in the not-too-distant future the science of medicine will be able to do far more for us than now. We should seek to preserve our Corporeal bodies and genetic material in anticipation of that time.

What is the primary difference between a mundane person and someone who has the sign of the Vampyre Current and thus potential for Zhep'r? The masses love death. They welcome it, often coming up with a multitude of reasons and excuses as to why they wish to expire. They cling to false hopes that they will be reborn into another body or enter an afterlife as themselves. However, there is no guarantee their personality will remain intact. Due to the law of conservation of energy, after the Second Death your energies will be recycled as a drop of water in the ocean. Is the soul recycled just like the energy and matter in your Corporeal body? No one living can say for sure. Why gamble on a mere improvable chance of Immortality?

As famous World War II general Erwin Rommel once said, *"I never gamble—I only take risks. A risk I can calculate. Gambles are completely random."* For the lifeloving Strigoi Vii, this gambling of "faith" is ludicrous. A Living Vampyre will not base their choices, for example, on a gospel that carries no proof other than badly translated two-thousand-year-old scriptures written from third-person viewpoints. Basically, if you have not validated something for your own Self, it is a gamble. Be wise and rational in your decisions and preparations for your extended future.

CHAPTER 16
THE QUEST OF FAMILY

"I have been and still am a seeker... I have begun to listen to the teachings my blood whispers to me. My story... has the taste of... dreams—like the lives of all who stop deceiving themselves."

—Hermann Hesse, *Demian*

Our Awakening can happen in many ways, from reading an enlightening book to meeting an inspiring individual from a similar esoteric system to having a Vampyre gather one's energy. Whatever the trigger, age of the individual, or how much experience they have, during Awakening they can only trust their instincts and the bits of information they have gathered. In the beginning, the process is as passionate and turbulent as falling in love, but with the passing of time we acquire a deeper understanding of and personal obligation to our Blood and Family. The un-Awakened may have the hardware for Zhep'r within their potential, but do they have the software of knowledge? The purpose of the Quest of Family is to "distribute the software" to those who are "compatible" with it. The goal of our great Quest of Family is to discover and welcome our future Sorors and Fraters.

Many will hear the Calling within their hearts and seek out the Family on their own through a variety of means. These range from attending our public events to trying to seek out our discreet international gatherings to meeting others of the Family on the Internet. However, there are still many who have not yet become aware of their potential.

The Quest of Family exists simply to provide an opportunity for Seekers to become aware of the tools for Zhep'r. The Strigoi Vii should not degrade the Family and the Quest by trying to forcefully convert, manipulate, or preach as do most mortal-minded cults and many religions. Strigoi Vii is not a closed-minded fundamentalist religion that seeks to brainwash individuals. Free will and the ability to come unforced are amongst the highest of all Strigoi Vii ethics and a sign of Vampyric Potential. This is how We show respect for all of our Family and other Awakened traditions.

Together We have built the OSV as a philosophical and spiritual movement to further the preservation and prosperity of the Current of Elorath. The OSV is a metaphorical Sanctum for Seekers, Initiates, Black Swans, and Elder Strigoi Vii alike. There is a bewildering array of organizations, societies, websites, and books claiming to know the "truth" about vampires. This can be confusing. These do not perceive the path of the Vampyre as we do. It is often hard to see through the propaganda and disinformation about what is Strigoi Vii tradition and Family and what is not. However, the true members of the Family will find us of their own free will, if the Family Quest is performed properly. Some elements of the Glamour can also be a part of our Quest of Family.

Identifying Potential Seekers

Many Seekers know they are different from other people and may explore a variety of lifestyles and spiritual paths. They most often find their way to the gothic, vampire, occult, Satanist, or neopagan communities, which intersect with the more public levels of the Family. When Seekers finally make the choice to come to the Family, they are often already dissatisfied and feeling a sense of loss or frustration.

Often they have begun to build a strong foundation by having spent the time to genuinely test and experiment with other systems. Sometimes their nature is right in front of them and, like a "closeted" homosexual or fetishist, they are filled with relief and pleasure upon discovering there are others like themselves.

Seekers are most often quite easy to recognize. They show a passionate and genuine curiosity by asking questions, being willing to challenge their beliefs, attending gatherings, and educating themselves. They will radiate the Dark Flame to others of the Family.

Be aware while pursuing the Quest of Family that only specifically appointed agents of the Synod are qualified to speak to the media or perform interviews regarding the Current, OSV and the Strigoi Vii Mysteries. These individuals have been Initiated into the Synod and are properly trained in dealing with the mundane world and communicating our ideals. Do not become overzealous in your pursuit of the Family Quest and thus place yourself and the Family in a compromising position!

When you see the Radiance in a potential, you must be circumspect, mysterious, and respectful. Play into the Seeker's curiosity and their awareness of their inherent difference from the rest of the world. However, Awakening can often be a challenging and confusing time, when the seeker will question their spiritual and philosophical perspectives. Let them lead themselves, and just spark the fire to show them the way along their own path.

Do not be disappointed if a Potential, who shows a strong Radiance does not hear the Calling. Many will come to the Family on their own. They may read the Strigoi Vii Codex and take days, months, or even years before actually taking the first steps of Zhep'r. Nature, as always, will cull out the weak and unfit so the strongest will have the best chance of survival.

It may be heartbreaking for the Immortal-minded to watch a loved one knowingly face the Second Death. It is their choice and not ours. We first must concern ourselves with our own individual Self and look to others who are passionate about the path of Zhep'r to surround and inspire Us. Never forget that, in time, the pain of loss does fade. In most cases, we can apply the old proverb "Time heals all wounds," especially since we welcome Immortality!\

A warning: It can be difficult to perform a mission like the Quest of Family without becoming overzealous. Be calm, discreet, and respectful. We are not a cult, and such a collective mentality does not benefit the prosperity and preservation of our Family. Dogma only becomes dogma if it is forced.

Realize that others, even if you perceive them as Family, may not be in agreement with you. Do not argue; let them believe whatever they like. They should come into agreement of their own free will through observation and personal validation, not because they are persuaded or coerced.

Remember, Strigoi Vii is not about mindless followers. We seek those who are beautiful of mind and spirit; the cunning and talented individuals who truly relate to our Mysteries. Do not apply the Quest indiscriminately to everyone you meet. Be patient, observe, determine if the Radiance is true, and then apply the techniques of the Quest of Family. Many of those who try to create a group of followers do so out of a deep-rooted sense of inadequacy and a need to be worshipped and adored. We are not a cult, and we are not interested in "recruiting" followers! We focus on independent, self-chosen like-mindedness and bonds of unity. Binding people together through desperation or intimidation is a mortal-minded trait and will only promote mortal-minded structures and hierarchies. Remember that only teachings and knowledge are only valuable for those who will live forever.

There are many ways to further the Quest of Family without violating the Strigoi Vii Principles, degrading the Quest of Family, or compromising your own personal privacy. These may be employed by any supporter, Initiate, or Black Swan to further and support the Current, the Family Quest with integrity and discretion.

First read the Strigoi Vii Codex and Black Veils: This is the first suggestion to make to a Seeker or anyone who is curious. Let them read it and make up their own mind. Never try to explain its contents through exposition or enthusiastic discussion. Allow a seeker to ask educated and informed questions on their own. The Strigoi Vii Codex was designed to clearly explain the elementary concepts of our Mysteries without revealing too much. This allows the individual to be presented with a common foundation and make their own choice.

When a Seeker asks about Strigoi Vii or the OSV and has not made the effort to at least read a book, they honestly are not interested, sincere, or ready. Let the Strigoi Vii Codex explain for you. Do not expend your energy or weaken our Mysteries by revealing too much verbally. We all have a foundation from this book. Reading is an internal experience, while listening is an external one, and thus not as intimate and personal.

Why do you think that reading is so often prohibited in science fiction and dystopian tales such as Fahrenheit 451 or 1984? The written word holds power and is a tool of transformation. Do not seek to transform others; let them transform themselves. Let the Seeker read, explore, and determine what works for them. If they then still have the Calling and a strong Radiance, they will come to Us of their own free will and with a strong foundation of self-sufficiency through dynamic and independent thought.

Place the book in your personal library or on your coffee table where it can be subtly visible to guests who you feel might have the Radiance. Put official Strigoi Vii Codex links and banners on your email signatures. If you are mysterious and tactful, it will strengthen the Glamour for you and the entire Family. If you are pushy or sensationalistic, you will simply weaken us all. Remember, everyone loves secrets, and we are an Open Secret hidden in plain sight! We are only there for those who are truly curious.

Quest Cards: Another practical technique is to use the Quest cards, which are about the size of a business card and have StrigoiVii.org printed on one side and "Are you Curious?" on the other. There are predesigned Quest cards available on the Synod-endorsed Strigoi Vii forums. You can subtly pass these cards out to Potentials in a social environment like a nightclub or a coffee house, or even post them on bulletin boards in occult shops, libraries, or esoteric bookstores. You might mail the card to someone or place one in a book in your local bookstore or library that might be of interest to Seekers. One powerful technique is to have another member of the Family send the card to a friend in the mail so as not to reveal your identity and to stay within the mystery of the Glamour.

Internet Banners and Signatures: When pursuing the Quest on the Internet, you can provide a link to a sanctioned Strigoi Vii website or where to find the Strigoi Vii Codex online by using one of the endorsed banners on your personal or business website or community pages. You can also put one of the Family Quest endorsements in the signature of your emails and profiles, such as "Are you curious? Sanctum of the Living Vampire: StrigoiVii.org."

Gifting: You can provide a Seeker you know personally with a copy of the Strigoi Vii Cod as a gift. This places the knowledge within their hands in a gracious gesture without imposing. If they are curious, they will read it on their own terms. You can even have it sent anonymously, which is less of an obligation and further leaves a sense of wonder.

Heritage Copies are personally owned copies of the Strigoi Vii Codex or Black Veils that are passed from a Strigoi Vii to a worthy Seeker. This is generally only done for those to who you are close. If there is someone in your life who you feel has the Radiance, and you would like to present them with the Strigoi Vii Codex, consider passing on your own copy to them as a gift. This is a very personal and familial experience that can be extremely rewarding, especially since you have consecrated the book. Please use discretion when revealing your Vampyre nature, especially if it is to a loved one. Once revealed, what you say can never be undisclosed.

Remember that doing anything beyond these recommended techniques can easily violate the secret Principle of the Strigoi Vii, and doing so will only be working against the Current. Never speak of the Strigoi Vii Mysteries with anyone who has not taken the time to read the Strigoi Vii Codex. Being willing to read and ponder a text on one's own shows maturity and responsibility. Those who are open-minded will try to understand us, even if they are not of the Current. Anyone who is not truly interested cannot even begin to comprehend our Mysteries and speaking to them will be a waste of energy on both sides.

We have no need to defend our Mysteries or force them on others. If someone is not of the Current, they will never fully understand our ways, as they cannot personally experience them. We must let the conditioning of the Glamour work its course. If, out of a dozen Seekers who read the Strigoi Vii Codex, only one feels the Calling and Awakens, then so be it. We are not concerned with sheer numbers, only with making contact with others of our Blood.

Some Testimonials of the Results of the Quest of Family

The following are examples of applications of the Family Quest and its results. These quotes are based on real-life testimonials of Family members. Their identities are kept confidential to protect their privacy. Many of these may seem familiar to you, as it may be the Quest has affected your life and brought you to reading this book.

"Many years ago, I was in Europe on a business trip. I had previously encountered an individual over the Internet who I felt had the Radiance and who had read the Strigoi Vii Codex and Black Veils. When I was in his country, I took the opportunity to have a drink with him. During the conversation, he realized he was with Family. Today he is a Magister and has served on the Synod." (Frater S.)

"For many years, I kept the secret of being Strigoi Vii from my wife. She knew I was into Vampyrism; however, she only knew about the social level of our world. She asked about the subject, and I replied, 'The book is on my altar. Read it when you are ready.' After a year, she read the book and began to ask questions. I told her to go to the StrigoiVii.org website. Today she is actively involved in the Family." (Mr. E.)

"I received the Strigoi Vii quest card back in 1997 at the Anne Rice Ball in New Orleans. One day, almost ten years later, I saw a vampire documentary on A&E and remembered the majestic individual who gave me that card. Now I am enjoying Zhep'r and challenging my beliefs, as I know I am Family. "(Soror L.)

"During an outing at a local gothic gathering, I noticed a lovely girl in a Victorian dress wearing fangs and a Legacy Ankh. I had never experienced the Radiance before, and I approached her. After spending a few days with her, I gave her a copy of [The Strigoi Vii Codex / Sanguinomicon] as a gift. She read it, questioned it, and became a Seeker. Now she has solved more of the Mysteries than I thought I could ever achieve." (Soror T.)

Beyond the Basics

Introducing someone who you feel has the Radiance to the principles of Strigoi Vii is only one part of the Family Quest, but there is danger in going too far. Too many groups and individuals distract themselves from their core purpose by trying to reinvent the wheel, write another "definitive" book on

Vampyrism, or start another order, clan, or coven. The purpose of the Quest is connecting with others of the Family, not glorifying oneself. Seeking personal notoriety by repeating actions and not complementing them or trying to redo things that already exist is a waste of energy and time. Rather, bring unique and new tangible ideas to the table—new ideas, new customs, fresh perspectives, new visions, and new rituals. Remember, the modernist poet Ezra Pound always urged his fellows to "Make it new!" instead of copying and regurgitating already-existing ideas and artforms.

Here are some further suggestions on how to further the Family Quest, contribute to the OSV movement, and strengthen Our Current. In all cases, be sure to consult with the Synod if there is any danger of copyright or intellectual-property infringement. The OSV was born of a collective of ideas and inspirations. Expand on this with courtesy and honor! The following is a list of suggestions for inspiring Strigoi Vii to further the Quest of Family.

Help organize a Convivium, Moot, Quabal, or gathering in your local area for practitioners of Strigoi Vii. Be aware that group ritual Communion should only be led by an Initiate who has completed at least the Morrah Ordeal. However, you certainly can take the initiative to contact one of these individuals, suggest your idea, and assist them as a Deacon.

Create a burlesque or performance art troupe using Black Veil Vampyre concepts and aesthetics.

Further the art of Black Veil Vampyre dance by choreographing a Strigoi Vii–specific dance piece.

Create Black Veil Vampyre / Strigoi Vii poetry or prose.

Offer to assist the Synod by translating the Black Veil Vampyre / Strigoi Vii into other languages. Please make sure you are qualified to undertake such a project and get proper permission from the Synod so as not to violate copyrights.

Encourage or sponsor the creation of Black Veil Vampyre / Strigoi Vii music, poetry, or visual art.

Organize discussion circles on esotericism on the Black Veil Vampyre / Strigoi Vii .

Open a Noir Haven if there is not one in your Halo or coordinate a Vampyre Ball. (Be cordial and make sure you do not conflict with other local events. Too many times, local groups and event coordinators do not coordinate, leading to divisiveness and unneeded competition. Try to compromise if events seem to conflict or help lead others to compromise. This is often a point of conflict in Halos, even with non-Family- coordinated similar events.)

Host an art gallery or viewing of Black Veil Vampyre / Strigoi Vii artwork.

Write a supplemental and complementary text to expand on the Mysteries or give your perspective on Black Veil Vampyre / Strigoi Vii and submit it to the Synod.

Write a review of a book that will inspire other members of the Family.

Compose music for meditation or ritual.

Start a Black Veil Vampyre / Strigoi Vii –oriented band or record label.

Contribute to the Black Veil Vampyre / Strigoi Vii presence at Burning Man or similar events.

Open a Black Veil Vampyre / Strigoi Vii –friendly bar or restaurant.

Magicians can use Black Veil Vampyre / Strigoi Vii Glamour techniques in their performances.

Belly dancers can add Black Veil Vampyre / Strigoi Vii elements to their performances.

Design clothing or robes for ritual and Black Veil Vampyre / Strigoi Vii fashion.

Develop or create a system of martial arts for the Mradu.

Breed capable Black Veil Vampyre / Strigoi Vii familiars and companions, such as cats or dogs.

Design handcrafted jewelry or artifacts with Strigoi Vii glyphs and symbolism.

Create Strigoi Vii–specific candles or incense for use in ritual.

Explore an ancient location or potential sacred space and write about your experiences. Share such sacred places by taking others to them.

Offer Black Veil Vampyre / Strigoi Vii and Black Swans special services or discounts if you own a business. For example, you might offer discounted admission to your Noir Haven for a Vampire Ball for those wearing an ankh or fangs.

If you are a fashion or pinup model, include subtle Strigoi Vii aesthetics in your images.

Create leather book bindings for personal grimoires.

Create food or drink recipes of interest to the Family.

Ask your local esoteric shop or bookstore to carry the Strigoi Vii Codex and Black Veils.

Open an online store or storefront offering Black Veil Vampyre / Strigoi Vii merchandise and services.

Tattoo artists can offer specially designed tattoos, including Strigoi Vii glyphs, symbolism, or the Legacy Ankh.

A Warning: Attempting to rewrite the Strigoi Vii Codex / Vampyre for one's own personal or communal group use, or misappropriating or misrepresenting it in whole or in part, constitutes plagiarism. Also, it is counterproductive to our Family unity and to the Current of Elorath and OSV movement. Attempting to replace the Legacy Ankh with another symbol is unscrupulous and undignified. The Legacy Ankh is the original symbol of the Black Veils and endorsed by the *Ordo Strigoi Vii*. The Synod has copyrighted and trademarked this symbol to protect it from misuse. Personal use of the Legacy Ankh or Legacy Ouroborous for purposes such as artwork is permitted; however, whenever in doubt, contact the Synod for direction. Our symbols and teachings must be used legally and ethically, with the intent of uniting and furthering Our Family. Misuse and violations will not be tolerated.

In the end, the Quest of Family is simply to suggest and direct individuals to read Strigoi Vii Codex as their starting point.

CHAPTER 17
VAMPYRE SENSUALITY

"We are not sexual as much as sensual."

—Magister Dimitri

"How much passion there is in you! It is that I feel in you. I do not feel the savant, the revealer, the observer. When I am with you, it is the blood I sense."

—Anaïs Nin, *Henry and June*

Strigoi Vii are most often, by nature, deeply romantic and sensual. This, combined with their love of life and awareness of the subtle levels of reality, brings to them a unique perspective on sexuality and intimate relationships. Sexuality is seen as a sacred act, as it involves an exchange of energies. The Glamour, sexuality, and courtship are sensual art forms for those who are part of the Current.

From the Dayside perspective of Strigoi Vii philosophy, the Vampyre is a libertine in the truest sense. The Vampyre libertine is far removed from the mass-media concept of libertines as sex-crazed, irresponsible, and hedonistic individuals. From the perspective of the Strigoi Vii, libertines advocate sexual freedom of the individual, whilst not imposing their values on others. Sexual freedom comes with a balanced respect for the free will of others and does not impose limits on the individual. If the individual finds homosexuality or bisexuality their nature, then it is their right; if they wish for heterosexual monogamy, then that is their choice as well, as long as it is true to their nature. Since We are responsible hedonists, there is no limit to Strigoi Vii sexuality as long as it is pursued safely and sanely, with the mutual consent of all involved. The Strigoi Vii seeks to be aware of their core primal nature, and if they feel empowered by expressing their fetishes, they should explore such desires without personal limits.

Elegance is most important to the Strigoi Vii, yet forwardness, as long as it is respectful, is absolutely embraced. Some even humorously refer to going out on the town as a "hunt," yet they never forget their True Nature. Strigoi Vii's will often find simple mundane sexuality limiting and uninteresting. The mundane world might assume painful sadomasochism and fetishistic bloodletting to be associated with those who adhere to what they would call a "Vampyric philosophy." However, this is yet another distortion perpetuated by mortal-minded society. The Strigoi Vii's sense of the arousing and the sensual is often associated with erotic symbolism, literature and poetry, aromatherapy, stimulating dance, feather play, masks and costumes, music, role-playing, and romance. The erotic predilections of the Strigoi Vii are often far more sophisticated than those found in "normal" pornographic films and magazines. The Strigoi Vii is playful, subtle, and seductive. Since the Strigoi Vii nature is often highly sexual, those who choose to embrace their sexual side will not shy away from practices or professions such as burlesque dancing or high-class erotic consultation. The Strigoi Vii Witch is often drawn to the artistically erotic burlesque striptease or belly dancer archetype.

Dominance and submission are mere games and roles of power exchange, which the Strigoi Vii may enjoy. While the Strigoi Vii is far too individualistic to truly submit their Self to any other, role-playing in this manner, with full understanding that it is merely a game of pleasure, can be liberating and highly enjoyable.

As mentioned in "The Strigoi Vii Prospectus," romantic chivalry is also a part of the Strigoi Vii sexuality for both ladies and gentlemen. The Vampyre Gentleman finds the ethics of the chevalier, Renaissance man, and Victorian gentleman to be powerful role models that often appeal to women. Yet the Strigoi Vii Knight is by no means limited to any seductive archetype, and he may deliberately pursue any number of romantic images. The Vampyre Gentleman may assume the character of a maverick rebel as embodied in the image of the rock star, cowboy, or pirate, whilst <u>always</u> seeking to maintain the deeper romantic and sensual undertones. These values are not simply limited to courtship between Strigoi Vii Ladies and Gentlemen. They also extend beyond Vampyre sensuality into codes of honor on how to deal with mortals, family, lovers, colleagues, and friends.

Many of the Vampyre Witches also maintain a sensual and highly sexual Presence. Lovers of the arts of seduction, the accomplished Vampyre Witch embraces Her sexual and sensual nature, no matter what her physical body type. The Vampyre Witch knows that the beauty myth disseminated by mortal society is no more than an artificial system. True feminine sexuality and sensuality encompass far more aesthetics than an unrealistic and prohibitive "Barbie doll" image. The Vampyre Witch taps into her own personal natural Goddess sensuality in courtship and seduction. Vampyre Witch maintains standards of honor and chivalry as do the Vampyre Gentleman. Strigoi Vii Ladies are far from dainty and submissive; they are often referred to as "Spartan women"! In a relationship, she demand active equality from Her consort, whether male or female, and form partnerships based on mutual respect.

Strigoi Vii prefer to address their lovers with discreet titles such as partner, lover, companion, or the more formal consort. Many of them reject mundane terms like boyfriend and girlfriend or husband and wife. The Strigoi Vii often finds the mundane terms quite limiting. As the mortal-minded conception of heterosexual courtship and marriage derives from a system of male ownership of women, many Strigoi Vii find following it puts up conditioned barriers to their individualistic sexual freedom. This is why many Strigoi Vii, in terminology and intent, take inspiration from the forms of homosexual partnerships.

Experimentation in polygamy or multi-individual relationships is not uncommon amongst the Strigoi Vii. However, this is not to say that all or even most Strigoi Vii engage in such practices! The realities and complexities of such couplings often cause irreconcilable difficulties for the Strigoi Vii. Some Strigoi Vii choose to engage in such practices only in very limited or short-term instances. Many Strigoi Vii also enjoy the deep intimacy found in one-on-one monogamous relationships.

Strigoi Vii sexuality absolutely does not involve rape, child molestation, underage sex, sexual relations with animals, or any other form of sex that violates free will or takes advantage of those who are too immature or unfit to give consent. Strigoi Vii philosophy on all levels calls for personal responsibility. No Strigoi Vii should ever manipulate or take advantage of another, whether physically, mentally, emotionally, or sexually. Should a Strigoi Vii become enamored of a minor, they must wait for the individual to mature. Aside from the obvious legal repercussions of a sexual relationship with a minor, patience and self-control are core Immortal virtues.

The Living Vampire seeks to be true to their Self. It only defeats the Self to ignore one's natural sexual preferences and desires. It is mortal-minded to lie to oneself. A great number of mundane religions encourage one to deny their natural instincts and conform to one standard of sexual behavior. With the reality of different sexual preferences among humans, there can be no uniform system that can be applied to all. For the Strigoi Vii, personal sexuality is accepted as a natural part of life and not ignored.

The Strigoi Vii employs the sensual side of the Glamour as a tool of courtship and seduction. This must be done carefully, as the Glamour must used for a specific purpose, not to fulfill a weak or damaged ego. Far too many unscrupulous individuals employ Strigoi Vii Glamour techniques to seduce Seekers or demand sexual favors for knowledge. This is a horrid abuse of our Glamour! The Glamour is much better applied ethically to the mortal-minded, as they love Us and are often freely drawn to those of the Current through both the Outer and Inner Glamour. Knowledge of psychology and body language is an empowering tool and must be used responsibly. There is an enormous difference between employing such tools in order to further our ethical Art of Gathering Energy, and using them to control a fellow Strigoi Vii! A comprehension of responsible Immortal and mortal-minded sexuality is a major component of Zhep'r.

Many, but not all, Strigoi Vii love BDSM (bondage/discipline/sadomasochism) and dominance and submission; however, they see such behaviors from a different perspective from the mortal-minded. They may view themselves as "SM artists" and often embrace the ritualistic aspects of BDSM practices. Due to their strong sense of Self, some Strigoi Vii prefer to use the terms active (the person performing or directing the activities) and passive (the person who is receiving or the focus of the experience), rather than terms such as dominant and submissive.

Of course, it is plain common sense that all individuals educate and inform themselves before engaging in any form of sensual or sexual play. There are many good sex and BDSM manuals available that detail the necessary precautions, from the use of a "safe word" to the proper and safe way to employ restraints, toys, and tools.

Flogging is the practice of striking another in order to provoke a sexual and sensual reaction, whether it be with a paddle, a scourge (a whiplike instrument comprised of multiple strands), or the bare hand. Flogging is a concept often associated with harsh beatings and rough play by the mortal-minded. However, flogging is a highly sensual exercise for those of the Family and does not involve torture or bodily mutilation. Many Strigoi Vii view flogging as an erotic performance and massage and do not perceive it in terms of dominance and submission.

However, some Strigoi Vii prefer a much more forceful and intense experience. They see flogging as an exciting tool to push their personal limits. This ritual is known as scourging and is not to be done by the inexperienced or timid. It is often used as a ritualistic behavior for testing the limits amongst those empowered by the word Mradu.

Bondage involves the physical restraint of another. It may include ropes, cords, handcuffs, or other restraining items. Often the active partner will sensually bind the passive partner. Again, amongst the mortal-minded, this is often seen as a show of dominance. The Strigoi Vii may employ it as a way to experiment with power roles and to enhance physical sensations. As with all such practices, bondage should never endanger the physical well-being of the subject.

The Vampyres' Hunt is a process of flirtatious courting and seduction that is often a joy for the Strigoi Vii, be it with a donor, potential lover within the Family, or simply for the purpose of gathering Ambient energies (which is often called the Vampyres' Safari). This courtship is often called the Hunt amongst members of the Family. One tradition amongst the Vampyre Witch is to gather a group of like-minded Witches for a "night on the town," during which the Vampyre Witch will tap the Ambient energy they draw to themselves by employing aspects of attractive dress, flirtation, and the Strigoi Vii Glamour. Of course, the Vampyre Gentleman do the same.

Red Magick is a form of sexual magick practiced by the Strigoi Vii, inspired by Eastern sexual techniques and linked to Tantric sex. Red Magick involves the denial or delay of sexual release. The sexual energies are then focused into fueling artistic or other creative or magickal endeavors. To practice Red Magick, one might stimulate oneself to the verge of release and then stop and focus on calming oneself. This rise and calming of energies can build up an immense amount of interior energy within the individual to the point of intense empowerment. It is thus an excellent way to raise energy for intense applications such as healing. However, be aware that prolonged sexual frustration is deleterious to the individual. The Strigoi Vii do not seek to mortify or deny their sexual urges or fulfillment. Thus, Red Magick should only be employed in specific and necessary instances for building and channeling energy, not on a constant basis.

Tantra and Sex Magick are part of the Nightside of the Strigoi Vii Mysteries. They involve a deep mastery of energy work and manipulation and are of high interest to the more sexual Strigoi Vii. Tantra and Sex Magick are employed by Strigoi Vii who seek to experience their pleasure and desire on every level. Kitra, by the nature of their attunements and practices within the Current of the Trinity, are often especially attracted to these practices.

At this point, we cannot fully explain the practices of Tantra and Sex Magick, as many of the details of how and why Strigoi Vii energy work can aid in sexuality are beyond the scope of this book. However, we can introduce the ritual of Chakra Kissing. Chakra Kissing occurs when two lovers kneel face-to-face and physically place their chakra points as close together as possible. They then meditate on the physical and energetic contact and feel their personal energies flowing through each other through their chakra centers. This is an enormously arousing experience and one with which the Jahira should experiment, if possible. Breathing exercises, self-stimulation, and other topics are also relevant to the Nightside of Strigoi Vii philosophy and will be discussed in the more advanced books of the Strigoi Vii Codex.

Do not think that any of these above definitions, terms, or examples are absolute. They are mere observations regarding general Strigoi Vii sexuality and sensuality. Each of us is unique on all levels! We must all put aside guilt for past "mistakes" or lack of conformity and have the courage to embrace our True Self.

CHAPTER 18

BEGINNINGS OF ENERGY GATHERING

"[Feeding] is no ordinary act... It is the experience of another's life for certain... It is again and again a celebration of that experience; because for vampires that is the ultimate experience."

—Anne Rice, *Interview with the Vampire*

Within "Liber Zhep'r: The Vampyre Prospectus," We explored the overall concept of the Art of Gathering Energy and how it is used within the Strigoi Vii Mysteries. Here in "Liber Jahira: Coming Forth by Day," We will begin to apply the most elementary application of drawing in and receiving energy, which We call the Ambient Art of Gathering Energy. The reason We are exploring the Ambient Art of Gathering Energy at the Dayside level is because it is the most basic and tangible method used by those who practice Vampyrism. The more advanced forms of the Art of Gathering Energy will be dealt with in the higher-level Mysteries, due to the complexity of their applications and the knowledge required by the practitioner. In brief, the Ambient Art of Gathering Energy makes use of the fact that large groups of people raidiate their excess Lifeforce into a vaporous cloud. The Vampyre can then gather this released Ambient energy and utilize it for the purposes of sating their spiritual hunger for life and increasing their Zhep'r.

All living things contain and radiate Lifeforce, best known to the Strigoi Vii by the Sanskrit name Lifeforce. There are many other names for this vital life energy, from *Ka* in Khem (Ancient Egypt), *Ki* in Japanese martial arts, and *Chi* in traditional Chinese medicine. Essentially, reality is comprised of a wide spectrum of types and frequencies of energies, from physical matter and energy in the Corporeal realm to the dream energies of the Astral realm. Lifeforce exists on the Ethereal plane and makes up of auras, chakras, and meridians and is the essential "energy of life." Ambient Lifeforce is "sweated" out or "radiated" by the subtle body of all living beings and thus may be absorbed or harvested by the Strigoi Vii.

As mentioned in "The Strigoi Vii Prospectus," Strigoi Vii gravitate toward professions in which they are the center of focus. It is not uncommon to find us working as performers, actors, politicians, tour guides, musicians, professors, or religious leaders! In such professions, the Strigoi Vii is the center of energy and attention, so they can forge subtle energetic links and gather the collective energy of the crowd without ever revealing their true identity. Ambient Gathering Lifeforce also allows the fledgling Vampyre to avoid drawing too deeply from one individual, by spreading their focus and attention across many people, harvesting a bit of Lifeforce from each.

Be aware that every living being naturally draws energy on this level. For example, the audience at an exciting blockbuster movie will leave the theater happy and animated. This is because each of them has unconsciously absorbed a little bit of the communal energy radiated by the other members of the audience. However, the Living Vampyre absorbs energy far more subtly and gracefully, with a focused conscious intent. Learning how to be aware of and control this process lays the foundation for all our other Arts of Gathering.

In order to gather Ambient energies, try to begin to sense energy. This can be simply done by breathing deeply and paying attention to your environment. It is not at all uncommon for Strigoi Vii to find themselves naturally sensitive to the quality of energy around them. Start by consciously opening your awareness to the subtle layers of the Corporeal world and try to intuit the collective mentality of people around you. Feel the "vibes," and allow the energy in the atmosphere to coalesce about you. At this point, straighten your spine, tighten your stomach, and meditate on your solar plexus; breathe in deeply, feeling the vaporlike energy flow into you. Visualization is a powerful tool that can help you in this process. As you breathe in, visualize the energy as shining, silver white, vaporous strands flowing into your solar plexus. You can also sit on the side of a crowd and, by deeply breathing in, slowly call forth the energy. You are essentially making yourself the focus for the energy in the vicinity, just as a magnet will attract nearby iron filings. Sit back and feel the energy penetrating your skin and flowing throughout your body.

Test this form of the Gathering Energy whenever there is a large gathering of mundanes in a specific mindset or focused on a specific intent. Recommended places for practicing Ambient Gathering include museums, shopping malls, sports events, concerts, public transportation, churches, nightclubs, busy streets, schools, or parks. Famous locales such as Times Square in New York or Piccadilly Circus in London are excellent places to experience massive amounts of Ambient energy. Innumerable mortal-minded tourists flock to these places, all energetically excited and exhilarated by the experience.

If you are lucky enough to have a profession or talent that brings you into contact with large numbers of mundanes, seize the opportunity! Be you a salesperson, bartender, customer service representative, or teacher, you are already interacting unconsciously with Ambient energy. During your next workday, try consciously gathering into the energy that constantly surrounds you.

When practicing Ambient Gathering, we recommend you meditate before beginning so to center your own energies. Also, it is usually helpful to dress in mundane garb. Be aware you may be doing this naturally already and not even know it. The difference between unconscious and conscious gathering is intent. Once you are Awakened to your True intent, bask in the energy!

Many of those new to Strigoi Vii, or coming from other Traditions to explore our techniques, may say to themselves, "I hate crowds! I can't do that!" Many of us are very solitary, so this is a common response. However, be aware that Ambient Gathering does not involve actually interacting with these crowds. Simply stand unnoticed within or near them and let the energy flow into and nourish you.

While this may seem obvious, always remember that the Strigoi Vii needs to consume both Corporeal and Lifeforce energy. In other words, Vampyric Gathering is not a substitute for physical eating! It is only in folklore that vampires are able to survive without eating. Since all levels of the body are connected, the Vampyric urge may sometimes manifest as physical hunger. Similarly, Ambient gathering may forestall physical hunger for a short time. However, it is necessary that you keep your body healthy on all its levels.

As the Strigoi Vii learns to transmute this harvested energy, they will be able to change the very shape of reality around them, as detailed in the Higher Mysteries of Strigoi Vii. However, the main purpose in obtaining Lifeforce is to fuel Zhep'r by exchanging it with the Strigoi Morte in Communion for Ambrosia (more highly refined energy). This concept and its application will be explained in "Liber Calmae: Coming Forth by Night."

Filtering and Shielding: These are protective and cleansing techniques that are of great use to the Strigoi Vii when employing the Art Gathering Energy. Most energy has levels of quality, or "flavors," from negative to favorable. In reality, Lifeforce is simply the pure fuel of life. There is no need to actually filter or shield from it, as it permeates all things and is transferred with every interaction. There is no such thing as negative energy—this would simply be an absence of energy. There is, however, "negatively charged" energy. Emotions from the Astral level of reality can become attached to Ethereal energy. It is these that must be filtered and blocked. For example, consider two people having a violent argument. They will release a great deal of energy into the atmosphere, but that energy will be "colored" by their anger and frustration. Any Strigoi Vii attempting to gather that energy will most likely sense the negative emotions of the people who have released it. However, be aware that you need only block the negative Astral attachments—the energy in itself is still energy. It may "taste bad," but it will still fulfill the same purpose as more "positively flavored" energy.

Blocking such Astral attachments can be very challenging for the Jahira. If you sense the quality of Ambient energy, you are gathering has a negative feel, simply break contact. Stop allowing the energy to enter into you.

This is the technique of "shielding," as you are shielding yourself from the unwanted energy. The flow of Lifeforce can be controlled through breathing techniques. These are quite similar to the techniques found in Lifeforceyama yoga. Simply stop breathing in the energy, hold your breath for a moment, and then push it out. This simple technique can be used to block these "negative energies." You may find it helpful to visualize a shield or protective bubble around yourself. When shielding, many Strigoi Vii like to visualize themselves behind a thick wall or surrounded by an iridescent "force field" that the energy cannot penetrate.

Filtering is a more advanced technique that will be discussed in full in higher-level teachings. It is much more effective than shielding, for while shielding involves simply blocking or stopping the gathering of energies, filtering involves choosing which energies are drawn to you and absorbed in your subtle body. As an analogy, you might think of passing water through a carbon filter in order to remove any dirt or impurities. Filtering is a technique beyond the abilities of most Jahira.

Many Jahira prefer to avoid the whole problem of "negative energy" altogether by gathering energy only in positive environments. It should not be hard to distinguish which locales will yield positively and negatively charged energy. As an illustration, the energy on a commuter train early Monday morning will be "colored" with the exhaustion, stress, and malaise of workers beginning a long workweek. Conversely, the energy of the crowd at a ball game where the home team has won a championship will be jubilant and celebratory. You should experiment to determine which environments yield the most favorable energy for you.

The Vampyres' Energy Ball:

This is a basic energy-work technique with which you should work to control energies. A visual reference that could serve as an example is a "raver" at a club, twirling glowsticks in their hands. In a darkened room, your eye will trace the moving glowsticks as spheres or waves of light around the dancer's body and hands. It may be helpful to visualize a similar image when performing this exercise.

Begin the exercise by simply cupping your hands into a ball. Envision all of your body's energies focused in your hands. Breathe slowly in and out to control the energy flow. Close your eyes and let the energy grow. Visualize this collected energy as a glowing mass within and around your hands. Move your hands to "shape" the energy ball. Experiment often to determine how you experience the energy collected between your hands. Many Strigoi Vii will feel a sensation of heat, pressure, or tingling in their palms. For group work, an energy ball can be passed around like a "hot potato," with each participant contributing their own energy. You should also perform this exercise after you have gathered Ambient energy and see how the absorbed Lifeforce affects your results.

It is not our intent to relist the variety of techniques available to the Living Vampyre that are enumerated elsewhere. There are already many excellent books on the subject, which can be found in the suggested reading section of the bibliography. Books on yoga and Reiki will also be extremely useful to the Strigoi Vii. This short chapter simply touches on the most elementary form of the Art of Gathering Energy. The next book, "Liber Calmae: Coming Forth by Night," will discuss intermediate applications of the Art of Gathering Energy.

Dayside Summation

The foundations of the Dayside are all but forgotten in too many esoteric systems. The path of Strigoi Vii realizes the necessity of a strong Corporeal foundation, as we have discussed here in "Liber Jahira." Your Corporeal body is the Temple of the Self. The Jahira must maintain a healthy and vibrant Corporeal Self and master the Dayside Principles before entering the magickal Nightside of the Strigoi Vii.

Remember that the True Strigoi Vii is sincere, focused, and dedicated. The Living Vampire loves life and the Self and follows their own path of personal evolution and Gnosis. Return often to the contents of this book and never cease practicing, testing, and experimenting with our Mysteries. You must develop your own mastery and understanding of your True Nature. This book is a key and a gate to your own evolution.

You have taken the first step toward Immortality of the Self.

"I celebrate myself and sing myself."

JAHIRA TESTIMONIAL

These are confidential and private questionnaires that are used within the OSV to evaluate the completion of an ordeal. This will only be seen by the Synod officers who will reply with notes and reflections will be sent back if one does not pass the evaluation. Please keep answers reasonably short and concise at most 300 words. If you do not understand something there is a lesson waiting to happen. These testimonials are based on the honor system and be truthful there is no rush for true Zhep'r. Submit these questionnaires with a freewill donation to synod@strigoivii.org.

1. Tell us why you are pursuing Jahira Ordeal: Coming forth by Day?
2. How have you manifested and applied the Cult of One Pillar?
3. How have you manifested and applied the Creativity Pillar?
4. How have you manifested and applied the Glamour Pillar and Dragons' Presence exercise?
5. How have you manifested and applied the Wellness Pillar?
6. How have you manifested and applied the Solvency Pillar?
7. How have you manifested and applied the Preservation Pillar?
8. How have you manifested and applied the Perpetuity / Immortality?
9. How have you manifested and applied the Ambient energy gathering?
10. Tell us of what pillar you are strongest in and weakest in?
11. What is your experience with the Dragons' Throne exercise?
12. What is your experience with the Dragons' Gaze exercise?
13. What is your experience with the Dragons' Presence exercise?
14. What is your experience with the Dragons' Will exercise?
15. What forms of meditation have you practiced, how often, and what are your results?
16. Any other comments or notes you would like to add.

BOOK II

LIBER CALMAE
"COMING FORTH BY NIGHT"

CHAPTER 19

THE CALMAE ORDEAL NIGHTSIDE INITIATION

I heard the sounds of sorrow and delight,
The manifold soft chimes,
That fill the haunted chambers of the Night
Like some old poet's rhymes.
From the cool cisterns of the midnight air
My spirit drank repose;
The fountain of perpetual peace flows there,
From those deep cisterns flows.

—Henry Wadsworth Longfellow, "Hymn to the Night"

Welcome to "Liber Calmae: Coming Forth by Night." In "Liber Elorath," we explored the elementary concepts of the Strigoi Vii tradition and Vampyre Current. Within "Coming Forth by Day," we explored the foundations of the Dayside and the functional principles of the Seven Dayside Pillars and Ambient Energy Gathering. In this book, we move into the Nightside, the supernatural and magickal world of the Living Vampyre. As before, you should enter into these Mysteries freely and of your own will, with an open mind free of stereotypes and blind belief. Continue to cast aside your residual mortal-minded perceptions in order to be able to truly understand and experience the full results of these Mysteries.

Breaking Free of Belief

We know the majority of the average mundane world is locked into a confining and limiting system of belief. A useful film analogy is that of the humans still willingly "plugged into" the Matrix. Recall that one of the villains of the first movie in the trilogy decided to return to the false virtual world instead of dealing with true reality. Many of the mortal-minded are virtually inexperienced and un-Awakened to the universe beyond what they experience through their five senses. According to Gnostic scripture, mortals accept only what they choose to see and are easily herded into a slave mentality. In contemporary society, this brainwashed and slave-like mentality is created by factors such as consumerism, oligarchies, drugs, and many organized religions. Being awakened to Zhep'r is to metaphorically open your "Vampyre Eyes," to see beyond these barriers and continue the Great Work of the Self on an independent and enlightened individual and collective level.

Yet, amongst the masses there are those who are different; they are the Awakened. The Strigoi Vii must carry the Promethean spark, or the "Dark Flame," within their Self. An important aspect of this Dark Flame is the potential to embrace the Immortal-minded perspective. Fully awakened Strigoi Vii and our spiritual cousins are within this Awakened minority. Such individuals strive for and require independent, critical thought and question the nature of the reality in which they live. These Awakened individuals have the potential for personal evolution and spiritual transformation. Throughout history, genuine mystics, yogis, prophets, saints, and others who touched spiritual and philosophical evolution showed similar potential. They were able to experience the subtle worlds beyond the Corporeal realm of the five senses. However, there are many other fraudulent individuals who claim supernatural powers and are only con artists and charlatans.

We encourage you to explore all possibilities for evolution, including systems beyond the Strigoi Vii Mysteries. Never limit yourself! Be wise enough to sift through the masses of available information. Do not lose focus. If you are a Vampyre in the Strigoi Vii perspective, you will always eventually come home to the OSV and know that you are Family. We Strigoi Vii recognize each other. our Radiance is unique. It is our energy signature, which makes each of us a part of our Promethean Blood, known as the Vampyre Current.

Obviously, if you are reading this far into the Strigoi Vii Codex, you are either extremely curious about Strigoi Vii or drawn to pur Current. You are most likely one of those individuals who are aware of the differences between themselves, mundanes, and others. Perhaps you have sensed this difference from an early age, feeling disconnected from or misunderstood by those around you. Alternately, you may be recently Awakened to your Nature. Strigoi Vii are unique, unconventional, and often very solitary. Through the word Calmae, the initiate should develop and refine their individual potential with confidence and tenacity.

Rejecting mundane belief systems and shifting from the mortal-minded to the Immortal perspective are the key challenges of those seeking to Come forth by Night.

Throughout history, the mundane world has always feared what it does not understand. This is where our Nightside truly begins. Due to the Glamour, many of our number may have been mistaken for nocturnal beasts and magickal beings of ages past, such as the werewolf, vampire, nephilim, or changeling. Born between two worlds, we have the potential to Ascend beyond the restraints of Corporeal perceptions.

The mundane often greet this difference with fear and misunderstanding. We have come to understand and utilize their fear on a more subtle level, forging a balance and equilibrium that benefits both ourselves and the mortal-minded. Humanity evolved to benefit from the symbiotic relationship with our Ancestors, and many vampire myths reflect this relationship. We have incorporated mortal-minded fear into our Glamour, and in recent centuries this fear has turned into a seductive, multidimensional construct that has sincerely aided our Glamour. Just compare the horrendous revenants of Eastern European folklore to the glamour of Anne Rice's vampires! Our Ancestors have evolved, and the Promethean Vampyre Current have set ablaze an indefinable yet unmistakable mark of creation, innovation, and discovery.

Be aware that many with the potential for Zhep'r, due to a failure of will, voluntarily remain in the bonds of oppression that have held the masses in a mental prison for so long. Religion, faith and belief, mind-numbing drugs, chemical and artificial additives, and multimedia "entertainment" are just a few examples of the conditioning that must be broken in order to experience Zhep'r. Most mortal-minded individuals resort to such props in order to numb their senses and forget the inevitable cycle of death that is their fate. The aspiring Calmae should fully embrace the opportunity of their own Immortality and reject mortal denial. You cannot let yourself be lulled into or continue to be bound by complacency. Break free and enjoy the pleasures of Zhep'r!

Science or Myth? Black or White Magick?

Throughout the ages, mortals have responded to the unknown with fear. It is often said that yesterday's magic becomes tomorrow's science. When Galileo first spoke of the Earth revolving around the sun, he was forced to renounce his claims, as they were considered blasphemy! Many of those burned as witches and sorcerers during the Middle Ages in Europe were in reality scientists, visionaries, skilled healers, and midwives. Various classic works of literature, such as James Joyce's Ulysses and J. D. Salinger's Catcher in the Rye, were banned upon their initial publication for being too "shocking" or "inappropriate." When looking deeply at great manifestations in art, architecture, philosophy, science, music, or performance, you directly witness the inspirations of the Awakened tribes and the spark of Prometheus.

We of the Family do not limit Ourselves to the perceptions of "black" and "white" magic or good and evil. Many mortals may choose to categorize us as "black magicians." Yet, in his own time, Galileo was considered a sorcerer! Recall the legend of Faust. Many of the un-Awakened simply cannot accept that brilliance or great wisdom can be achieved without blasphemy or "deals with the devil." We, as Strigoi Vii, inherently know better! We refuse to let changeable mundane standards limit Us. To further genuine Zhep'r in your mind and heart, come to accept your true freedom from the slave bonds of the mundane world and experience Awakening—you hold the potential in your Blood!

As Strigoi Vii, be aware of the grain of truth in every metaphor. Such vigilance is especially necessary when exploring the Nightside. We are not just creatures of darkness. The vampire who must skulk in the shadows and cannot survive in the sunlight is a creation of Hollywood and nothing more. Many of Us simply enjoy the quiet of the night so that we may avoid the endless hum of mundane world. We might choose to live like the nocturnal predators we revere and embrace the night due to our connection with the unknown. Some of us also find Communion more efficient at night. However, we are not pandering to the contemporary occult and gothic mentality that associates the night with all things forbidding and "spooky." Many of us are also equally drawn to the light of day.

Why, then, bother with the distinction of the "Nightside"? Darkness is a powerful symbol. Since the beginning of time, humankind's collective unconscious has identified the night as representing that which is hidden and mysterious. The un-Awakened cannot pierce the Corporeal or symbolic darkness, so they populate it with monsters and demons, exclaiming, "Here there be dragons!" To Plato, the sun was the light of reason that dispelled the shadows of ignorance and delusion. Even psychologist Carl Jung viewed the "shadow" as the aspect of the human psyche that is secret, repressed, and verboten.

For the Strigoi Vii, darkness and the night are powerful psychological tools. However, the Strigoi Vii Master is truly free of all limiting associations and knows, indeed, that the light is no less powerful than the dark. Nevertheless, the evolving Vampyre may find they are more easily able to let go of mortal constraints under the midnight sky. We never scorn to use the tools at our disposal! Although part of building Zhep'r is seeing through the Veil of illusion, another essential part is recognizing the power of symbols and archetypes.

The Nightside, simply, symbolizes all in our nature that is hidden from the light of un-Awakened eyes. To explore your Nightside is to take the first steps on a journey of exploration of your own soul. The true Calmae must be able to stare unflinchingly into the depths of the black mirror and embrace what they see there.

Furthering Zhep'r

Igniting Zhep'r comes when you sincerely endeavor to pursue your own path. However, keep the following in mind: the True Strigoi Vii wisely never proselytizes, argues, or tries to convert others to our Mysteries. An individualistic and solitary nature is a major characteristic of the Blood, and We must always allow nature to take its course. Those Strigoi Vii just beginning their journey should learn to take the initiative and manage their own distractions. Thus is the never-ending experience of Zhep'r individually and independently enhanced and furthered.

The Order is not like any organization, political party, church, temple, or occult lodge you have yet encountered. The Strigoi Vii Family cannot be "joined" in the mundane sense. You cannot "purchase" the true understanding of Initiation. It is a process that begins with a shift from the mortal-minded perspective of the sleeper to the Immortal-minded perspective of the awakened to the Self. It is a profound autonomous journey of Selfhood.

The Strigoi Vii lives by the laws and hierarchy set forth by nature, in which the strongest and most fit shall survive and thrive. Yet We of the Family are not in competition with each other or with the mortal-minded. We are in competition with the individual We each see when we gaze into the mirror: our True Self. While the path of Strigoi Vii is a path for the individual, be aware that your Sorors and Fraters of the Family are your teachers, students, and fellows.

Be loyal to the Quest of Family, uphold the Strigoi Vii Principles and you will always be loyal to the Family and the Self! In the end, you are your only judge. Only you must judge and live with the consequences of your actions. Raising Zhep'r can be achieved once you have realized the principles of the Mystery of night and established mastery of your Dayside. You are now ready to make the next step of pursuing your Nightside Zhep'r!

The core of raising one's Zhep'r in the Nightside is Communion with Vampyre Current, in which you give an Offering of Lifeforce to the Strigoi Morte, and they return a gift of the highly refined energy we call Ambrosia, which advances your personal Zhep'r. Coming to realization of this is a significant challenge, as the Strigoi Morte only grant Zhep'r to those They deem worthy of Their gift.

Spending time in Sanctums and Quabal, where you are free to be exclusively in the company of members of the Family, is a valuable opportunity if you are able and choose to embrace it. This environment, whether it be a small or large gathering, provides more than just an opportunity for socialization. It is a forum for teaching and advisement and is a powerful way of furthering your own Zhep'r. What better way is there to reinforce and be exposed to new ideas than teaching and aiding others in Zhep'r? Of course, do not violate the Strigoi Vii Principles by speaking of the core Mysteries to those individuals who have not had the opportunity to read the appropriate section of the Strigoi Vii Codex and reflect on its contents. If you can inspire them to further their experiences or direct them to validation, you both will benefit. Most of all, encourage others to ask questions. This will be more beneficial than forcing the information on them. Of course, advising others beyond your means and level of experience is not wise. The Calmae, while honing their own skills as inspirators within the family, should not attempt to advise Strigoi Vii beyond the word Jahira.

How to avoid a cult mentality

Many mortal cults and religions discourage spending time with your mortal family if they are not in agreement with your path. More than once, we have heard the grumblings of Satanists, Wiccans, pagans, or occultists who say members of their family "do not approve of their path" or try to convert or "save" them. We find humor in the fact that those of fundamentalist religions and cults are jailed by their own faith and beliefs. Those strong in their faith should be appreciated for their offerings to the Ancestors! If your mortal family cannot accept your nature as Strigoi Vii, wisdom dictates you are better to "agree to disagree" with them and still appreciate them for the benefits they may bring to your life. You may choose to simply listen to them and enjoy their ramblings while you gather their energies to fulfill your thirst for Lifeforce! If the negativity of those with whom you are speaking becomes overwhelming, simply disengage, or walk away. If you are in a situation where you must cohabit with a hostile mortal-minded or psychic vampire who is family member, practice discretion and recognize their limited perspective. Being a discreet individual, you have no need to be flashy about your nature. Secrecy is a far more powerful tool.

Enjoy your time with mortals, and love your family. Live and let live! Do not be emotionally injured by their personal choices. A bond with birth family can be extremely fulfilling and can indeed help further your Zhep'r. Do not neglect your mortal family over petty differences of opinion. You never need justify to those not of the Blood your personal spiritual views nor reveal your True Nature as Strigoi Vii. The legally protected freedom of religion in many countries allows you to maintain your own spiritual perspective. Even should you not live in a country where this freedom is your legal right, it is always and forever your personal right. Employ and embrace this freedom and remind others of your rights when they try to confront you in disagreement.

There are many inhibitions to Zhep'r. One of the most significant is dying before you reach the level of evolution to defeat the Second Death. Violating the common sense of the Strigoi Vii Principles is an obvious way to inhibit and limit your Zhep'r evolution. Feeding into the melodrama and politics of psychic vampires is another roadblock. Prospectii and Jahira commonly fall into this trap. At the Calmae word, it is important to learn to practice discrimination and maturity and form strong associations with those persons who will further your Zhep'r.

Relying on belief and faith before personally experiencing results is a common error of the mundane! Test and validate everything in the Mysteries for yourself. You are the only one who can judge the validity of your path and your results on it. Experiment and personally deter- mine what is true on your own. This is a solitary Quest which, once begun, is as important as eating or drinking. The Path of the Mysteries is not a system of threat and punishment. The only "punishment" for feeding into distractions will be less attention and Recoiling from the Strigoi Morte in Communion. The more you deviate from the path of Zhep'r, the more likely you are to be deprived of the opportunity for Vampyric Immortality. This is where focus and inward sincerity are best applied.

The Nightside Initiation (Calmae Initiation Rite)

This is an Initiation into the Nightside of the Strigoi Vii Mysteries. For some Strigoi Vii, this is the most challenging Initiation of all and requires dedication, patience, and willpower. Of course, the Calmae Initiation is only for those who have made the Jahira Ascension and have read "Coming Forth by Day" as well as "Coming Forth by Night." The following steps are the traditional method of formal understanding from Jahira to Calmae within the Strigoi Vii Mysteries.

First: Practice the Surjaah.

This is a personal ritual for Calmae Seekers and Initiates. It should be performed every morning in order to prepare oneself for the day's achievements of Zhep'r. It involves several phases, which include a mix of yoga, meditation, grounding, physical exercise, and mental planning for long-term and short-term Dayside goals. The Surjaah should take about twenty to forty minutes per day and is divided into three separate parts as detailed below. It is recommended that the aspiring Calmae adopt the Surjaah as a regular part of their daily morning routine.

First, you should, upon awakening from sleep, sit quietly in a comfortable position and meditate. If possible, the lotus position may be assumed. You should spend five to ten minutes meditating and grounding yourself. Adopt a slow, steady breath during this step and focus on pushing all negative thoughts away with the exhalation of the breath. Focus on and think about personal Dayside goals. If you are skilled in yoga, specific poses may be utilized during this step to help facilitate concentration.

After the first step is completed, you should initiate a program of positive physical exercise. Any standard workout routine will suffice; however, we suggest trying aerobics, Pilates, dance, various martial arts, or some such system that does not unduly strain the physical body yet helps build strength and endurance. There are many excellent workout videos and books available for inspiration.

Third, and finally, you should rest in a comfortable position (per- haps the lotus position) and concentrate on your goals for the day. Focus on how you may apply the Dayside Pillars and work toward furthering Zhep'r through them. You should then concentrate on long- term goals and plan how you shall apply your will toward Dayside mastery. You should then spend a few minutes meditating on your Nightside goals and allow the energy of Lifeforce and the Current to flow freely through you.

This simple exercise should be done every day. It is of prime importance in the evolution of Zhep'r and will help establish a short-and long-term set of objectives and goals. You should feel free to customize it according to your own needs and tastes. When going to rest for the evening, meditate on the Surjaah for the next day, so that one day leads to the next with the bridge of the night in between.

Two: Obtain the Tools of the Calmae.

At this level of Ascension, tools are powerful elements of psychodrama. However, be clear in regard to what is solid fantasy and tangible reality, as these regalia are only useful tools and not essential requirements. Thus, if you wish and are able, procure a quality black robe, attractive mask, personal grimoire, ar'thana (black-hilted ritual blade), chalice, wand, and speculum (black mirror that acts as a portal to the subtle world). Many of these items can be obtained at occult or new-age shops. Internet websites, including online auction sites, are also useful sources. Collecting these tools is a meaningful and personal process. Of course, if you possess the skills, personally crafting, blooding some or all of these items means they will be more attuned to you. It is a ritual unto itself and mentally prepares you for the next step in evolution.

Practice Gathering Energy in Ambient and Surface levels. Take an afternoon or evening to fill yourselves with Lifeforce. Setting aside a time for nothing else but gathering energy is a powerful personal ritual. Do this alone if you can, as the presence of another Vampyre can be distracting. Going alone allows you to completely focus on your intent and experiences. The Art of Gathering Energy should be performed consciously every day, or as often as possible. When you feel you have personally verified and experienced the flow of Lifeforce and learned to draw energy to your own satisfaction, you may attempt the Communion with first the Strigoi Morte, then the Current directly.

Three: Perform the Sanguine Mass.

This is the essential aspect of the Calmae Ascension, which should be completed alone many times. Results must be achieved before even considering entering group ritual. Communion is the most sacred of all Strigoi Vii acts. Be warned that only truly experienced individuals should enter group

Communion; the inexperienced individual will taint the experience for all present or simply become a source of energy for another's Offering. The Sanguine Mass (provided later in this text) is a formulated ritual containing a set of tools, steps, and systems that are proven to yield results for many Strigoi Vii.

Many Strigoi Vii agree it is best to memorize the standard rituals as presented later in this book. However, as ritual is a highly personal experience, feel free to modify them and experiment with different formulations. Not everyone is expert with the same exact formulae or elements of ritual. Most of Us do not participate in group ritual, so being flexible within your own ritual format is a powerful solitary tool.

Do not get discouraged if you do not achieve immediate success in Communion ritual. The Ancestors will judge you on your potential and the sincerity, quality, and quantity of your Offering. Some Initiates have had to perform Communion at least a dozen times before achieving a successful Recoiling, whilst others received it the first time. Some even received Recoiling subtly over a period of time after the actual ritual. Every experience is different, and you should not judge your own ritual results by those of others. Also, do not be overzealous and delude us that you have obtained ritual results if you have not! Communion is a deeply sacred and hallowed aspect of our Mysteries that requires time and dedication to master.

You are only truly Calmae and have "Come forth by Night" if you have successfully received a True Recoiling. Be patient, sincere, and dedicated to your goal. Do not give up after the first few unsuccessful attempts, as often the results are cumulative and contribute to a successful Communion Day, weeks, or even months afterward. True Strigoi Vii know this reality!

Fourth: Perform the Oath of Calmae (Nightside Oath).

This is very important as a personal tool and marker of Ascension. It is a sincere communication and testimonial to the Ancestors that the Seeker is beyond the stage of testing and is exploring the Dayside and Nightside Mysteries. This Oath should be spoken in ritual during Communion, after an Offering of Lifeforce has been made to the Strigoi Morte. As in the Jahira exercise of "Vampyres' Throne," the Initiate should look directly into their own eyes through a mirror, preferably set at eye level. Of course, if desired, active members of the Family can request an Priest/ess or Magister or other Strigoi Vii be present within a formal Quabal to observe their Oath of Calmae. Sharing this experience before the Sorors and Fraters whom you honor and respect can be an empowering and rewarding experience. As with the Oath of Jahira, you may submit a written testimonial of your Oath of Calmae to the Synod if you wish it to be formally recognized by the Family and the OSV.

The Nightside Oath

Ancestors, hear me now!

I, The Vampyre [Sobriquet], come into this Sanctum of my own free will, to stand before my Sorors and Fraters, in love and loyalty, with the full intent of reaffirming my Jahira Oath and entering into the Nightside of the Strigoi Vii.

This Ascension is my testimonial to the reality of the Nightside and the existence of the Ethereal realm of reality.

I have been touched by the Current in sacred Communion, and in my heart know I stand here proudly amongst Family!

I vow to become a shield in defense of the Family.

I vow to be a sword to protect from the enemies of our Family.

I vow to be a pillar of strength, passing on the Mysteries of Strigoi Vii to those who hear the Calling of our Quest.

Does anyone oppose my Ascension? Speak here and now!

Thus, I now declare myself Calmae [Nightside name] of the StrigoiVii.

CHAPTER 20

BEYOND THE MIRROR

How do you know but ev'ry Bird that cuts the airy way, Is an immense world of delight, clos'd by your senses five?

—William Blake,
"The Marriage of Heaven and Hell"

For the vast majority of mortal-minded humans, the only world they have truly experienced is the physical world of what they can see, touch, hear, taste, and smell. They call this "reality." We call this Corporeal layer of reality Maiiah, adapted from the Hindu term maya, or "illusion." This physical or "solid" world is merely an illusion covering multiple subtle layers of reality. These layers are often called realms or planes in various esoteric systems. The Living Vampyre and other Awakened beings see beyond the Maiiah and seek a more diverse personal and spiritual worldview. Those of Family have the potential to Awaken lucidly within the dreamworld and thus experience and interact with subtler layers, realms, and planes of existence such as the Ethereal and Astral realms. These more subtle layers of reality intersect and coexist with the physical world and are akin to the different dimensions of perception. Consider the familiar fable of the blind men attempting to describe an elephant. Each man perceived but one aspect of the elephant, and each one had a different theory about the elephant's nature. The man who seized the trunk was certain the elephant was like a snake. The man who touched the tusk thought the elephant must be like a spear. The one who felt the side was convinced the elephant was like a massive wall. None were correct, yet none were wholly wrong. All the dimensions of their perceptions were required to form a picture of the truth. This ability to see the larger picture of reality is known as the Awakening.

We Strigoi Vii and our Awakened cousins have the potential to see beyond the limitations of the Maiiah from a unique perspective. Many mortal-minded psychics, witches, and magicians obtain results in their occult endeavors yet miss the grander equilibrium of Twilight and thus become ungrounded and lost in the Nightside. Most remain truly un-Awakened to their limitless potential, as they are only able to solve half of the equation of reality. Even if they can detect layers of reality beyond the Maiiah, many remain bound by restricting belief and faith. They do not take the necessary steps or possess the vision to obtain Ascension to True Immortality of the Self. Many will make excuses for going to their deaths without a solid guarantee of Immortality or rebirth.

The mortal-minded thus fall into the trap of faith and belief. They provide a variety of pretexts for their willingness to die, claiming their souls will ascend to a dubious afterlife or that Immortality is "unnatural" according to the boundaries of mortal-minded ethics. Like the prisoners in Plato's cave, these individuals choose to be blinded to the broader perspectives of reality. They accept what is presented to them by "gurus" and spiritual leaders as pure fact, without any solid proof or evidence. Thus, the vast majority of the mortal-minded are seduced by beliefs and religions that lull the masses into complacency. The Strigoi Vii must strive to be different. See the world as your science lab, experiment with everything, and come into agreement for yourself! Validation may take time, but patience is truly an Immortal virtue.

Having a genuine love for life, members of the Family are willing to strive for Zhep'r, fully embrace the complete nature of reality, and take the necessary steps to solidify their own Immortality. This is the most difficult challenge of Zhep'r. We deeply resent the Second Death and consider it our only true enemy. Those who deny their own evolution, from a lack of spiritual confidence, pure weakness, or a simple love of self-destruction, face what We call the death of the Self, or the Second Death. Only the truly Awakened amongst us who embrace their heritage will experience Immortality of the Self.

Evolving and continuing to build Zhep'r is the true agenda of all Strigoi Vii. As our personal Zhep'r grows, We experience the associated evolution of our perceptions, thus laying the foundation for our transformation from the mortal-minded perspective to that of the Immortal. Few have potential for genuine and complete Zhep'r, as only those willing to discipline and apply themselves will be able to achieve Communion with the Strigoi Morte and the Vampyre Current.

Mortal scientists and artists may catch glimpses of the deeper nature of the ultimate reality at this stage in mortal spiritual and scientific evolution. Yet many such perspectives have been known to those of the Family and other Awakened beings throughout the ages. The rise of modern physics, such as relativity and quantum and chaos theory, as well as the contemporary popularity of science fiction, only confirms what we already know. Consider the scientific notion that there are several dimensions to our universe. For example, physicist Albert Einstein spoke of "multidimensional space," which must be defined by more mathematical variables than those of the three-dimensional space that our senses normally perceive. Some physicists currently believe that the fully descriptive structure of the universe may contain more than twenty dimensions! This is an example of mundane science becoming increasingly aware of the subtle levels of reality. Einstein published his theory of spatial relativity in the early twentieth century. H. G. Wells, widely considered the first science fiction writer, published many of his famous tales in the late nineteenth and early twentieth centuries. As humanity evolves, We evolve as well, and the ultimate realities become validated in the Dayside. As the Promethean Awakenings filter through the collective human consciousness, we benefit. The mortal-minded may believe they discover new truths, but they are only beginning to discover what many of us already understand.

The multiple layers of reality are not alien to Us. They are all an intrinsic part of the world that We inhabit. These layers constantly interact with each other. All living beings exist simultaneously on these different levels.

You have already, perhaps unknowingly, experienced these different levels. For example, with every thought, emotion, or memory, you are interacting with the Astral realm. When you breathe or work with Chi or Ki (as energy is called in martial arts), you are carrying with you the Lifeforce of the Ethereal realm. At the time of this writing, mortal sciences have explored the Corporeal but only touched on the Ethereal and Astral layers of reality. The layer of most interest to the prospective Calmae, as explored in this book, is the Ethereal Nightside.

Strigoi Vii define the basic geography of reality as consisting of five layers, which are most often called realms or planes. Each has its own characteristics, density, and frequencies of energy. As we know, the scientific law of conservation of energy states that energy is never destroyed, only transformed. Energy comes in many forms, such as heat energy, atomic energy, and potential energy. It may also function at different intensities and frequencies. The Corporeal world is made up of specific frequencies of energy and is denser and less flexible than the higher realms. According to the Outer Mysteries, what might be possible in one layer of reality may not be possible in another. For example, shapeshifting is generally impossible in the physical world; however, it is completely possible to shape and transform Ethereal matter through the application of energetic will.

The Hindus believe that the veil of the maya must be penetrated in order to achieve *moksha*, or liberation from the cycle of death and rebirth, which is our ultimate goal in defeating the Second Death. Ego-consciousness, or *ahamkar*, is one of the forces that binds the un- enlightened to the maya. In Strigoi Vii terms, ahamkar could be seen as another expression of the externally gratified ego that is fixated on a mortal mindset.

Be aware that a complete description of these layers is extremely difficult to understand without firsthand experience. Hinduism, Buddhism, and other religions and philosophical systems have concepts similar to the Maiiah and present a well-considered depiction of the geography of reality. However, most religions and spiritual paths involve prescriptions for enlightenment that involve Corporeal deprivation and varying levels of asceticism, including the proposed elimination of the individual Self. We understand that existence is far more complex. All of reality is a dream or illusion, beginning with the Maiiah. The Awakened members of our Family have the ability to be "lucid dreamers" within that illusion. However, the un-Awakened essentially live their lives as sleepwalkers. They allow themselves to be deluded and enslaved by illusions and can never Ascend to the great heights of understanding and enlightenment.

The Strigoi Vii does not see the Maiiah as something to be overcome, but rather as the first piece of the puzzle of reality that must be assembled in order to achieve Zhep'r. The Maiiah is the surface reality and our first level of perception. The Strigoi Vii can shift their perceptions and thus have the potential to become aware of all the planes of existence. With such awareness comes a mastery of reality and a realization of the mortal constraints of perception. Thus does the Vampyre achieve the necessary freedom to move from one of the mortal-minded to an Immortal.

The layers of the reality and the Self, as defined within the Strigoi Vii Mysteries, are as follows.

The Corporeal, or the Maiiah, is the realm of the Dayside, physical matter, and the tangible reality experienced through the five senses. This is the world of the mortal-minded, where energy and matter are bound by the known laws of physics. For example, in the Corporeal realm it is impossible to transform or shapeshift into a bat. The Jahira Initiate focuses on this realm, as it is the most easily and commonly experienced. The Corporeal body is the physical body containing flesh, organs, and blood. The physical death is the First Death, and when the physical body dies, the other layers of the Self begin to break down.

The Anatomy of the Subtle Body

The Ethereal is the beginning of the Nightside, the mirror reflection of the physical world. It is the first layer beyond the mirror and is the focus of the word Calmae. It is also the subtle framework on which the Corporeal realm is based. Known as Chi, Ki, or Lifeforce, Ethereal energy is the level of pure Lifeforce. Personal Ethereal energy is analogous to the Ka of Egyptian mythology, which was understood to be the Lifeforce of a human being. In the ancient Egyptian Book of the Dead and other iconography, the Ka was often depicted as a ghostly double of the deceased person. Through advanced techniques, the Ethereal body can be manipulated and is the vessel for shapeshifting. One element of Ethereal energy is our "Blood," which is of use for the Art of Gathering Energy and in making Offerings to the Strigoi Morte. The death of the Ethereal body is the Second Death and may follow days or weeks after the death of the Corporeal body. Upon the Second Death, the Ethereal body shatters into countless fragments and is released into the universe and the cycles of creation, to be transformed and recycled in accordance with the principle of conservation of energy. This is one of the reasons why the spiritual philosophy of Khem hinged on the process of mummification, which preserves the Corporeal body.

The Astral is the realm of the Twilight, which is the concrete consciousness, encompassing dreams, emotions, thoughts, and imagination. It is this realm on which the Morrah focuses. The Astral body, closely related to the Ancient Egyptian concept of the Ba, is far less dense than the Corporeal and even the Ethereal body and is not bound by space and time. Therefore, the Astral body is the perfect vehicle for out-of-body experiences, telepathy, and what are considered by mortals to be "psychic powers." The Astral body is perhaps closest to the Egyptian concept of the soul, or the essential Cartesian Self. The death of the Astral body comes with the Second Death.

An understanding of these layers of reality is the basis for exploring the Nightside and is required for furthering Zhep'r. Collectively, the subtle reality begins with the Ethereal layer and ends with the Spirit layer (not detailed here and explained in Higher Mysteries) and is, at first, best perceived with a dark mirror, as will be discussed in later chapters of this text.

Between the physical world and the subtle layers of reality exists a frontier, which is a Shroud Between Worlds (SBW). To the un-Awakened with magickal potential and those Vampyres with limited Zhep'r, this is as strong as any physical hurdle and is most effectively traversed through meditation, altered states of consciousness, and ritual in sacred spaces or at certain times of the year. This limitation is only a perception conditioned in our minds due to the programming of the mundane world and can be overcome. Eventually, through the growth of Zhep'r, the Strigoi Vii will be able to achieve magickal results with a simple thought. It takes time and practice, but do not be deterred by this fact. Any destination is reached by a journey of many steps.

The foundation of Zhep'r is the gathering of radiated Lifeforce from the Ethereal bodies of humans, which is then offered to the Strigoi Morte in exchange for higher energies. This simple circuit of Communion is the key to the evolution of the subtle body for the Strigoi Morte. The Lifeforce of the Earth and lower animals and plants is generally not useful as an offering in Communion. Due to its low frequency and energy level, it is of little use to the Strigoi Morte. The Ethereal energy of the human subtle body is the only energy of use to Us, with the exception of Ambrosia from our Ancestors. If the Offering of Lifeforce is strong enough and the Strigoi Vii is deemed worthy, they will receive a direct gift of highly refined energy from the Strigoi Morte. This energy will function as "fuel" to aid the Strigoi Vii in reinforcing and preserving their memories, experiences, and personality after the First Death and to help them avoid succumbing to the Second Death. This is analogous to the union of the Ba and Ka in Egyptian mythology and results in a state known as the "Shining Ones," or the Akh.

We see evidence of some understanding of these layers of reality in almost every ancient culture's mystic tradition, including Sumerian, Babylonian, Chinese, Assyrian, and Egyptian. The Egyptians knew of these patterns, and their entire religious system was devised to avoid the Final Death by preserving the patterns found in the *Khat* (Corporeal body), *Ka* (Ethereal body), and the *Ba* (Astral body). Their temples were designed for Communion with the Ascended beings and the Egregores that were god-forms of the Ancient Egyptian pantheon. Some may say the process of the Art of Gathering Energy and Zhep'r is unnatural. The vast majority of the mortal-minded, who possess an externally focused ego, understand survival in terms of blind faith, religion, and belief. The Strigoi Vii has an inwardly empowered ego and places personal survival of the Self above all else. We focus on our own Zhep'r and our associated Immortality.

CHAPTER 21
ANATOMY OF THE SUBTLE BODY

[T]he radiant world [is] where one thought cuts through another with clean edge, a world of moving energies 'mezzo oscuro rade,''risplende in se perpetuale effecto,' magnetisms that take form, that are seen, or that border the visible, the matter of Dante's Paradiso, the glass under water, the form that seems a form seen in the mirror...

—Ezra Pound,
"Mediaevalism and Mediaevalism (Guido Cavalcanti)"

T he Ancient Greeks used the term Aither to refer to the upper reaches of the sky and the heavens, which they considered the pure air breathed by the gods. The word is derived from the Indo-European root word aith, meaning to burn or shine. Over time, the word was changed to Ether or Aether. In mediaeval alchemy, the Aether was the fifth element, or Quintessence, that was seen as being the key to the Philosopher's Stone. It was often associated with the topmost point in the pentagram. Victorian occultists, notably Madam Blavatsky, viewed the Ether as corresponding to

Akasha (the fifth element in Hindu metaphysics). Blavatsky saw Ether as being related to the Hindu concept of Lifeforce, or the Lifeforce of all living beings. In the nineteenth century, before electromagnetic and quantum theory were fully understood, scientists coined the term luminiferous ether to mistakenly describe a proposed substance filling empty space, through which they thought electromagnetic waves propagated.

The Calmae Mystery of Coming forth by Night focuses on working with the Ethereal plane, whilst the Morrah Mystery deals with the Twilight perspective and Astral plane. Confusing the Ethereal and Astral levels of reality is a common mistake of the neophyte StrigoiVii and occurs in multiple paradigms of occultism and Vampyrism. Such confusion is perpetuated by the fact that many esoteric sources conflate the two. This is why in "Coming Forth by Night," we focus our perspective on the Ethereal realm.

The Ethereal plane is the layer of reality which lies between the Astral and the Corporeal. It is the beginning of the subtle realms of reality. Energy is eternal but takes different forms in each layer of reality. The Ethereal realm is slightly less dense than the Corporeal. It cannot be perceived by the five senses; hence, the concepts of the "sixth sense" and seeing with the "Third Eye" refer to perception of this layer. If the Corporeal realm is that of solid energies (analogous to ice), the Ethereal realm is the place of liquid moving energies (analogous to water). Ethereal energy flows from and between all things, suffusing everything we know in the physical world with its eternal dance. The Ethereal is a realm of pure vital energy and Lifeforce on which the Strigoi Vii gathers and draws. Strigoi Vii commonly call this Ethereal energy Lifeforce. Living things, especially humans, are the prime generators of Pranic energy. Lifeforce is produced by the body's natural functions and can be manipulated by breath and will. Ethereal energy is influenced by the moon, which creates tides in the Earth's Ethereal atmosphere. In accordance with the Gaia hypothesis, the Earth is itself a living being and thus possesses an Ethereal field as well.

The Ethereal body is strongly influenced by breath. Indeed, the English word spirit is derived from the Latin spiritus, meaning "breath." The word *ruah* in Hebrew means "breath," "wind," "air," and "spirit" simultaneously. Many cultures have legends of vampires stealing not blood but breath from their victims. Echoes of these beliefs remain in the enduring legend that cats can kill infants by stealing their breath whilst they sleep. Lifeforce may be seen as corresponding to Corporeal blood; thus, the metaphor "the blood is the life" may be understood. While the Corporeal blood may be the living fluid of the physical body, Ethereal energy is truly the essential vitality of all living things.

The Ethereal body, or the double, is a mirror image of the Corporeal body that exists in the subtle realm. It has its own anatomy, which partially reflects the Corporeal body. Lifeforce is analogous to blood, meridians to the arteries and veins, and the chakras to vital organs. Each type of being has its own anatomy. Some types of beings do not even possess a Corporeal body, so their existence begins in the Ethereal realm. Some entities have only chakras, whilst others have different paths of meridians and flavors of Lifeforce. Strigoi Vii have subtle bodies very similar to those of humans, although different from each other. Of course, here we only focus on the subtle body of the "normal" human and the Strigoi Vii.

The subtle body is linked to the Corporeal in many ways, and due to this linkage, the subtle and the Corporeal body are causally joined. Breath and will are the most powerful tools of manipulating Lifeforce and the flow of energy in the subtle body. Wounds in the Corporeal body will affect the Ethereal body, and, conversely, Ethereal wounds may manifest physically. Some Ethereal ailments can also affect Corporeal health; likewise, physical diseases can also weaken the Ethereal body. The Corporeal body is the material anchor within the universe and provides shape and form for the subtle body. Without this anchor and a conscious application of will, the subtle body will lose shape. That is why many seemingly "ghostly" beings and effects, which are remnants of mortals who have not faced the Second Death, do not hold their shape easily and are flexible like an amoeba. Practices such as Reiki and traditional Chinese medicine (TCM) specifically focus on treating the Ethereal body through its relation to the Corporeal body. With the growth of Zhep'r, the subtle body of the Strigoi Vii also evolves and grows stronger, eventually achieving a state where it is strong enough to exist and survive on its own without the Corporeal body. At this point, the Strigoi Vii is prepared to conquer the Second Death. This is why the un-Awakened beings and neophyte Strigoi Vii will have an undeveloped Ethereal body, whilst the subtle bodies of advanced Strigoi Vii can be likened to what an un-Awakened individual would describe as an angelic being. Just as with the Corporeal Self, maintaining the health and strength of the Ethereal body requires exercise and persistence.

The Signature is the subtle equivalent of one's personal scent or fingerprints. Each person has their own unique Signature, whether they are Awakened to the subtle reality or not. This Signature leaves an imprint on all things the being touches and with which they interact. When a Strigoi Vii practices the Art of Gathering Energy from another being, the Signature can be sensed as a "flavor" or "taste."

Since each being has their own Signature, it can also be used to differentiate between types of energy, such as human Lifeforce or Strigoi Morte Lifeforce, or that of a dog or cat. After much experience in Communion, the Strigoi Vii can grow to identify Strigoi Morte from other subtle beings by identifying Their unique Signature. All beings are drawn by and attracted to different Signatures. For example, some people may be drawn to certain individuals and repulsed by others. Compatible Signatures result in this experience of seemingly "knowing" or being attracted to another whom you have never previously met. Also, Signatures may even slightly change in regard to the being's moods or environment, while staying fundamentally the same at the core. The Signature is not only Ethereal; it contains elements of the Astral, such as emotions and mood.

The aura is the "radiated" energy and outer layer of the Ethereal body of living beings. The aura may be compared to light radiated from a light bulb or heat from the body. This outer shell of the aura is very flexible and layered. The aura is densest closest to the body and slowly becomes thinner and thinner as it radiates outward. On a surface level, the Art of Gathering Energy depends on aural contact. The aura is also a protective device that screens out harmful energies and welcomes beneficial ones. The subtle body is constantly interacting with the universe on all levels, cycling energy in and out through the aura. Auras often have specific shapes and colors, and those who are Awakened can perceive the mood, health, and nature of a being based on its aura. The aura of a Strigoi Vii generally appears radiant and bright, especially once their Ethereal metabolism is raised and they are full of energy. The aura can be changed and modified through will, and adept individuals can mask their own aura and Signature.

Tendrils are parts of the aura that can be created by the use of will and projected beyond the normal constraints of the subtle body. They begin as small filaments, akin to hairs on the arm, which can be controlled and extended by the will. Once extended like the arms of an octopus or the pseudopods of an amoeba, these tendrils can be used to touch others, defend oneself, and create links with other beings. Most importantly, tendrils are used in the Art of Gathering Energy and are extended out at a distance in order to interact with the energy of other beings.

Tendrils are exclusively native to Vampyric beings, and their presence can be easily used to identify those of Vampyric nature. Other entities may possess the ability to form tendrils in a limited fashion if they are advanced in energy work; however, for the Vampyre, they are a natural and identifiable feature of the subtle body.

"A hundred and one are the arteries of the heart, one of them leads up to the crown of the head. Going upward through that, one becomes immortal."

—Chandogya Upanishad

Meridians are akin to veins and arteries and function as channels for the flow of vital energy through our subtle bodies. These are akin to the meridians of traditional Chinese medicine, which are a main feature of practices such as acupuncture, acupressure, and qigong. Meridians intersect with the chakras and control the flow of Lifeforce throughout the body.

Practices such as Lifeforceyama, breathing alternatively through the left and right nostrils, can help control and stimulate the flow of Lifeforce. Links are subtle connections to everything and everyone with which you have ever interacted. These links vary in strength and intensity. The Norse concept of the "Web of the Wyrd," or the cosmic linkage of the ebb and flow of energy and destiny, is analogous to our understanding of links. Links are akin to strings of Ethereal energy through which Lifeforce and Astral energies, such as emotions, flow. Links can be formed from physical contact, such as touching someone's personal possession or wearing someone else's clothing, sharing intimate experiences, or even drawing energy through the

Art of Gathering Energy. Links can also be created by nonphysical contact, such as emotional conversations over the phone or making eye contact with someone. Common experience often creates links.

For example, links that are formed and reinforced between lovers will allow emotional energies to flow between them, causing a feeling of "connection" even when physically separated. Thus, links are direct connections and channels to another being, place, or object. Links are excellent tools for employing the Art of Gathering Energy and for gathering energies.

Within esoteric systems such as Voudoun, objects that are connected by links can affect another person at a distance. Most powerful links come from the physical body, such as hair, fingernails, or skin. These links can be used to draw energy even when the individual is not present, bypassing the illusion of space and time by functioning in the subtle world where these things have less meaning. Voodoo dolls, when created and used properly, are an example of such phenomena. Links can be broken. However, the effort required to break a link depends on its strength. All living beings create links to those with whom they interact. The more frequent and intense the interactions, the stronger the links. For example, breaking a link with a casual work acquaintance would probably not require a great deal of energy. In contrast, breaking a link with a former lover would take a much larger effort. Within the Art of Gathering Energy, links are easily formed by drawing energy directly from a specific donor. Drawing large amounts of energy creates very powerful links. This is why many Strigoi Vii prefer Ambient Gathering, as it does not cause direct or strong links.

Links are useful for empathy and telepathy. If two people have strong links with each other, such as often happens in the case of close identical twins, they may be able to sense the pain or emotional state of the other. Two lovers who are deeply in love will possess a strong level of empathy for each other, creating heightened emotional states. However, it is sometimes necessary to break links. This may be accomplished through ritual or energy work. Be wary and careful in your intense interactions since links of which you are unaware can be used against you. Sometimes links cause damage or subtle wounds, which must be healed and treated.

Chakras have been embraced by various belief systems, especially new-age and neopagan groups. They are an excellent beginning point for those seeking to increase perception and manipulation of their Ethereal bodies. They can also be used as a tool of focus in meditation. Strigoi Vii work with a series of chakras within the geography of the Ethereal body. The Hindu Tantric Shakta system practiced by the Theosophists is partially reflective of our own. The Theosophists and other contemporary occult orders were largely responsible for introducing the system of chakras to the mundane world. The system of chakras employed by Strigoi Vii includes the following.

Crown (AK)—Located at the top of the head, the Crown Chakra is the connection to the higher planes of existence beyond the Maiiah and to the Dragon (higher Self and intellect). This is the seat of the Immortal Self, free of the perceptions of time and space. It is the core of identity and the key to self-actualization as a deity. It can be used for gathering energy in conjunction with Flight of the Succubus, as explained in Higher Mysteries, or for Astral projection when in meditation or deep sleep. In meditation it is used to communicate with one's Dragon. It is the seat of the will, balance, and wisdom.

Third Eye (AH)—Located right above and between the eyes, this chakra is the seat of perception and the "sixth sense," or the vision of the subtle levels of reality beyond the Corporeal, such as the Ethereal and Astral realms. Clairvoyance is seeing with the Third Eye. The Third Eye may be used for drawing in energy at a distance within the subtle world and is considered the "Eyes of the Throne." Mal'acchio, or the "Evil Eye," is a Morrah-level form of Vampyrism and employs this chakra. In meditation, this chakra can be used in some forms of divination and for connecting to the consciousness of others. The Third Eye Chakra is related to the Strigoi Vii aspect of Ramkht, the Oracle.

Throat (AY)—Located in the throat, this is the chakra of self-expression, power, voice, and creativity. To speak with the Throat Chakra's voice is to speak prophecy. When used in the Art of Gathering Energy, the Throat Chakra facilitates contact via tendrils created by the seduction of the voice. For personal self-realization, the Throat Chakra may be utilized for vocal seduction and persuasion.

Heart (SA)—Located in the upper chest area, the Heart Chakra corresponds to emotional states and social identity and is focused on self-acceptance. This is the middle chakra of the seven employed by the Strigoi Vii.

This chakra is used for feeding from Ambient energy at a distance within social environments. For personal meditation, the Heart Chakra relates to self-love, the balance of ego, and intelligence.

Solar Plexus (TA)—Located near the navel, this is often called the Center Chakra and is the core of the Self, as well as the seat of the Dark Flame. Here is where the difference between the mortal-minded human and the Immortal Vampyre begins. Self-empowerment is focused in the Solar Plexus Chakra. Focusing on this chakra aids in contemplation of the Self.

Sacral (AE)—Located near the pelvis and sexual organs, the Sacral Chakra deals with self-gratification, instincts, and sexuality. This chakra can be used as the link in cycling energy in Vampyre sex with another Strigoi Vii. It can also be employed for feeding as a "Succubus" or "Incubus," either through tactile contact involving actual intercourse or through sexual arousal without direct contact. In meditation, this chakra can be used for knowledge of one's emotions, prowess, and endurance. The Sacral Chakra is related to the Elorathian aspect of Kitra, the weaver.

Root (NE)—Located between the genitals and the rec- tum, the Root Chakra relates to the element of earth and is linked to the grounding of the Self and the Corporeal body. When gathering energy, this chakra is used for draining through tactile contact. It is useful in meditation in regard to set- ting goals and being grounded. The Root Chakra is related to the Elorathian aspect and Current of the Mradu, the warrior.

The Need AKA the Hunger

The Need is the necessity for the Strigoi Vii to gather and process large quantities of Lifeforce. This comes from the growth of Zhep'r and the high frequency of energy of the Strigoi Vii's subtle body. Think of the Vampyre subtle body as having the equivalent of a very active metabolism. Thus, it is beneficial to fulfill that metabolism by absorbing Lifeforce. The Need is not analogous to psychic vampires who have an energy deficiency such as weakened chakras.

Our thirst for Lifeforce is a different condition and is not a result of damage to the subtle body. It is an evolution and enhancement. The Need is intimately associated with the possibility of Immortality, for when the Strigoi Vii absorbs Lifeforce during their Corporeal life, this absorbed energy allows the Double to maintain a high vibrational frequency and maintain cohesion, thus preventing the Second Death.

Many Strigoi Vii feel the Need as a sort of physical thirst or hunger for Lifeforce and will instinctively seek out situations where they can obtain large amounts of Lifeforce. As previously mentioned in the Strigoi Vii Codex, the Need may sometimes be interpreted as Corporeal hunger or thirst, especially by un-Awakened Strigoi Vii. These un-Awakened individuals often subconsciously employ elements of the Art of Gathering Energy even before their Awakening. Strigoi Vii who have Awakened to their nature become more consciously aware of their Need for Lifeforce and gather energy on a very regular basis.

Of course, as the Strigoi Vii evolves in Zhep'r and becomes more practiced in Communion, their "reservoirs" of Lifeforce increase. However, the entire process of Zhep'r requires Lifeforce as fuel, so the Strigoi Vii will experience the Need to absorb energy at every step on their path of evolution. This Need is purely spiritual; however, since all layers of the body are connected, not fulfilling the Need to gather Lifeforce can deleteriously affect the psychological and physical health of the Living Vampyre. The solution is practice, development, and mastery of the Arts of Gathering.

When a Strigoi Vii's Need for Lifeforce is fulfilled, their aura will contain bright and vibrant colors, alive and radiant with the fire of life. In contrast, the traditional psychic vampire will have a dark aura, often giving the impression of illness. The fact that we Need Lifeforce in order to enhance and further our evolution, not to fulfill any sort of deficiency, is the main difference between psychic vampires and Strigoi Vii.

CHAPTER 22
INTERMEDIATE ENERGY GATHERING

[T]hink me not cruel because I obey the irresistible law of my strength and weakness; if your dear heart is wounded, my wild heart bleeds with yours. In the rapture... I live in your warm life, and you shall die—die, sweetly die—into mine. I cannot help it; as I draw near to you, you, in your turn, will draw near to others, and learn the rapture of that cruelty, which yet is love; so, for a while, seek to know no more of me and mine, but trust me with all your loving spirit.

—*Carmilla*, Joseph Sheridan Le Fanu

Liber Zhep'r" introduced you, the reader, to the Art of Gathering Energy from the Strigoi Vii perspective. In "Coming Forth by Day," We learned the most basic application of our Art, known as Ambient Energy Gathering. Here, within "Coming Forth by Night," We move further into intermediate levels of our Art: surface and deep feeding.

Since all living things exchange energy with every interaction, these energy exchanges can be directly applied to the intermediate applications of Vampyrism. Mortal society is comprised of constant energy exchanges between individuals, ranging from casual eye contact to a friendly conversation to intense sexual contact. Within the animal kingdom, animals eat plants and other animals, and, near the culmination of the cycle, humans eat both animals and plants. This "food web" is a never-ending exchange of Lifeforce energy, with humans seemingly sitting atop the hierarchy. Thus, humans produce the most refined form of Lifeforce because they have taken in the life energies of all living things below them in the exchange cycle. Gathering is the act of obtaining this highly refined energy for the purposes of furthering alchemy, Zhep'r and employing *Clavicula Sangraal*, which is vibrational high magick or, simply, Strigoi Vii Sorcery.

To the mortal-minded, the Strigoi Vii practice of absorbing Lifeforce may seem very much akin to traditional psychic vampirism; yet the Strigoi Vii do it with a different intent and purpose. The absorption of Lifeforce enhances the subtle metabolism of the Strigoi Vii and fuels Zhep'r. It is also a necessary practice so that the Strigoi Vii may then offer forth the collected energies to the Strigoi Morte in Communion. During Communion, the Strigoi Vii receives a higher form of Lifeforce from the Strigoi Morte, which We call Ambrosia. Practicing Communion is the primary manner of increasing Zhep'r. Also note that regularly taking in large amounts of Lifeforce from humans promotes physical, emotional, and spiritual health in the Strigoi Vii.

Strigoi Vii enjoy a mutually beneficial, or symbiotic, relationship with the vast, teeming masses of humanity and take full advantage of the more than six billion donors on our planet. At first glance, it may seem that what a Vampyre does is unethical and harmful. To the contrary! The Immortal-minded simply has a different perspective than the mortal-minded. Mortal ethics are most often artificial constructs and are different from the laws of nature. Civilized morality is a synthetic construct, not a natural or inherent law. Consider how the accepted codes of conduct and morality have varied between historical periods and cultures. In truth, the ruling class almost always prescribes behavior in order to better control their subjects.

For example, the antiquated Western European constraints prohibiting anyone other than clergy from reading and interpreting scripture were merely a way to keep power in the hands of the church. Europe and America, women could not vote, own property, or work in most professions until relatively recently. These were primitive mortal- minded concepts that were eventually overcome as mortal-minded ethics evolved. In contrast, natural laws are pragmatic and innate. As Hermann Hesse wrote in Steppenwolf, "look at an animal, a cat, a dog, or a bird, or one of those beautiful great beasts in the zoo. You can't help seeing that all of them are right. They're never in any embarrassment. They don't flatter and they don't intrude. They don't pretend. They are as they are, like stones or flowers or stars in the sky."

While the kingdom of nature is quite often *"red in tooth and claw,"* its brutality is impersonal, unlike concentrated deliberate malice. The Calmae should look both to the positive elements of human civilization and the naturalism of the wild. The philosophy of the Strigoi Vii Art of Gathering Energy achieves a harmonious balance between the two, embracing the best aspects of each.

With large amounts of Lifeforce and concentrated will, the Strigoi Vii can raise their Ethereal metabolism. Due to their un-Awakened minds and the conditioning of the Glamour, the mortal-minded are mostly unaware of our process of Gathering. The tales of "blood-drinking vampires" in literature and folklore are but echoes of the true Art of Gathering Energy. We, as Strigoi Vii, are so subtle in our Vampyrism that most humans never truly realize nor are harmed by our intentions. In fact, they benefit from the process!

Interacting with and exchanging energy is something humans do every day. Gathering on the level needed for fueling Zhep'r requires effort and intent and, at higher levels, a significant energetic exchange. Purchasing an item with cash or credit represents an exchange of energies and creating links. Continual and prolonged contact between two humans often results in Ethereal bonds of familiarity, and thus produces links. Advanced Adeptus of Vampyrism benefit significantly from learning how to consciously gather and draw out the energy of the human's Lifeforce through these links. The Vampyre then uses the acquired energy for their own purposes.

Maintaining large reservoirs of Lifeforce aids the Strigoi Vii in dream recall, promotes physical health and emotional well-being, increases memory, improves vision and psychic awareness, and increases the ability to draw in and store larger amounts of Lifeforce. It is also essential to Communion, as the collected energies are offered up to the Strigoi Morte. Drawing in this Pranic energy is the Art of Gathering Energy. It is one of the most beneficial things a Strigoi Vii can do.

"Donors" are those from whom We draw energy through the Art of Gathering Energy. From some donors, we only draw residual and excess energies; from others, We draw deeply and consensually. Either way, donors must never be harmed and always respected, as they are our source and deserve our regard.

The ethics of Vampyrism from an outsider's perspective might seem like a paradox, as the mortal-minded might consider us predators or parasites. While there are many things We can learn from predators, We are not truly analogous to the lion or the hawk. The Art of Gathering Energy is not a brutal form of predation! It is a much more refined, elegant, and ethical system of energy acquisition. We are evolved beyond the beasts of the wild as well as what many vampire Traditions call "predatory spirituality."

The mortal-minded, in their blissfully distracted and comfortable lives, believe they sit at the top of the food chain. They are highly mistaken. The Strigoi Morte and the rest of the Ascended Masters are more highly evolved beings than humans and even the Strigoi Vii. They are also the supreme sentient beings with whom the Calmae is concerned. From the perspective of the average mundane, the Strigoi Morte may seem to be angelic or spiritual beings. From the perspective of the Vampyre, they are our Elders, Sorors and Fraters, teachers, and parents. The Strigoi Vii do not worship such evolved beings but instead experience a student and mentor relationship with the Strigoi Morte. As you progress in your journey of Zhep'r, it is important to fully understand that Gathering Lifeforce is an act which at first might seem morally difficult. Embracing your potential is one of the most challenging aspects of your own personal spiritual evolution. It is beneficial to overcome such mundane conditioning! The wolf preys on the deer and, in order to survive, humans eat animals such as cows and chickens and other living organisms such as plants. This process is part of the natural web of life, and no one would call it wrong or unethical. Even passionate vegetarians or vegans admit the necessity of eating plant matter in or- der to survive.

Gathering Lifeforce is a much more evolved form of the same action, albeit one that is performed in a completely different way.

We, as Vampyres, have no need to physically kill our "food" as predatory animals do. There is more to being a predator than simply surviving on the life energy of others. An essential element of the life for the predator is the hunt. The wolf does not ask the deer's permission to eat it. Most human ethics do not usually require a journey to the slaughterhouse to obtain the cow's consent before ordering a hamburger in a restaurant. One of the reasons why people living in countries such as the United States eat so much meat is because they are distanced from the process of obtaining it. They usually have never killed an animal for food or even witnessed such brutality acted out by another. Most people are desensitized by going to the supermarket and buying a nicely packed piece of meat from the butcher's counter. Similarly, it is highly unlikely that the mortal-minded would ask permission from an ear of corn before attending a summer picnic luncheon! We do not physically harm those mortals from whom We draw energy. This is one of the distinctions between the death-accepting mortal and the Vampyre. Nor are We as coldly and inexorably vicious as natural predators in the animal kingdom, such as the lion or the bird of prey. The Strigoi Vii takes a far more civilized and artful approach when performing the Art of Gathering Energy. We fully admire and embrace the philosophy of the Native American hunters who would give thanks and praise before taking the life of their intended prey.

Many humans would say Gathering Lifeforce is theft. However, does not the human steal the life of a cow whenever they take a bite of hamburger? Vegetarians kill or harm plants for sustenance, which are also living beings. There is no creature in the world that does not survive by consuming energy of other beings. Even plants absorb sunlight and the minerals of dead animals present in the soil and convert them to useable energy to fuel the plant's growth. However, unlike the actions of the mortal-minded meat eater, Gathering Lifeforce is far less harmful. We know it is actually beneficial to the health of the human.

Donating Corporeal blood is healthy because the loss of the donated blood forces the body to generate newer, healthier blood. The old blood then goes to serve the well-being of humans who are less healthy and in need of a transfusion. It is no different when the Strigoi Vii draws in human Lifeforce. Gathering too much Lifeforce from a mortal may cause minor and temporary damage, just as draining someone of too much blood will cause dizziness or weakness. Therefore, be careful not to draw too much Lifeforce from one donor. There is an additional disadvantage to drawing too much energy from a single mortal; it may result in something commonly known as "sympathetic vampirism." Any human whose Ethereal body has been too deeply drained of Lifeforce will unconsciously seek to replenish it by taking it from another human's subtle body. This is not an actual evolution into Strigoi Vii, but rather a purely instinctual response of the subtle body. It is, in fact, a common cause of temporary traditional psychic vampirism and the myths of the vampires "bite" turning their victims into vampire minions.

From the Immortal-minded perspective, it is not an ethical violation to take energy from others. The wolf does not ask the rabbit or the lion ask the gazelle if they can eat them. However, the lion has the instinctual common sense to not overhunt their prey, as that lion's pride cannot survive without the herd of gazelle. These simple laws of the wild are examples of Vampyric ethics. We want mortals to multiply and live long, happy, and healthy lives, generating more Lifeforce so we can both mutually further our respective evolution. The human race only truly benefits from a respectful coexistence between us.

Different frequencies of energy occur depending on the nature and source of the energy. A common misconception is that lower forms of Ethereal energy, such as that of plants and animals, are of a high-enough frequency to be useful to the Strigoi Vii. These low-grade energies cannot, by themselves, sustain the Vampyre. The low-frequency energies of the Earth, as well, are not enough to provide fuel for Zhep'r. When a Vampyre seeks to gather only these energies, it is like a carnivore trying to survive solely by consuming plants. The system of the carnivore is simply not constructed to endure in a healthy state without eating meat. Human Lifeforce is the best and most potent form of Pranic energy of use to the Strigoi Vii.

Vampyric Cannibalism and Rape is the procedure of drawing energy from other Strigoi Vii, Awakened beings, or ethical psychic vampires without their knowledge and consent. These practices are extremely unethical. Gathering energy from those who are Awakened and/or have attained Zhep'r is equivalent to cannibalism. As an analogy, while humans consume lower animals, consuming human flesh for sustenance is one of the most universal and deep-rooted human taboos. It is also unethical to drain a donor to the point of temporary impairment, especially if the draining is severe enough to produce sympathetic vampirism.

To the neophyte, it may seem like cannibalism when two Strigoi Vii exchange energy. However, energy exchanges between Strigoi Vii are for the purpose of cycling, not drawing on energy. This can be done in playful games, during ritual to amplify an Offering and raise more energy, between two Strigoi Vii as part of a healing, or for Vampyre sex and Tantric practices.

Surface Gathering occurs through direct physical contact or any form of social interaction. This form of Gathering may be simply accomplished through the application of intent and will. Since all living beings exchange energy and form links in this manner, it is a natural process that does not require consent, just directed intent. In surface Gathering, the Vampyre does not draw energy from below the surface of the aura and definitely not deeply and directly from the subtle body. Any basic link can be utilized for surface Gathering, such as a simple touch, kiss on the cheek, handshake, discussion, or casual and "accidental" physical contact. Be respectful and elegant with touch. Everyday social settings and interactions are forums for such indirect forms of the Art of Gathering Energy. Surface Gathering is a simple surface draw of energy in order to satisfy the general and immediate needs of the Strigoi Vii and should be done discretely and subtly.

To understand the role of physical contact in surface Gathering, remember that any time your aura directly interacts with that of a donor, immediate Ethereal links are created between the two of you. Physical contact can create some of the strongest and most energetic links. However, even if you are at a distance and have a conversation with another individual without physical or even visual contact, links are formed. The more prolonged and interactive the contact, the more links are forged and, therefore, more energy can be drawn in.

Once contact is achieved, the Vampyre must simply focus their intent on using the tendrils to pierce the aura. These "Ethereal fangs" open the aura slightly, allowing the Vampyre to gather the subsequently freed Lifeforce. To aid this process, you may wish to visualize shining tendrils or tubes connecting you and your donor, each tube filling with Lifeforce, which you then draw toward yourself. You can inhale deeply and rhythmically or even clench your abdominal or sphincter muscles to facilitate the process.\

Many of Us perform this type of Gathering instinctively, but like all arts, you must consciously and repeatedly practice in order to become a Master. When performing surface Gathering, make a silent statement to yourself regarding your specific intentions. This will solidify your intent and engage your will. Once the process is concluded, the Vampyre must extract their tendrils and break all links between themselves and the donor in order to prevent an unwanted reversal of energies. Many Strigoi Vii choose to visualize the tendrils "fading away" or slowly disengaging and dissolving.

Indirect surface Gathering should be a brief and shallow form of gathering. Take only a small amount of energy from each donor and do this from as many donors as required to satisfy your needs. This is one example of why being in an urban setting can be beneficial for the Strigoi Vii. If you live amongst a large number of people, there is no lack of energy and no reason to ever gather too deeply from any one donor. As explained in "Liber Jahira," when you deeply absorb energy from the subtle body of another, you may likely also absorb their emotions and moods. Try instead to focus on directing the tendrils toward the shallower Ethereal layer, as you may suffer distasteful effects from absorbing another's emotional sensations. This process is part of the skill of filtering.

Deep Gathering is the process of penetrating deeply into a donor's subtle body, beyond the aura, and directly into the core of their Subtle Body. This is where the most concentrated Lifeforce is located. Deep Gathering is a process that must only ever be performed with great caution and care and by those advanced Strigoi Vii who have mastered the process of gathering. It is a process too sophisticated for the Calmae. Deep Gathering can negatively and harmfully drain the donor and may quickly cause symptoms of sympathetic vampirism. Strigoi Vii Adeptus who are skilled in this process, if they choose to practice it, will often develop a consensual and informed relationship with a specific donor before gathering from them deeply.

When you cannot maintain a constant physical contact with a donor, it is possible to simply touch an individual as in surface Gathering and let the tendril root deeply into them. Once this is done, and if the Strigoi Vii is expert in the Art of Gathering Energy, they can forge a strong link and draw deeply. However, this is not recommended, as some consider it vampiric rape. It may also be extremely exhausting to the donor. Experience and practice with surface Gathering is required to master this technique. Also, if you were to practice this form Gathering on a powerful and skilled Awakened being, they might be aware of what you are doing and fight back consciously or unconsciously. The Strigoi Vii makes sure to refine and develop ethical tactile Gathering, as it is subtle, respectful, and not harmful to the donor.

Direct Gathering is actually beneficial to the donor! When the link is established and the energy drawn from the donor, their subtle body interacts directly with that of the Vampyre, thus stimulating the donor's energetic system. This stimulation may cause a faster flow of Lifeforce throughout their subtle body, thus cleansing them of stagnant energies and increasing the vibration of their subtle metabolism.

Direct Gathering can be best equated to many healing practices, such as "laying on of hands," energetic or therapeutic massage, and Reiki techniques. Studying and experimenting with these practices is a good way to master this form of our Art of Gathering Energy. You will also offer your donor pleasure and healing energy work whilst drawing on their energy.

Consecutive or repeated interactions may lead to a powerful bond between the Vampyre and their donor. In such a case, the two will form lasting links, which the Vampyre can then use to gather energy from the donor. This is similar to deep Gathering. Obviously, in such a case the Strigoi Vii must take care to not draw too much from their donor. We strongly advise that this form of the Art of Gathering Energy be consensual.

Sensual Gathering is an aspect of both surface and deep Gathering and can include any combination of sexual elements, such as seduction, erotic stimulation, and Tantric techniques. Intercourse need not be part of sensual Gathering. Of course, because of the ethical implications of this form of our Art of Gathering Energy, the Strigoi Vii must obtain consent if physical contact is to take place. There are two main forms of sensual Gathering:

Surface Sensual Gathering is used in intimate situations to stimulate the donor to release Lifeforce. Sensual or erotic arousal creates an incredible amount of available energy. Surface sensual Gathering may include body massage, dance, masturbation, erotic performance, or a multitude of other situations. The most common technique is to sexually arouse the donor into a state of heightened stimulation. Examples include a dancer doing a striptease, a burlesque performance, or even reading erotic poetry to a lover. Through these and many other techniques, energetic links are forged through which the donor is unconsciously offering Lifeforce.

Deep Sensual Gathering requires sexual intercourse and is a deeply penetrating form of interaction. This, of course, is an extremely intimate technique that should only be performed between two consenting adults. Deep sensual Gathering often involves stimulating the chakras and moving deeply into the subtle body of the donor, as during this process the subtle bodies of the Vampyre and donor are deeply and profoundly connected. This form of Gathering is often extremely empowering for both the Vampyre and their donor, as there is a direct flow of energy from the donor to the Vampyre. Deep sensual Gathering often produces a great deal of intense stimulation in the donor. This technique should only be attempted by the most skilled Strigoi Vii in the Arts of Gathering, as it requires great skill to filter the immense flood of Astral energetic residue that may be released by the process. The Calmae should be aware that deep sensual Gathering and other forms of deep Gathering are only discussed here for informational purposes. These are techniques that require a large degree of practice and evolution in Zhep'r to master. The Calmae, at this point, should focus on practicing ethical and responsible surface Gathering.

Commencing is the equivalent of surface Gathering and the most elementary application of cycling. It involves a variety of techniques such as mutual erotic dance, energy wrestling, mutual performance, BDSM practices, martial arts sparring, or many other activities. The participants collectively create a "circuit" of energy between them, in which they both give and receive energy.

In summation, the Art of Gathering Energy requires that you shift your ethics and perspectives from those of the mortal-minded to those of an

Immortal. Immortal ethics are based on natural laws, the survival of the fittest, and a deep sense of personal responsibility. Remember, it is only the Lifeforce we desire from the hyle, never their physical blood! Lifeforce is the key to defeating the Second Death.

Consider deeply and wisely. Do you wish to experience the fullness of eternity as your Self, retaining your memories, free will, knowledge, and experiences? Or would you rather be "reincarnated" as a thousand disparate shards spread among a thousand new beings? Gathering Lifeforce will fuel your Zhep'r and build your own Immortality.

Defeating the Second Death is genuine Immortality of the Self. Choice is freedom. The choice is yours. You hold the tools this very second in your own hands.

CHAPTER 23

THE ANATOMY OF DEATH

"That is not dead which can eternal lie, And with strange aeons even death may die."

— H. P. Lovecraft, "The Nameless City"

For all living beings, life begins with the divine spark of conception and continues outward to physical manifestation. Upon the First Death, or the death of the Corporeal body, the Ethereal body, being inextricably married to the Corporeal, begins to lose its pattern and shape. In most cases, the survival of the Ethereal body is aided by preservation of the Corporeal body. That is why the Ancient Egyptians were so concerned with preserving the physical body through mummification. We, as Strigoi Vii, realize this extreme possibility, and the health and preservation of the physical pattern is correspondingly important (see Wellness and Perpetuity Black Veils). Systems such as cryonics, DNA preservation, and the potential option of cloning are powerful advantages for the modern Vampyre.

The death of the Ethereal body, or the Second Death, occurs when the patterns anchored by the Corporeal body begin to lose density and cohesion. Regard the Corporeal body as a drinking glass. Imagine the glass being filled with water (the Ethereal body). When the glass is shattered, the water spills and will eventually be dispersed into the universe through evaporation. Similarly, when the Corporeal body deteriorates, the process usually takes days to weeks, depending on the strength of the individual's Ethereal body and their mental and spiritual health.

Since the Ethereal body is the Vessel for the Astral, the Astral body is, in turn, jeopardized by the destruction of the Ethereal body. Re- member that all levels of the Self are connected. Without the solid foundation of the Corporeal body and the Ethereal body, all dreams, memories, and experiences evaporate like water vapor. During the Second Death, the Astral body and its associated characteristics are dispersed across the universe as a thousand shattered crystal shards or disappear like a drop of water into the ocean. Rebirth or reincarnation beyond the Second Death cannot be validated by any spiritual path or religion beyond the assumption of belief and faith. We do not choose to gamble on an unproven theory. The aim of the Strigoi Vii is to avoid the Second Death and therefore achieve Immortality. Those consciously existing between the First and Second Death might thus be known as "Undead."

The separation that occurs between the First and Second Death is often the cause of near-death experiences (NDEs). NDEs involve a form of Astral projection during which the subtle senses of the individual are heightened. People who have experienced NDEs often report phenomena such as looking down on their Corporeal bodies from above, seeing bright lights or entities, and other Ethereal sensations. However, there is a strictly biological dayside explanation for many of these experiences. The "bright light" reported by many individuals during an NDE is often just random neural firing in the optic nerve and brain. The peace and comfort commonly associated with such experiences is due to the release of chemicals and subtle substances that create a feeling of euphoria. Strigoi Vii are always very skeptical of all accounts of near-death experiences, as we know how unusual it is for mortals to be able to maintain the higher levels of their body beyond the death of the Corporeal.

Sometimes, however, a human's Ethereal and Astral energies will be caught between the First and Second Death due to a variety of circumstances. This occurs mainly due to Ethereal links, such as strong emotional ties to a specific place or person, which are maintained across levels of reality to the physical world. Violent or sudden deaths can forcefully separate the Ethereal body from the Corporeal, and the strong emotions of the individual involved will forge links to the specific location. These circumstances comprise much of what we know today as ghostly phenomena. However, such occurrences are quite rare, and a persistent Ethereal link is hardly a "ghost" in the commonly known sense of the word. Most of these links are little more than a semiconscious collection of emotions, like an accumulation of dust beneath a bed. Many cultures have rituals for releasing these clogged partial entities, such as exorcisms or funeral rites.

We Strigoi Vii wisely choose to master knowledge of the Anatomy of Death and to keep survival of the entire Self as the first and fore- most goal in our lives. As lovers of life, what other option could there possibly be for us?

[B]ehold a new cycle of life and mortality. Your genius will not be allotted to you, but you will choose your genius; and let him who draws the first lot have the first choice, and the life which he chooses shall be his destiny. Virtue is free, and as a man honors or dishonors her he will have more or less of her; the responsibility is with the chooser.

—Plato, *The Republic*

Reincarnation does not mean the same thing to the Strigoi Vii as it does to the mortal minded. Mortals only detect a bare echo of the truth of our reincarnation. Various forms of reincarnation in mortal-minded belief systems focus on the continuation of a "soul" rather than continuation of the Self. What, then, is a soul? It is not memory or experience or identity. Instead, the mortal-minded see it as a loosely defined concept that is closely affiliated with their idea of God.

Imagine, for a moment, waking up tomorrow morning in a completely unfamiliar house. You do not know your name or personal history. You have no idea if you have a family. Any occupation you might hold is also a mystery. You also have no sense of your personality—are you a weak or strong person? Do you take pride in your accomplishments (whatever they may be)? Are you physically abusive or charming to those close to you? Are you intelligent or mentally challenged? Imagine looking at your own face in a mirror and not recognizing a single feature, as if you were staring at a photograph of a stranger.

Now consider forgetting, absolutely, everything that ever mattered to you in your life—your parents, your profession, your lover, your hobbies, your children. Imagine passing the one whom you love best on the street and having absolutely no idea who they are.

Such is the mortal-minded conception of reincarnation. The mortal-minded individual who believes in reincarnation sees their rebirth as a moment of complete, ultimate forgetting. Their experiences, dreams, and ideals are completely shattered into millions of energetic shards and recycled throughout the universe. Their KA the essential spark or "soul" has been transferred into a different body. They have become an entirely different person. Hindu doctrine maintains that humans can even be reincarnated as animals or insects! Mortals see themselves as helpless on a wheel of rebirth that inevitably grinds their consciousness through incarnation after incarnation. This is no more than an extension of a slave mentality. They cannot conceive of truly taking control of their own destiny and believe it to be ordained by chance or by higher forces that "punish" them for transgressions against some artificial moral or religious code.

In "Coming Forth by Day," We discussed Corporeal Immortality. Spiritual Immortality is Immortality of the entire Self, not just one portion of the Self. The myth of the undead, undying vampire derives from the truth of our reincarnation and the prevention of the Second Death. We have no interest in rebirth as an endless process of memory loss. We value the treasures of experience and knowledge we have collected during this life! Why struggle toward Awakening and strive for spiritual evolution if all understanding and advancement will be lost upon the Second Death? Imagine having centuries to obtain experiences and knowledge to develop the Self.

Vampyre Immortality is one of the Mysteries of Strigoi Vii, and something the mortal-minded can rarely even begin to comprehend. As long as we can conquer the Second Death, We live forever in a timeless existence, free of the constraints of time and space.

Vampyre Immortality is to never forget, to break the cycle and to remember who you are. This is a True Awakening, and together We shall remember and not forget who we are.

CHAPTER 24

THE STRIGOI MORTE

Honor thy mother and father... so that your days may be long and that it may go well with you...

—Deuteronomy 5:16

The Strigoi Morte are the spirit guides of the Strigoi Vii. They are often known within the Family as Whisperers or the Ancestors and are said to be our disembodied Elders, Sorors, and Fraters who have conquered the Second Death and thus exist in subtle form. They are thought to have once been human and, through manifestation, can still influence the Corporeal Dayside world by such means as inspiration, visions, and possession. Once a Strigoi Vii is Awakened to the Vampyre Current, the possibility of direct contact with and validation of the Strigoi Morte becomes possible.

In Romanian mythology, the Strigoi Vii were the Living Vampires, and the Strigoi Morte were the undead spirits who haunted the living. In actuality, some of these myths may derive from the partially Vampyric beings known as Ethereal revenants. Only the namesake is employed here, as our true Strigoi Morte differ greatly from their mythological counterparts. The wisdom of the Strigoi Morte can survive throughout the eras with the continuation of their conscious Self. They are an essential part of the Current of Elorath and the Family. Our Mysteries state that They are the keepers of the ancient knowledge and secrets of True Immortality of the Self.

Mortals throughout history may have caught faint glimpses of the Strigoi Morte and possibly interpreted them as angels, miracles, spirits, faeries, gods, and demons. From a spiritual and religious mortal-minded interpretation, the Strigoi Morte are on the same level as beings who have Ascended to a higher plane of spiritual existence. Mortal religions and spiritual paths speak of Ascended Masters such as the Great White Brotherhood, Secret Chiefs, or the Order of Blessed Souls. These Masters are individuals who have spiritually advanced beyond the Corporeal to a transcended state that many mortal-minded would call Buddhahood, sainthood, nirvana, or enlightenment.

More recently, such contact could be possibly interpreted by the mortal minded as some of the sources of alien encounters. Occultist Aleister Crowley claimed to have contacted a particular entity, known to him as Aiwas, who may indeed have been a Strigoi Morte. Crowley always claimed it was from Aiwas that he received The Book of the Law. Prior to his death, Crowley drew a picture of his visions of Aiwas, which looked quite similar to what new-agers and UFOlogists describe as a "grey," or an alien. Crowley created and led the occult organization known as the *A∴A∴* (Argentium Astrum, or Silver Star) for the purpose of spreading Aiwas's teachings.

As Strigoi Vii, We use the potential of our heritage to aspire to Ascend and join the Strigoi Morte in what humans consider eternity and the Mysteries consider timelessness. Through self-mastery and the esoteric technology of Zhep'r, the Strigoi Morte truly have achieved a conscious state not bound by space and time. They are our catalyst for Zhep'r and our guides through the Mirror Gates of Immortality.

The manner in which Native Americans and various Asian cultures honor their Corporeal ancestors is loosely analogous to our respect for the Strigoi Morte. We see them as guides and inspirators. The Ancestors are said to have achieved a point in Zhep'r where They are able to maintain the Self at a point between the First and Second Death. Legends amongst the Family tell of some Vampyres who have been able to achieve this state during their Corporeal existence, and thus have easily made the transition to Strigoi Morte upon their First Death.

Many Strigoi Vii speak of finding the transition very challenging and even more ultimately have failed. Ascension to undeath and Immortality in a timeless state is the ultimate agenda of Zhep'r for the Strigoi Vii. Only thus may the Self pursue Zhep'r and continued evolution on grander levels of existence.

Although disembodied, the Strigoi Morte can theoretically manifest Corporeally if They so choose. They can assume physical form through possession of a human. This is known as "skin riding." A Strigoi Vii may perform the same process via Astral projection upon proper development of their Zhep'r. This is explored more thoroughly within the Higher Mysteries.

Many Strigoi Vii encounter the Ancestors throughout their entire lives, directly or indirectly. Some Strigoi Vii have reported experiencing whispers, hints, or inspirations that directed them to the archetype of the vampire or the Family. These Seekers have used such clues and tools to begin the foundations of Zhep'r. Many simply felt a general Calling of sorts and finally took their first steps on a path leading to the gates of the OSV. A great number of Strigoi Vii have said they came upon the Family and the Mysteries in ways that seemed oddly synchronistic or almost mystical. While the mortal-minded would say such experiences are simply blind coincidence, We know they may be the result of a Patron Strigoi Morte guiding the Seeker and creating circumstances to prepare them for their Awakening. The Strigoi Morte are a powerful element of Vampyre ritual and esoteric workings. They give guidance and inspiration not just to the Family but to individual Strigoi Vii. One Vampyre may not have just a single guide but a group of them, known as a Pantheon.

Before the Order, the Family had highly intimate and solitary relationships with the Strigoi Morte. Many Strigoi Vii theorize that the Ancestors would even orchestrate the birth of a potential by arranging the union of humans possessing the "Vampyre gene" or implanting a piece of the Current during conception. The Strigoi Morte would then guide the chosen potential as they matured by taking the form of apparitions, spiritual guides, inspirators, or visions. As the potential Strigoi Vii grew older and began to realize their true potential, the Ancestor would formally reveal Themself and begin teaching the Mysteries to Their chosen student. Some Ancestors would even have several potentials, knowing only a few would truly Awaken and show promise for success within Zhep'r. Today, the Strigoi Morte not only guide individual Strigoi Vii, but they also guide and inspire the entire Current of the Family as a whole.

One of the qualifications for advancing within the Central Mysteries is to personally validate the existence of the Strigoi Morte in ritual Communion. Learning of the Secrets of the Strigoi Morte is one of the key principles in experiencing Zhep'r. One cannot simply be told of and believe in the existence of the Strigoi Morte. Declaring belief upon receiving secondhand information is a very common mortal-minded trait. Be skeptical always and seek validation. Moreover, there are not sufficient concepts within human language or experience to describe a true encounter with the Strigoi Morte. You must experience and come to know Them for yourself in order to validate their existence. Such Gnosis comes from making intimate contact with the Strigoi Morte during Communion, where you contact them and personally verify their existence. The wisest approach for validating the existence of the Strigoi Morte is to keep an open yet skeptical mind. Observe the results of your investigations objectively and make judgments later. If you are courageous and tenacious, you will thus explore and fulfill your True Nature. One may ask how to distinguish Strigoi Morte from other disembodied beings. Various lower or parasitic entities exist within the subtle layers of reality. However, as the Strigoi Vii intrinsically recognize others of the Family, so do we recognize the Strigoi Morte. Thus, do not fear that you will be "tricked" by other entities falsely claiming to be Strigoi Morte. If you are Strigoi Vii, you will simply know their Radiance and experience a deep feeling of love as you would from a fellow Strigoi Vii. The Strigoi Morte have such a focused energy Signature that it is impossible to mistake Them for anything but Family.

In a deep sense akin to love, We build relationships both individually and as a Family with the Ascended. Strigoi Vii can consciously and successfully make Communion with the Strigoi Morte through ritual, meditation, trance, and divination. The True Strigoi Vii creates an intimate bond with the Ancestors. This is one of the things that distinguishes us from Others such as ethical psychic vampires and other Traditions. The Family's relationship with the Strigoi Morte continues to evolve, as does the Order.

The Strigoi Morte in Their True form cannot be perceived in a practical mundane sense. Instead, they lend us a sense of blessing and of being chosen and guided. The Strigoi Vii allows for more than one possible explanation of the reality of the Strigoi Morte, and each Strigoi Vii may have their own interpretation of contact with them.

Many amongst the Family theorize that our Patron Strigoi Morte may also be an aspect of our higher Self that is free of time and space. In that sense, the patron is an aspect of our Ka, Immortal soul or Divine Spark. Becoming conscious of all levels and facets of the Self is a grand Awakening of personal awareness. Thus, our experiences with the Strigoi Morte may indeed be simply like looking into a universal mirror and making true and Deep Communion, which is Communion with our Higher Self. The Strigoi Morte, free of time and space, are thus perceived as having personality, shape, form, and image so that our minds may comprehend the Dragon Itself.

We leave it to you to validate Their existence. The Strigoi Morte are highly discriminating in regard to whom They reveal Themselves. Only the most dedicated and sincere Vampyre will benefit from the vast possibilities of the Vampyre Current.

The Vampyres' Rovance

The Rovance, or the Patron introduction or acknowledgement, is an exercise in self-meditation and communion during which a Strigoi Vii begins to contact their patron Strigoi Morte. Begin this exercise during a day of solitude, after having gathered Lifeforce to your fill. If possible, try to perform this ritual isolated from the mundane world, such as in a pleasant rural locale. If not, you should at least find a room or residence that can be secured from intrusion. It is important that you not be disturbed or interrupted during this exercise. Be sure to turn off all communication devices so you will truly experience solitude. Tap into the energies of the world and begin establishing a sacred space known as a Sanctum. Once the Sanctum has been established, begin the Rovance by relaxing yourselves from your feet to your head, then center yourself by imagining a serpent from deep within the Earth coming up and wrapping around your spine, slowly sliding through each chakra. As the snake coils up your spine, it moves toward your *Vampyres' Throne*.

Once this has been established, let your Lifeforce flow through your body. Visualize oneself in a long tunnel, on a path in a dark forest, or any other route that manifests in your imagination. Feel yourself walking down this path. Notice what is around you with all your five senses and listen for direction. Your Dragon will guide you. As you continue the exercise, you will begin to perceive signs on your path. They may take the form of voices, lights, symbols, or even road plinths. These signs have been established by your Patron for you. Heed them, and take note of what they say, following their direction. Do not be discouraged if you do not perceive any signs on your first experience with the Rovance. It may take several attempts to finally perceive the markers your Patron has set for you on your path of evolution.

The following descriptions represent some of the impressions members of the Family have received upon performing the Rovance. Use these as examples and inspiration only, as your personal Patron may provide you with a completely different experience.

On this path, you will gradually notice a grand temple far in the distance. You will be magnetically drawn toward a set of immense double doors. The temple looks different to all of us. Some have seen a large obelisk, while others have seen a cathedral, a pyramid, or ancient Greek temple. Through the cracks in the door, you will notice a beautiful and calming, yet alluring, light. You knock on the door three times, and it swings open with a unique alien creaking sound. As you enter, you are surrounded by darkness while bathed in the subtle lights you noticed from outside. The light becomes brighter, and before you, in the halls of this temple, one or more figures will be revealed. These will be your Patron Strigoi Morte.

Kneel before them as a Knight before their sovereign. Look Them directly in the eyes and introduce yourself. They will often not speak. You will experience their words as whispers or visions inside your mind. Whatever the case, they will find the best way to communicate with you to achieve understanding. Take this opportunity to ask them their names, your purpose within the Family, and your personal sigil. This sigil will be your key to calling on them in meditation and for Communion. At this point, they may choose to reveal a sacred image to you that will be the sigil. Once you have contacted your Patron, you can call on them for guidance, advice, and support. Also, they will often be drawn to you in sacred Communion rites such as the Sanguine Mass.

CHAPTER 25
STRIGOI VII RITUAL

There is a single main definition of the object of all magical Ritual. It is the uniting of the Microcosm with the Macrocosm. The Supreme and Complete Ritual is therefore the Invocation of the Holy Guardian Angel.

—Aleister Crowley, *Magick in Theory and Practice*

R itual is a strong formula for energetic workings. It creates a "theater of sequences" through the tools of psychodrama by utilizing a system of regimented steps and actions, all for a specific purpose. If the celebrant applies proper will and intent to the ritual formulation, it can be a powerful tool for raising and manipulating energies. The varied tools and symbols of ritual will aid less experienced practitioners, such as the Strigoi Vii Calmae, in entering into non-ordinary reality and achieving different states of consciousness. Ritual may also be used to celebrate a specific rite of passage or achievement, such as Initiation. Below are some of the benefits and purposes of different types of Strigoi Vii ritual:

Communion with the Strigoi Morte
Contacting and awakening the higher Self (the Dragon)

Raising energy
Entering alternate modes of consciousness
Creating sacred spaces (Sanctums)
Focusing will and intent to achieve a specific goal
Reaffirmation of the Self
Reaffirmation of collective agreement
Consecration of tools
Personal transformation
Celebration of Initiations and Ascensions
Celebration of festivals and holidays

A significant benefit of any Strigoi Vii ritual is reaffirmation of the individual Self and the collective Family Pact. In the past, there have been many different variations of Strigoi Vii rituals presented in various forums. These rituals had their value; however, they were generally tailored to the needs of a particular individual or group and thus did not have widespread applicability. We now present a more generalized formula for ritual with which the Initiate can experiment as they choose. We encourage you to work with this ritual formulation on your own terms, adapting it as best fits your needs. It is a template from which you can make your own system, which will be best suited to you personally.

In "Liber Elorath" and "Coming Forth by Day," we explored Initiations, psychodrama, and the aesthetics of rituals. Keep these concepts in mind as you now prepare for more advanced rituals. The ritual formulation that follows incorporates the philosophy and the ceremonial aspects of Strigoi Vii ritual. Any modifications you make to this general ritual format should always be in keeping with the spirit of Strigoi Vii ritual, for it is thus that you will gain the most effective results.

However, be aware that anyone attempting Strigoi Vii ritual should be firmly grounded in the Dayside. Mastery of the Dayside is the foundation on which the rituals of the Nightside rest. Without this foundation, the celebrant simply is not prepared to enter ritual, and they will not obtain results. We suggest the celebrant review "Coming Forth by Day" and the Black Veils if they are unclear or uncertain about the foundational principles underlying ritual and the Strigoi Vii Nightside.

The Sanguine Mass

The Sanguine Mass is the most central of all Strigoi Vii rituals of Communion with the Vampyre Current and the Strigoi Morte and is the standard on which many others are based. This is a more advanced edition of the Red Mass, found in the Black Veils. It is especially empowering for unifying a group ritual into a formulated ceremony to direct and focus energies. There exist many different variations on the Sanguine Mass, but the nine steps below comprise the standard core formulation and are detailed later in this chapter.

Prelude (or preparation)

Entering the Sanctum

Invokation

Invitation

Offering

Recoiling

Closing

Return

Celebration

Although the Sanguine Mass is the cornerstone of all Strigoi Vii ritual, there are other ritual forms. Some forms of Strigoi Vii Communion ritual are akin to a séance, where the celebrant establishes direct communication with the Strigoi Morte. The celebrant may request the Strigoi Morte contact them through various proxies, such as the tools of divination. Some Strigoi Vii use the ritual format as a tool of inspiration, in which they request revelation and insight regarding a specific problem or for a particular personal or Family endeavor. Even if the celebrant does not wish to perform a full ritual, they may apply various elements of our general ritual format to other workings. Always experiment and discover what best works for you!

Solitary Ritual

The vast majority of Strigoi Vii are solitary and independent and often don't even meet their Sorors and Fraters in person. Thus, solitary ritual is the most commonly practiced form of ritual within the Family. The Sanguine Mass is primarily written from the solitary perspective for this reason. However, it is easily adapted to group ritual if necessary.

Group Ritual

Group rituals, most importantly, act as a tool of unity in which all the ritual celebrants are in agreement. Group rituals can be intensely significant psychological markers in situations such as Ascensions and Initiations. The presiding member in group ritual must be a Adeptus, Priest/ess, or a Magister, as only these individuals are properly trained and experienced enough to channel the flow of energies. The only exception to this rule is if a Strigoi Vii couple wants to perform the ritual together.

Within group ritual, individual celebrants may assume specific roles. The leader of the ritual is known within Strigoi Vii as the presider or presiding member. The Deacons are individuals who are charged with assisting the presider by taking up specific roles or duties. For example, the presider may request that the Deacon inform the other celebrants that the ritual is about to start and help them prepare their robes and masks. The celebrants are those who are directly involved in the ritual, either by contributing energy or being present to celebrate the ritual.

There is no set number of celebrants for group ritual. Traditionally, in witchcraft, the ritual format called for thirteen members. From an Outer Circle perspective, this requirement mainly arose from mortal- minded superstition. Moreover, we Strigoi Vii know that a ritual can be just as effective when held by two people as by twenty! Large numbers do not necessarily make a more powerful ritual. We also suggest that the ritual be limited to the number of celebrants that can comfortably fit in the ritual space and can effectively participate in ritual. A smaller group creates a more intimate and personal experience, often leading to a greater Offering of Lifeforce for the Vampyre Current or Strigoi Morte than does an unmanageably large group.

Performance Ritual

Even though rituals are mostly done in private, there are occasions where some rituals can be done publicly if they are incorporated into performances such as fetish or burlesque shows, dominatrix sessions, DJ sets, or live music or theater performances. One can take example from the "Theater of the Vampires" in Anne Rice's novels. In performance ritual, the audience should be stimulated to produce extra Lifeforce to act as donors to fuel the ritual. For example, as a band performs a live show, the audience will be energized, perhaps singing and dancing along with the music. They will be directing their attention and energy toward the performers in an energetic circuit. This circuit is similar to the Art of Ambient Gathering, but in performance ritual the performers are directly involved in raising the energy of the crowd, instead of standing aside and simply gathering it. Such rituals should always employ the Glamour in order to disguise the true intent of the performance and not violate the sacredness of Communion. It is recommended that performance rituals only be performed by Strigoi Vii who are quite experienced in ritual, and who are capable of being discreet in their performance so as not to violate the Principles.

A fetish performer might, as an example, wear fangs and traditional "vampire" attire. The audience will merely see the performance as exciting and exotic, while the performer will be utilizing disguised elements of Vampyre ritual. The exception, of course, is during the Endless Night Festival when public rituals can be performed openly, as mortals who are in attendance are more than willing to be the "victims of vampires"!

Timing of Ritual

For those of the Outer Mysteries, this ritual is best done when the Veil between worlds is thinnest, so distractions from the Dayside are at their least intrusive. Strigoi Vii magick and sorcery are two entirely different applications. Magick depends on timing, tools, and psychodrama and can be utilized to create powerful change. Sorcery comes from within the practitioner and needs no tool except the will to master the universe itself. To generalize, Vampyre Magick as performed by those of the Outer Circle is a thaumaturgic system, based on ritual actions and tools. Clavicula Sangraal or Vampyre Sorcery, the province of the Inner Mysteries, may be likened to theurgy, is internally and instinctually based, and often uses no props at all save the willpower and Lifeforce of the Sorcerer. The abyss between magick and sorcery is both as profound and as simple as the distinction between the Dayside and Nightside.

Adeptus Strigoi Vii can directly apply Clavicula   Sangraal Sorcery whenever they choose to gain results. However, even the Master does not disdain a useful tool! The main difference is that the apprentice requires the tool, while the Master chooses it. Specific times of day and dates on the Wheel of the Year have power within the collective human consciousness. The Strigoi Vii Adeptus and initiates alike can tap this power in order to fuel many of their rituals. For example, there still exist numerous legends of sorcerers calling forth demons and ancient gods during their midnight Sabbats for dark orgiastic rites. Playing on such psychological tropes can aid the psychodrama of Strigoi Vii ritual and thus energize it, especially for those of the Family Initiated into the Outer Mysteries.

The Witching Hours

The Witching Hour, according to a twenty-four-hour daily chronology, begins at the stroke of midnight and continues for the first three hours of the new day. Various writers have called this time the "dark night of the soul." From the Outer Circle perspective, during the Witching Hour, a "door" or "passage" opens between the Corporeal and subtle realities, and Astral beings such as the Strigoi Morte can more easily make contact with the Corporeal world. Mortal legends claim that this time is when predatory spirits such as the Incubus, Succubus, and old hag come to steal the Lifeforce of mortals. The Witching Hour is also an efficient time for practicing higher forms of the Art of Gathering Energy, since mortals are asleep and naturally projecting into the Astral by dreaming. We use the belief stamped on the mortal-minded collective unconsciousness through superstitions and legends as a tool to empower our ritual.

The Dark Moon

The Dark Moon (also called the New Moon) is an appealing time for ritual since this is the darkest time of the month. As viewed from Earth, no moon appears in the sky since no sunlight reflects from it in a manner that is visible from our planet. Psychologically, the Dark Moon aids in a deep Nightside experience where the Outer Circle Strigoi Vii is more easily able to enter the supernatural Nightside.

The Wheel of the Year provides an annual framework of holidays and festivals that may be applied to Strigoi Vii ritual and magick. The holidays on the Wheel of the Year either fall on cross-quarter days, such as equinoxes or solstices, or on other chronologically significant days. They are of ancient origin and have been celebrated by humanity for thousands of years under different names and in slightly different forms. For example, Nightside Festival or the winter solstice (which falls on December 21 or 22 in the Western Hemisphere and marks the longest night of the year) was celebrated by the Druids thousands of years ago. Now, a huge amount of mortal-minded individuals celebrate this holiday on December 25 as Christmas. On this day we tap the huge amount of excess Lifeforce collectively released by the common focus of all the mortal-minded Christmas shoppers! We make use of this and similar days of power to fuel our ritual intent.

For the purposes of the Strigoi Vii, there are two significant holidays on the Wheel of the Year, as discussed in "The Strigoi Vii Prospectus." The first is Samhain, All Hallows Eve on October 31. On this festival day, secular humans and occultists alike turn their collective thoughts and energies to supernatural creatures and denizens of the night. The second is May Eve on the night of April 30, known in Germany as Walpurgisnacht or Hexennacht. German legends say that on this night, witches would meet on Brocken Mountain to commune with their gods and hold unholy ritual. These and many other dates throughout the year are ideal focus points for aiding ritual due to their prevalence in the human consciousness. Refer to "The Strigoi Vii Prospectus" for more information on each of the festivals.

Again, ritual timing is mainly an aid for gathering the human collective consciousness and helping the celebrant focus. Clavicula   Sangraal Sorcery is not reliant on these concepts of Strigoi Vii magick and ceremony.

Location of Ritual

Strigoi Vii rituals are best done in secure and private Sanctums that are free of distractions from the mundane world. For group ritual, it is best to choose a neutral location. For this reason, as well as issues of personal privacy and confidentiality, it is best not to hold group ritual in a private domicile. Public rituals, both group and solitary, are discouraged in most situations because of the associated distractions and lack of privacy.

The majority of Strigoi Vii who participate in group ritual reside in urban settings, so indoor Sanctums are preferred for two reasons. Firstly, it is very difficult to find a private, isolated space outdoors in a large city. Secondly, an indoor Sanctum screens the rite from mortal-minded eyes while still allowing the celebrants to tap the large repository of excess Lifeforce that surges all about them. If a group of Strigoi Vii wishes to perform an exclusively outdoor ritual, such as the Rite of Bast, they should consider renting a private campsite outside the city or making a trip to a secluded wilderness area. It is also possible to rent cabins or houses in rural areas on a short-term basis.

Some solitary Strigoi Vii have the luxury of setting up their own permanent private temple in their home. If possible, this is ideal. If this is not possible due to cohabitation, or simply because of lack of space, we suggest at least choosing a particular area of your residence for ritual use, even if it takes some preparation to ready that area. For example, a living room can be easily adapted to a ritual space once chairs are moved out of the way, the floor cleared, and the coffee table cleaned off for use as an altar. Strigoi Vii tools can be discreetly stored in a chest or drawer when not in use. A space in which rituals are repeatedly performed will build up energy over a time, thus aiding future ritual workings.

For group rituals, we suggest choosing a neutral location. In the old stories, vampires had to be invited across the threshold before they could enter a private home. While this is only a legend, it contains a grain of common sense. Most obviously, it is simply wise to be discriminating in regard as to whom you invite to your home!

However, on a subtle level, your personal ritual space is also a place of power. When you invite others to join you in that space, you are allowing them to tap into the energies you have invested in it, and they, in turn, will be investing some of their own energies. Instead, We suggest renting a space that is convenient and affordable for all the participants. Such spaces may include hotel rooms, rehearsal rooms in a dance or music studio, or even a short-term apartment or house rental. Online websites and the classified section of newspapers will list such rentals.

Many Strigoi Vii wish to do rituals in public places such as the Ancient Egyptian wing of a museum or in sacred sites such as the Pyramids of Giza, Stonehenge, or the Mayan pyramids in Mexico. While such locations may yield powerful results, they are also highly public. In such places, the Strigoi Vii must be extraordinarily discreet and careful to blend in with the crowds. Otherwise, they are likely to face unwanted mortal-minded intrusions such as suspicious security guards or curious tourists. Controlled environments are best for ritual. It is difficult to achieve and validate results with constant interruptions.

It is possible for the Strigoi Vii to perform ritual within their own mind by utilizing visualization only. Silent Communion, detailed in Liber Morrah, is an example of one such ritual. A Strigoi Vii may choose to perform this type of ritual in very energetically charged locations, such as in churches or tourist destinations like the Eiffel Tower. In this case, the Strigoi Vii gathers the vast amount of Lifeforce swirling about them and immediately offers it to the Strigoi Morte before any of it has had an opportunity to dissipate. This sort of ritual is one possible solution to the problems of performing ritual in a public place. However, it is still possible for the Strigoi Vii to inadvertently call attention to themselves during this type of ritual, especially if they begin to "lose themselves" in the offering or Recoiling. Public ritual should always be veiled from the eyes of the mortal-minded and attempted only if it can be "hidden in plain sight."

Regalia: The Tools of Ritual

Regalia are items and tools used within ritual to focus the will and direct energies. The term was originally used to refer to the insignia and privileges of a ruling sovereign. The word regalia itself derives from the Latin regalis, which is in turn derived from rex, or "king."

Here are some common tools used within Strigoi Vii ritual. Not every Strigoi Vii will use each of these tools in every ritual, but all the tools listed below (save candles) are used in the Sanguine Mass.

The Altar is the center point of the ritual, and on it the tools are placed. Traditionally, the altar faces west and is covered with a black cloth. An altar is usually a sturdy table about four feet high, six feet long, and three feet wide. However, any suitable and available table may be used.

The Ar'thana is a black-hilted, double-edged knife or sword that symbolically represents the drawing of blood. It is used for controlling the movement of Lifeforce in the Subtle. It is important to note that the ar'thana is never used to draw physical blood. Its function is metaphoric only.

The Bell sets the Corporeal patterns and mood of the ritual. Any material save gold is acceptable. Crystal bells often produce a most delicate chime. Some Strigoi Vii like to use temple bells or other similar instruments, such as gongs or Tibetan singing bowls. When a bell is not available, the celebrant may briskly and loudly clap their hands as an alternative.

Candles are used for lighting and mood in many rituals. However, note that if a Communion with the Strigoi Morte is to take place, candlelight should be avoided. The preferred lighting for rituals incorporating Communion is explained below. Symbolically, red candles represent Lifeforce and blood, white candles represent the Dayside, black represents the Nightside, purple the Twilight, and silver the moon.

Chalices or goblets are symbolic in that they represent the Offering of Lifeforce and the Blood of the Family. Silver or pewter are the preferred materials, although glass, pottery, or china are also acceptable. Ornamental designs that include Dragons or Strigoi Vii glyphs are best for decoration. Gold is discouraged. Red wine is the traditional drink contained by the chalice in ritual, but any natural liquid such as fruit or vegetable juice, milk, or even water may be used, according to personal taste.

The Black Mirror is the gateway to the subtle reality; hence, the Strigoi Vii phrase "beyond the mirror." It is traditionally set at eye level on the western wall, on the altar, or on the floor so that the celebrants can peer into the subtle realities as if they are sailing in a glass-bottomed boat. The speculum may be set in an ornate frame or simply rendered, according to the tastes of the Strigoi Vii. Many Strigoi Vii prefer to obtain a speculum in which the glass is convex, or curved outward, which may create interesting visual impressions. If a black mirror is not available, then any readily available mirror may be used.

The Wand represents the direction of the Will. It can be made of any type of wood, metal (except gold), or other substances, such as crystal. The wand will often have Strigoi Vii glyphs engraved on it to focus will.

The Mood

The Outer Sanctum is a preparation room and is not used for the actual ritual. This room should be open to light. Here, members change into their ritual attire, discuss the elements of the ritual, and meditate in preparation. If Black Swans are present, they should be welcomed in the Outer Sanctum. The Outer Sanctum represents the Dayside world.

The Decompression Chamber is a gate or portal. It should be a doorway or a hallway between the Outer Sanctum and the Inner Sanctum. The Decompression Chamber is where the participants psychologically journey from the Dayside into the Nightside toward the Inner Sanctum.

The Inner Sanctum is the actual chamber where the ritual takes place. The Inner Sanctum should be established in a private chamber, secured from any mundane intrusion. Additionally, it should be completely blocked from outside light. If the Inner Sanctum is an outdoor location, it should be as private and isolated as possible. Either way, it should be separate and secure from the mundane world, so that the Shroud Between Worlds can be safely broken down and crossed.

Lighting is extremely important for ritual in which Communion with the Strigoi Morte is to take place. In this case, any light present in the Inner Sanctum should be that which does not disrupt Ethereal patterns, such as the light from a red bulb as used in a photo lab, the blue light used for night activities in the military, or a Sterno candle. Other light sources, such as sunlight, white light bulbs, or normal candles may disrupt the crossing between worlds. If candlelight is absolutely necessary, it should be kept to a minimum.

Music is a powerful tool in setting the mood of ritual. Drums, rattles, bells, and gongs are common tools in large group rituals incorporating live music. If live music is not available, prerecorded music such as the chanting of cloister monks, tribal rhythms, or ambient or gothic music also will work well. Any music chosen should be appropriate and in accordance with the tastes of the members performing the ritual. Make sure that the music does not drown out the voices of the presiding member and the celebrants.

Incense is an important tool, as scent is sometimes considered the most powerful of the five senses. Any incense scent chosen should be pleasing and should aid in the ritual atmosphere. Suggestions include frankincense or myrrh. Many different varieties of commercially prepared incense are readily available.

Ritual Garb

See Vampyre Aesthetics & Motifs in Liber Jahira. Clothing within Strigoi Vii ritual can be just as important an aspect as meditation or ritual tools. It is often said that the "clothes make the man," and certainly changing one's clothing changes one's mindset and can be considered shapeshifting. Consider the mortal-minded leaving behind their ordinary identities and inhibitions upon donning a costume on Halloween. When an actor applies their makeup and puts on their character's costume, they have "become" that character. Think of the office worker who changes her clothing be-fore heading out for a night on the town! Garments, to a great extent, determine one's mood and way of thinking. Therefore, the Strigoi Vii can utilize this tool of the Glamour to their advantage in ritual. Here are some forms of ritual garb to inspire you.

Nightklad (seek Nightklad Black Veil) is best used for solitary ritual and groups of individuals who are well-acquainted with each other and comfortable with nudity. Wearing nothing other than darkness is an excel-lent tool for experiencing and stimulating the free flow of energies. Being Nightklad helps create a psychological and sensual freedom seldom experi-enced elsewhere. However, always make sure that nudity is used for ritual intent and not abused by those who might try to manipulate others or induce unwanted sexual situations.

Masks (see *Masks Black Veil*) often add an element of anonymity to those wearing them, in both solitary and group rituals. They are thus a popular tool for increasing the drama of ritual and separating the celebrants from their Dayside. Masks come in a variety of styles, ranging from theatri-cal characters to predatory animals to fantasy creatures such as dragons and griffons. One example of inspiration popular amongst many Strigoi Vii is the masked sex ritual performed in the film *Eyes Wide Shut*.

Robes are an alternative when a Nightklad ritual is not possible or desired. Long, hooded robes effectively mask the identity of the wearer when anonymity is a focus of the ritual. Generally speaking, a simple black robe is most popular ritual attire among Strigoi Vii. The robe should have a large hood and be loose and comfortable. Often, individuals will choose to customize their robes with glyphs significant to the Strigoi Vii. While no material is preferred, be aware that synthetic fabrics are often quite flammable, which may be a concern if an open flame is present in the ritual chamber.

Costumes can range from the theatrical to the erotic and may include an ensemble "transforming" the wearer into a deity, stimulating garments of latex or leather, or the attire of an ancient Roman or a Druid priestess. As detailed in Liber Jahira, in group ritual celebrants who identify with the Pulses of Ramkht, Mradu, and Kitra may choose to wear garb that reflect a particular aspect of their Current. Costumes can aid in the psychodrama of ritual and stimulate the subconscious. Often a costume can be used to "tap into" a particular thoughtform, thus enhancing the experience of ritual.

Jewelry and Artifacts can assist in communicating the role or duty of each celebrant or help in enhancing the persona of each individual. All participants should proudly wear their Legacy Ankhs in ritual, as this communicates dedication to the Family and to life and is a symbol of respect and kinship with the Ancestors. Iron and gold jewelry should be avoided; silver is the preferred material.

Phases of the Sanguine Mass
Depending on the individual, group, resources available, and type of ritual, there are many phases of ritual. The following are the general steps taken in a wide variety of Strigoi Vii rituals, including the Sanguine Mass.

1. The Prelude
This involves the preparation of the Inner Sanctum and the ritual celebrant(s). The celebrant(s) should have gathered their fill of Lifeforce in the days preceding the ritual in order to prepare themselves for the Offering or fueling the ritual. It is best advised that the celebrant(s) not drink or ingest any form of mind-altering substances for at least twenty-four hours before the ritual.

Before the ritual can begin, the celebrant (or presiding member or appropriate Deacon in group ritual) must prepare the Inner Sanctum and tools of ritual. The Inner Sanctum, as explained above, must be an isolated environment free of distractions. Only those who are Initiated or attuned to the Mysteries of Strigoi Vii should enter the Inner Sanctum from the time of its preparation to the end of the ritual. The presence of the un-Initiated will cause unwanted distractions and lead the Strigoi Morte to ignore the ritual and refuse the offering. However, this obviously does not apply in the case of performance rituals.

The ritual is best performed in darkness and with as little electromagnetic interference as possible. If indoors, electronic devices such as cell phones should be turned off in the chamber where the Inner Sanctum is to be erected. The lights should be turned off, and all sources of outside light, such as windows, should be covered as completely as possible.

Tools and regalia should be prepared and laid out for ease of use. Getting dressed (or Nightklad) helps induce the mindset of the ritual and serves as a meditative preparation for the celebrant(s). In the case of group ritual, the presiding member should assign ritual roles and make sure everyone knows their place and duties. Assigning duties is essential if the ritual is led by more than one person.

Meditation, yoga, or minor energy work before the ritual can also raise energies and help bring the celebrant(s) into the mindset of the ritual. In the case of group ritual, a communal meditation will also aid in the group agreement and focus. The celebrant(s) should also tend to any Corporeal needs that may interfere with the ritual. Remember that proper planning and preparation can be just as important in achieving results as the ritual itself.

The Sealing and Banishing is very important and should be done within the Inner Sanctum before any celebrants enter. In group ritual, the sealing and banishing is usually conducted by a celebrant associated with the Mradu Pulses. The celebrant points their blade toward each wall, tracing its borders and thus erecting a subtle barrier. They then state, "By my will I seal this wall." The process should be repeated for each wall, including the floor and ceiling. The celebrant should then repeat the process for any reflective surface in the room, including mirrors, television sets, computer screens, and so on. While pointing the ar'thana toward the reflective surface, the celebrant should state, "By my will I seal this portal." At this point, the Gate from the Outer to Inner Sanctum should be left open. Once the celebrant has sealed all walls and portals, they should then, using the flow of their breath and the energies of their subtle body, banish all negative energies toward the Gate, pushing them out with their own will. Once this is done, the Inner Sanctum is prepared, and the Cleansings can begin.

Cleansings are powerful tools to prepare the mind, body, and spiritual centers before ritual. In solitary ritual, the celebrant should cleanse themself by taking a bath or shower before ritual (if possible), or at least washing their hands and face. They should also meditate, focusing on directing stagnant energies away from their subtle bodies, thus allowing an improved energy flow. The solitary celebrant may also choose to utilize a cleansing solution, such as Florida water (a cologne used as a cleansing agent in many South American and Caribbean spiritual paths such as Santeria and Voudou), as a Corporeal sign and trigger. In group ritual, the celebrants should be cleansed at the Gate to the Inner Sanctum. Again, this is traditionally done by those who associated with the Mradu Pulse. The individual doing the cleansing may focus their intent and "push" away stagnant energies from each celebrant, or "anoint" them with Florida water.

A celebrant, preferably one attuned to Mradu should, with the ar'thana or wand, touch each wall, finishing by reaching toward the gate, and state, *"By my will I seal this Sanctum."*

2. Entering the Sanctum
This should take place only once everything has been properly prepared. Only then is it time to enter the space where the Inner Sanctum has been established. Within the Inner Sanctum, the participant passes from the Dayside of rationality, materialism, and logic into the Nightside, where everything is permitted.

As the Gate is the entry from the Outer Sanctum to the Inner Sanctum, the Portal between the Corporeal and the subtle worlds is the speculum, or black mirror. Thus, the Inner Sanctum is a place between worlds, where the subtle and physical realities touch and merge. For best results in ritual, the celebrant(s) should fully accept that they are at the crossroads of worlds once they enter the Inner Sanctum. Anything that is possible in any world is possible in the Inner Sanctum. These potentialities include extraordinary experiences, the revelation of magickal realities, and, of course, tangible manifestation of the Strigoi Morte.

The presiding adeptus or priest/ess or an assisting Mradu should point a ar'thana a the chest of each celebrant and ask *"Do you come in love and loyalty? If you own free will? State your Vampyre Name."* If they say yes, then they are permitted to enter.

3. The Invokation

This serves dually as the Invokation of the Current within the celebrant(s) and the declaration of intent and purpose for the ritual and the focus point of will by which the Sanctum will be consecrated. Due to the lack of light in the Inner Sanctum, for best results this and all future spoken parts of the ritual should be memorized or done spontaneously. The presider should face toward the west. Clapping hands loudly twice or ringing the bell a few times is a good way to focus the mood and cleanse the air. Then the words of the Invokation should be spoken slowly and with deep passion. As a sample, the Invokation of Vampyre Current is as follows:

> *Hear me! I stand within this Sanctum.*
> *Tonight I celebrate with my True Family.*
> *Blood calls out unto Blood, and the Blood of Vampyre Current within*
> *me cries out to be heard.*
> *Let nothing keep me from my purpose, for I am Strigoi Vii!*
> *I turn my gaze to You, the Fraters and Sorors of Our Family.*
> *You, who share Our Immortal inheritance, are welcome here with me*
> *in this sacred space.*
> *I have gathered the life of mortals.*
> *I offer this greatest of gifts to You, the true Elders of Our Family!*
> *I call You forth so I may receive Your Ancient energies and thus join You*
> *in the glory of Immortality!*
> *I am here to escape death and seize eternal life!*
> *Drink from me, and We shall live forever!*
> *Ancestors, come forth into this chamber!*
> *Vampyre Current, I invoke Thee! Hail Elorath!*

4. The Invitations

This is mainly used for Communion rites such as the Sanguine Mass or rituals where the Strigoi Morte and the Current are invited to aid or protect a ritual. This should be done after the preparation and Invokation. The Invitation is similar to processes to the the LBRP (lesser banishing ritual of the pentagram) in occult and neopagan paradigms. For each of these directions, the celebrant calls the associated Pulses. In group ritual, the Invitation is often sent by those individuals associated with the Pulse Ramkht.

Once the Inner Sanctum has been sealed and the Invokation declared, the Invitation to the Vampyre Current of Elorath is sent forth. The celebrant performs the Invitation by holding the wand upright whilst standing at each angle and then ringing the bell or clapping their hands after each. The Invitations are sent to the south, concluding in the west. A sample template for the Invitations to the Strigoi Morte follows:

> Before Me — *Mradu, I see the gate of stone. Let my own inner power open that gate! Mradu, guardians of the Current, I humbly request your presence. Protect and strengthen me. Hail Mradu!*

> Behind Me — (this sets up the axis of materiality) *Kitra, I face the gate of fire in passion and love. Kitra, weavers of the Current, I turn my gaze to you. Come now with beauty and delight. Hail Kitra!*

> To My Right —*Ramkht, I gaze upon the gate of the Zhep'r, the breath of life. Ramkht, I call on your wisdom. Come to this sacred chamber and lend me your insight. Hail Ramkht!*

> To My Left — (this sets up the numinous axis) *Elorath! Let the Gates open between the worlds! It is my True Nature that wills it to be so! I look upon you, and I see no beginning and no end; I look upon the Greatest of all Dragons, and I see my Self. Ancestors, I humbly invite You to this Sanctum, where You are welcome. I have prepared an Offering! Come forth and feast! Hail Elorath!*

5. The Offering

This takes place after the aeonic words of power have been spoken and an invitation to the Strigoi Morte have been sent for them to come with the Vampyre Current. This can also be used to offer the Strigoi Morte energy in exchange for support in any specific ritual. The celebrant(s) should subsequently focus all their energies into the speculum, recognizing it as a portal to the subtle world. This is the most sacred of actions; the time when we offer our most precious gift to our Ancestors for their use as well as ours.

In order to release the stored Lifeforce for the Offering, it is often helpful to control the breath on which it is carried toward the black mirror. The celebrant should inhale deeply through the nose, then release the Offering in an outward, extended breath, exclusively through the mouth. Vocalizing a long vowel sound, such as hoooo, with each outward breath may aid in the process.

Placing the speculum on the floor can give the effect of a glass-bottomed boat, whilst putting it eye level on the western wall presents the horizontal view into the subtle world. Some Strigoi Vii prefer to hold the speculum in their hands, so as to bring it close to their face. Various positions should be tried, as some may be more effective than others.

The greater the offering, the more likely is it that the Strigoi Morte and Vampyre Current will manifest and return pure and refined energies to the celebrant(s). Smaller offerings are not as effective, since the entire process of Communion takes a certain amount of energy to perform.

The process of releasing the Lifeforce should be continued as long as possible, even if it means working to the point of exhaustion or experiencing discomfort. The release of Lifeforce should continue until the Strigoi Morte manifest and accept the offering. Be careful about your own health, as this process is strenuous and those with serious health problems may experience negative results. If you have any doubt as to your own physical ability to participate in ritual, you should refrain from taking part. Similarly, those who are ill, physically hurt, or who are taking prescription medication should abstain from ritual, as these factors will interfere with energy flow and can cause detrimental results to the individual.

In group ritual, the presiding member should be careful to monitor the other celebrants and ensure no one is in danger of being overcome by the offering process. If a celebrant is overcome to the point of distress or collapse during the offering, whether in solitary or group ritual, they should immediately stop the offering and sit quietly or lie on the floor until they have recovered. If the celebrant is drained to a point where they are physically unable to continue with ritual, they should bring a halt to the ritual (if in solitary ritual) or disengage and wait until the other celebrants have finished (in group ritual). In either case, afterward the celebrant should take special care to restore their energies and maintain their health. They should drink water and eat food high in energy, such as carbohydrates or sugars, and of course absorb energy as soon as possible to replace that which was depleted. Often, when a celebrant is overcome during ritual, it means they did not build up a large enough fund of Lifeforce before the ritual. That individual should be careful to absorb a larger amount of Lifeforce when preparing for future rituals.

6. The Recoiling

In Communion rituals, this is where the real Nightside experiences begin. If the Strigoi Morte have responded to the Invitation and accepted the offering, they will show signs of their presence through actual manifestation. In return for the Offering of Lifeforce, they will send a gift of Ambrosia to the celebrant(s). Ambrosia is highly refined energy that is essential in building Zhep'r and achieving Immortality. Achieving a successful Recoiling is an honor and a sign that one is truly of the Family. Only those worthy will be privileged to experience a Recoiling, during which there is an immense reverse flow of energy into the celebrant's subtle body. The Recoiling of energy can be great or small if it occurs at all. If the Strigoi Morte have not been satisfied, little or no Recoiling will take place. However, this does not mean the ritual has been a failure, as the simple experience of being in the presence of the Strigoi Morte is enough to potentially increase the Zhep'r of any Strigoi Vii.

The Recoiling of energies will be a fresh infusion of pure Ambrosia and Zhep'r from the veins of the Ancients into the celebrant's depleted subtle body. There are many signals of a successful Recoiling, which vary from person to person. Some common signals include a tugging sensation on the solar plexus, the sensation of being touched, the impression of tingling in the fingertips, ringing in the ears, hearing whispers of one's name or other words, or a plethora of heightened emotions such as love, joy, or fear. Some celebrants experience a change in environmental temperature, see sparks of light or after-images (as if they looked at a bright light and then went into a dark location), or perceive images of shadowy phantasm-like figures. It is not uncommon, especially in solitary ritual, for the celebrant to experience a spontaneous and prolonged orgasm during the Recoiling. The more powerful the experiences, the greater the degree to which the offering has been accepted.

The Communion ritual is the most basic form of interaction with the Strigoi Morte and Vampyre Current is an experience that will result in Zhep'r for the Strigoi Vii. It is necessary to achieve a successful Communion, including Recoiling, in order to complete the Mystery of Calmae.

7. Closing

This marks the formal end of the ritual. Upon the completion of the ritual, the Ancients & Vampyre Current should be honored as They depart. During the closing, the celebrant(s) bid the Ancestors farewell and thank Them for Their presence. The celebrant or presiding member should raise the chalice toward the portal and state in a firm and empowered voice these or similar words:

> *"I raise this chalice to You, oh Ancients. Let it symbolize the Blood that is Our life and Vampyre Current! I drink in remembrance of the eternal Pact of my True Family, and my True Nature! I drink in love and loyalty, for I am Strigoi Vii, the Living Vampire, and I am Immortal! Hail Elorath!"*

The presider should look into the mirror and into their own eyes, then drink deeply from the chalice. Then the presider should clap their hands twice or ring a bell three times to signify thanks. In group ritual, the chalice should then be passed to the next celebrant counterclockwise, until each celebrant has drunk, each speaking words of thanks, if they so desire.

The presider should point the tip of the ar'thana or wand into the mirror. They should then extinguish all light and, in the absolute darkness, sincerely pronounce: *"So now it is done!"* followed by clapping the hands, a Howl or ringing a bell thrice to mark the conclusion of ritual.

8. The Return

Once the ritual has been finished, it's time to return to the Dayside. The lights should be reignited, the ritual tools removed, and the altars covered. Everyone moves on to the celebration.

9. The Celebration

After the ritual is completed and the celebrant(s) have returned to the Dayside, they need to acknowledge the need for restoration and balance. Drinking or eating is a good way to restore one's equilibrium after an especially intense ritual. Foods containing carbohydrates, such as bread, cakes, or rice provide high levels of Corporeal energy and are especially grounding. Chocolate is preferred by many Strigoi Vii, as it has been long considered a delicacy and associated with magick and ritual.

Summation

In the preceding pages, We have presented the core elements and traditions of Strigoi Vii ritual, including the format for Communion ritual within the Sanguine Mass. The aspiring Calmae should assiduously experiment with these ritual formulations and elements. Each individual and group is different, as we of the Family are all individuals; therefore, no one form of ritual will be most effective for all celebrants or ritual groups.

The guidelines we offer here are tested and proven to yield results for those of the Family with dedicated practice. However, you should always feel free to adjust them as suits your needs. Discuss your ritual experiences with others of the Family and contribute your own. The Family evolves both individually and collectively. However, the aspiring Calmae should first experiment alone and achieve results be- fore progressing to communal ritual work. Remember that you cannot solve the Mystery of Calmae until you have achieved a successful Communion with the Strigoi Morte. For in the end, only results matter.

CHAPTER 26
ENERGY MANIPULATION TECHNIQUES

"Change your thoughts, and you change your world."

—Norman Vincent Peale

The Strigoi Vii is more attuned to the subtle layers of reality than the average mortal, due to the higher vibration of their subtle bodies. This is spiritual alchemy; even before an awakening, the potential Vampyre may have experiences that are undisciplined uses of energy manipulations. With training and discipline, "techniques" can be used to focus and amplify these abilities. Those who are of the Current, awakened or un-Awakened, are sensitive to fluxes in subtle energies and have what would seem like latent psychic abilities. Some potential Living Vampyres un-Awakened to their nature have become professional psychics, healers, and mediums. Many turn away from their nature, attributing these experiences to delusion, and never taste the fullness of Zhep'r. They deny themselves this freedom out of social conditioning or a sense of displacement. To them, the apprehension of the subtle nature of reality keeps them from "fitting in" to mortal society.

They will create excuse after excuse as to why they do not rise into their own opportunity of accepting their potential for Immortal-mindedness. These individuals are the iconoclasts of Strigoi Vii society—they reject their own potential and continue to identify with the mortal mindset.

Knowledge of the difference between Invokation and Evokation is an essential step toward mastering techniques. Evokations are outside the subtle body, whilst Invokations are internal. Grounding, for example, is an evocation because is deals with pushing energies and manifesting external workings, whilst centering is an invocation and works inward.

For many of the un-Awakened, potential Vampyres or not, the process of seeing beyond the five senses can be a terrifying prospect. The perceptions of children are usually not considered "normal," as the child does not hold the agreed-on adult perceptions of what is "real" and what is not. Instead, the child simply perceives and experiences without measuring their experience against a standard of what is deemed possible, normal, and rational. It is not uncommon for children to see spirits or "invisible friends," engage in psychic activity, or have premonitions and lucid dreams. Some other markers of the potential to sense the subtle realities include an intrinsic sense of geography, a unique sense of humor, love of life, strong sense of empathy, love of ancient cultures, interest in the mysterious or supernatural, and an abiding sense of personal strength. However, one must realize there is no one set of these markers. Strigoi Vii are often well-rounded individuals who have many varied interests, many of which are strongly rooted in the Corporeal, such as sports or other physical activities. This reflects our need for a powerful connection to the Corporeal, which is the foundation for the flow of energies.

While the Vampyre is wise to solve the Outer Mysteries, it serves to bring their understanding toward the first steps of Mastery. This intimate connection to the subtle realms offers the Strigoi Vii the experience to interact with energies most mortals will never experience. There are many mortals, other species of Awakened beings and, of course, other tribes of vampires/Vampyres, who also interact with these energies. Most Strigoi Vii have a strong and unique connection to these subtle realms.

Here are a few of the "techniques" that are essential for the Nightside perspective to be fully embraced and for Zhep'r to flourish. Meditation is at the center of all successful energy work and manipulation techniques. We have already explored a standard regimen of meditations such as the Vampyres' Throne and the Vampyres' Surjaah. A meditation is a shift in consciousness and focus from the normal reality to one of relaxation and alternative states of consciousness, usually achieved without the influence of drugs. It brings our energy into focus and creates equilibrium between the layers of the Self. One does not have to be in a lotus position or use charms or chants to "properly" meditate. There are many forms of meditation, which the average mortal-minded person does not consider. For example, intense and focused activities such as dance, performance, yoga, running, sex, creating art, and even driving can allow your mind to move into these alternative states. What is most effective for each individual depends on their nature and the state they wish to enter.

Once the shift has come, meditation is essential not only for higher levels of energy work, but the most basic steps of filtering, grounding, and centering energy. Breath and breathing are the most basic elements of meditation. Breath controls your flow of Lifeforce in and out of your body, and breath control naturally centers and grounds you.

Deep breathing should begin any meditation. Many breath techniques advise you to begin breathing in through your nose and out through your mouth, expanding your diaphragm and using it as your focal point of control. This simple technique, if practiced correctly and continuously, will result in relaxation of the mind and body as the two come into balance.

Once breathing has been mastered, bring the mind into the equation. Begin Throning or simply sit still in a relaxed position for as long as you can. Let your mind wander for a while, then try and bring it into focus. Cleanse your mind of all random thoughts and visuals. Focus on the pleasure and calmness of just existing. If you have a specific focus for meditation, which you often have prepared beforehand, bring it forth when you feel it is the best time to focus on it.

Rituals are meditations and can be truly empowering. Many paradigms and groups employ ritual, from African tribes to Voudou practitioners. Meditative states can be created through dance, scent, melodrama, and music. These are done to achieve a trancelike state that can be used for Astral projection, dreaming, celebration, or Ascension, among many others.

Chanting is a powerful way to evoke trance but is best done in a group as it depends on harmonizing with others' voices.

There are many levels on which we can achieve meditation. Most effective meditation comes from sensory modification, stimulation, or deprivation. One can simply meditate, such as in the Surjaah, in order to plan their day and harmonize themselves. A deep level of meditation and trance can be achieved by body suspension and similar procedures practiced by modern primitives. Tattooing and permanent body modifications are also a powerful experience. However, deep meditations should be prepared in advance in order to be truly meaningful. The Strigoi Vii should also use good judgment when embarking on any process, such as tattooing or piercing, which is not easily reversible.

In closing, explore and test, experiment and validate. Each of us is a unique being and what works for one person will not be of benefit to the next.

Perceiving is the ability to discern subtle energies to which We are Awakened, such as auras of the Ethereal body and the flow of Lifeforce. Perception of deeper forms of energy are most often done through Astral projection and dreamwalking, as they are less tangible. Use of psychic abilities is actually perception on this level, and many use the Astral as their gateway, especially when working over long distances, as time and space are perceived differently in the subtle layers of reality.

Energy can be also perceived in ways analogous to the Corporeal senses, such as a scent or sound. This is most often the case with Ambient energy. One can simply "smell" or "listen," and even those who are only slightly Awakened can sense such energies if they pay attention.

The aura is the most basic form of energy sensing beyond Ambient energy. Auras are the excess energy radiated from the outermost Ethereal layer of the subtle body. Astral energies such as emotion appear as colors and can be used to determine the nature of the being emitting the aura, their emotional state, and their state of health and spirit. There are countless books on this, so we will only go into basic details on aura perception.

Vampyres' Halo Hands Technique

The first and foremost technique is manifesting energy into the hands and holding them up toward a dim light in order to perceive the energy. Of course, first try this on the most convenient subject: yourself! Push the energy into your hands and begin to focus on them. Once you have begun to feel heat and vibration, you will begin to see a dim and blurry halo a few inches off the skin. Like a mime, hold your hands upward toward an invisible wall, and the halo will become visible. You will also be able to feel the energies between the hands as a subtle pressure and resistance. This is the thickness of the focused and dense Lifeforce in the Ethereal body.

One experiment involves manifesting tendrils of energy. What differentiates a human aura from that of a Vampyric spirit is these tendrils, which are in effect the "subtle fangs." Once you have learned to perceive auras, this will allow you to differentiate between mortal and Vampyre. More advanced techniques will allow you to actually read auras and determine the nature of a being. Strigoi Vii have radiant and powerful auras of swirling colors with a high rate of vibration, almost alight with what could be perceived as a divine fire. The auras of psychic vampires are dark and often contain small streaks of purple and very disparate tendrils. More advanced ethical psychic vampires have been able to manage their auras and heal them temporarily as they feed properly. This is their curse and shows their true nature. Human auras vary in comparison to the consistent nature of the auras of Awakened beings.

Auras also vary in size and health according to the individual. Divinely empowered individuals can be as radiant as Strigoi Vii; this is how they channel their abilities either consciously or unconsciously. Auras vary in distance from a few millimeters to about a meter away from an individual, again depending on the health and strength of the individual's subtle body. The auras are also layered, with the core being the actual double of the individual, their "second skin." Layers of aura move out and become imperceptible to all but the most sensitive. When we perform the Art of Gathering Energy on a surface level, We are making contact with the outer layers of the aura. Deeper forms of Gathering Lifeforce must pierce these layers to draw energy directly from the source, or "soul" of the human.

Perceiving the aura with your hands is entirely possible. A good example is "energetic play" between two individuals. You can use the force of the aura to "disarm" the other individual, or to experiment with pressure. You can touch the outer layers of the aura or mix them. This is one of the ways in which we penetrate the aura. Remember, aura contact between two individuals is subtle body contact.

There are many tools which the un-Awakened use to scientifically attempt to perceive the aura. Approach such tools with a skeptical mindset, as they are not fully scientifically validated. Some examples include Kirlian photography, which was accidently discovered and pioneered by Semyon Kirlian in the 1930s. It is often used to photograph the subtle body, most particularly the aura. Scientists working with Kirlian photography were able to photograph a portion of a leaf, working under the assumption that all parts of a living thing possess a residual energetic aura of the whole. The "phantom limb" showed up as a complete leaf. There was even an experiment involving Kirlian photography in 2006 for a History Channel special called "Vampire Secrets." In this experiment, a Kheprian priest showed a darker aura than a Strigoi Vii Kitra, who had a radiant, fiery aura. Brighter and more vibrant auras are the signatures of Living Vampyres, whilst the darker ones are often the signatures of psychic vampires. The touch of the psychic vampire left a black mark on the subtle body of the Kitra, which of course healed quickly.

Utilize the applications and techniques listed here, and experiment to discover your own methods. Each of Us has our own talents and abilities. We should focus on and hone those manipulations.

Vampyres' Energy Filtering Technique

Filtering is a defensive technique for Vampyres selecting which energies to procure. The Adeptus Living Vampire never shields, because shielding partially blocks and cuts off the Strigoi Vii from the flow of energy, which they must interact with at all times, as every being must interact with energy at all times. However, sometimes there are energetic attachments that we do not wish to bring into ourselves, and we must be selective with them. The foundations of filtering are important at the Nightside level and for more advanced forms of the Art of Gathering Energy.

In order to properly filter, one must have an understanding of the difference between Lifeforce and emotional energies, as we are filtering out the negative emotions and keeping the Lifeforce. This is the difference between a traditional psychic vampire who feeds on emotion and a Living Vampyre who gathers pure Lifeforce. Emotional "baggage" such as negative emotion can be absorbed into our subtle bodies and affect us if we do not filter properly. Filtering is often unconscious and varies with the stability of mind; however, as with the Art of Gathering Energy, we benefit from directing this consciously with the will as a manipulation. We can choose which energies benefit us the most, and the others are simply converted. Of course, not all filters will be perfect, and this technique takes time to master and develop. Filters can also be reversed to project "negatively charged" energy to ward off psychic attacks and subtle beings.

To consciously filter, one must ground and center, then envision a bubble or focused layer of the aura, which is like porous parts in the Corporeal skin. Fuel the filter with Lifeforce and shape your Ethereal body into a bubble-like shape, often visualized in a violet color. This technique is facilitated by Ambient Gathering, as the absorbed Lifeforce will give your Ethereal body strength and form. One advantage of filtering is that it keeps out harmful energy such as that of diseases and drugs. Filtering is the first technique used to protect the Vampyre and their spiritual health. There are more advanced techniques, such as converting energy, which eliminates the need for filtering in most cases.

Once the energy bubble has been created, apply will, visualize, breathe, and pull inward to the contours of the Ethereal subtle body. This will become like a suit of armor through which you can choose to allow specific energies in and out. Let the filter function like a wetsuit, keeping "warmer" energies in and keeping out the "colder" energies. More advanced filters can act as environmental suits that can open and close according to your preferences and how much energy you wish to absorb.

Filtering can also be used to cleanse yourself of specific energies already in your system. Simply visualize the filter going through your subtle body like an X-ray scanner. It will push out the negative energies.

Vampyres' Grounding Technique

Grounding is the process in which one brings energy under control and releases the stagnant or unwanted energies. We use a system similar to grounding in the Throning exercise. Strigoi Vii grounding is more about direct energy than focus and is metaphorically equivalent to grounding an electrical wire. Grounding is very important, especially for the more advanced Vampyre working with large amounts of energy. Most people use the Corporeal Earth as a grounding tool; however, this is only one example, as the zenith and the heavens can also be used in what can be seen as reverse lightning. There are many people who are naturally grounded and do it instinctively, whilst others have difficulty grounding themselves. Of the Strigoi Vii Currents, the Ramkht are the least grounded; Mradu are commonly exceptionally grounded individuals. Due to the intense interactions with and cycling of energy, the Kitra are often most in need of grounding. The Vampyre Middle Pillar exercise found in Liber Morrah "Coming forth by Twilight" not only stimulates energy flow, but it is a powerful grounding tool.

Even with filtering, the emotional and negative energies will some- times seep through. Grounding helps get rid of these and is almost a personal cleansing. It is possible to ground others and to ground in group ritual. This is exactly where the Mradu are most proficient. The Mradu can ground others through a laying-on of hands and then grounding themselves. This is why they are most powerful at filtering and are naturally larger.

Grounding is essential for preparing for ritual, for practicing healing, and for after practicing the Arts of Gathering. One of the most effective techniques for grounding amongst the Strigoi Vii is known as the Serpent Spear. Visualize at the base of your spine a coiled snake.

Then imagine it's eyes opening as it begins to uncoil up your spine and through your chakras until it becomes a long lightning rod which extends deep into the earth. The top of the rod ("zenith" or "up") can release energy like lightning into the heavens, and the lower portion of the rod can release energy into the earth. However, be aware that being too focused on the ground does not create buoyancy. This is done by also releasing these energies into the heavens, where they will offer a balance as a reverse lightning leaving the tree. Of course, these techniques work from both a Dayside and Nightside perspective; however, they contribute to a balanced energy of the Twilight.

Grounding is most effective when you are around traditional psychic vampires and you are overloaded with excess emotional energies. It allows you to more firmly defend against their energies and more efficiently absorb the Lifeforce they offer to you through normal interactions. One can use metals as symbolic tools for grounding. This technique is like using a rod, blade, or wand for directing energy.

Vampyres' Energy Centering Technique

Centering, as it is called in most esoteric paradigms, is a different form of controlling energy and is the next step beyond grounding. At its core, centering is a meditative application of energy manipulation. With focusing, you bring your energy into a specific state of relaxation. This can be done in conjunction with grounding or separately, depending on the situation and goals. The best formal use of centering is meditation and breath work, including forms of yoga. In *Coming Forth by Twilight* we will explore the Vampyre Middle Pillar, which is in itself a grounding, focusing, sealing, and centering exercise that can be broken down or used efficiently to inspire other forms of energy manipulation. Centering is different than focusing, as it is used for bringing energies together, whilst focusing is for directing energy toward a specific goal.

To begin centering, focus on your Center Chakra, the solar plexus, and then bring your energy into a vibrational swirl around this chakra. Do not let it be static, but alive and fluid, moving and rotating like the sun. It is best to begin Throning partially at this time, but if this is not possible, focus on a specific point, such as a point on the wall, for as long as you can. Focus on the Self and do not get lost in selflessness in the eternity of Throning. Create a balance between eternity and the focus on the Self.

Once you have achieved this, center your hands around your solar plexus as if you were holding an energy ball. Then, like a puppeteer using a marionette, pull the energy outward until it fills the inside of your body. This should be molded inside your Ethereal double and line the inside of your aura.

Maintain this for as long as you can and ground out any distracting energies. This may be done sitting, standing, or reclining, and can be used to begin to apply the technique of focusing energy and even sealing.

Vampyres' Cycling Technique

Cycling is a form of communion and a direct exchanging energy between two Vampyres and can be used for energy play or exercise, sexual and erotic encounters, and many other things. Such practices essentially involve the conscious exchange of energies between two consenting Strigoi Vii. This does not always or even often involve intercourse but can be aided with physical contact. Since the Art of Gathering Energy requires intent, cycling involves two individuals applying the Art to each other with specific and mutually informed consent. The process is called "cycling" because the flow of energy will cycle back and forth between the two Strigoi Vii, like a pendulum swinging between two points in an arc. Each Strigoi Vii, as they absorb the energy at their point in the cycle, will enhance and augment it.

Vampyres' Sealing Lifeforce Technique

Sealing is the technique of preserving Lifeforce so as to stop any leakage. Many Vampyres know how to draw in energy, yet they do not really know how to keep it. There are many things that may cause a practitioner of the Art of Gathering Energy to lose Lifeforce.

Just consider water poured into an uncovered bowl. Over time, unless the bowl is covered and sealed from contact with the air, the water will evaporate. Any liquid poured into a container with small holes will eventually drip through those holes. Numerous factors, such as personal worry, stress, anger, and ill health of the Corporeal body can cause a leakage of Lifeforce, just as a crack in a vase will cause the water inside to leak away. The Strigoi Vii focuses on metaphorically "covering the bowl" or "repairing the holes or cracks in the vessel" in order to preserve the precious Lifeforce within.

The Sealing is a powerful tool to reduce Lifeforce leakage, as a calm and centered mind does not waste energy on unneeded worry and destructive thought patterns. When the mind is functioning in a healthy and productive manner, the Ethereal body often follows suit. Since the Corporeal body is connected to the Ethereal body, maintaining the health of your physical body will help ensure your Ethereal health. Energy practices such as chakra work or Reiki may also help you sense any "holes" in your Ethereal body, so you can turn your attention to "repairing" your Double.

Sealing is important for the digestion of energies. It allows the digestion of Lifeforce so the physical body can rest and recharge. Such a process can be seen on Thanksgiving, when humans eat large gluttonous meals and become sleepy. During sleep, the body is free to concentrate on digesting and processing the large amount of food consumed. After eating, one must digest, and sealing is that technique. Sealing slows leakage and creates a contained energy pool. Once an individual is sealed, they can then proceed to more efficiently focus their energies.

Summation

The techniques listed here are the most elementary of energy manipulations and should be practiced and developed as skills. Not every Vampyre will be able to master these immediately, whilst others will find they come naturally and can be improved on. They are the foundations of full Initiation, and more advanced versions of these techniques are explored in the Higher Mysteries.

CHAPTER 27
EMBRACING THE VAMPYRE CURRENT

But when Zarathustra was alone he spoke thus to his heart: "Could it be possible? The old saint in the forest has not yet heard anything of this, that God is dead!"

—Friedrich Nietzsche,
Thus Spake Zarathustra

The Vampyre Current manifests as an egregore tangibly and in a modern form, focused through the aeonic word of Elorath. This is our spiritual Blood, collective consciousness, group mind and will, mutual "high guardian angel or spirit," and the united karma and dharma of the Family. Those who Initiate into the Mysteries, pursue Zhep'r, and gain results are activating and attuning to this Current, consciously, and willingly. We as a Family are aware of the nature of Elorath and know It is not like any previous or future concept of "blood ties" or divine being. Our Current is unique, and thus we do not worship Elorath as the mortal-minded would a deity. The totality of Our Current is far more unique, and at its foundation is the Trinity Pulses of Kitra, Mradu or Ramkht, which are supporting Aeonic words of power.

The Strigoi Vii Initiate need not concern themselves with the precise source or origin of Elorath. This is indeed a very deep and sacred Mystery, which only generates more questions with every answer. Elorath is alive and flourishing, growing and self-aware, sentient yet not in the manner in which sentience is commonly understood. The Current of Elorath flows around and through us, ever speaking to us in our dreams and Calling the members of the Family together for the purpose of a conclave of Awakening.

The Nature of an Egregore

The word Egregore derives from a Greek word meaning "watchers," which is also sometimes translated as grigori. Egregores are elemental beings created by a collective spiritual consciousness and group mind, and thus they manifest specific characteristics. Each Egregore has its own individual personality traits, karma, dharma, function, and will. The precise nature of an Egregore depends on who created it and for what purpose. Its function is unique and sustained. Younger Egregores are dependent on the energies of sacrifices and offerings provided for them by their creators or worshippers. Once an Egregore is established and reaches a specific level of momentum, those who helped create it commonly make offerings to it in exchange for resources and favors. The Egregore can also be tapped as a source of guidance and power for the members of the creating group, with the appropriate offering of collected Lifeforce.

Many Egregores die or lie dormant when they are no longer fed by belief and thus receive no Offerings. Many "dead gods" from ancient religions are simply Egregores who weakened when they lost their worshippers. These are a specific type of Egregore known as a godform. For example, for many years the ancient Greek gods and goddesses had no worshippers as Christianity overtook Europe. However, the memories of these gods were kept alive through art, poetry, and literature. Even if the poet did not believe in Pan, she still composed an ode in his honor. Therefore, these Egregores did not "die" but no longer maintained the level and frequency of power and manifestation they once had. Yet these dormant Egregores can be revived, as has recently happened with the contemporary occult and neopagan interest in ancient godforms. Now thousands of people hold rites to invoke and honor

Pan and other such deities! For example, when performing ritual, many pagan groups "feed" these deities by projecting their collective energy and intent. The more people who do so, the greater the strength of the Egregore.

Elorath, in its current form, is effectively a modern incarnation of the same Egregore established by the members of Our Family in a time so ancient it retains no record, and which is only truly known to the eldest and wisest of the Strigoi Morte. Elorath, like our own higher Dragon Self, has no shape, no gender, and no graven image. We would not disrespect Elorath and worship it as what It is not: a god! Rather, We respect and honor it as the focus of the collective soul of the Strigoi Vii. As a member of the Santeria religion would esteem their Orishas, so do we esteem Elorath, as It is the deepest connection and the most spiritual Blood bond between the members of our Family!

Dealing with the Egregore of Elorath is something that always should be done with respect, and only by those who are initiated. Those inexperienced in the Mysteries of Strigoi Vii should not attempt to work with Elorath directly, and even experienced Strigoi Vii should always exercise utmost caution and respect. Elorath solely exists on the subtle layers of reality and can be invoked and interacted with as a source of power. Advanced summoning and direct manipulation of the Current of Elorath is magick too advanced for the Calmae level of Initiation and is one of the Higher Mysteries. At this stage of Zhep'r, the Calmae should attempt to merely familiarize themselves with the idea of Egregores and the nature of Elorath at the most introductory and elementary level—through the Trinity Pulses.

There are three base Pulses of Elorath. Each is a balanced and actualized sub-Current within the whole of Elorath. As an analogy, you might consider a research team working on a scientific project—each member of the team has their own unique scientific specialty, but they all strive toward the successful completion of the overarching project. Within Elorath, the first Choir is the Singularity Choir, which represents Elorath as a unified representation of the soul and Blood of the Strigoi Vii. The second is the Duality Choir of the Vampyre Witch (feminine) and Vampyre Gentleman (masculine) aspects of the Vampyre Currents of Elorath.

Many Strigoi Vii possess aspects of both the Vampyre Witch and Vampyre Gentleman, and there are Vampyres who are even "spiritually transgendered." In other words, a Strigoi Vii need not be a female to strongly identify with the Vampyre Witch Current! Additionally, many Strigoi Morte have blended aspects of the Duality within Themselves. Understanding and working within the Duality Choir is part of the evolution of Zhep'r for the Strigoi Vii. Finally, there is the Trinity Pulses, comprised of the Currents of Elorath, entitled Kitra, the lovers and weavers; Mradu, the warrior guardian; and Ramkht, the magician. Some Strigoi Vii view the Trinity by how the specific Strigoi Vii interacts with or is attuned to energy.

As stated in "The Strigoi Vii Prospectus," all Strigoi Vii have these three Pulses running within their soul; however, only about one in five members of the Family truly and strongly resonate with one of these three basic Pulses. Those Adeptus who ordain to a specific Pulse are known as Kharrus. Most Kharrus can function outside their Pulse and perform the duties of another Pulse, yet without quite the same level of expertise. Kharrus tend to be much more social and drawn to interaction with other members of the Family. The Strigoi Vii can view the Trinity Pulsesas a fluid framework of initiatory optional roles that may be adopted and developed by an individual Strigoi Vii.

Within ritual, individual Kharrus of specific Currents are often assigned particular ritual tasks. However, the importance of the Trinity Choir reaches far beyond ritual roles. The Trinity Pulses describes the spiritual predilections of the individual Strigoi Vii, which in turn may be useful in a ritual format. During ritual the celebrant calls on the Choirs during the Invitation to the Strigoi Morte. This is no coincidence. Remember, the aspects of Elorath are not gods and do not represent the totality of the Strigoi Morte. They are instead aspects of the Current's archetypes inherent in each of Us, as well as within the Strigoi Morte. This may be confusing and hard to understand, but it is an essential aspect of our Mysteries. However, these are teachings that must be left for higher levels of Ascension. The Calmae is most rewarded when they first experience Communion with the Strigoi Morte, before beginning to perceive the multiple facets of Their Blood through the aspects and Choirs of Elorath. The Calmae is thus taking the first step on the path to a deeper and more profound apprehension of the great Secrets of Our Blood.

Together, three Strigoi Vii who each identify with one of the Currents of the Trinity Choir can perform a special form of Communion known as the Vinniculum.

In the early days of Strigoi Vii, the Family used rudimentary applications of the Kitra, Mradu, and Ramkht Pulses. When We encountered the Kheprians, they inspired the evolution and re-envisioning of Our Trinity Pulses. Therefore, Our Trinity Pulses is similar in some ways to the Kheprian castes. However, the significant difference is that the Kheprians view their castes as direct modifications of the actual subtle body, while the Pulses are expressions of a natural energetic attunement on the part of the individual Strigoi Vii.

Kitra

The Pulse of Kitra is that of the weaver, councilor, healer, and lover. The Kitra cycles energy easily and frequently acts as the "con- science" of the Family. They often are highly drawn to sensual acts and are catalysts of Pranic energies. In Hebrew, Kitra also means "crowned one." Kitra are drawn to the Ethereal plane and thus their Ethereal bodies are the most developed, adaptable, and active of the three Pulses. This is why they are the most attuned to healing, cycling, and sensual techniques within the Arts of Gathering . Kitra are often called weavers because they are constantly cycling Lifeforce energy at an extremely high rate, always pulling in and releasing Lifeforce. Therefore, they are often the best suited of all Pulses to act as donors, if necessary, and contributors of energy in ritual. With such a deep connection to the Ethereal and a high flow of energy coming in and out of their subtle bodies, Kitra can also recover energy more quickly than individuals of other Pulses.

The Corporeal form of a Kitra is often attractive and fey, as this image best suits their duties. However, as with the other Pulses, each Kitra is a unique individual and thus they cannot be said to absolutely conform to any guidelines of appearance, profession, or predilection. Many Kitra may seem initially to possess a passive and agreeable personality. However, most Kitra are ultimately very forceful and emotionally intense. When they disagree with others, they can be very assertive about their own preferences. They are naturally resourceful and play a creative role within the Vampyre Current of Elorath.

Due to their extremely active subtle bodies, Kitra must learn to filter out energies and may succumb to emotional overloads if they are not skilled in such techniques. This is why so many Kitra seem to have emotional outbursts and forge emotional links with others so easily. Yet, in reality, such sensitivity makes the Kitra extremely adaptable to different situations. A Kitra may seem giving and altruistic at one moment, self-centered the next. Such seeming contradiction is due to the constant flow of energy through their subtle bodies, which in turn may be reflected in their emotions and associated behavior. The Kitra functions very well when balanced by the other Pulses, as that balance prevents them from neglecting their Self.

Since they form links so strongly and rapidly, Kitra may become extremely attached to those with whom they connect. The Kitra must be wary of jealousy, as they have the potential to become very obsessive when links reach too deeply. However, once lasting and profound links are formed over a prolonged period of time, they will be loyal and passionate in their relations. This is why they have an intense need to be loved and can be very talented in regard to lovemaking and sensuality. Kitra are known throughout the Strigoi Vii for being intense lovers.

Out of all the Pulses, the weavers and lovers are the most social, due to their deep need for affection. They are also the most common of all the Kharrus. This ratio may seem unbalanced, but in actuality it is not, since the Kitra provide the most important of all functions: the weaving, cycling, and flow of energy throughout the Current of Elorath.

The energy signature of the Kitra is very much charged from the Current, yet there is a definite streak of Vampyre Gentleman within their souls. As a consequence, many male Kitra are "dandies" or manifest typically feminine characteristics, while female Kitra are often extremely feminine in their behavior and personal predilections.

In group Communion rituals such as the Vinniculum, the Kitra usually are charged with stimulating the flow of moving energies, as they are more skilled in processing energy than Strigoi Vii belonging to the other Pulses. During group ritual, the Kitra enter the Inner Sanctum immediately after the Mradu (who enter first), as they must begin the flow of energy. Within the Family, Kitra often find themselves in the role of advisor and confidant, as they are known to possess a quick wit and a poetic way of stating their opinion. Those who attune to the Current of Kitra often will find cycling energy from the Mradu to be quite beneficial, as individuals of these two Currents of- ten complement each other.

Throughout history, many members of the Current of Kitra acted as sacred priestesses or temple concubines, serving the gods and goddesses of various religions. They could be seen amongst the temple maidens of the Second Temple in Jerusalem, the Maenads or the female worshippers of Dionysus in ancient Greece, or as priestesses of Isis in Ancient Egypt or Greece.

Mradu

The Pulse of Mradu is that of the warriors and guardians. Of all the Currents, the Mradu are most intimately connected to the Corporeal plane. Mradu are not as common as Kitra, yet are much more common than Ramkht.

The Mradu are renowned for their honesty, loyalty, and dedication to the Family. However, for most Mradu, a strong streak of stubborn- ness manifests alongside these traits. The core purpose and instinct of the Mradu is to protect and defend the Family against all threats, external and internal. Somewhat contradictory in their nature, the Mradu may be seen as a "two-sided coin," as their strong protective instinct may lead to personal inflexibility and obstinacy. Partially for this reason, some Mradu are anti-social and withdrawn. However, they may also be extremely charming and gregarious when they so choose.

The Mradu are primarily grounded in the Corporeal plane and are very much creatures of the world of the five senses. Nevertheless, they are still connected to and skilled at manipulating the Ethereal and Astral layers of reality. Their groundedness and the way in which they channel energy is often reflected in their physical form. Physically, the typical Mradu is broad-shouldered and muscular, and many Mradu are larger than average. Due to their subtle metabolism, the Mradu generally are of excellent physical health and may even possess overdeveloped immune systems.

Their Ethereal bodies are composed of very dense Lifeforce, which flows slowly and almost thickly. Some members of the Family have jokingly dubbed the Mradu "Strigoi Vii Camels," because they have the lowest need for Lifeforce to fuel Zhep'r and the most efficient subtle bodies within the three Pulses. They are able to go for long periods without employing Gathering consciously and can even combine Lifeforce with elemental energies in connection to the Earth to fuel their needs.

Mradu naturally filter, ground, and shield energy, which makes them the best-equipped defenders and protections of the Family. Quite often, they are skilled in martial arts or other forms of combat and gifted in military strategy. Mradu are well known for their tempers and, due to their intense loyalty, hold powerful grudges against those they see as betrayers. They will present a very hostile face to anyone who has betrayed or angered not only them, but their Family or close associates as well.

Some of the Mradu find themselves facing a conundrum, for while they have an intense need to give love, it is often difficult for them to forge links and cycle energies deeply. In response, the Mradu may adopt an "old-world" romantic or chivalrous personality. Once they bond with someone, they are completely dedicated and loyal to that individual. Knowing this side of a Mradu is truly an honor, as they are often very slow to open themselves to others and very selective about whom they choose as friends and associates. The loving, outgoing nature of the Kitra thus often complements the steadfast, reserved Mradu.

The Mradu often have difficulty with out-of-body experiences and Astral projection but have great success in limited shape-shifting on an Ethereal level. This is why so many Mradu are often drawn to the totem of the wolf, predator bird, great cats, or bear. Even though they may have difficulties with Astral projection, they are still able to be highly effective in the Astral realm. Mradu are renowned for banishing and combating hostile subtle entities.

A Mradu with a fully manifested Zhep'r will project a very strong presence. They excel in tasks of guardianship, as these roles are fulfilling to them. It is dishonorable and even unthinkable for a Mradu to turn down such a duty when they are needed. No task that requires protection, grounding, or active defense is foreign to the most dedicated and sincere Mradu, as they take the initiative to find all the potential threats to the individual, group, or Family, and respond quickly and effectively.

Within ritual, Mradu are called on to ground energies and are always the first to enter and begin establishing the Inner Sanctum. Throughout history, examples of Mradu-like groups have served as templars, holy warriors, and temple guardians. The Knights of the Round Table in Arthurian mythology is a well-known illustration of legendary Mradu.

Ramkht

The Pulse of Ramkht is known to us as the magicians and inspirators. The Ramkht are the rarest of all the Pulses yet are the most influential in regard to their impact and role within the Family as a whole. Ramkht are known for their talents in energy manipulation, spiritual guidance, and the ability to fuel intent and inspiration into manifestation. Since the members of this Pulse prefer the role of ritual leader, they often preside over rituals, group Communions, and other Family functions, such as Ascensions or weddings. Ramkht focus their talents on providing intent and direction in ritual. Foresight and intuition are common characteristics of the Ramkht Pulse.

Ramkht are most deeply tied to the Astral plane and least connected to the Corporeal. This is why they are often called the "Dreamers." The Ramkht can easily fall into the trap of neglecting their Corporeal development or physical body and will thus have to consciously remember to ground themselves. The Ramkht will sometimes choose to spend as much time as possible dreaming, creating visions, and dancing within the Astral realm. However, this does not mean that Ramkht are dissociated from everyday concerns or seek to "escape" the physical world! They often choose to work within the Astral realm so as to manifest their goals and desires into reality. Many Ramkht are as at home in the Astral as a bird is in the sky, and thus, of all Pulses, they have the best potential for mastering Astral Flight.

As their Zhep'r advances, Ramkht develop a very strong "thirst" for Lifeforce due to a specifically developed subtle metabolism. Unlike Kitra, who cycle energy constantly, Ramkht draw energy in and expend it, due to their specific frequencies and energy attunements. They also have the greatest potential for Inviting the Strigoi Morte during group ritual and are often skilled in communication with subtle entities. When employing the Arts of Gathering, Ambient Gathering rarely sustains them for long periods of time, and they require larger doses of energy from deep Gathering or other forms of the Art.

Physically, many Ramkht tend to be somewhat hermaphroditic in their appearance and demeanor. Many see the Ramkht as "bi-gendered" or "androgynous," a perception that is in many ways due to the Ramkht being equally balanced between the Kitra and Ramkht Pulses of the Current of Elorath. Even if they first appear solidly grounded in one gender, many

Ramkht assume traits or behaviors commonly associated with the other gender. Male Ramkht, for example, may be drawn to appearances or pastimes normally considered feminine, while the female Ramkht may be correspondingly drawn to seemingly masculine behaviors.

When in ritual, Ramkht are most drawn to the energy of the Kitra, while the Mradu is strongly drawn to the Ramkht. You can see examples of the Ramkht Current throughout history in the high priests and priestesses of many religions, from Catholicism to the ancient pagan temples of Egypt and Mexico. Several legendary philosophers and sages have also borne traces of Our Ramkht Current, from St. Augustine to Jeanne d'Arc (Joan of Arc).

Summation of the Currents is one which must be taken seriously. Remember that not all Strigoi Vii are Kharrus, and only a minority of Us resonate with one of the Trinity Pulses. Those who are not Kharrus can, of course, practice and become skilled in these roles if they so choose. The path of Kharrus requires focus and dedication in order to successfully reach Mastery.

Conclusion

Within the Nightside, one revels in darkness and the unknown. In the Nightside, the Strigoi Vii will experience that which the mundane world considers magic, legend, and superstition. The aspiring Calmae should stride firmly and confidently into the darkness of the Nightside, personally testing and validating the wonders that lie within. There are no "rules" or "musts" for this journey of exploration—it is a journey of the Self, a process during which the Initiate comes into agreement within their Self and with others of like mind.

Coming Forth by Night is a journey that can only be made with personal dedication and a firm foundation in the perspective of the Dayside. All beliefs must be cast away and dangers accepted. Truly, then, in the Nightside "there be Dragons," for agreement with the Dragon is the only truth.

With this foundation, the Initiate is then prepared to take the next step and investigate the deeper challenges beyond mere mortal survival. You are on a glorious Quest for genuine Immortality of the Self and personal divinity! Embrace the duality of your nature—civilized, spiritual, and noble as well as primal like the predators in nature!

Zhep'r! Hail Elorath!

CALMAE TESTIMONIAL

These are confidential and private questionnaires that are used within the OSV to evaluate the completion of an ordeal. This will only be seen by the Synod officers who will reply with notes and reflections will be sent back if one does not pass the evaluation. Please keep answers reasonably short and concise at most 300 words. If you do not understand something there is a lesson waiting to happen. These testimonials are based on the honor system and be truthful there is no rush for true Zhep'r. Submit these questionnaires with a freewill donation to synod@strigoivii.org.

1. Tell us why you are pursuing Calmae Ordeal: Coming forth by Night?
2. How have you manifested and applied the Beyond the Mirror teachings?
3. How have you become sensitive to life-force and what are your experiences with it?
4. How have you experienced and experienced the Etheric Double / Subtle Body?
5. What are your reflections on the anatomy of death and Vampyric Re-manifestation vs Mortal Reincarnation?
6. Tell us of an encounter with a Strigoi Morte?
7. What are your experiences with Sanguine Mass and Ritualistic Communion?
8. How have you manifested and applied Energy Manipulation?
9. Tell us of which pulse of the Current of Elorath calls forth to you and why?
10. What is your experience with the Dragon's Eyes exercise?
11. Any other comments or notes you would like to add.

BOOK III

LIBER MORRAH "COMING FORTH BY TWILIGHT"

Beyond the masque of the Outer Circle lies the foundation of the Higher Mysteries. These reveal a Self that is evolving into a noble and elegant yet predatory being who is truly in agreement with the Laws of Nature and is the master of Civilization. Within the Higher Mysteries the Strigoi Vii is free to remove their mask of humanity, practice genuine Vampyre Ethics, and truly walk the path of Personal Immortality.

—Magister Dimitri to Soror Raven, Summer 2002

CHAPTER 28

COMING FORTH BY TWILIGHT
THE MORRAH ORDEAL

Twice each day a crack opens
between night and day,
Twice twilight
slips through that crack.
It stays only a short time
while night and day
stand whispering secrets
before they go their
separate ways.

—Ralph Fletcher, "Twilight Comes Twice"

Welcome to Strigoi Vii Book III: Liber Morrah "Coming Forth by Twilight." You now stand at the threshold of the Inner Mysteries of Strigoi Vii, steping into the role of the Adeptus.

The most profound difference between the Outer and Inner Mysteries is the evolution from the mortal-minded to the Immortal perception. The Morrah is a Vampyre Adeptus is equipped to embrace Their primal nature: that of the elegant, evolved, honorable, and Noble Predator.

The Morrah make decisions from a Twilight perspective and are in full contact with Their Higher Self. They may espouse convictions that seem bizarre or confusing to the mortal-minded; however, beyond the Strigoi Vii Principles, the Morrah are answerable only to Their own survival and success toward attaining Immortality of the Self. The Vampyre disassociate themselves from the ideology of the prey-victim mentality so common amongst the mortal-minded both spiritually and mentally and adopt the perspective akin to a predator. The Morrah have begun to fully actualize Their potential for Immortality of the Self.

The word Morrah is derived from the term for spirit, ghost, or vampire in Romanian folklore. In Croatian the word mora means nightmare; therefore, the Morrah sometimes are known as Mora within the Family in regards to their focus on astral work and Dreams. The feminine of this word is Moroaică. In Romanian mythology, the Morrah is sometimes described as a sort of phantom that rises from the grave to draw energy from the living. In folklore, Morrah are often unbaptized children or the offspring of two Strigoi.

These and other myths have inspired our use of this term to describe the final level of ascension within the Outer Mysteries of the Strigoi Vii. Ascension to Vampyre Adeptus is the foundation of formal initiation into one of the Trinity Pulses of Elorath and the last step before pursuing initiation into the Inner Mysteries. Once the Strigoi Vii has completed the Morrah ordeal, They gain the opportunity to pursue the deeper and more profound Higher Mysteries.

The Morrah has mastered the Outer Mysteries and now focuses on achieving a balanced Twilight. They have gained experience with lucid dreaming, astral projection (also known as Flight), dreamwalking, Apotheosis, Predatory Spirituality, and the Advanced Arts of Gathering energy. In order to achieve a true balance of Twilight, the Morrah must possess a solid foundation in the Corporeal Dayside and the Ethereal Nightside.

At the heart of the Morrah Ordeal is a true and genuine personal evolution from the mortal-minded mentality to that of an Immortal.

This involves completely bidding farewell to unverified gambles with one's life, serious disengagement from mass media brainwashing, and an active commitment to the preservation of the Temple of the Self as demonstrated by actions such as totally abandoning unhealthy personal habits. The Adeptus should also be dedicated to preserving and bettering Their Corporeal Dayside world by living in an ethical and nobly responsible fashion and acting to further the quality of corporeal life for Themselves and Their loved ones. The Morrah should practice personal mastery of the Dayside principles while planning for the possibility of an Immortal future. The Morrah is a fully mature Vampyre as They embrace Life in a consciously positive manner largely unknown to the mortal-minded.

Ronin, of course, is welcome to read this volume and test and experiment with the teachings it contains. Ronin who feel satisfied with Their own Zhep'r then can testify to "Having Come Forth by Twilight." Strigoi Vii who wish to have Their mastery of this important level of ascension formally recognized within the Family may, as with the Jahira and Calmae Ascensions, submit a written testimonial to the Synod. As one Strigoi Vii Magister stated, "If you meet a Strigoi Vii Ronin who has truly Come Forth by Twilight without formal initiate it will be obvious in their actions and knowledge." Since Strigoi Vii is an inwardly oriented system, the vast majority of Ronin who have achieved mastery of these mysteries will never try to flaunt Their achievement, nor require outwardly centered approval from others.

Some Morrah will have the makings of potential Magisters. However, it is important to note that formal validation of this ascension is necessary before the Morrah or Ronin who have Come Forth by Twilight can pursue the path of Magister within the Scale of Ascensions and Ordeals of the Strigoi Vii. Hence, many Strigoi Vii, even those who consider Themselves Ronin, choose to request that the Synod formally validate the Morrah Ascension.

The Morrah seek to align Themselves with the great thinkers of the world and look toward achieving mastery and enlightenment similar to that of Plato's "philosopher-kings." The Morrah may wish to closely study and emulate the great philosophers of history, such as Socrates and Plato, Hypatia, St. Thomas Aquinas, Thomas Hobbes, Bodhidharma, Pascal, Lao Tzu, Mary Wollstonecraft, and many others who exhibit the nature of the Immortal–minded life.

The Morrah is fully dedicated to Immortality of the Self and has chosen it as Their primary focus in life. They not only wish to survive, but to thrive. Without the foundations of the Dayside and Nightside, no Strigoi Vii can Come Forth by Twilight, nor have the stamina for personal Immortality or individual Nobility. The Strigoi Vii is free of the Culture of Distraction that permeates the mortal world. Awakening to one's Strigoi Vii Nature is to Awaken from harmful distractions and completely embrace the opportunity for Immortality. The remaining Strigoi Vii texts beyond this book will be privately disseminated within the secret mysteries and teachings of the Ordo Strigoi Vii. Morrah are welcome to aspire to join this order and be formally initiated as a Strigoi Vii Adeptus.

Beginning the Morrah Ordeal and the path to Strigoi Vii Adeptus:

First: Make the Dedication to Begin the Morrah Ordeal

Second: Reinforce Apotheosis

At the very core of Strigoi Vii Vampyrism is the drive to achieve Immortality of the Self. Apotheosis is the core of this concept and is about aligning oneself with the concept of personal divinity and deification. This marker is an essential step of ascension in that the individual sees no other god before themselves and their own ego.

Third: Equilibrium of Twilight

This rests upon mastery of the Morrah skills and the comprehension and application of the Dayside and Nightside elements of Strigoi Vii. Twilight is not a static condition, but rather one that must be constantly maintained and explored. The initiate of the Morrah Mystery must have the courage to face this eternal challenge. They can never neglect Their Dayside or Nightside, for once that balance is gone, so is Twilight.

Fourth: Awakening to Predatory Spirituality

This is one of the most difficult and profound steps of personal evolution. The Predatory Spirit must rise and be freed. Only within Twilight can this primal force be fully released. The Morrah must learn to fully embrace Their predatory nature.

Fifth: Freedom in the Astral

This is an absolute requirement for genuine ascension and understanding of the Morrah Mysteries. At the core of Touching the astral is lucid dreaming, followed by Flight and dreamwalking. Only within the astral is the Strigoi Vii truly liberated, as mortal-minded moralities, inhibitions, and barriers that exist in the corporeal world are simply not present. There the Strigoi Vii can fully realize their potential and behave as a truly evolved Spiritual Predator, utilizing the skills They learned in earlier levels of ascension.

This astral freedom comes with associated power and responsibility. In the Dayside and corporeal worlds, the Adeptus is established in conventional morality and the Strigoi Vii Principles. In the astral plane, the Strigoi Vii has the opportunity to Ascend and rise as a true Divinity of the Self through an entirely new perspective, which must be responsibly practiced and mastered. With this newfound freedom, the Strigoi Vii is able to embrace the fundamentals of Clavicula Sangraal (Strigoi Vii Sorcery), as They can actively touch and interact with the Web of Wyrd and navigate the Labyrinth of Kaladra. These are the interconnecting astral webs and the universe of links between all things corporeal and Spiritual. The Web of Wyrd can be manipulated in accordance with properly applied Will and Sorcery. As part of Their evolution of Zhep'r, every Strigoi Vii must eventually tread the sacred paths of the astral Labyrinth of Kaladra. These concepts are the foundation of all Sorcery of the Inner Mysteries and will not be further explained here.

Sixth: Practice the Vampyre Middle Pillar

Seventh: Master the Advanced Art of Gathering Lifeforce

Eigth: Morrah Ascension Rite

The Oath of Morrah is the affirmation of success in and absolute understanding of the markers of the Twilight Condition and the central validation of becoming a Strigoi Vii Adeptus. The Oath of Morrah must be performed during a Sanguine Mass before the Ancestors after formal recognition from the OSV. Alternately, the Rite may be performed as a solitary ritual and a written testimonial sent to the Synod for validation (if the Strigoi Vii is an active member of the StrigoiVii.org Forum).

The initiate performing the Rite should prepare Themselves with all the tools of the Sanguine Mass. Traditionally, for the Rite of Morrah the speculum should be a black bowl or vessel filled with water, not a mirror. This is to represent the primal waters and the Mirror reflection of the world, as well as the Mirror Gate into the deep astral realm.

The Oath of Morrah:

Ancestors, Hear Me Now!

I, (Vampyre Name / Sorbriquet), come into this Sanctum of my own free will, to stand before the Vampyre Current, in love and loyalty, with the full intent of reaffirming my Oaths of Jahira, and Calmae, thus entering into the Twilight of the Strigoi Vii Mysteries.

This Ascension is my testimonial to the reality of the Astral Realm, Predatory Spiritualism, and Apotheosis.. I dedicate myself to my personal Quest for Immortality and freedom from mortal bonds.

I have been touched by the Ancestors & Current in sacred Communion and in my heart know I stand here proudly amongst Family!

I vow to become a shield in defense of the Current. I vow to be a sword to divide Truth from fallacy.

I vow to be a pillar of strength, passing on the Mysteries of Strigoi Vii to those who hear the Calling of Our Quest.

Does anyone oppose my Ascension? Speak here and now!

Thus, I now declare myself Morrah (Vampyre Name / Sorbriquet) of the Strigoi Vii.

Hail Elorath!

CHAPTER 29
PRIMAL SPIRITUALISM

*To the enlightened there is no god and no
devil, just you and the universe.*

—Magister Dimitri

The Strigoi Vii Adeptus is by nature an evolved, elegant, and primal, yet Noble Predator who is very much as in touch with Their animalistic primal nature as well as master of Their civilized conditioning. The core of Primal Spirituality is to be in touch with one's primal nature, destruction of the victim mentality, and acceptance of the laws of nature: that there is no higher law than survival. Awakening the Primal Spirituality is the most difficult barrier the Strigoi Vii must overcome in order to truly Come Forth by Twilight. Being an evolved predator to the Vampyre Philosophy is far beyond physically harming, torturing, or abusing humans or animals. To be Truly Adept in Vampyism, one must fully and completely accept this fundamental principle to Rise into higher levels of Zhep'r.

Without the predatory and primal perspective, Zhep'r is simply impossible, and those who remain bound to their mortal ethics cannot fully embrace their nature. There is simply no other source of energy that is as efficient, refined, and potent as human Lifeforce, and this is the fuel of Immortality. Few of those who come to the Mysteries of the Family have the courage, strength, and Will to genuinely embrace the concept of Primal Spiritualism. The Morrah who fully accepts Primal Spiritualism must move beyond the human perceptions and ethics with which They have been raised. The Key to Zhep'r beyond Coming Forth by Night is Awakening and realizing the primal Predatory Spirit within.

Note: What one must realize is that the Primal Spirit from the Vampyre perspective does not mean that one should be a violent criminal who preys on others. It is a metaphor for the will to survive, to embrace the primal nature, and to thrive beyond the barriers of the limited perceptions which society has conditioned us to believe and put our faith in.

The Primal Spirit

The Primal Spirit and attaining the Dragon's primal perspective are the foundation of the Immortal Mind. From the Dragon's perspective, one can reawaken the dormant survival instincts lost in the conditioning of civilization. This primal spirit brings forth natural survival skills which lie within the reptilian brain. A single human body alone does not generate enough refined Lifeforce by itself to fuel the higher levels of Zhep'r. Without harvested human Lifeforce, the Vampyre cannot raise the necessary energies to make Offerings to our Ancestors in Communion and fuel Vampyre Magick to defeat the Second Death.

This mindset and perspective in nature is the historic dividing line between predator and prey, ruler and servant, immortal and mortal-minded. The Vampyre Adeptus no longer accepts the role of prey and realizes that survival of the fittest is the highest law of nature, which is no different in human society.

Primal Nobility

From the Dayside Perspective, Primal Nobility is an ideology in which the Vampyre takes example and inspiration from rulers and the noble apex-predators of the wild, such as the lion, tiger, hawk, wolf, bear, and many others. These creatures are the ultimate predators and lords of their realms. The

Strigoi Vii radiates an aura of mastery that is projected from every element of Their Self, even in the most challenging circumstances. Predatory Nobility for the Strigoi Vii involves seeing Themselves above the food chain and fully embracing the reality of that position. However, the Noble Predator accepts the doctrine of *noblesse oblige* and does not use their mastery to torment or torture, only to ensure their spiritual survival.

As the lion lives in the jungle and hones its instincts in accordance with the laws of survival, so does the Strigoi Vii. The Vampyre, however, lives within the jungle of human civilization. To survive in this jungle, the Vampyre must look to the most successful members of human society as exemplars. Success in the human jungle depends upon one's wits, intelligence, enduring spirit, and creativity. Some examples of those who have succeeded in human society through Primal Nobility include Julius Caesar, Cleopatra, Benjamin Disraeli, Alfred Hitchcock, Margaret Thatcher, General Patton, Oprah, Napoleon Bonaparte, Queen Elizabeth I, Thomas Edison, Winston Churchill, Eleanor Roosevelt, Stanley Kubrick, Alexander the Great, even Bill Gates, and many other notable historical and contemporary figures. One modern example of Social Darwinism on a Dayside level is the founder of Facebook, Mark Zuckerberg as seen in the film The Social Network. Taking on the mindset of Primal Spiritualism means achieving mastery of the Dayside principles and thriving in the jungle of humanity by only bending the laws of society, and not breaking the laws overtly.

From the Dayside Perspective:

The Dayside philosophy of Primal Spiritualism is akin to Social Darwinism. From the perspective of the Strigoi Vii, it is obvious that nothing and no one is created equal. As Charles Darwin noted, variation abounds in nature as well as the human world. Organisms that possess variations most favorable to their survival will thrive and pass those advantages to their offspring. Of course, within human society the concept of "favorable variation" is much more complex than within the animal and plant kingdoms. Moreover, humans have the ability to adapt to their circumstances and either change inherent detriments into advantages or hone latent gifts into powerful tools of mastery.

The most successful humans are those who are able to both utilize their inborn talents and develop skills that prove them superior to others. Consider professional athletes who are born with a superior body type but must train assiduously to develop their skills. Or Stephen Hawking, who is possessed of a genius level intellect, yet suffers from ALS (amyotrophic lateral sclerosis). He has survived beyond all predictions for his life expectancy and is one of the most brilliant and groundbreaking physicists in history. Best-selling writer Stephen King endured years of discouragement and rejection slips until he published his first novel. The Noble Predators of the human culture succeed through inherent advantages, innovation, cunning, overcoming challenges, determination, and constant hard work, just as the predator must do in the wild.

From the Nightside Perspective

From the Nightside Perspective to fully Awaken the Vampyric Condition of Zhep'r, the shift to a primal survivalist mentality must take place deep within the psyche. This Awakening must be done in order to fully mature and have the necessary skills for achieving spiritual immortality. Many un-Awakened Strigoi Vii will naturally embrace the characteristics of Their primal nature and understand the necessity of Gathering energy without training. However, this is far from perfect, and the purpose of the convergence of the Family through the Order is to achieve a conscious collective Awakening and a think tank to further this nature in a way never done before. For others, embracing a primal viewpoint seems harsh, selfish, or out of balance with the morality of modern society. Shouldn't we all produce enough Lifeforce on our own to live a fully functional life without gathering the energy of others? The answer is yes, we all do produce enough Lifeforce for a short period of time. However, it is not enough to sustain cohesion of self-awareness when the corporeal body ceases to function.

At some stage, after the corporeal First Death, the consciousness will become disembodied, without a living, breathing body to produce Lifeforce. The human body Vessel is an energy-producing machine and is our consistent source of energy. Even before the First Death, those Vampyres of higher Zhep'r require far more energy than the mortal body can produce, and They cannot fuel offerings in Communion, achieve higher levels of astral projection, or be used to mold various applications of sorcery that We require for survival as disembodied entities. All such actions increase Our Zhep'r and, therefore, help Us stave off the Second Death. When We Ascend of Our own efforts to defeat the Second Death, it is the result of Our spiritual vibration being very high, so We must learn to store massive amounts of Lifeforce to keep the subtle self-awareness and cohesiveness without a corporeal body. Without the Arts of Gathering energy, We simply cannot achieve cohesion, and We will enter what is known as the Dream Matrix and face the Second Death. In short, We are not satisfied with producing just enough energy to survive. We absorb enough energy to thrive and advance Our evolution! The best part is that this is not illegal, nor will it be; it is, however shunned by mortal-minded science as a point of fiction, and few would even believe such a possibility to be true. The Strigoi Vii wishes for this to be true and is not daunted by those who disagree or disbelieve; in fact, the Strigoi Vii does the opposite and promotes the idea that it is a possibility.

Modern medicine is no stranger to the practice of replacing, modifying, and enhancing parts and systems of the human body. Doctors replace joints, transplant organs, and perform blood transfusions daily. In light of this, the practice of Gathering energy should appear just as sane, reasonable, and useful as any human who opts for a necessary fluid transfusion or organ transplant. A key marker of evolution is finding and utilizing tools to advance and enhance life. The Vampyre is not only interested in enhancing their corporeal life, but is also devoted to advancing their eternal life and personal Immortality!

The Prey Mentality

The Prey Mentality is the concept associated with prey animals who are genetically programmed to accept their fate in the jaws of the predator. This is the nature of the food chain.

Their survival instincts are drowned and dulled by the comforts of human society and by mass media. They simply exist, being brain- washed by the opiates of television and other forms of mass media. In the time since the great wars of the mid-twentieth century, technology has provided such conveniences as mass-produced and inexpensive food, affordable and comfortable accommodations, and much improved medical care. Long gone is the need to go into the forest to hunt game or into the field to harvest food by hand. These luxuries trigger the reflex in the mind of most humans to no longer fight to survive. As a result, they have become more accepting of the prey mentality.

Ethics of the Noble Predator

For the Strigoi Vii, the ethics of Vampyrism come down to intent and action. The Strigoi Vii, educated in the social benefits and moralities of human culture, never harms humans or animals physically. Our intent is to further Our own evolution and personal Immortality, not harm Our Source. We embrace Our role as We embrace Our Primal predatory nature without breaking the law or endangering Our corporeal existence. The evolving Vampyre quickly learns that drinking blood is a risky and inefficient form of Gathering energy to satisfy our Zhep'r. Vampyres scoff at taking part in illegal or socially reprehensible activities, or directly involving the fragile and unestablished Dayside minds of minors in Strigoi Vii Mysteries. Such acts only limit Our kind within human society.

It is possible that the mortal-minded may perceive Vampyre ethics as often contradictory and hypocritical. Although most mortals profess to value human and animal life, they secretly still see them- selves as superior to others and pretend to show equality amongst each other in the games of political correctness. Many mortals who claim to espouse brotherhood/ sisterhood would at first deny, and then not hesitate to sacrifice, a fellow human if their own survival was on the line. Some of the most strident animal and environmental rights supporters selfishly engage in activities that directly or indirectly harm the ecosystem. Many so-called "humanistic" organizations have openly or covertly supported genocide, oppression, rape, torture, and imperialism. Mortal nations that publicly claim to respect personal freedoms and social justice nevertheless invade and colonize other nations whose governments do not agree with them or who lack the military strength to defend themselves. The Strigoi Vii rejects and is contemptuous of this self-serving Jekyll and Hyde mentality and sees reality as survival of the fittest. We are self-actualized beings who act responsibly and do not engage in self-delusion. We are evolved Noble Predators who never kill, torture, or harm other beings for pleasure. Instead of denying our role, We embrace and accept Our place in the hierarchy of living things. Nature does not embrace the concept of political correctness; it only sees the survival of the fittest.

To the Vampyre, humanity is a virtually unlimited Source of Lifeforce, especially in these modern days with billions of humans generating a massive field of refined Lifeforce over the planet. In the food web of life, the Vampyre must harvest the subtle life energy radiated by humans but also must transcend to a new set of ethics and morality in order to achieve an advanced evolutionary state through spiritual focus and practice. The Vampyre was born and raised in human culture with human origins and experience. Yet the un-Awakened Vampyre has always possessed the potential. Even before Their realization of Their True Nature, They may have felt "different" from those around Them in a deeply profound way. The path of Zhep'r for the Vampyre includes fully exploring the depths of this difference. This evolution can be accomplished within the confines of mortal civilized society. The Vampyre is wise to apply untrammeled Predatory Spiritualism on the etheric and astral levels of reality alone and wear the mask of human ethics and morality in the corporeal realm whilst still recognizing Their Primal Nature.

Summation

In conclusion, the Vampyre accepts Their role as a Noble Predator of the mortal-minded. We refuse to engage in the self-deluded elements common to the mortal-minded mentality. The Strigoi Vii, looking through the Eyes of the Dragon into the Mirror, is only genuine once They embrace Their Noble Primal Spirit.

CHAPTER 30

APOTHEOSIS
SELF-DEIFICATION

Wilt thou love God as he thee? then digest,
My soul, this wholesome meditation,
How God the Spirit, by angels waited on
In heaven, doth make His temple in thy breast.
The Father having begot a Son most blest,
And still begetting—for he ne'er begun—
Hath deign'd to choose thee by adoption,
Co-heir to His glory, and Sabbath' endless rest.
And as a robb'd man, which by search doth find
His stolen stuff sold, must lose or buy it again,
The Sun of glory came down, and was slain,
Us whom He had made, and Satan stole, to unbind.
'Twas much, that man was made like God before,
But, that God should be made like man, much more.

—John Donne, "Divine Sonnet XV"

Tat Tvam Asi. (Thou Art That).

—Chāndogya Upanisad

One question has long been used as a test amongst Vampyre Seekers wishing to distinguish between genuine Potentials and curious mortals. This question is simply, "Do you wish to be Immortal?" Without fail, the mortal-minded will respond in the negative. They may offer a number of justifications for their response, ranging from "I couldn't stand to see my friends and family die" to "I would get bored" to even "Death is a natural process."

However, the subtext behind all these answers is the same: the mortal-minded worship death and simply do not have the capacity to conceive of, much less embrace, the possibility of Immortality. Like sheep, they would rather meekly "go gentle into that good night" and dare merely to hope that an omnipotent deity might grant them a semblance of continued existence according to their religious beliefs. Some mundanes will even confess that they have no wish for an afterlife; they want only to cease existing in their current state or to be reborn as a completely different person through Reincarnation.

The Strigoi Vii always strives for personal Immortality of the Self. They align themselves with divinity, or numina (from the Latin). The Strigoi Vii is the god/dess of Their personal reality and celebrates the Self and worships Themselves as Their own god; that is one reason the mirror is a powerful symbol in Vampyrism. There is no greater purpose than the Survival of the Self. Once the complete Self is gone, there is no free Will, no perception, and no Zhep'r. Therefore, exaltation and preservation of the Self is the utmost priority for the Strigoi Vii. Moreover, by accepting Their personal Divinity, the Strigoi Vii also fully accepts their rightful place as one of the most evolved of all living beings and finally casts off all mortal-minded bonds in celebration of their True Divine Self.

Apotheosis
The Strigoi Vii furthers the Quest for Immortality of the Self with the process of Self-Deification or Apotheosis. This term comes from the Greek word

apotheoun, meaning "to deify." The Latin word *deification* and the Italian word *gióvino* both mean "to be made divine."

Apotheosis can also be seen throughout history in ancient and modern "imperial cults." For example, the Ancient Egyptians initially saw the Pharaohs as mortal incarnations of the gods. In Roman legend, Romulus and Remus, the founders of Rome, were the sons of a god. The Ancient Romans believed that their Emperors would ascend to godhood upon their death. Even during their lifetime, they were often worshipped as divine by their subjects and became the centerpiece of state religions. During the Middle Ages in Europe, kings were believed to rule by Divine Right; they were supposedly chosen by God and therefore were God's representatives on Earth.

Within the mysteries of Strigoi Vii, Self-Deification is a matter of worshipping the Self above all else. In order to achieve Apotheosis, the Strigoi Vii must be entirely free from traditional mortal-minded religious faith and belief. The first commandment appears in Exodus in the Judeo-Christian Bible as *"I am the Lord your God, who brought you out of the land of Egypt, out of the house of slavery; Do not have any other gods before me."* The Strigoi Vii knows that They have brought Themselves out of the slavery of the mortal-minded mentality; moreover, to the Strigoi Vii the Self is the premier deity above all else! The Strigoi Vii achieves personal godhood by Awakening to perceptions which, are the breath of the Promethean Fire of the Inner Dragon God. The Vampyre is free to align Themselves with Their own perceptions of divinity. Beyond faith and belief, there are some other concepts that are key to understanding Apotheosis and Self-Deification.

Dharma

Dharma is a concept that comes from Indian traditions and is a core notion within the more advanced mysteries of the Strigoi Vii. It is linked to the concept of Karma, but this link has frequently been forgotten or outright ignored by modern Western culture. Dharma is the equivalent of the Tao in Taoism. The term Dharma loosely means "one's righteous duty" and is the focus of understanding the "Higher Truth," akin to hearing the whispers of one's own Dragon.

Those Vampyres who choose not to embrace and listen to the Higher

Self are simply subject to the self-imposed limitations and curse of the Khaskt and will never achieve personal self-aware Immortality. Dharma is a profound purpose and is first expressed within the Current as one's Calling to the Mysteries. One example is that for some Vampyres, being True is responding to and mastering a Calling, a specific Pulse of the Current. In most general terms, Dharma is simply understanding and accepting one's own purpose.

In a mundane sense, following your Dharma is the quest to understand your own life path and purpose. One example in Western esoteric studies is Aleister Crowley's concept of the True Will, upon which he elaborated in his novel Diary of a Drug Fiend and other writings. Crowley believed that every person has a genuine calling in their life and that it should be everyone's ultimate purpose to discover and follow their True Will. A life lived without realization of one's True Will is, according to Crowley, a life full of quiet desperation, anomie, and apathy. Those who have not discerned their True Will often despairingly turn to self-destructive activities and habits. They are not true to their own nature and thus not Strigoi Vii. Obviously, the majority of the mortal-minded never succeed in discovering or following their True Will. Part of Zhep'r is the search for one's true purpose and therefore one's True Divine Self.

Karma

Karma is often also misunderstood in Western culture and is sometimes rather misinformed, embraced, and redefined by many newage philosophies. The Strigoi Vii understanding of Karma is more akin to the original Hindu concept than the Three-fold Law of the Wiccans, which ignores Dharma. Deleterious or "negative" Karma results from not realizing or adhering to your Dharma. For the Strigoi Vii, a prime example of negative Karma is denying one's natural potential. Simply doing so is ignoring the opportunity for Zhep'r and Immortality. Some who are of the Current nevertheless choose not to embrace their nature due to fear, lack of will, or other reasons of their own, ignoring their potential. These individuals cling to their mortal-minded perspectives and truly do not have the endurance for the Path of Immortality.

Luck

Luck is at best a mortal-minded concept followed by the Strigoi Vii as a part of the mortal's Culture of Distraction. Nothing happens by pure chance. Things that appear lucky only occur due to hard work or opportunistic behavior. An "unlucky" situation can almost always be manipulated in order to achieve a positive outcome. What is perceived as luck often results from a concerted application of Will, whether that Will be of the individual Vampyre or of the Family as a whole.

Summation

For the Vampyre Adeptus are varied individuals who have the potential to walk path of Zhep'r and Apotheosis. The Strigoi Vii focuses on their own personal evolution and divinity of the Self and does not become pulled into the drama that abounds vampire obsessed mundanes. The Morrah should strive to see mundanes as individuals for what they are: sources of Lifeforce for the Strigoi Vii.

CHAPTER 31

THE VAMPYRE
MIDDLE PILLAR

*To those who feel the call to make this effort, comes the Order with a
series of pictures, symbolic of the growth of the soul to new life. The
meditations given…are designed to lead the mind toward ideas which
will assist in self-knowledge—universal impersonal ideas which each
must find in his own way—"the secrets which cannot be told save to
those who know them already."*

—Israel Regardie, *The Golden Dawn*

The Vampyre Middle Pillar technique is a variation of a meditation
that was used by the Hermetic Order of the Golden Dawn and discussed in the book *The Golden Dawn* and other publications by Israel
Regardie. The exercise presented here is the Strigoi Vii version employed
within the syllabus of the OSV. The Middle Pillar is used to know your Self
and learn about and control the mind and body, thus controlling the energy
within your body. Most importantly, it focuses on grounding and centering
of the Self, which allows you to build consecrated energy centers in the body.

The Principle of Vibration states that "nothing rests and everything moves." Every form of energy actually vibrates. Modern science states that everything is composed of vibrations, from subatomic particles to the most complex collections of corporeal matter. Many contemporary scientists believe that the fundamental structure of the universe can be described as an assembly of vibrating strings. The Principle of Vibration was known as far back as Ancient Egypt where there was no differentiation among science, religion, and magick. Even whilst talking, you feel the vibrations of your chest. When concentrating speech into a specific part of the body, that portion of the body vibrates more intensely. If you concentrate enough on one portion of the body, it will focus the vibrations. This Middle Pillar exercise thus makes use of the vibratory principle.

The Middle Pillar will relax you on a mental, spiritual, and physical level, balancing the imbalanced aspects of your corporeal and subtle bodies. As you develop more advanced meditations, you will notice the side of the body you use most will take longer to relax than the other side. For example, a right-handed person would most likely need more time to relax their right side, and vice versa for a left-handed person. That is a natural effect; during meditation just be sure to be aware of such imbalances so as to gain maximum benefit from this and similar exercises.

Once the body is relaxed through the Middle Pillar exercise, energy will be able to rise up through your chakras and make its way to your brain. In Raja Yoga (more recently called Kundalini Yoga), the Yogi raised energy up through his spine and into his brain to attain the full potential of his mind and body. Through relaxation, concentration, and repetition, the Yogi brought the energy into focus. With repeated practice your body will remember the relaxed state you have achieved. In order to program body and mind to remember the relaxed state, do the Middle Pillar exercise immediately upon waking up as a part of the Surjaah and just before going to bed. This is when the mind is most susceptible to suggestion.

The Middle Pillar technique is performed best while sitting upright in a comfortable chair and breathing rhythmically. This pose can also be performed standing with both feet on the floor, knees together, and hands on your thighs.

First, focus on a brilliant, purifying light penetrating your skull, glowing from just above your Crown. This light should be envisioned as a radiating, revolving sphere of light the size of a small melon or grapefruit. Form it on the astral and etheric levels. Next you must implant the divine word "Ah" into the sphere. As you inhale, say this name in your mind, and as you exhale, say it with your voice out loud so you can corporeally experience the vibrations and concentrate them in the sphere. Deep concentration will help the ball vibrate.

Now, repeat this step for the other chakras. Imagine a tube or ray of light going into your Third Eye chakra. Repeat the word "Ah" mentally as well as verbally. Continue for all the other chakras; Throat (AY) Heart (SA), solar plexus (TA), Sacral (AE), and Root (NE). Once this is accomplished, your chakras will be linked together so as to plant energy deep into the corporeal and subtle earth.

ELORATHIAN
ANATOMY OF THE SUBTLE BODY

ASTRAL BODY
ETHERIC BODY
CORPOREAL BODY

Artwork © 2022 StrigoiVii.org by Zuriel

To ground yourself, concentrate on the energy beneath your feet and breathe rhythmically for a count of four seconds in and four seconds out as you imagine your chakras radiating energy throughout your body. Imagine the energy from the right side of your feet flowing up your body as you inhale and down the left side as you exhale.

Now visualize the energy rising up your front as you inhale and down your back as you exhale. This can be visualized as the energy rolling up and down an egg that encloses your body. Now imagine the energy riding up the Middle Pillar through the center of your body as you inhale and out the top of your head like a fountain as you exhale. The energy should saturate all sides of your body as it flows down to the bottom of the egg surrounding you. Imagine this egg of Lifeforce forming around you as it flows downward. Repeat until you feel the energy strongly flowing around you.

To conclude the exercise, focus the energy into a specific chakra, using the divine energy. The chakra you choose will depend upon the desired result. For example, should you seek to strengthen yourself and your understanding of your Immortal-minded nature, raise the energy to your Solar Plexus. Visualize the energy coming from your foundation (the ground) and flowing up to your Solar Plexus. As you inhale, imagine the energy expanding, and as you exhale, imagine it contracting. This can be done for as long or as short a duration and as many times as you wish. You may also alter the visualization and mantra depending upon your personal preference.

CHAPTER 32
ADVANCED GATHERING OF ENERGIES

...and looking out [at me were] the hungriest eyes in the world... those eyes. Nothing vulgar, but all the same they're looking at you with a hunger. There was the faintest dizzy feeling like something was being drawn out of me. Just a little bit.

—Fritz Leiber, *The Girl with the Hungry Eyes*

Within the previous tomes of the Strigoi Vii Codex and the chapter on Primal Spiritualism, we explored the elementary aspects of the Art of Gathering Energy, including ethics, applications, and practices such as Ambient, Surface, Sensual, and Deep Gathering . Here in Coming Forth by Twilight we explore more advanced forms of gathering energy. We will focus on breath control and the applications of Psychometric and Visual Gathering Energy. Astral Gathering, or Flight, will be discussed later, because its practice requires a significant and more advanced set of skills.

The ability to employ these Advanced Arts of Gathering Lifeforce ultimately depends upon the sincere intent of the Strigoi Vii. Those who do not possess significant experience in the lower techniques of Gathering energy and the genuine purpose of moving beyond mortal-minded ethics while drawing in Lifeforce will not have achieved the perceptions necessary to employ Advanced Gathering. If the aspiring Morrah feels any uncertainty upon these points, We recommend They review the previous books of Strigoi Vii Codex before attempting these Advanced Arts of Gathering.

While the Advanced Arts of Gathering are natural processes that fall solidly within the boundaries of Immortal-minded ethics, it is especially necessary that the aspiring Morrah fully let go of any residual mortal-minded perceptions of gathering Lifeforce as "unethical theft." This is our nature, and as the lion feeds from its prey, We must feed from the herds of humanity. However, unlike the savage animals of the wild, we wish to foster content amongst humans as well as happiness and satisfaction in their day-to-day lives. Worshipping their gods, idols, and celebrities will then keep them in a seduced state of Lifeforce generation. These distractions are the brush in which we lie and wait, gather their energies, and encourage them to further expand their numbers in order to provide us with an unlimited Source of Lifeforce.

Our Psychometric and Visual forms of drawing energies involve the direct intent to practice Gathering by looking at a mortal, attaching a tendril to their subtle body, and drawing out their Lifeforce in large quantities. There is nothing unethical about gathering energy in this manner to fuel Zhep'r. It is a necessary process within the evolution of Strigoi Vii, and full and complete acceptance of the Art of Gathering Energy is necessary to approach Immortality of the Self and avoidance of the Second Death.

Even if a mortal became aware of your intentions in gathering their energy, which is unlikely, most mundanes would not believe you were feeding upon them because they rarely have perceptions awakened beyond the corporeal. Conversely, those mortals who have the Vampyre Current in their souls or who manifest genuine psychic abilities may be able to notice your actions. Be cautious of such individuals and avoid them if possible, unless you have consent to draw upon their energies. A Strigoi Vii can recognize such Awakened or semi-Awakened individuals by observing their energy signature.

Advanced applications of the Art of Gathering Energy are much more challenging than the simpler forms of our Art. The Advanced Art of Gathering Energy draws upon deeper energies as the Strigoi Vii draws directly from a target's etheric body at a distance. Since the Strigoi Vii's etheric body is not directly touching that of the target, the connection must be made through more diverse layers of reality that have not been discussed before this teaching. Such acts require a significant shift in perception.

Breath Control

Breath control is an essential part of managing and controlling the flow of Lifeforce. Lifeforce is carried and directed by the breath and by application of the Will. For example, imagine you are a dancer in a club and come face-to-face with your donors on an intimate basis. Look them directly in the eye as would a lion or wolf and subtly breathe in their energy while they are distracted by your performance. You do not need physical contact, just visual contact. This technique works well for any Strigoi Vii who is regularly the focus of people's attention, such as a college professor, public speaker, tour guide, exotic dancer or performer. This technique can also be used when seducing a mortal. Feel their aura and, when you are at a sufficient distance, breathe directly in, taking their energy. You should experiment and practice to determine at what distance you find this application most effective. At first, the Strigoi Vii will most likely find it is easiest if they are physically near their donor, while later they will be able to perform this technique from a large distance.

Psychometric Gathering

It is essential to work on your breath technique. This is the foundation of these more advanced forms of Gathering. When you are applying Psychometric Gathering, your breath will guide and direct the energy. Psychometric Gathering requires the Strigoi Vii to shift Their perceptions to break down the illusion of time and space. This concept comes from the idea of "sympathetic" or "imitative" magick, as described by scholars such as James Frazer in The Golden Bough. Psychometric Gathering energy is a form of Gathering based upon correspondence. It requires a corporeal bridge, or an item that is connected to the donor(s). Practices related to Psychometric Gathering include psychometry (reading objects), voodoo dolls (when created and used properly), and sacred contagion.

The mention of contagion does not come from the concept of contagious diseases, but a positively conceived interpretation of the theory of Sacred Contagion envisioned by French sociologist Émile Durkheim in his book The Elementary Forms of Religious Life. Such a definition of contagion is that the spiritual properties of an object can be passed to another object, person, or place through physical contact. We Strigoi Vii use this concept of contagion to transfer energy through the Art of Gathering Lifeforce.

Psychometry is the ability to read energetic impressions within objects such as a piece of clothing, jewelry, or other powerful personal possessions. The skilled psychometrist can hold such an object and receive impressions of the person(s) who owned it, under what conditions the object was used, and even, in advanced workings, locate the owner(s). Psychometry depends upon the fact that everything creates energetic links as it comes into contact with other objects or is used by a living being. Not only will people create links with others with whom they associate, they will create links with personal objects. For example, a wedding ring that is worn every day will have a strong link with the wearer. When practicing Psychometric Gathering, the Strigoi Vii must be able to manage these links over a large distance without the donor being physically present.

Psychometric Gathering thus allows a remote connection with the donor. However, from the astral perspective, the donor is not actually absent, since space is simply an illusion when perceived from the astral. Therefore, the donor is simultaneously at a distance yet directly in contact with you through the personal object to which they are linked. These pieces are known as Viss and contain immensely strong links to the donor.

With the Viss you can make a bridge between yourself and the donor that bypasses corporeal distance and contains many subtle links upon which to draw. When practicing Psychometric Gathering, the Strigoi Vii is simultaneously subtly "touching" the donor through the links and corporeally reaching them through the physical Viss. Viss may include any item that has had time to form a significant number of links with the donor. The most basic would be a favorite article of clothing, piece of jewelry, lucky charm, cell phone, and so on. The most effective Viss are those items to which the donor has a strong emotional attachment or those with which they have had prolonged physical contact. However, the best Viss are actually pieces of the individual such as fingernails, hair, blood, or skin. These have been generated by the corporeal body and maintain intense links to the donor.

At this point we must issue a warning for those who seek to master this level of the Art of Gathering Energy. From the Strigoi Vii perspective, Psychometric Gathering is not a violation of the Principles because the Strigoi Vii has no need to ingest or even physically touch the corporeal blood of the donor with their bare skin. Of course, physical elements of the donor should be obtained in an ethical fashion and without physically harming the donor. Each Strigoi Vii will have to determine for themselves to what degree they wish to practice this particular application of Our Art and exercise responsibility in obtaining the necessary Viss. For example, a Strigoi Vii might develop an informed and consensual relationship with a particular donor and request a securely sealed vial of safely drawn blood in order to practice Psychometric Gathering with this donor. The donor may send them a gift of a Viss (such as a lock of hair or vial of blood). Of course, it can be dangerous for the Strigoi Vii to place themselves in direct contact with any bodily fluids! For this reason, many Strigoi Vii who practice Psychometric Gathering in this manner prefer to use items such as a lock of hair or nail clippings as a Viss and completely avoid the entire issue of corporeal blood.

It is also necessary to note that excreted waste products, such as urine and feces, are not suitable for Psychometric Gathering. Not only does contact with such excretions represent a potential health risk, but they are also the discarded waste products of the corporeal body and as such do not have a strong energetic link to it.

A great example of this art is voodoo dolls, which originated in some practices of Haitian Vodou. The practitioner creates a poppet in an individual's likeness that contains elements of that person, such as their hair or clothing. The poppet is thus linked to the individual. In theory, any harm that comes to the poppet will also affect the individual. However, in many practices, the poppets are used solely for positive functions such as healing.

An echo of this practice exists in the concept of phylactery, or when the life of an individual is transferred to an outside object. There are old folktales of individuals who have hidden their heart in a secret location and thus achieved immortality. The traditional Russian story of Koschei the Deathless is one such tale. These all represent examples of links and how they can be manipulated on a subtle level for various purposes.

Once the Strigoi Vii has obtained the desired Viss, They simply link to the item by holding it or touching it and beginning to visualize Their donor. In the case of a Viss involving blood or corporeal portions of the donor, for safety's sake it is advised to first place the Viss within a sealed container or touch it only with sterile protective gloves. For physical objects such as a piece of clothing or jewelry, it is preferable to simply hold the Viss with the bare hands. The Strigoi Vii should then take a deep breath inward, clenching Their abdominal muscles if desired to help maintain Their focus on the individual and the Viss. They should then begin to draw Lifeforce through the Viss. Some Strigoi Vii report that the Viss may begin to "feel warm" or subtly begin to vibrate as energy is channeled through it, and others report the sensation as a sort of "energetic glow." As long as the target is alive, no matter where they are, these links can be used to draw in their energy. Of course, the more carefully constructed and personal the Viss, the stronger the links.

Our Art of Psychometric Gathering Lifeforce can also be applied with individuals you have not met. For example, suppose you find a purse or wallet some unknown person has lost (of course you shall shortly bring it to the lost and found or the police). Whilst you are holding the item, simply meditate on it, feeling the links stretching out through the Web of Wyrd in the subtle reality. Once you feel you have made contact with the donor at the other end, simply apply breath control and draw in the energy like liquid through a straw. Again, make sure not to take too much, as you may harm the donor or alert them to your intentions. During this process you may find that you gain some psychometric impressions of the person who lost the item, potentially even where they went after they dropped it!

Experiment with Psychometric Gathering as much as possible. Try touching your colleague's chair when they are not at their desk, a glass a nightclub patron left on the bar or table, or a coat in a cloak-room. Note your impressions during these experiments. However, common sense dictates that it is not a good idea to handle or examine a stranger's personal possessions. That is why neutral objects such as desk chairs or abandoned tableware may best serve as a Viss. In the case that you construct a Viss from highly personal or cherished possessions, it is advised to obtain the donor's consent to use these things instead of just taking them.

These links will dissipate and weaken over time, as the corporeal and subtle connections will disperse. Ergo, take advantage of strong and recent links that can be employed powerfully.

Visual Gathering

Visual Gathering can only be attempted after the initiate has mastered Psychometric Gathering, since it requires touching exclusively through the ethereal and astral levels without even the corporeal link- age of a Viss. The term Mal'acchio comes from the "evil eye" cast by witches in many myths and folktales. However, Our Visual Gathering is not an evil curse! Instead, it utilizes links formed by visual eye contact between the Strigoi Vii and the donor. There is an old saying that "the eyes are the windows to the soul," and for the Strigoi Vii, this is literally true!

For example, it is possible to single out an individual standing in a crowd or walking down the street by making eye contact with them. Eye contact is initially a great tool for creating a weak distance link, yet this is not enough to satisfy the thirst for Lifeforce a Strigoi Vii experiences. The Strigoi Vii must make subtle contact with the donor. However, how can this occur when there is no direct contact between the etheric bodies? The answer is simple: the Strigoi Vii must learn to create the link through the astral realm, in which time and space do not present the same limitations as in the corporeal world.

Once you have made contact with an individual and wish to initiate Visual Gathering, begin to feel their presence at a distance with your aura. Stretch out a tendril as far as you can toward them. You will then begin to start finding the links that will guide your tendrils into contact with their subtle body. This is a difficult technique that takes time and practice to master. Some Strigoi Vii find that it is helpful to visualize a luminous ray or beam emitting from Their Third Eye chakra and penetrating into the donor's subtle body. This process may also be made easier at first by choosing a donor with whom you have some ostensible reason to make eye contact, such as if they are making a public announcement or wearing an eye-catching outfit. Many people, especially in urban areas, avoid eye contact with strangers and may break that contact before you can establish a link. With dedicated practice you will eventually be able to form a link even with a split-second glance.

Once the Strigoi Vii overcomes barriers of time and space and sees distance as only an illusion, They can reach directly through the astral and "touch" Their donor. This process is called the vampiric gaze when used in combination with the Glamour technique of the Vampyre Presence. Visual Gathering is similar to what many new-age theorists and occultists call telekinesis, which is the process of touching with one's mind or subtle body in order to affect the corporeal world. Since space and time are different in the astral realm, the Strigoi Vii can simply look at Their donor without any physical connection, make subtle contact through the astral realm, and draw forth the desired Lifeforce. The Strigoi Vii must be able to project both ethereally and astrally simultaneously to effectively practice Visual Gathering. Mastering Mal'acchio gathering is the necessary foundation for moving on to Flight.

Warnings

Certain warnings do apply to this Advanced Art of Gathering Energy. Due to the intimate astral and etheric connection with the donor, the Strigoi Vii should be careful to make sure there is no reverse flow of energy, in which the donor actually absorbs energy from the Strigoi Vii! This is no danger in more basic applications of our Art such as Ambient Gathering, for in that case the Strigoi Vii simply consciously disengages from the Ambient Lifeforce. However, in Mal'acchio gathering, the tendril that links the Strigoi Vii and the donor can potentially transmit the energy both ways. In that case, the Strigoi Vii should consciously disengage and break the tendrils that link Them to the donor. As an analogy, when one is breathing in foully scented air, they can simply hold their breath to avoid the stench. This is similar to disengaging when Ambient gathering. However, if drinking spoiled milk through a straw, one must consciously stop sucking at the straw, and even may choose to remove the straw from the cup. Such is disengaging from Visual Gathering, as the tendrils (or straw) do not enter into the Ambient Art of Gathering Energy.

Be sure to filter the Lifeforce upon which you draw, because it is best to remove the static of astral attachments such as emotions or thoughts. If you fail to do this, you may absorb confusing bits of the donor's memories, mentality, or emotions. During this application of the Art of Gathering Energy, the Strigoi Vii seeks the pure Lifeforce only, not the associated astral attachments. However, more advanced techniques within the Clavicula Sangraal Sorcery practiced by Magisters include deliberately gathering energy with astral attachments.

Traditional psychic vampires (asarai) are parasites who on positive emotional energy over gathering Lifeforce. Many accounts of the curse of the evil eye may actually have their roots in asarai practices of feeding on emotions. This is not our intent. As with other more advanced applications of the Art of Gathering Energy, the Strigoi Vii should be careful not to draw too deeply from a single individual; this may result in what we call a conditional, or sympathetic vampire. The donor's depleted energetic body will instinctively seek to replenish itself, often by causing a reverse flow of energy, as mentioned previously. There is no reason to and no sense in drinking the cup of Lifeforce to its dregs! As ethical Strigoi Vii, We always seek to preserve the health and well-being of Our Source. There is an endless surplus of Lifeforce in the world, and no reason to ever tap one individual donor to the point of potential harm.

Some Strigoi Vii prefer to practice Visual Gathering and other Advanced Arts of Gathering with consensual, informed donors. However, such an arrangement is not necessary in Our ethical practice of Gathering energy and is merely an individual preference. As predators, We need feel no guilt regarding any of Our Arts of Gathering Lifeforce. As well, there are potential disadvantages in gathering exclusively or primarily from certain donors. For example, repeatedly drawing energy from the same donor over a prolonged period of time may result in sympathetic vampirism. Also, many of the individuals who eagerly "offer" themselves as donors are actually asarai in disguise! They voluntarily act as donors in order to draw energy as they are tapped! There is no honor in such an arrangement, and it is antithetical to the Strigoi Vii nature. For these as well as other reasons, the majority of Strigoi Vii do not rely on specific donors or accept offers from potential donors when practicing Our Art of Gathering Energy.

Summation

Our Advanced Arts of Gathering Lifeforce require dedication, practice, and Will to master. As Strigoi Vii, the world is yours to enjoy! Life is everywhere. Test these techniques for yourself, explore, and enjoy the results! Like all aspects of Our Mysteries, these applications may take time to master. However, do not be discouraged and never forget your purpose. Zhep'r is the practical road to personal Immortality of the Self. Focus the Lifeforce you collect into positive intentions and mold your personal reality as you wish. Most of all, continue to offer your collected Lifeforce as an offering in sacred Communion with our Ancestors and Vampyre Current. By doing so, you will be more easily able to gather and store ever increasing amounts of energy, reinforce your subtle body, and Ascend to higher states. Do with it what thou wilt!

CHAPTER 33

THE ASTRAL REALM

When I survey the bright Celestial sphere;
So rich with jewels hung, that night Doth like an Ethiop bride appear:
My soul her wings doth spread
And heaven-ward flies
The Almighty's mysteries to read In the large volumes of the skies.

—William Habington, "Nox Nocti Indicat Scientiam"

Above the corporeal and ethereal is the astral plane; this is where dreams, emotions, visions and thoughts reside. The very word astral means "of the stars." The astral layer is comprised of the most abstract and least dense energies of the three outer layers of reality. It is also the vastest of the three outer planes. It may be seen as a central realm between the lower corporeal and ethereal and higher mental and divine planes of existence. In mortal-minded religions and esotericism, the astral is related to the Yetzirah in Lurianic Kabbalah or the third world in the Tree of Life, sometimes called "the world of formation." The astral plane is similar to the concept of the Spirit World in occultism and spiritualism. It is also associated with the land of Faerie in Celtic folklore, and Pan's pastoral

Utopia, Arcadia of Peloponnesus, in Greek mythology. From the perspective of modern science and mathematics, the astral may also be seen as the fourth dimension beyond the corporeal x-y-z Cartesian plane.

As the center point between the higher and lower planes of existence, the astral plane is a virtual world where the laws of space-time are very different from those experienced in the corporeal or even the etheric world. The astral plane exists on a higher vibrational frequency than the corporeal and ethereal plane. It is the realm of spirits, because such entities have no physical form and exist only as certain frequencies of energy. The astral may also be apprehended as the luminous gateway to the higher realms of existence and perception. Thus is it that Coming Forth by Twilight is concerned with the astral plane. Once the Adeptus Vampyre has gained and validated their understanding of the astral world, they will have the foundation pass the Mirror Gates into the Inner Mysteries and explore the higher levels of initiation.

Time and space do not have the same meaning in the astral realm as they do in the corporeal and even the etheric realms. The astral world is nonlinear and cannot be fully understood from the perception of Euclidean geometry. When Albert Einstein conceived his theory of relativity, he may have been inspired by a glimpse into the astral plane. In the astral realm, truly, a straight line is most often not the shortest distance between two points! The contemporary mundane sciences of quantum physics, chaos theory, and even psychology are beginning to describe the geography of the astral plane. However, the true and entire cartography of the astral is still far beyond the domain of mortal-minded science and understanding. It is vast and contains many domains and dimensions that can only be consciously reached through skill, deliberately freed perceptions, inherent ability, or, in certain cases, permission from the guardians of those domains. As a Strigoi Vii, you should begin to learn how to develop your natural aptitude and "fly" within the astral realm. The astral realm is also sometimes called "the realm of emotions." As with any other sort of energy, emotions are vibrations, and of a type that are extremely potent and much more highly charged in the astral realm than in the lower layers or reality. In previous books, we have counseled not to draw energy from the astral layer, because the Strigoi Vii who does so will likely also absorb emotional energies and impressions contained within this layer. Also, the mortal-minded pass through the astral layer upon the Second Death. As they do so, their emotions of guilt about their life are most amplified. This is one reason why people who have suffered true NDEs (Near-Death Experiences) often feel the compulsion to change or amend their lives thereafter.

Within the astral plane, corporeal objects possess counterparts, or doubles, just as they do in the ethereal plane. In fact, this mirroring is related to the potentially holographic nature of certain aspects of reality.

The Astral Body

The astral body is the least dense of all layers of the Self and is the vessel of the aspect of the Self sometimes mortal-minded call this the "spirit" by the mortal-minded. The term astral body originates from nineteenth-century Theosophists and neo-Rosicrucians. Many contemporary new-age and occult paths have also adopted the concept of the astral body. The astral body may also be seen as the far reaches of what is sometimes known as one's "concrete consciousness." Like a spiritual processor, the astral body functions as a vehicle for desires and emotions. It is also the seat of imagination, Will, and memory.

The astral body is located above the etheric body (although such linear concepts have less meaning in these higher layers of reality), and thus mutually supports the existence of the etheric body. Similarly, the etheric body supports the corporeal form. From the Strigoi Vii perspective, the mutual existence and interaction of these three layers of the body comprise what is normally viewed as "life." Upon the Second Death, the entire astral body dissipates, because the corporeal and etheric bodies no longer hold their cohesion and thus do not support the continued existence of the astral. The astral body relies on the energies supplied to it by the etheric and corporeal bodies and when they decay, so does the astral envelope of memory, imagination, and Will. Upon the dissolution of the astral body, the Self essentially ceases to exist. The Living Vampyre seeks to avoid the Second Death at all costs and, therefore, is concerned with physical and energetic preservation of all layers of the body. Just as taking physical care will help preserve the corporeal self, absorbing Lifeforce and making the circuit of Communion will help preserve the energetic and True Self.

It is possible for the astral body to manifest corporeally without the physical shell. Upon occasion, the Strigoi Morte have appeared to certain members of the Family using this method. Mortal-minded tales of ghosts or divine apparitions may also have some basis in these manifestations. It is not impossible for a Strigoi Vii to also manifest Their astral body in this manner, but the process for doing so is a highly advanced technique of the Inner Mysteries. Corporeal Manifestation of the astral body is a very different process than Flight, because during Flight (or astral projection), the astral Self is not perceptible to others, whilst in Corporeal Manifestation the astral body appears as if it had physical reality. Highly skilled Strigoi Vii, as well as the Strigoi Morte, can also, through application of Will, shape Their astral body into any pattern They choose, whether it be a mist, bat, or wolf. This art is known as lycanthropy or shapeshifting. Very advanced techniques of shapeshifting also involve extending the shape into the etheric and corporeal bodies through the mirroring of the layers of the Self.

Much mortal-minded folklore about vampires may actually derive from manipulation of the astral body. For example, astral Energy is not fully or generally detectable by corporeal means. Therefore, a Vampyre traveling or projecting through the astral would not cast a reflection or appear in a photograph! Similarly, shapeshifting of the astral body may be the basis for the old tales that vampires can dissipate into mist, or transform into animals like cats, bats, or wolves.

Since the astral body is composed of energy that is at a different frequency than the matter of the corporeal world, in most cases the astral body cannot be harmed physically. However, it would be potentially possible for an entity to energetically charge or attune an object that could function as a weapon in the astral. Again, this is the seed of the superstition that vampires can be killed by holy objects such as crosses or "blessed" weapons. Since all layers of the body are connected, wounds sustained upon the astral body will be mirrored in some fashion on the corporeal body. In a similar fashion, physical wounds will have an analog in the astral. It is possible, to a certain extent, to heal corporeal wounds by embarking upon processes to heal the astral body, but this is a skill that takes talent and dedication to master.

If a Strigoi Morte chooses to corporeally manifest their astral body, a great deal of Lifeforce is required. They may appear visually and audibly present, but generally will only be able to achieve limited tactile contact with the corporeal plane unless they posses a body. However, the Strigoi Morte can easily effect ethereal contact in this manner and can tap and draw Lifeforce from the subtle bodies of mortals. In this way, along with Lifeforce offerings made to Them during Communion, the Strigoi Morte sustain their existence and avoid the Second Death. It is also possible for a Strigoi Vii to perform the Art of Gathering Energy in a similar manner during astral projection. However, it is necessary to make clear that the nature and sustained existence of the Strigoi Morte is much more complex than this simple explanation. As the Morrah approaches the gates of the Inner Mysteries, They should continue to deepen and develop their relationship with the Strigoi Morte so as to better know our Ancestors and apprehend their Secrets.

Astral Projection

Astral projection is fully detailed in the chapter on Out of Body Experiences or "Flight." In brief, it is the ability to separate the astral Self from the corporeal body and then return to the corporeal self at will. The result is sometimes known as an Out of Body Experience (OBE) and represents a pinnacle of freedom for the Strigoi Vii. Note that astral projection is very different from etheric projection. When a Strigoi Vii is actually projecting, they are separated from the energetic links of the ethereal world and can fly freely within the astral plane. Some of the advanced forms of the Art of Gathering Energy might be viewed as etheric projection.

The Akashic Records

The Akashic Records are a compendium of the entire history of the cosmos and the collection of all sentient learning and knowledge that exists in the astral world. The records are essentially the ultimate omniscient library of all existence. Carl Jung's theory of the collective human unconscious may be seen as a very limited version of the Akashic Records. The term Akasha means "space" or "sky" in Sanskrit, and in Hindu philosophy, it is the element of spirit, one of the five basic forces in the universe. This term found its way into Western Magick through the Theosophist movement and eventually was assumed by the Hermetic Order of the Golden Dawn. Since the nineteenth century, many esoteric and spiritual leaders have claimed to have visited the halls of the Akashic Records and say they have found occult wisdom or inspiration within these "halls." Within the halls of the Akashic Records, all the secrets of creation may be revealed.

Even the mortal-minded occasionally may visit the Records unknowingly during altered states of consciousness or particularly vivid dreams. Conscious and deliberate exploration of the Akashic Records is an Inner Teaching of the Strigoi Vii.

Extra Sensory Perceptions

Extra Sensory Perceptions (ESP) are the astral "senses" that correspond to the five corporeal senses. Of course, this is only a rough correspondence because the astral senses function on a different and more subtle energetic level. Generally speaking, these are the senses through which the Strigoi Vii experiences the astral world. However, with training in the Inner Mysteries, the Strigoi Vii can come to extend these senses into etheric and even corporeal perceptions. Some reported instances of psychic powers such as mind-reading actually occur when a Strigoi Vii or other psychically sensative individual can employ these subtle senses within a corporeal framework.

Subtle Sight "Clairvoyance"

Clairvoyance comes from the French words clair, meaning "clear," and voyance, meaning "seeing." It refers to seeing within the astral plane. Amongst the Strigoi Vii this clairvoyance must be first developed in the astral and then projected outward to the vibrational levels of the ethereal and finally the corporeal.

Subtle Touch "Psychometry"

Psychometry comes from the Greek words psyche, meaning "spirit" or "soul," and metron, meaning "measure." In Strigoi Vii parlance it refers to touch and feeling in the astral. Unlike corporeal touch, psychometry is not limited by physical distance. Applications of this astral sense were discussed in the chapter on Advanced Arts of Gathering.

Psychokinesis comes from the Greek words psyche and kinesis, meaning "motion." Psychokinesis is the ability to move objects within the astral plane. This is very difficult to translate to the corporeal world and requires a great amount of skill and Lifeforce directed by the Will. Most popular reports of psychokinesis (such as the story of the Amityville Horror) are the products of hoaxes or wishful mortal-minded thinking.

Subtle Hearing "Clairaudience"

Clairaudience is astral hearing, as clairvoyance is astral sight. The ending of -audience in the word is from the French for "hearing."

Subtle Voice "Telepathy"

Telepathy comes from the Greek words tele, meaning "distant," and patheia, meaning "to be affected by." Telepathy is the ability to speak or communicate in the astral world. Such communication can include transference of feelings, images, or memories rather than a direct mirroring of corporeal speech.

Dreams

> "Dream! Dreams shape the world. Dreams create the world anew every night. Do not dream the world they was it is now… Dream a new world."
>
> —Neil Gaiman, *A Dream of a Thousand Cats*

Dreams fall within the territory of the astral realm. When all sentient and semi-sentient beings fall into the grasp of sleep, they unconsciously interact with the astral plane. Talented humans are more skilled at moving within the astral than many other beings, because all humans experience REM sleep nightly. Furthermore, the Strigoi Vii, with Our innate talent for lucid dreaming, have an even greater potential for exploration within the astral realm.

Lucid Dreaming

Mastering lucid dreaming, or conscious control over one's dreams, is a marker of the Vampyre Adeptus. As We Strigoi Vii are masters of Our corporeal realities, so must We be masters of Our dream-realities!

Lucid dreaming occurs when the dreamer is (1) aware that they are dreaming within the dream ("awake within the dream") and (2) able to shape the dream to their Will. To some, lucid dreaming comes naturally. To others, it requires devoted practice.

Upon going to sleep, the Strigoi Vii should keep Their intent to experience lucid dreaming fixedly in mind. It may be helpful to devise a mantra ("I will experience lucid dreaming," for example) and repeat it mentally. Some Strigoi Vii report a greater rate of success when They meditate or perform a chakra-opening exercise before sleep. You should also ensure that you will not be disturbed or rudely awakened. While light background music may help, try to minimize disruptions such as television; outside influences may be overheard by the corporeal body and incorporated into the dreaming. In all cases, alcohol and medications that promote sleep should be avoided, because they disrupt the normal sleep cycle. Historically, opium was often regarded as facilitating the passage to the Dreamworld, but in reality it simply causes harmful effects and limits the abilities of the astral body.

The Strigoi Vii should seek for Their sense of Self within the dream, and attempt to consciously remind Themselves, "This is a dream." Most people are the leading actor in their own dreams, usually playing themselves! If you can maintain this knowledge of Self, you will find yourself free to act as you will within the dream and even shape the astral environment of the dream. With the conscious knowledge of this freedom usually comes an incredible exhilaration as you realize you can do whatever you want within the world of the dream, from "calling up" fantastic creatures such as dragons to flying through the air! Many lucid dreamers report increased dreaming sensory awareness upon mastery of lucid dreaming, to the point where they can actually "taste" and "feel" things consumed or experienced within lucid dreams. Remember lucid dreaming is practice for OBE but happens exclusively with your own head yet can be a good practice and launching point for astral projection.

It is often helpful to have a notebook where you can easily reach it upon waking to record your dream experiences. Expertise in dream recall is closely linked to expertise in lucid dreaming and may be difficult for novices. Too many dreams are gone and forgotten by the morning's first cup of coffee!

Astral Entities

Astral entities range from the astral bodies of corporeal beings such as humans and animals to entities that mortals generally perceive as ideas or dreams. The astral realm is also the dwelling-space of egregores and the Strigoi Morte. There is endless variety to its inhabitants, so the possible encounters are essentially countless. Since the astral is the realm of ideas, astral entities represent the manifestation of mortal and Immortal ideas and inspirations throughout history. As well, there exist amorphous entities that may be likened to pure "dream-energy" or unformed ideas. The Strigoi Vii Adeptus, during their practice of lucid dreaming and Flight, should begin to familiarize themselves with the cornucopia of fantastic entities within the astral realm.

As a rough analogy, consider the book and film *The Neverending Story*. The main character, a young boy, journeyed to a land called Fantasia by reading a story in an enchanted book. Within this land dwelt all the fantasies ever created by the human mind. Later in the story, he was given the power to shape the land of Fantasia with his thoughts and create his surroundings in that world. While this comparison is not perfect because the author's concept of Fantasia was limited by his mortal perceptions, it serves as a useful beginning point from which to start to apprehend the astral.

Among the Strigoi Vii Priesthood will typically have specific interactions with subtle beings, depending on their attunement within the Trinity Choir Pulses. Kitra, for example, are channelers and thus often draw subtle entities to themselves, both consciously and unconsciously. Ramkht, due to their natural affinity with the astral, are generally the most successful at perceiving and interacting with astral beings. Finally, Mradu, due to their intensely grounded nature, are sometimes less initially proficient at interacting with these subtle entities. However, because of their corporeal grounding, they are often talented at forming long-lasting bonds with particular astral beings.

One specific type of astral entity of interest to Strigoi Vii is known as a servitor. A servitor is an elemental being created for a specific task, such as guardianship or ritual assistance. The main difference between a servitor and an egregore (a collective group mind) is that a servitor is not self-aware and self-actualized in the manner of a well-established egregore. Often, as well, servitors are called upon for specific, limited purposes and then released back into the fabric of the astral plane when their purpose has been fulfilled.

Summation

The astral plane is like a multifaceted gemstone, constantly revealing new glittering images to one's perception. It is the realm of the Morrah and the border between the more concrete "lower realms" of the corporeal and ethereal and the abstract "higher realms" of the mental and divine. Within the astral realm the corporeal laws of time and space do not apply in the same manner, so the Strigoi Vii can boundlessly fly and dance within the astral world of memories, inspiration, ideas, and emotions. While the Minoan labyrinth revealed to Theseus only the deadly Minotaur at the center, the labyrinth of the astral realm discloses new wonders and delights at every turn. Explore!

CHAPTER 34
SILENT COMMUNION

"No longer knowing whether time existed, whether this display had lasted a second or a hundred years, whether there was a... Self and others, wounded deeply by a divine arrow which gave him pleasure, deeply enchanted and exalted, [he] stood yet a while bending over [the]... peaceful face... which had been the stage of all present and future forms."

—Hermann Hesse, *Siddhartha*

S ilent communion is a solitary Communion Rite performed without the trappings of ritual attire, speech, or other objects and tools. It is Communion performed by application of Will and activity in the mind alone—the physical body does not move. This requires intense concentration. It may be either less distracting or more difficult than formalized ritual, depending on your personality, level of concentration, and skill in energy work. Formalized ritual is a tool to prepare and focus the mind, and many Strigoi Vii find it initially necessary to use such tools. Silent Communion, however, is an essential skill that must be mastered before Ascending to Adeptus.

To perform Silent Communion, lie face up on the floor in a private, darkened, and quiet room. If desired, use earplugs to block out-side sounds and a sleeping mask to cover your eyes. Lie with your arms at your sides, palms facing upward, and your entire body relaxed. Your legs should be slightly apart, not crossed or overlapping. In yoga, this pose is known as *Shavasana* or the "corpse pose." Rub your solar plexus briskly for a short time to prepare your subtle body.

Prepare your mind for ritual. Put away distracting thoughts and focus on the task at hand. Your breathing should be steady and regular. If you wish, with each outward breath, mentally "banish" any distracting thoughts, and with each inward breath, draw peace and calm into yourself.

When you are ready, focus on your intent to perform Communion. Make a strong mental statement that you are offering your collected Lifeforce to the Strigoi Morte for Their use. Envision yourself speaking this out loud and push this intent outward through your Third Eye. At the same time, begin to release a little Lifeforce through your solar plexus. Wait for a response from the Strigoi Morte. If They do not respond, refocus and repeat this step. When you feel Their presence in response to your statement of intent, forcefully direct a stream of Lifeforce out through your solar plexus and directly upward, or in the direction of the Strigoi Morte if you can sense Their presence in a specific area. Continue until you are exhausted or receive a Recoiling.

When you are finished, linger in the ritual chamber for a while and contemplate your experiences. It is not uncommon to have visions or fall asleep following this ritual. It is often used as a jumping-off point for Out of Body Experiences.

CHAPTER 35

FLIGHT OF THE SUCCUBUS (OBE)

I didn't quite dream, but it all seemed to be real... something very sweet and very bitter all around me at once; and then I seemed sinking into deep green water, and there was a singing in my ears, as I have heard there is to drowning men; and then everything seemed passing away from me; my soul seemed to go out from my body and float about the air.

—Bram Stoker, *Dracula*

The Strigoi Morte have been able to conquer the Second Death and secure Their Immortality through, among other factors, Their mastery of the astral realm. To begin to gain this familiarity with the astral you must master Flight. In modern occult parlance Flight is sometimes known as an Out-of-Body Experience (OBE) or astral projection. Astral Flight is a natural skill for those of the Current and an important step in Zhep'r that is required of the Strigoi Vii Adeptus. It is the basis for higher levels of ascension.

However, this is not to say that mastering Flight will be easy! Even though you are inherently capable of Flight, you must practice and learn by concerted application and not be discouraged by early failure. A child inherently knows how to walk yet must stumble and fall many times before becoming ambulatory. To fully experience the freedom of the astral layer and Come Forth by Twilight, the Strigoi Vii must solve, experience, and, finally, apply the technology within this mystery.

Until the Strigoi Vii achieves such mastery of Flight, They are essentially imprisoned within the fleshy bonds of the corporeal body. Even though the Vampyre may have the ability to fully interact within the ethereal and be skilled in the Arts of Gathering Lifeforce, they still lack the necessary skills to truly defeat the Second Death and achieve Immortality of the Self. Achieving successful Flight is a challenging task, yet once it is fully consciously realized, the Strigoi Vii will truly Ascend above the more restricting corporeal and ethereal layers of reality and partake in the freedoms that only a genuine Flight experience can offer. In Flight the Strigoi Vii can dance within the wider universe, enjoy the companionship of the Ancients of the Family in Their natural environments, and for the first time enjoy the pleasures of direct contact with the Ascended Elders. Only through a successful grasp of Flight can the Strigoi Vii truly experience the astral realm and Come Forth by Twilight.

Applications

Once you shift your perspective, you change your worldview. Flight offers endless realities and possibilities that cannot be achieved from the limited perspective of the Dayside or Nightside. During Flight, the Strigoi Vii is freed from the dense energies of the corporeal world as well as the moving liquid energies of the ethereal. Echoes of the reality of Flight, transformed by the Glamour, can be found in folklore and legends. The tales of vampires turning into bats and taking flight into the darkness or dissolving into a cloud of mist and traveling through a keyhole all have their origin in the truth of our Flight. Astral Flight is intimately associated with Vampyric shape changing, as evinced in the folk belief that vampires must change shape before taking flight.

From the Twilight perspective, Lifeforce gathered by the Vampyre during Flight is much easier to draw upon, delectably sweeter, and more intensely potent. The contact between the subtle body of the Vampyre and their donor is direct and unhindered, especially when the Vampyre draws Lifeforce from a sleeping mortal. Throughout history mortals have been dimly aware of this and have concocted legends of incubi or succubae who fed upon sleeping victims as an explanation. The experience of being fed upon during a Vampyre's Flight can be exquisitely intense for the mortal as well, which is why so many legends depict the vampiric creature as a seductive sexual predator. Mortals simply derive pleasure from such experiences!

Technology

All layers of the body are generally closely interwoven. Energy is required to effect the conscious separation of the astral body from the corporeal body for any length of time. Before practicing Flight, the Vampyre must first separate a portion of the Lifeforce contained in their etheric and astral body for use in Flight. This Lifeforce must be sealed and condensed into what is known as a "double," or a projection of the corporeal self. With this foundation, the Vampyre is free to leave the corporeal realm and move freely in the astral.

For successful Flight, astral projection must be done consciously and with full application of the Will, or else it is simply pipe-visions and fantasies. Daydreaming that you are flying away from a boring workday is not Flight! One of the most common pitfalls for the Strigoi Vii beginning to experiment with Flight is that of self-deception. It is possible to so vividly imagine an episode of astral Flight that you convince yourself it actually happened!

We recommend assiduously following the exercises listed below as well as researching the vast body of occult knowledge on astral projection before drawing hasty conclusions about personal success. As with everything else, the Strigoi Vii will achieve success in Flight only through experiment yielding verifiable results. Above all, do not be discouraged! The knowledge and memory of Flight are in your Blood. It is your responsibility to unlock the gates of this mystery to experience true Zhep'r.

Mortal Perceptions and Near-Death Experiences

As discussed, Near-Death Experiences (NDEs) can usually be explained by simple biological processes. As well, sometimes the mind of the hyle (Aristotle's concept of matter), when the body is near death, will invent a convenient fiction to mask the reality of death. Many Near-Death Experiences have similar features, such as the mortal moving toward a "healing white light" or experiencing intense feelings of well-being or safety. Some mortal minded or "hyle" even report "seeing" the gates of heaven during these experiences! The great majority of Near-Death Experiences are based upon lies that have been planted in the mortal-minded consciousness to comfort them in the face of death. Most mortals cannot face the reality that they will eventually cease to exist as an individual and their energy will consequently be recycled in the great cycle of life. Thus, the Strigoi Vii do not, in general, consider Near-Death Experiences to be full experiences of Flight.

For mortals, after the First Death their corporeal body ceases to produce new Lifeforce in order to sustain the links to the etheric body, which in its turn slowly begins to decay. Since all levels of the Self are linked, during this time the astral body begins to evaporate. The decay of the corporeal, ethereal, and astral bodies can actually be a very pleasurable trap for the mortal. When the corporeal body is in the process of dying, it releases chemicals that reduce pain and promote feelings of contentment (DMT). The etheric body, when dying, produces equivalent effects. For mortals, this is a natural process, and they lack the ability or potential to forestall the inevitable First and Second Death.

However, it should be obvious that should the Strigoi Vii be able to separate Their astral body from Their corporeal body, They will be able to continue existence in the astral realm after the First Death and even continue to maintain their etheric body by utilizing Lifeforce collected in the astral realm. This is an important aspect of True Immortality for the Strigoi Vii! As we have noted in Coming Forth by Day and Coming Forth by Night, this process is greatly simplified if the corporeal body can be preserved; there are strong ties between all layers of the body, and maintaining the astral body will become more difficult if the corporeal body is destroyed.

Warnings

Be wary! The corporeal and ethereal layers should not be ignored or thought of as irrelevant once you have truly experienced Flight. Such a mentality can be very tempting and seductive for the beginner. How- ever, all layers of the Maiiah are part of the Self. Ignoring other layers of the Self in favor of the astral may have its origins in the infamous mind-body dualism of Descartes, the foundation for a great deal of Western thought and religion. Descartes, like so many after him, viewed the physical body as essentially separate from and inferior to the spirit or soul. Experience and existence are valuable on all levels! The Strigoi Vii does not seek for a limited life or limited Immortality! While the pleasures and advantages of Flight are manifold, you must not let these pleasures distract you from the equally compelling pleasures to be experienced in the corporeal and ethereal realms.

So many mortals seek to mortify or deny their physical body because they see it as a prison and something unclean and profane. Perpetuation of this belief is another example of the Glamour of the Ancients, for with such a mindset the mortal-minded are slaves to their own ignorance and thus are never able to enjoy the security and benefits of Immortality. Free of these beliefs, the Strigoi Vii can truly embrace Their own nature and enjoy the pleasures of Zhep'r.

Without the balance of all three layers of the Self, the Strigoi Vii will not be sufficiently established within the Maiiah to defeat the Second Death. This balance is essential because it is required for the Immortal to shift perceptions from Day to Night and, finally, achieve Twilight. These anchors are the three foundations of the Self. Without mastery and equilibrium of the Corporeal Dayside and Etheric Nightside, there is no foundation for Zhep'r within the Twilight. Balance is truly the key to self-actualization and Immortality of the Self.

Keys and Exercises

Perhaps the best way to begin your exploration of the astral is through lucid dreaming, detailed earlier in this text. Dreams are one of the gateways to the astral realm, and each time you dream your astral body separates from your corporeal body and roams throughout the astral realm. To a great extent, the confused events and symbolism of most dreams are no more than your residual mortal-minded perceptions and expectations placing limitations upon your experience in the astral realm because the substance of the astral is quite malleable. You must learn to separate the mere dream-reflections of personal events and predilections from true Flight.

Once you are experienced in lucid dreaming, you are ready to attempt short astral Flights. This does not necessarily have to be done before sleep but should be attempted in the same sort of environment in which you experienced lucid dreaming.

For many, the most difficult part is the conscious separation of the astral body. Make a concerted effort when beginning the separation to feel as if you are climbing out of your body as a scuba diver would remove their wet suit. If needed, take a deep draught of Lifeforce to encase and sustain your astral form. Those who need more help might want to envision a rope dangling above them and, hand over hand, pull their astral body out of their corporeal form. Others like to visualize a ghostly silver "astral double" separating from and floating above their physical body. You must experiment and determine which method is most effective for you.

Envision yourself leaving your corporeal body. Focus on experiencing all the surrounding area from the astral perspective through the subtle senses of clairvoyance (sight) and psychometry (touch). Once this is achieved, you should feel a sense of floating, which many Strigoi Vii liken to drifting in the weightlessness of space. Others have spoken of it as effortlessly swimming though a crystalline pool.

Once again, it may be difficult to determine when you are just imagining Flight and when you have truly achieved it. Some experience a "click" upon separating from their corporeal body, but many do not. Following are two exercises that can be used to verify the validity of an astral experience.

The first, cited in many different discussions of astral projection, is ideal for the beginner. Before beginning the separation from your corporeal body, place a playing card face up on top of a shelf or any other raised location where it cannot be seen. Do not look at the card as you do so. Then, once you begin your Flight, "fly" over to where the card is placed and "look" at it. You will quickly find that your senses in the astral realm correspond, though not exactly, to your corporeal senses. "Seeing" in the astral is a different experience from seeing in the corporeal world.

You may return to your corporeal body by traveling back to it and merging the astral and the physical bodies or by strongly concentrating upon your corporeal Self. Despite much discussion to the contrary, it is nearly impossible to get "lost" from your corporeal body whilst astrally projecting! Similarly, the corporeal and etheric bodies have self-sufficient sustaining mechanisms during the relatively short duration of Flight (recall, as well, that time is infinitely variable in the astral) so there is no worry about your body dying or ceasing to function while your astral consciousness is not in it.

Upon returning to your corporeal body, check the card. Was it the card you saw during Flight? Once you have successfully completed this exercise, you should move on to longer Flights.

For a longer Flight, separate your astral body from your corporeal as before, but this time choose a more distant destination that is well known to you, such as a friend's or relative's dwelling or a familiar street. Time and space are not constants in the astral realm, so you do not have to worry about your destination being too far for your astral self to travel! The only caveat besides familiarity in your choice of destination should be that you should be able to easily and quickly verify your astral impressions of that location.

Try very hard to "see" and not simply remember the location! Look around and take careful note of anything that is changed from your memories. Does your friend have a new rug on the floor? Is there a sale taking place in your favorite store? If there are people present in the location you have chosen, what are they doing? Do not worry about being found out while astrally flying. Most mortals cannot detect astral beings, and even the most sensitive mortals usually have no more than a faint sense of something else being present.

As soon as possible upon returning to your corporeal body, verify your experience. Call your friend and ask if they have bought a new rug! Take a trip down to your favorite store and see if there is a sale going on! This exercise can be facilitated by the aid of a sympathetic partner who is willing to position themselves in the location you have chosen and immediately verify or discount your impressions.

At first, you will find it easier to fly to places of which you have foreknowledge. However, as your expertise in Flight grows, you will find yourself able to astrally visit locales all over the globe!

Finally, the Hunt of the Succubus/Incubus is an advanced exercise in gathering energy astrally. It should be done with serious intent before going to sleep at night, in the conditions noted previously. The target of the astral gathering should be predetermined and can be anyone, but it may be helpful to pick someone with whom you are familiar and with whom you can verify the experience. Note that you should not disclose your intent to them and can verify your results without doing so. Once you have gained your astral form, astrally visit your target whilst they sleep. You may find it helpful to "hover" directly above their corporeal body. Then use the Advanced Art of Gathering Energy technique of Visual gathering to draw from their ethereal body and enjoy the fulfillment of bountiful Lifeforce. The astral gathering is not an experience that can be easily described. Strigoi Vii who have mastered this art report strong sensations of bliss and gratification, both during the process and upon returning to their corporeal bodies. Some say it is, when recalled, like an episode in a particularly pleasurable and vivid dream. It is something you must experience for yourself.

If possible, the next day contact the person from whom you chose to tap Lifeforce. Often the person will report dreaming of you or thinking of you suddenly in the night or upon awakening! Very frequently they will also recount enhanced and enjoyable dreaming experiences as well.

Please note that, since maintaining the cohesion of the astral body requires Lifeforce, it is recommended that you gather energy before attempting these exercises. Once you have mastered the Hunt of the Succubus/Incubus, you can use the Lifeforce thus gathered for other astral Flights.

Mastering Flight can be a frustrating and tedious process. However, if practiced with diligence, it will yield unimaginable benefits for the Strigoi Vii.

CHAPTER 36

DREAMWALKING

Adieu! adieu! thy plaintive anthem fades
Past the near meadows, over the still stream,
Up the hill side; and now 'tis buried deep
In the next valley glades.
Was it a vision, or a waking dream?
Fled is that music: Do I wake or sleep?

—John Keats, "Ode to a Nightingale"

D reamwalking is a more advanced technique employing elements of astral projection and lucid dreaming; Walking the Dream can be done on all layers of reality, not just the astral. It requires that the Living Vampire be conscious and "awake" within all dreams and realize the Principle of All Realms. For the Truly Awakened Vampyre, all the layers of reality are a dream. In contrast, the normal mortal-minded consciousness perceives the corporeal world as the only and unassailable reality and all other experience or existence as a dream, or "untrue." The Strigoi Vii sometimes refer to Strigoi Viis as the "Awakened" and to mundanes as "Sleepers." Dreamwalking is the most sophisticated of all the techniques of the Outer Mysteries and may take significant time and effort for the Strigoi Vii Adeptus to master. It requires a significant shift of perception and, of course, cannot be achieved until the Morrah has gained successful results in lucid dreaming.

The foundation of dreamwalking is the Principle of All Realms. The Principle states that everything is "real" across all levels of reality and ranges of experience. Thus all experience is real and genuine, just with varying levels of tangibility. According to the Principle of All Realms, every different experience has different levels of tangibility and is defined by the positionality of the one(s) experiencing it. If someone experiences something, it exists in their perceptions, and their perception makes it "real." Thus, everything is equally real or, in the converse, equally a dream. As Edgar Allan Poe wrote, *"All we see and all we seem/ Is but a dream within a dream."*

The concept of dreamwalking is why We consider Immortals "Awakened" and mortals "Dreamers." Thus the Vampyre must feed on the life of the dreamer to maintain our Awakened state. The Vampyre must work to be Awakened at all times to all layers of reality, knowing that fact is tangible and valid, and fantasy is a loose collection of experiences which cannot be validated or made tangible in the same sense.

The Principle of All Realms is perhaps more simply illustrated than explained. Consider a dreamer having a particularly vivid yet non-lucid dream. While they are dreaming, they believe everything within the world of the dream is real. If they are frightened within the dream, they truly feel fear. If they are physically attracted to a character in the dream, they feel aroused. If that character then dies in the dream, the dreamer feels grief and misery. All these experiences and the associated emotions are valid as long as the dream lasts. Then, once the mundane awakens to the corporeal world, they tell themselves, "It was only a dream." They then resume what they think of as their "real" life, and anything that happened in the world of the dream is dismissed.

However, what makes the events and characters within the dream unreal and less valid than events and characters within the corporeal realm? Dreams can elicit responses every bit as strong as events in the corporeal realm. Someone having a horrid nightmare about being attacked by a maniac will awaken shaking, covered in sweat, and just as terrified as if they were being attacked in the corporeal world. Nocturnal emissions are physical orgasms triggered by erotic dreams. Someone who dreams of the death of a close friend or relative will be devastated and may even wake up crying.

Mortals will brush away even the most profound of dreaming experiences by saying, "It's only a dream—it's not real." We Strigoi Vii experience this perception differently. When dreaming, the dreamer engages directly with the astral world. What makes the astral realm any less "real" than the corporeal realm? What makes experiences in the astral any less "true" than corporeal experiences? Many mortals will attempt to limit reality to that which they can detect with the five major corporeal senses. However, We know there is an analog to each of these senses in the astral realm, as previously discussed. How, then, can the corporeal senses be the only and ultimate marker of reality and truth? The mortal-minded limit themselves to their corporeal worlds and thus enslave themselves with somnambulant disregard of all other aspects of reality.

All experience is truth. The great physicist Albert Einstein touched on this aspect of our Mysteries in his theory of relativity. Einstein stated that observers in different reference frames will observe their environment differently. Time passes differently for someone moving at a greatly accelerated velocity than for another person who, relative to the first, is at rest. Physical quantities such as length are seen differently by accelerating and non-accelerating observers. According to Einstein, there is no preferred reference frame; in other words, there is no one "correct" observer in these situations. The person accelerating makes observations that are true within their frame of reference. The person who, relative to the first, is not moving makes observations that are true within their frame of reference. Each of their experiences is "true."

As a rough analogy, consider someone riding in an airplane. Unless the plane suddenly gains or loses acceleration or altitude, the passenger will feel as if they are not moving and will be able to walk around the plane as if they were on the ground. In their frame of reference, they are stationary. If the passenger looks out the window, they will report that they are indeed moving at a very great velocity, but only because they are thus able to see the ground beneath them. They might as well say the plane is motionless and it is the Earth that is moving. However, people on the ground looking at the plane will report that the plane is moving at a great speed and it is they who are motionless. Yet the observers on the ground are not motionless—the Earth itself is moving at a great speed through space, as could be seen by an observer in a spacecraft.

Or, as another example, imagine that you receive a tearful call from a trusted family member telling you that your mother is dead. You will react with shock, anguish, and sorrow. You may begin to cry or even become hysterical. In your reality, your mother is dead, and the experience of grief is as real as anything else in your life. Although you have not yet received corporeal verification of her death (such as seeing her dead body), you have succumbed to the belief that she is dead. However, if the loved one were to then admit to playing a cruel joke on you, your perception of the real would suddenly change. What was real and true just a moment ago would suddenly become false. Your subsequent outrage at the deceitful caller would be just as real as your distress of an instant past. However, now that you have validated the situation, you shift from belief into reason. Yet even though you have validated corporeal truth, the emotions of grief may linger. You may have nightmares in which your mother dies or begin to anticipate her death with dread. Every time the phone rings you may experience panic, expecting it to be news of her death. The experience lingers in your emotional and mental state and thus continues on in the astral plane. There it is real even if your mother's death is not "real" in the corporeal world.

One final example of the Principle of All Realms may be seen in the famous Schrödinger's Cat thought experiment. The physicist Erwin Schrödinger posed this supposed paradox in 1935 to illustrate the quantum principle of uncertainty. In an article entitled "The Present Situation in Quantum Mechanics," published in the German magazine Naturwissenschaften ("Natural Sciences"), he wrote:

> *A cat is penned up in a steel chamber, along with the following device (which must be secured against direct interference by the cat): in a Geiger counter, there is a tiny bit of radioactive substance, so small that perhaps in the course of the hour, one of the atoms decays, but also, with equal probability, perhaps none; if it happens, the counter tube discharges, and through a relay releases a hammer that shatters a small*

flask of hydrocyanic acid. If one has left this entire system to itself for an hour, one would say that the cat still lives if meanwhile no atom has decayed. The of the entire system would express this by having in it the living and dead cat (pardon the expression) mixed or smeared out in equal parts.

It is typical of these cases that an indeterminacy originally restricted to the atomic domain becomes transformed into macroscopic indeterminacy, which can then be resolved by direct observation. That prevents us from so naively accepting as valid a "blurred model" for representing reality. In itself, it would not embody anything unclear or contradictory. There is a difference between a shaky or out-of-focus photograph and a snapshot of clouds and fog banks.

In most general terms, Schrödinger was addressing the basic corporeal indeterminacy present at the smallest level of matter. The state of any specific subatomic particle can be described as a superposition (combination) of wave functions. However, the wave function does not collapse until the particle is observed; the presence of an observer affects the outcome of the experiment. It is not until the box is opened by an observer that the particle is forced to "choose" a state and the nucleus either does or does not decay and, correspondingly, the cat dies or lives. The Schrödinger's Cat puzzle is closely related to the Heisenberg Uncertainty Principle, which states that either the position (location) or momentum (power residing in an object, calculated by finding the product of the mass and velocity) can be exactly determined, but not both. Once one is determined, the other can be calculated only within a particular range of uncertainty. The implication is that there is a fundamental indeterminacy "built in" to the physical world. Schrödinger's paradox extends this uncertainty from the microscopic world to the macroscopic.

From the perspective of the Strigoi Vii, there is no paradox or uncertainty. When Schrödinger talks about a "blurred model" for reality, he is speaking from a mortal-minded corporeal perspective. While he was one of the greatest physicists of the twentieth century, as a mundane he was still limited to corporeal perceptions. There is no puzzle when the problem is considered across all layers of reality. The uncertainty lies in the corporeal realm only; the very fact that there seems to be a paradox merely shows that these corporeally-limited theories are incomplete. In fact, many contemporary physicists have begun to grasp this fact with theories such as the many-worlds interpretation of quantum mechanics. Briefly, the many-worlds interpretation implies the possible existence of all alternate histories and futures—a concept in direct dialogue with Our Principle of All Realms.

We, the Strigoi Viis, have the potential to Awaken to full awareness of all realities. We are Lucid Dreamers, bending reality in accordance with Our True Will, apprehending the realms from the perspective of the Dragon. We are free of time and space. We can view the median point of all possible worlds. The Morrah should strive to free Their perceptions from dependence upon the corporeal world. They should continue Their explorations in the astral plane so as to gain experience with the mutability of perspective across the realms. The Morrah should begin to reject accepted definitions of what is "real" and "unreal" and instead rely upon the Eyes of the Dragon for guidance.

Time

Time is something the Strigoi Vii seeks to escape. As Einstein showed, time is a mortal perception and a relative concept. From the perspective of the astral realm, time does not even exist. It is possible to have a fully developed, vivid, and lucid dream within the space of no more than a few minutes by a corporeal clock, even though within the astral, hours, days, or even years have passed. A useful concrete validation of this fact involves timing yourself during Flight. Before embarking upon Flight, notice the time recorded by a clock. When the Flight ends and you return to your corporeal body, before checking the clock again, honestly ask yourself how long it seemed to last. Very likely you will feel as if a long span of time passed whilst you were in the astral realm, only to discover that a comparatively short time has passed in the corporeal world.

The Strigoi Vii seeks eternity through timelessness and independence of time. Once the Adeptus has validated the Principle of All Realms, They will have begun to Awaken to ultimate nonexistence and mutability of time. These remarks are but the beginning of a very profound evolution of Zhep'r that is further explored in the Inner Mysteries of Strigoi Vii.

The Dream Matrix

The Dream Matrix is the state that exists between the First and Second Death. This is akin to the collective subconsciousness and collective consciousness described by Carl Jung. The Dream Matrix is a subtle state that corresponds to the corporeal process of natural death. When the physical body is near death, it releases chemicals and other substances that create a feeling of corporeal euphoria. The Dream Matrix is the analogous state of euphoria on the etheric and astral planes. Since it is a subtle instead of a corporeal process, it is even more seductive and pleasurable. It can be extremely difficult for the Vampyre to resist.

What is the enduring grace of the Living Vampyre? Their sheer Love of Life and the Self. With a sincere yearning for eternity and Immortality, the Vampyre can master the Principle of All Realms, resist the Dream Matrix, Walk within the Dream, and fully Awaken.

Summation

Thus concludes the Outer Mysteries of the Strigoi Vii. Once a Vampyre has solved these mysteries, They have Ascended to truly "Come Forth by Twilight" and become a Vampyre Adeptus. Those who wish to pursue the Higher Mysteries must be initiated into the Inner Court of the Family: the Ordo Strigoi Vii (OSV). This order is by invitation only. All prospective OSV members must be personally invited by the Synod and sponsored by a current member of the Order.

You have only just begun. ... .

MORRAH TESTIMONIAL

These are confidential and private questionnaires that are used within the OSV to evaluate the completion of an ordeal. This will only be seen by the Synod officers who will reply with notes and reflections will be sent back if one does not pass the evaluation. Please keep answers reasonably short and concise at most 300 words. If you do not understand something there is a lesson waiting to happen. These testimonials are based on the honor system and be truthful there is no rush for true Zhep'r. Submit these questionnaires with a freewill donation to synod@strigoivii.org.

1. Tell us why you are pursuing the Morrah Ordeal "Coming forth by Twilight" and become a Strigoi Vii Adeptus?
2. How have you applied Primal Spirituality?
3. How have you what progress have you gotten with Apotheosis?
4. How have you manifested and applied the Vampyre Middle Pillar?
5. How have you manifested and applied Advanced gathering of energy?
6. How have you manifested and applied the what are your experiences with touching the Astral Realm?
7. How have you manifested and applied the Silent Communion?
8. How have you manifested and applied the Dragon's Flight / Flight of the Succubus?
9. How have you manifested and applied the Dream Walking?
10. Tell us of what Morrah teaching you are strongest in and weakest in?
11. Any other comments or notes you would like to add.

VAMPYRE MAGICK

INTRODUCTION TO VAMPYRE
MAGICK BY MICHAEL W. FORD

Vampyre Magick is a core foundation in what I call "Adversarial" or "Promethean" ideology; the inner drive toward self-evolution and willed change. Many tend to think of the mental state of the predator as being malicious and harmful to society. The predator is a beautiful example of the natural instinct for survival. If you ever have the chance, observe the feeding of a rat to a snake of appropriate size. You do not see the serpent obtaining "pleasure" from restraining the rat, nor does the predator prolong the moment any more than necessary. The serpent without hesitation feeds to survive. Humans do not kill others for food, yet the world is a consistent "survival of the fittest" environment.

From the daily grind of work, like seeking a promotion or trying to get an account before a competitor, it matters not. The world still operates according to the law of the predator. Society is made great from those who are able to operate within the contract of human contact: do not harm others unless in defense, don't steal from or cheat others, and seek excellence in yourself while helping those around you. The Predator is not a sociopath; rather it is the point of connectivity which leads us toward excellence. Magick is the exact motivator in this process; it creates change and allows us to seek the powerful therionick reserves in our deep unconscious. (Therionick is a term representing "beast," found in my books, Akhkharu: Vampyre Magick and The Bible of the Adversary. It represents the dark or primordial instinct that is expressed in our basic desires and lusts.) Shaping that darkness into productive behavior in accordance with the will is the purpose of Vampyre Magick.

For those seeking the essence of the so-called Black Arts, you need not look toward some abstract, tired concept of "demonology" with inverse designs; rather, look within. We are the mirror of the worst in the world, yet also the best within it. If you can establish your Temple or abode to the dark gods within, then your foundation begins and ends within. The Vampyre realizes that to be successful in magick, responsible thought and action must be consistent in accordance with the will of the individual. Don't allow yourself to be whitewashed into thinking nature is fluffy, kind, and nurturing in entirety. Understand the predatory, often violent, and dark aspects in nature and then look for the balance! This is evident everywhere around us; when something is destroyed, another creation emerges from it. Only in the lack of balance found in some avenues of humanity do we see more destruction than creation: oil spills in the ocean, disregard for education in cities, allowing violence against the innocent to go unpunished by law, and so on.

The Vampyre must be willing to exist within the world and the laws that society has established. Remember that the majority of humans in a mass are like sheep; they believe what they are told consistently, and it is only reasonable to observe that there can be few leaders. Many like to be led and told what to do; that is found in all things from democracy to socialism. It depends upon the level of restriction that the so- called "leaders" wish to impose.

Vampyre Magick will allow you to learn to be comfortable and find nourishment in the darkness, yet at the same time offer the strength to ascend as a god. The Adversarial Path, as I have defined it in recent years, has been the result of my initiation in the Vampyre mysteries, yet applying them in accordance with my will. Success has been a continual result, which has taught me the significance of control, thoughtful reflection, and the continual testing of my will and core aspects of Self. Father Sebastiaan is one of my brothers of the vampyric mysteries; his works will allow the inspired initiate to achieve their own level of vampyric Awakening. Sebastiaan by experience is quite aware of the predatory, self-deified instinct and the potential of the Awakened Vampyre. No matter if I call it "'Azal'ucel," "daemon," "dragon," or as Sebastiaan has shared with us, "Elorath," the vampyric instinct, or divine spirituality some call "soul," is found with our circles of power. Let me remind and caution you, however. Imagination and will are essentials to our sacred arte. When you enter the ritual chamber, you must use your imagination to fully see and feel what you are summoning; allow your mind to be free here and find the belief to then see your desires becoming real in the world around you. Belief can cause any change desired to manifest as long as it is within parameters of "reason." In the ritual chamber, however, reason is less frequent. Those deep fantasies and desires must be allowed to move in accordance with our lusts; then is anything possible to us within our living world.

Upon the path of the Vampyre, your spirit will go forth upon the West wind into twilight realms, reaching further into the darkness. From the path of Zhep'r will you begin a process of self-transformation, which will allow you to experience this life more intensely and with a deeper hunger for more of that which life offers. Zhep'r, in my own experience, allows a certain type of "nostalgia," with which you will be able to recognize the subtle experiences of a life that seems to be ever- lasting. Feed the Dragon, transform your mind and body into the careful balance of the Vampyre; life will never be the same for you again.

In short, welcome to the possibility of Zhep'r.

Michael W. Ford, Akhtya Dahak Azal'ucel of the Black Order of the Dragon

CHAPTER 1
ELEMENTS OF VAMPYRE MAGICK

Is it not more sensible to worship a god that [man], himself, has created, in accordance with his own emotional needs—one that best represents the very carnal and physical being that has the idea-power to invent a god in the first place?

If man insists on externalizing his own true self in the form of "God," then why fear his true self, in fearing "God,"—why praise his true self in praising "God,"—why remain externalized from "God" IN ORDER TO ENGAGE IN RITUAL AND RELIGIOUS CEREMONY IN HIS NAME?

—Anton Szandor LaVey, *The Satanic Bible*

Vampyre Magick has many elements, ranging from small rituals and ceremonies, which are conducted every day, to the secretive rituals of the Inner Court. Within Strigoi Vii Magick We know belief is a tool, so We always focus on the positive and remain aware of the negatives. This attitude truly brings an empowering spirit to workings. We see magick as "psychological technology" from the Dayside, and from the Nightside, a spiritual and abstract concept. Learning how to differentiate reality from fantasy is one of the most difficult hurdles for the neophyte Vampyre to overcome. Only wisdom and reason can be employed in the Dayside of Vampyre Magick, which almost always has a psychological or scientific rationalization. The Nightside relies on results and flexibility of beliefs; even more complex is the Twilight, which accepts and lies between both perspectives. Here, once Twilight is experienced, is the Immortal Mindset truly realized.

Agreement

One of the Inner Mysteries, the Principles of Vibrational Vampyric Sorcery and mastery of the three layers of reality, delves into the Principle of Agreement. Without agreement, magick is lost and lacks any power. All of reality, be it the marketing propaganda of corporations, the confusion of politics, or the stage performances of a magician, requires agreement for success. Group ritual is a point of agreement. If individuals are not in sync, they will only fall out of the experience and potentially ruin the ritual for all others. This is why true initiation at the basic level is a statement of agreement; many systems of spirituality and even culture have such rites of passage. Democracy is an agreement of the majority, and the rest must follow, but the agreement can be manipulated and changed. This is why the Strigoi Vii validate reality and experiences as individuals, and when They join together for workings, the magick is most powerful.

Astral Travel

Mastery of Out-of-Body Experiences (OBE) and astral travel, known to the Strigoi Vii simply as "Flight," are at the core of raising Zhep'r and achieving Nightside Immortality. The Morrah level of ascension and higher begins to focus heavily on these workings and techniques. Astral travel is simply projecting the consciousness away from the body into the vast astral layer of reality. This is more deeply handled in the *Strigoi Vii Codex Book III, Liber Morrah "Coming Forth by Twilight."* However, we will touch on this within this book to supplement those mysteries. So please refer to Liber Morrah for more information on the core of these techniques.

Astral travel is heavily important for higher levels of Gathering Lifeforce and deeper face-to-face meetings in the realms where the Strigoi Morte exist in their natural habitat. The astral is an abstract reality, the place of dreams, visions, and knowledge. Here lies the Akashic Records, the astral layer of the Self, and the place of emotions and thoughts. Being in the astral is akin to being in space or under the sea, which is an alien environment. Lucid dreaming is an internal experience solely in the mind in which the dreamers are aware they are within a dream and astral projection is an external experience away from the physical body. Mastering lucid dreaming will be a good foundation and launching point for out-of-body experiences. The Strigoi Morte have mastered OBE and learned to maintain an etheric body of Lifeforce.

Belief

Since the Strigoi Vii Vampyre operates as a chaos magician, belief is a tool. The flexibility of belief is essential for a Vampyre to achieve Zhep'r. In ritual the Vampyre finds most results when belief and disbelief are both suspended; this is the true nature of the Twilight experience. This state of consciousness is the major benchmark of Zhep'r and is the state in which Communion is best experienced. The more the Vampyre experiences results, the more they begin to focus on such over the common systems of beliefs. This is where reason comes forth.

Neophyte Vampyres, those of Prospectii and Jahira levels of initiation, will have the most difficulty achieving this state of disbelieving and believing. Most Jahira, when first performing the ritual of Communion, will find that they will not receive "results," and this is due to the reality that they cannot experience, even for a short while, true Twilight. However, as Zhep'r builds through stronger consensus, through experience, and through results, validation will gather within the mind of the Vampyre. Not believing in something is the natural rationality of a mortal-minded skeptic and essential for the Vampyre's Dayside perspective.

Blood

Many claim that drinking corporeal blood is the only way a Vampyre can obtain the energies they need for their emotional, physical, and spiritual balance. Of course, the Strigoi Vii respects free will but sincerely disagrees with this perspective as an application of the act of Gathering Lifeforce. We Lifeforce Vampyres have discovered and learned to be free of these perceptions and look toward more subtle forms of energy gathering. It will become clear which form of feeding is valid, safe, and efficient. For the Strigoi Vii, it is impossible to prove the need to drink blood, and there is no scientific evidence that consumption of corporeal blood provides tangible health benefits. Even though blood can in itself be a powerful and romantic ritual or sexual symbol and tool, it simply does not provide Lifeforce that is of use for the preservation of the self beyond First Death. When you are disembodied or within OBE you cannot easily gather lifeforce from corporeal blood. From the Strigoi Vii perspective, blood-drinking is most emphatically not an efficient technique for gathering Lifeforce.

At its core, the vampire archetype in legend, myth, and most literature is about Immortality and surviving death as an Undead. If one cannot preserve the Self beyond the First Death, they are either mortal or have not succeeded with true ascension. Attaining Immortality depends on the very basic principle of surviving while disengaged from the body. Once an individual defeats the First Death and has no corporeal body, of what use will be the consumption of blood? What skills will benefit them when they exist in a completely subtle state? Moreover, how does one attempt to drink blood when they have no physical mouth? Those Living Vampyres who espouse blood drinking must consider a more pragmatic and achievable route to furthering Zhep'r.

Medical science has proven that diseases such as HIV can remain dormant in the blood for upward of ten years. Draining one individual will provide two major impractical issues from the perspective of the Strigoi Vii's interpretation of Gathering Lifeforce. First, one must have a screened and healthy donor from whom to feed. This requires extreme trust in a donor, who must wait years to prove their health in a quarantine of sorts. If this donor leaves or turns on their Vampyre, the only result is the Vampyre is out of a source until They can safely screen and build a relationship with another donor. Human relationships are quite complex and not all humans, as free-willed beings, are as obedient and loyal as man's best friend. They change their minds. Feeding sessions must be frequent to satisfy a proper Thirst for blood and certainly, blood-drinking is not efficient for the Strigoi

Vii. What of two Vampyres in a relationship? Do they feed on each other? It is against common sense for predators to consume each other, and it is considered spiritual cannibalism. Secondly, why would such an independent and individualist spirit be able to depend on anyone but themselves? Does this limit the Apotheosis of the individual? Absolutely!

The Strigoi Vii may wonder how Blood Magick relates to this discussion. Quite simply, Blood Magick is different from feeding on corporeal blood. Blood Magick includes body modification, sacrificial rites in Caribbean and African religions such as Yoruba and Santeria (in which animals are sacrificed in a fashion little different from your neighborhood butcher), and such forms of art as blood paintings. If done in a sterile medical and safe fashion, no different than the butcher shop, these rituals do not involve the risks that come with the consumption of blood.

Intent and Sincerity

Without intent and sincerity, all is lost in magick. As important as agreement, one must be honest and come with a sincere intent to be able to direct Will and energy. The Strigoi Vii hold high standards in individual and community. When you go to perform a ritual, be it the most sacred Communion or the simplest arts of Gathering, you must put aside the humor and fantasy and bring into full realization your own focus.

Invocation

Invocation is the internal summoning of energies, forces, or entities into the magician, equivalent to possession or self-identifying with certain spirits. This term hails from the Latin verb invocare, which translates as "to call on," and Magus Crowley put it perfectly: Crowley states that Invocation is to "invoke," to "call-in," just as to "evoke" is to "call forth." This is very applicable within the Strigoi Vii system of magick in that we use it for the Arts of Gathering and in certain Communion rituals where we invoke the Undead to "skinride," or invoking and raising the Vampyre Current. The one exception, the Invokation of the Dragon Rite, is not as much invoking the Dragon Within as it is more or less recognizing its presence as the core of the Self and the throne of perception. Invocation can also be employed to identify with complete, or aspects of, god forms, spirits, or entities, such as the Trinity Pulses of the Current, where the initiate becomes an embodiment of that aspect of the Current of Elorath. For example, if a Strigoi Vii initiate wants to invoke the strength of the Mradu or the sexual energies of the Kitra, They would take aspects of those and invoke them.

To successfully invoke, one must have their consciousness attuned and opened to welcoming that specific energy or entity. This is done with trance, sexual stimulation, fasting, deprivation of sleep, pain, SM, dance, and ritual, which clears the mind to a primal state where transmissions, visions, and voices can be brought through the initiate.

Evocation

The direct opposing action of an invocation is an evocation, which is to bring an entity or energies external to the summoner. This is often looked upon in mortal magicks as calling a spirit into a container, circle, ritual chamber, etc. Then in a literally face-to-face situation, the summoner can interact with the entity in person and ask for favors, make pacts, or gain information. Historical examples of evocation are found in ancient grimoires such as The Lesser Key of Solomon, The Greater Key of Solomon, The Dragon Rouge, and The Sacred Magic of Abramelin the Mage. This involves heavy systems such as symbolism, fire, dance, offerings, tools, and environment.

Within Strigoi Vii and other Communion Rites, we use evocation in the Sanguine Mass to invite the Ancestors to come feed from our amplified offered sacrifice of Lifeforce, which we have fed from. Evocations are best used for group rituals and will gain a common experience; on the other hand, an invocation is more about one central magician performing the ritual and having the deepest experience.

Meditation

There are several forms of meditation, each containing specific benefits and focuses. The primary purpose of meditation is to achieve an altered state of consciousness. The two most commonly used within Strigoi Vii and Vampyre Ritual are active and passive. Passive meditation is what people most think of like meditation, which is a more relaxed trance state with eyes closed and with little or no movement. Active meditation is when the subject is moving and can take place during dance, sex, running, physical exertion, sport, performance, painting, etc. Both have their specific benefits and applications. *See the Black Veil: Meditation.*

Necromancy

The esoteric process of speaking with the spirits of the dead for divination is known as necromancy. The Strigoi Vii Vampyre is a natural necromancer, and these practices, which are Communion with the Undead, are at the core of Strigoi Vii Mysteries on spiritual immortality. However, there are other uses; the Vampyre can tap into the Dream Matrix of dead souls and pull out information; some Strigoi Vii have mastered the practice of exorcising spirits of humans, animals, demons, elements, or even Renegade Strigoi Morte. We hear in human legends the tales of Haitian Vodou priests making zombies, witches dealing with demons, and necromancers capturing and containing entities and spirits of the dead. Necromancy is often considered taboo and forbidden to the mortal-minded, yet since it is natural to the Strigoi Vii Vampyre, this becomes a powerful tool of self-deification. These transmissions and messages from "the other side" can come forth in ritual, spontaneously, elementary divinations, or visions. This is one of the main ways in which the Strigoi Morte communicate with us.

Sex Magick

Sex in Vampyre Magick is a very powerful tool just as it is in many systems of magick and esotericism. The symbolism goes even deeper, as sensuality, BDSM, fetishism, romance, mystery, and seduction are all strong elements of the vampire archetype and can be used within this paradigm. Initiation offers a rebirth from mortal to Immortal-Minded perspectives, and the ritual chamber is similar to a womb from which we Rise from death into Life.

"Sacred Marriages" take place when sexual congress occurs with the involvement of a Strigoi Morte, godform, entity, or one of the Pulses of the Vampyre Current. This can be done in ritual or trance or it can, especially in the case of the Strigoi Morte, be similar to a possession experience. Legends of incubi, succubi and demons mating with humans may be, in fact, sexual sacred marriages. It is common for a Strigoi Morte to possess a mortal and be a "second seed" in order to increase the chances of a child with Vampyric potential. Other times a Strigoi Morte will make love to a human woman or will skinride during sex. These experiences are highly energetic and often extremely stimulating. Such encounters are often used to create trance states for meditation or increasing Zhep'r. One example of a Sacred Marriage is the Temple of Kitra ritual presented in this book.

Orgasm in sex magick has been a powerful tool throughout history for focusing and raising energies. Kundalini Yoga techniques are very similar to Riding the Dragon in Sexual Congress and can be used to come closer to the Dragon Within. Two Vampyre Sex rituals are presented in this book for you to experiment with.

SHAPESHIFTING

Vampires in legend are known to shape-change into a bat, wolf, or mist, but in reality, this is virtually impossible to achieve within the corporeal layer of reality and can only be done in the ethereal and astral realms. Within the perspective of Strigoi Vii, shape-shifting can be done by many Awakened beings, but it is predominately on an astral plane since this is the most intangible energy frequency of all the realms. Once shape-shifting has been mastered there, it requires more energy to shift the etheric body and enormous amounts of energy to change shape to the hard and inflexible energies of the corporeal. Refer to Chapter 5 on Shapesifting for more information on how shape-shifting is achieved and handled within the Strigoi Vii tradition.

Sacrifice

The word sacrifice comes from the Latin sacrificium, or "sacred rites," and the old French facere, "to do, perform." In mortal-minded terms, it refers to offerings such as animals, plants, money, gifts, or even living humans to the divine in exchange for favors.

Living Vampires respect the free will of sentient beings and never harm humans or animals (except when hunting or slaughtering for corporeal food). However, in the most sacred Communion Rite, the Sanguine Mass, Vampyres offer up their life energy plus that obtained from the practices of the Art of Gathering Energy, in exchange for Ambrosia, which is the energy of a spiritually immortal and divine frequency. This process of free will releasing energies in ritual to the Strigoi Morte is known as the "Offering." This circuit of Gathering and Communion with the Ancestors is the central act of energetic exchange within Vampyrism and perpetuates the conscious-ness after the First Death and strengthens the etheric and astral bodies so that they are able to exist consciously in the undead state of existence (not dead or not alive but timeless) and prevent the Second Death.

It is inefficient and against Vampyre Principles for the Vampyre to destroy life because the Vampyre seriously distinguishes between roasting kitties on the BBQ for fun and entertainment and humanely slaughtering cattle for sustenance. We are catalysts of the flow of life, and the murder of an animal or human is the destruction of life and a source of Lifeforce. When a living being is destroyed, their excess Lifeforce is released into the subtle world where it dissipates and is recycled, often changing frequency. This is worthless to a Vampyre. The only exception is when killing animals to sustain the need for corporeal food.

For the Strigoi Vii, offering this energy to the Ancestors is a natural process, which many Vampyres have been doing naturally since we were children with our Patron Spirits, Strigoi Morte mentors, and spirit guides whom some Vampyres call Whisperers. What differentiates the initiate from this subconscious act is intent, which can increase the amount of energy provided in an Offering. The Strigoi Morte seek only the highest quality of Lifeforce and wish not to sit at a table of scraps. If deemed worthy, the Whisperers will manifest within the sanctum in which the ritual is being performed, feasting upon the Offering and providing the energies of the Zhep'r in return. Since energy is the currency of the Vampyre, this is the most sacred form of sacrifice, and the Strigoi Morte have no interest other than the Lifeforce, which a Vampyre harvests and refines.

The more the Communion is performed with honesty and intent, the more Zhep'r is evolved.

Servitors

As with many other powers, vampires of legend are known to have many servants such as beasts of the night and supernatural creatures at their com-mand. Reality is far from these legends. The Living Vampire seeks to master Life and Belief; therefore, by balancing both of these traits, They can make servitors, which are created by beliefs and thought patterns on a specific frequency that are conscious entities and programmed for a specific purpose.

The human mind will often fuel these servitors through fear, faith, worship, or even by acknowledging that they exist simply by the Will of the Vampyre. Marketing, advertising, and propaganda engineers put forth similar concepts into the human collective consciousness as magicians use to make egregores and servitors into human cultural programming. This is effectively creating a miniature elemental made of will and intent that is programmed for a specific purpose. Servitors can be used to protect, harm, or achieve a specific task. What makes Strigoi Vii servitors different from those of other magickal systems is that they are imbued with Lifeforce directly from the Vampyre and at the same time the elements of the Current itself. This is the "Blood," which is required to initiate their existence and attunement as being Vampyre Servitors.

The Shadow

According to Carl Gustav Jung (1875–1961), Swiss psychiatrist and the founder of analytical psychology, the Shadow is the portion of ourselves that is the catalyst for all our negative emotions and self-destructive tendencies. The Shadow is comprised mostly of repressed emotions, uncontrolled ego, and primitive urges.

This Shadow is like a great beast within all sentient creatures— even more so for us because we reject the eternal optimism and placidity offered by "white light belief. We must at all times keep the Shadow from becoming overwhelming and causing our Selves and those around us to be wrapped in negativity. The Strigoi Vii is more susceptible to the Shadow than the mortal-minded because we are more in touch with what humans call our "dark side." This is especially true for those who are still de-identifying from their mortal-minded roots. Controlling the Shadow can be a challenging process for many of us, and it takes sheer Will. Do not become hardened and jaded in your rejection of belief and illusion and turn to despair and nihilism. Remember that there is still much life, love, creativity, and joy in this world. Your existence is what you make of it. Choose to be the catalyst of all good things in your life. Choose to be empowered. Choose enjoyment. Remember always—you are your own god and divinity!

CHAPTER 2
PARADIGMS

Magick is fueled with will, agreement, and intent. Yet in the end, only results matter.

—Magister Dimitri, 1995

Strigoi Viis are by nature chaos magicians, striving to be free of faith and belief to focus completely on the results of Their actions. This concept is hard to grasp for many newly Awakening Vampyres who are unfamiliar with it, but as Zhep'r evolves, the shift from belief to knowledge to gnosis begins to set in if they are truly of the Vampyre Current. At the core of this chaos magic, there is a specific concept called paradigms.

Paradigms are schools of thought and belief systems most often created by agreement on traditions, faith, belief, philosophy, and spirituality. Each paradigm has its own flavor of rituals, theology, symbolism, and perspectives. Even some schools of magick are considered paradigms; for example, Phil Hine, chaos magician, and contemporary of chaos magick founding father Peter J. Carol see chaos magick as a paradigmless system. In contrast Mr. Carol sees chaos magick as a meta-paradigm, in that it can "become" any paradigm and be molded into it.

Strigoi Viis\ who are open spiritually and true to Their nature can adopt various paradigms just as mortals change clothing styles to accommodate their own tastes and situation. There is no limit to the number of paradigms an individual can draw power and inspiration from; it is a matter of the personal taste and interests of each Vampyre. Some Vampyres even experiment for a time with a paradigm or perform a specific ritual of that paradigm to "taste" the experience.

Many paradigms cross over amongst each other, evolve as their members do (the Catholic religion is not the same as when it started), have spinoffs, and often birth new paradigms. Vampyres of the Strigoi Vii Tradition see themselves as a part of a movement that promotes spiritual and philosophical evolution, which is deeply rooted in the soul, not just a specific singular religion or paradigm. Once Awakened there is no turning back; the Current is alive within the individual. This reality will never change and cannot be taken away unless one consciously begins to break the Strigoi Vii Principles and Zhep'r ceases, which is equivalent to final death.

Strigoi Vii Vampyre philosophy encourages exploration of one's paradigms, experimentation with the methods of those paradigms, and assimilation of what produces the best results. Because Strigoi Vii less a religion, and more a sacred spirituality based on the utilization of belief as a tool, elements of reality can be bent and morphed through Will. Each paradigm can be mixed with other paradigms, customized, and specialized for each individual interpretation. Chaos magick can be considered from a neo-pagan perspective as an eclectic system of magick. So, in a sense, the Vampyre is an eclectic magician.

Most of the paradigms found amongst the Vampyre of the Strigoi Vii Tradition were brought in with new members, established and developed by the individual, and formally recognized by Magisters. Here are some example paradigms that are known to exist amongst the Strigoi Vii Vampyre Mysteries and a sampling of how diverse and compatible with other belief systems Vampyres can be.

Asatru
by Kaedrich Olsen

The Asatru paradigm was created in the late 1960s or early 1970s in Iceland to resurrect the belief structure of the Old Norse. The term Asatru literally means "true to the gods." Asatru is rooted firmly in the literature of the Old Norse, the primary sources being the Poetic Edda and Prose Edda. Several translations of these Eddas are readily available. Far from being a bible, or a source of dogmatism, the Eddas are seen as a loose guide by which to direct one's deeds. In addition to the Eddas are the Sagas. The saga's primary purpose is to tell the story of an ancient family line, or a particular region, over the course of several generations. Some notable Sagas is Egil's Saga, Vinland Saga, and Hrolf Kraki's Saga.

As the paradigm developed over the next few decades, several tenets were culled from the literature. The most famous of these tenets are the Nine Noble Virtues, as declared by Edred Thorsson in his book A Book of Troth. These charges are Courage, Truth, Honor, Fidelity (not to be confused with monogamy), Discipline, Independence, Industriousness, Perseverance, and Hospitality. These Nine Noble Virtues gave Asatru the sense that it is a living religion. This came to mean that the gods care less for the sacrifice of ritual and more for the individual living a noble life.

Asatru is a polytheistic religion mixed with ancestor worship, fatalism, and two branches of magick. There are too many deities to name in this article, but you already know four of them. The days of the week are named after them: Tuesday—Tyr's day, Wednesday—Odin's Day, Thursday—Thor's Day, Friday—Frey's Day. For each of these gods, one will find elaborate stories.

One who is new to Asatru is often cautioned not to Romanize the Norse gods. That is to say, there is no one god of war or one goddess of love. Each of the deities has multi-dimensional facets of strengths and weaknesses. For example, Thor, though the protector of mankind, is mocked in most of his stories.

The two branches of Norse Magick are Seidhr and Galdr. Seidhr is a shamanic type of practice that covers everything from oracular workings to shapeshifting. Galdr is the magick of runes. There are many sources to learn of these practices. Two recommended sources are *Trance-Portation* by Diana Paxson and *Runes for Transformation* by Kaedrich Olsen.

Followers of Asatru easily embrace the Dayside Pillar of Material

Mastery. The highest of all tenets in Asatru is to seek to increase might and main. That is, one looks to become more influential and affluent in their life. This, then, tied into hospitality, means a successful leader shares their wealth and power so the community, as a whole, can increase in might and main.

Community is a strong point for Asatru. It is believed that all who follow the ways of the Old Norse share one common folk soul. This folk-soul is not dependent upon corporeal genetics as some would insist. Rather, the folk-soul is like the Vampyre egregore of Elorath. If all Asatruar conduct themselves in noble ways, the might and main of all Asatru can be increased. If anyone acts ignobly, by breaking laws or letting their honor be defiled, the power of the whole of the community is diminished. Thus, one must always strive to conduct themselves most valiantly.

Many Asatru, like Strigoi Vii, are very independent and strong willed. It is strongly encouraged that every follower of Asatru pursues a scholarly study of the primary texts and secondary scholarly interpretations. This independent study paired with the natural boldness of the Asatru leads to many divergent opinions at Heathen gatherings. Lively discussions ensue, to the point where gatherers must agree to disagree.

The main ritual of Asatru is called Blot (pronounced "bloat"). It is very similar in nature to the Strigoi Vii Communion Rite. Blots are seasonal rites, with intentions similar to the seasonal rites of the Strigoi Vii. During the blot, a warding takes place, and then a particular god and the ancestors are called. Then mead is blessed, passed around to the gatherers, and poured into a bowl for an offering. The passing of the mead is a two-fold process. The folk gathered load their own energy into the mead that is then poured into the bowl. The blessed mead, from the bowl, is sprinkled upon the folk, bestowing the blessings of the gods upon the people. It must be noted that the blot is a devotional rite, but it is not one of supplication and subservience. The Asatruar stand boldly before their gods and ancestors calling upon them with respect and treating them as if they were all equals—like members of an extended astral family.

Death plays heavily in the Norse tradition. One does not live to die as is believed by many who think of Asatru as a Viking way. The followers of Asatru seek to live life to its fullest in every moment. In doing so, they do not fear death. The Eddas tell us that all who die to travel the road to Helheim, the land of the dead. At the pit of Helheim lies the great well

Hvergelmir. All who are cast into Hvergelmir are destroyed, and all rivers flowing through all the worlds run from Hvergelmir. This parallels what we Strigoi Vii know as the second death. The soul that is committed to Hvergelmir is destroyed, and the essence of its being is returned throughout all of our shared existence.

Not all who walk the road of Helheim, however, are doomed to perish. If one is fully conscious of their death, truly loved their life, and passionately seek to continue their existence, they avoid the great seething cauldron. Instead, they find themselves in one of the many halls of the gods (such as Valhalla). Even more continue their existence as a Dísir.

The Dísir are very similar to what we know of the Strigoi Morte. They are human beings who have ascended from their mortal coils to attain immortality in the astral. The Dísir are often seen guiding the fate of those in their own family line, communal groups, or of the whole of the Asatru egregore. They offer guidance, direction, and the occasional kick in the butt. Out of respect, and with gratitude for their guidance, these ancestors are highly honored in blots and other personal rituals similar to our Communion Rite.

To the untrained eye, Asatru may seem like a group of barbaric individuals bent on hedonism and self-destruction. In reality, most Asatruar are very well educated and can debate their understandings with scholarly deftness. What is most important to know is that they live as they expect to die: honorably and boldly with no regrets. This love of life, of self, and of community paves the way for them to take their places among the Dísir and the gods... as every Strigoi Vii that valiantly pursues Zhep'r will take their place among the Strigoi Morte.

Christian

Many would think of the notion of a Christian Vampyre as a contradiction and that Vampyres by nature are directly opposed to Christianity. This is far from the truth. The obvious answer is that one will think the concept of such a combination of perspectives is not compatible and the individual would be a heretic.

However, from the perspective of the Strigoi Vii, who is a chaos magician, why couldn't a Vampyre be a Christian or use its elements as a tool? Vampiric symbolism is highly prevalent throughout the Bible, including this quote from the King James Bible, which can be interpreted as a direct example of the Blood Principle:

> ... for it is the life of all flesh; the blood of it is for the life thereof: therefore I said unto the children of Israel, Ye shall eat the blood of no manner of flesh: for the life of all flesh is the blood thereof: whosoever eateth it shall be cut off (Leviticus 17:14).

Obviously, in this quote, it says never to eat physical flesh, for the spirit is in the blood. Also look at the communion ritual of the Catholics, which is to drink of the blood of their god, which turns directly from spiritually charged wine to the corporeal Blood of Jesus.

The Sang Grael or the Holy Bloodline in humanity has many interpretations; one of them is the bloodline of Jesus Christ. Some might even think if you look more deeply into the legends of ancient Sumer, you would see the Anunnaki, who were gods who came to earth and had children with humans.

One can see the blessing of an angel (Strigoi Morte) in the story of the Archangel Gabriel carrying the divine seed to impregnate Mary. Joseph could have been the corporeal father and a Strigoi Morte a divine or spiritual father. This is looked at in many older traditions with angels and demons possessing a father and impregnating a woman and the resulting child being the offspring with divine blood. Can this story be related to the story of the Nephilim? Could it be that Jesus was a Nephilim, a member of the Sang Grael Bloodlines? The Book of Genesis mentions Nephilim:

> Now it came about when men began to multiply on the face of the land, and daughters were born to them, that the sons of God saw that the daughters of men were beautiful; and they took wives for themselves, whomever they chose. Then the LORD said, "My Spirit shall not strive with man forever, for he is indeed flesh; nevertheless his days shall be one hundred and twenty years." The Nephilim were on the earth in those days, and also afterward when the sons of God came into the daughters of men, and they bore children to them. Those were the mighty men who were of old, men of renown (Genesis 6: 1–4).

DARK PAGANISM

Amongst the various religions of influence within the esoteric community, the one that has had the greatest impact is Wicca. This is a neo-pagan reconstructive religion claiming to be one of the original pre-Christian pagan religions in the English Isles. What is most interesting is that as a modern incarnation, it was either founded or popularized by Gerald Gardner after he claimed to be initiated into a coven in New Forest, England in 1939. Whatever the origins, which cannot be proven, many have been introduced into the esoteric world with the endless variety of books, gatherings, websites, and resources for Wicca, which we do not need to get into here. However, we are going to explore the reality of those who are Vampyres and find Wicca an empowering paradigm.

Some occult historians claim that Gardner actually was inspired by Crowley's (whom he knew personally) Thelema for the basis of Wicca. Some even claim that Crowley even created the religion, manipulating Gardner for his last hurrah before he died. Yet, even with the controversial origins of Wicca, what is most important is the actual workings, theology, and focus on magick and rituals, which are empowering and functional.

At the core of Wicca is a duality of gods: the masculine Horned God and the Triple Goddess. This easily relates to the Kitra and Mradu aspects of Elorath and, like many other thoughtforms, can be tapped and used in relation to Vampyrism. Outer court magickal workings of the Vampyre can also be strongly related to the use of moon cycles, which the Wiccans find useful in their workings. The Wheel of the Year and the eight Sabbats easily are conjoined in the workings of the Vampyre Festivals because they come from similar origins. These Sabbats are comparable to the Festivals in many ways, but merging them together through symbolism is often difficult in every case. The ritual element of the Wiccans, known as a Circle, has tools and elements similar to the Sanguine Mass. These origins are considered to be based on rituals of the Hermetic Order of the Golden Dawn, which is the foundation for most Western magickal traditions and is taken from ancient magickal systems. There is no reason these two rituals can't be merged or crossed over, but this depends on the personal tastes of the individual(s) performing them to select which works best for them. The Wiccan Book of Shadows is identical in concept to the Vampyre Grimoires of being a personal book and journal.

These similarities make for a strong compatibility between Vampyrism and Wiccan paradigms, but the rational mind of the Dayside Vampyre usually shies away from the exclusively Nightside tendencies of the new-age community, which Wicca is so closely tied to. An excellent book, which might be of interest to Dark Wiccans is Out of the Shadows by John J. Coughlin.

Discordianism

Discordianism is a paradigm and religion created in the late 1950s by Greg Hill and Kerry Thornley or unleashed to them late one random night in a bowling alley in Los Angeles by a spectral chimpanzee. This paradigm stands somewhere in the realm between a religion of chaos and a practical joke. The central focus is Eris, the Greek goddess of discord, chaos, and confusion.

This paradigm remained a small movement limited to close friends of the founders as a private joke until the early 1970s. This changed when San Francisco's Ripp Off Press first published a version of *Principia Discordia*, the tome which details the philosophies, scriptures, and teachings of Discordianism. Within Principia Discordia, one will find many unique oddities which range from the Book of Uterus to the Epistle to the Paranoids and the feared Discordian Turkey Curse. Further enhancing and expanding the paradigm, Robert Shea and Robert Anton Wilson authored the Illuminatus! Trilogy, a sci-fi spoof that drew great inspiration from the scriptures of the Principia Discordia. Thus these two texts brought Discordianism into the spotlight of underground subcultures throughout the world.

May I say there are many benefits of being a Discordian! You have a downright excuse to whatever insanity you like as long as it is within reason, and you have a solid and practical reason behind it. Because it involves being a worshipper of chaos, evolution, and change, the teachings of Discordianism naturally sit well with many Strigoi Vii. These must be downright impossible or obviously ridiculous enough so that people laugh so hard you can get away with anything! Humor is a great seducer and aid to the Glamour.

One example of a Discordian Quabal had as their main activity—to invade a bowling alley dressed as clowns. They got away with running down the lanes and knocking pins down, putting makeup on people, and making people trip over themselves. Many even flirted with girls in the alley, one of whom had clown phobia, and they were strangely turned on. A few weeks later a Strigoi Vii couple went and randomly had a picnic in the middle of a nightclub dance floor. These unexpected behaviors do not seem like "Vampyre activities," but in fact they draw subtle attention and are excellent tools for ambient Gathering energy. Remember to keep within the Principles because a Vampyre who gets arrested in the cause of Discordianism will have the burden of a criminal record and less freedom the next round. Reference the Zombie Con or SantaCon event guidelines of behavior for a good set of rules on how to be discordant without being arrested. One of the arts of being a Discordian is to subvert normal taboos and customs without offending or attacking someone.

Self-initiation is the only way to become a True Discordian, and with a flurry of Strigoi Vii becoming what we call brothers and sisters of Eris throughout the world, it is not surprising how common Discordianism is within the Strigoi Vii, even without people realizing it! Beyond the standard systems of conventional thought, the systems of Quabal are perfectly suited and reflect the Discordian nature; many Strigoi Vii tap into the Current of Eris easily.

Randomness, contradiction, and chaos are central tools of the Discordian Vampyre. For example, Discordians are forbidden from eating hot dog buns, but during their initiation self-wise into the paradigm, they are encouraged to eat an entire bag of buns without hot dogs. Eris Esoteric, one of the mortal Discordian orders, provides a good example of Discordian initiation: their dictate states that each member must write out five times the Erisian Affirmation. They must then put their nose print on it and sign it, and then send the first copy to the President of the United States and the second to a minor California government office. The third is to be nailed to a telephone pole, the fourth hidden, and the fifth burned.

Even though Discordianism may seem like a bunch of insane individuals wishing for an excuse to go wild, it has a more sinister purpose. It actually takes tremendous creativity, intelligence, and freedom from social conditioning to remain true to Discordianism.

Draconian

The Draconian Path is a term that is used amongst the Strigoi Vii to describe an amalgamation of ideas. The inborn harshness and reality are what make a Vampyre naturally Draconian, but those who embrace this paradigm bring it further. Such Vampyres see this Blood of the Dragon as the source for an inborn potential for personal divinity and godhood.

Those who adhere to this path see the world as beautiful and harsh at the same time. The focus is ultimately based upon the pursuit of knowledge and spirituality. The Draconian seeks to rise to the heights of the universe and descend into the depths of the underworld unbeknownst to mortals.

The "Fire of the Dragon" is a term used by those aligned with the Draconian Current to destroy all obstacles within their path which would deny them their own deification of the Self.

Vlad Dracul and the Order of the Dragon often act as the most obvious example of the Draconian Path. He was born in a horrible time when Walachia was on the front line of the war with the Ottoman Empire. He had to use psychological warfare on such a level of harshness it was considered Draconian. During this time many of the Eastern Nobility were indeed considered Strigoi Vii by many of the gypsy tribes. Some sources say the Order of the Dragon was actually, on some accounts, an organized collation of Strigoi Vii Nobles fighting to protect Europe. This order came from the word Dracul, which in many sources translates to demon, dragon, and vampire all in one.

Another source for the Draconian Vampyre is the Greek lawmaker Draco, who lived in the seventh century BC. He replaced the blood feud and oral law system with one that could only be enforceable by a court of law. The Draconian constitution, which was the first written law of Athens, detailed his laws. So that no one could refute the laws, they were written on clay tablets and dispersed throughout Greece. What stands out most is his harshness; even smaller offenses were commonly met with capital punishment. For example, Plutarch stated: "It is said that Drakon himself, when asked why he had fixed the punishment of death for most offenses, answered that he considered these lesser crimes to deserve it, and he had no greater punishment for more important ones."

Within this paradigm a select few humans have the "Blood of Dragon," and this relates to the Vampyre concept of the Dragon Awakening.

Kemetism

Kemetism is the term most commonly used to describe the religion of Ancient Egypt and is translated as "Of the Black Land." The Kemetic Vampyre embraces the ancient rites and mythology of the Kemetic religions. Such an approach is not unlike the pagan reconstructionist religions and revival cults, which came along with neo-paganism around the 1960s and 1970s. This flavor is extremely empowering for many Vampyres as a paradigm so old it has a depth and mysticism that is imbedded in the human consciousness.

Prominent Vampyre theological components that come from the Egyptian Kemeticism are the ankh and the word kheper, which is used within Strigoi Vii as Zhep'r. The ankh represents eternal life and immortality, while the term Kheper means to become and transform.

In the modern era, Egyptian mythology truly embraced the concept of vampires originating in Egypt, especially with the invention of Akasha from Anne Rice's Vampire Chronicles. There is little in the way of truly blood-drinking beings in Egyptian mythology, save the priestesses of the lion-goddess Sekhmet, who are known to drink blood in their rituals, and spirits of the dead who were not fed with offerings, which causes their spirit to come back to haunt the living.

The relations of Kemetic theology and spiritualism can be brought into the Vampyre perspective with the correlation of many aspects. First, of course, is the ankh symbol meaning life; second is the *Egyptian Book of the Dead*, which offers a variety of tools for transcending death. Within the Vampyre culture are two dominant godforms and traditions, which have sprung up relating to Kemetic religions:

Asetians in the Kemetic Mysteries draw upon the goddess form of Aset, which is the older and Kemetic term for Isis. This term roughly means "The Throne" and is considered the force and power behind the Pharaohs and Kings. Since the early times of the Kemetic religions, Aset has also been considered by many to be the "mistress of magic" because she is highly skilled in the concept of Heka, or Egyptian Magicks. For the Strigoi Vii, the Current of Aset relates to the aspect of the Kitra and many a Strigoi Vii strongly find their relationship with her as a Patron.

Setians are the older, yet not as common, relation within the Vampyre culture as the Current of Set is very much embraced by modern Left Hand Path occult traditions. In fact, the very first organized Vampyre order, the Order of the Vampyre within the Temple of Set, shows how strong this godform is. Set is the god of the desert, the "red god," and has other names known as Sutekh and Seth in various writings. Set is often considered to correspond with the Greek god Typhon, and many consider magick of the Setians Typhonian magick. Set, even though not considered inside Kemetic Mysteries, is thought a necessary force within the universe. Set has not been able to be identified with any known animal within the culture or of the times. Set is seen as an animal with square ears and a forked tail, which to this day remains a mystery to Egyptologists. This animal may or may not have actually existed. It is known as a Typhonian or Set animal.

Many consider the Setians the opposite of the Asetians because Set was the god who murdered Osiris, husband of Isis. However, in modern culture, these are simply two different Kemetic Currents that are applied in various ritual aspects depending on their usage. They are not commonly called upon at the same time because Set was demonized as the murderer of the Lord of the Black Land and has been related to many modern concepts of the Devil.

Of course, there are many other elements of the Egyptian religion that come into play within the Vampyre community. These range from a variety of interpretations and influences but remember there is no unbroken tradition of Kemeticism (contrary to claims of some groups) from ancient times.

Lovecraftian

The Cthulhu mythos from the writings of H.P. Lovecraft is all the rage within the occult community these days and is even considered slitheringly sexy, especially amongst those interested in chaos magick. The true Cthulhu magician knows for a fact that Lovecraftian mythology is not based on any historical or mythological background, but on the reception and experience of dreams and transmissions from the human collective subconsciousness.

Lovecraft's works dealt with the Beyond, alien gods known as the Great Old Ones, so out of the scope of human consciousness and interpretation getting too close or interacting with them too much will drive the normal human mind insane. At the core of this mythos is the dreaded and fictional book Necronomicon, which was the inspiration behind the name for the Sanguinomicon. Said to have been written by the "Mad Arab" Abdul Alhazrad, this book first appeared in Lovecraft's story "The Hound," written in 1922. Necronomicon is about summoning and the history of the Old Ones.

Various editions of Necronomicon have been released over the years from mainstream publishers, including the best known, very controversial, and most popular, Simon Necronomicon by Avon Books. The author was never known to anyone except by the name Simon. This edition focuses on Babylonian and Sumerian mythology more than the Old Ones.

Within Lovecraftian magic you will find a specific approach to necromancy, conjuration, incantations, sigil work, shape-shifting, pacts, amulets, dreamwalking, summonings, invocations, and opening the gateways to other subtle visions of the Beyond. There are also various orders dedicated to Lovecraftian magick rising in recent years, including the Magan Lodge from the Dragon Rouge, which is very much dedicated to many of these sorceries.

Within the most notable Lovecraftian godforms are, of course, Cthulhu who is the high priest of the Old Ones, but there are many others including Nyarlathotep, the Crawling One; Yig, the Father of Serpents, Azathoth, "the hideous name"; and Dagon, a major Semitic god. Within the Simon Necronomicon are scarce references to vampire-like entities and how to summon and control them, but since this book draws more on Babylonian mythology, it really has nothing to do with the Cthulhu mythos. This book does touch on the subject of the Lilitu and the children of Tiamat as vampire-like beings. The Shadow does have a lot to do with the concept of Lovecraftian vampires because it is a part of the mortal spirit, which can be turned into a demon-like being and shape-shifted under the control of the sorcerer, then sent out as a predatory being to feed on the energies of their victims.

Whether these entities exist in historical human consciousness or not, they do exist now as thoughtforms within the esoteric cultures because they are worked with as legitimate godforms. The Lovecraftian Vampyre embraces this mythology as a tool and understands the reality of fiction from fantasy, using the psychodrama principle of the chaos magician and, when in the

Nightside, embraces these concepts and taps the energies of the Great Old Ones from the subconscious of humanity.

Kalistree: Path of the Dark Goddess

The Dark Mother, Maiden, and Crone, The Queen, and Vampyre Witch & Divine Feminine Current goes by many names from Lilith to Hekate to Kali. Her divinely feminine spiritual Current manifests through the word Kalistree amongst the Vampyre Current. These are those who are Vampyre Witches and embody the feminine of the *Vampyre Queen Within Black Veil* with a defined enthusiasm. Lilith, mother of the night, seduction, feminism, and empowerment is the most common representation of this Current, but this energy goes by many names including Kali, Hel, Sekhmet, Aset, Isis, Ishtar, etc. Like Lilith, the Vampyre Witches are very much in touch with their femininity and sexuality.

The concept of the "Vampyre Witch" is as a powerful and emancipated individual who has embraced the Vampyre Current as a tool of empowerment from a feminine perspective. This form of Witchery is not inspired by the modern Halloween Witch template with broomsticks, black cats, and cauldrons. The Vampyre Witch sits upon the throne of the Dragon Goddess Within as a serpent of Draconian inspiration. They scoff at the cultural limitations put on the feminine, and use seduction, charm, cleverness, beauty, sensuality, intellect, alternative thinking, reason, knowledge, and glamour as elements in their lives.

See the Vampyre Witch Black Veil for more details.

Luciferianism

The Luciferian Vampyre, from the Vampyre perspective, identifies with the pursuit of knowledge or illumination, and they thus are called "Illuminati" within the Family.

Symbolically embracing the spiritual Current of the Morning Star, or Venus, which is known as Lucifer the Light Bearer, amongst the themes attributed to this paradigm, which mimic the pursuit of the light, are high levels of self-discipline, the predatory pursuit of knowledge, and spiritual excellence. At the core of the Luciferian Vampyre is a deep-seated desire for knowledge, and they are thus very focused on the concept of Gnosis.

This desire is also mixed with a personal quest to become Illuminated and cannot ever be fulfilled due to the vastness of the universe, thus attributing to the reality that "the Road to Success is Always Under Construction." Excellent sources of knowledge on this path can be found in the writings of the founder of the Order of Phosphorous, Michael W. Ford.

Thelema

The word Thelema is translated from the Greek word "Will" and is the name for a paradigm and religion founded by the Great Beast, Magus Aleister Crowley (1875–1947). The original scripture of Thelema is *The Book of the Law*, which was revealed to Crowley on April 4, 1904, by a spiritual intelligence he addressed as Aiwass, possibly a Strigoi Morte. Crowley forbids discussion of this book in the Ordo Templis Orientis (OTO) because he felt each person should figure it out for themselves.

After his death, Crowley's followers, especially those within the OTO, have kept his teachings alive in the Gnostic Catholic Church. Crowley took over as Grande Master of the OTO in the 1920s and evolved the order to become a vehicle for Thelema. The Gnostic Mass is the central ritual of Thelema and is often performed by members of the OTO as it was written by Crowley himself; it is one of the inspirations for the Sanguine Mass.

Thelema teaches that all souls are eternal, and each possesses a "True Will," which is that soul's essential purpose, very much akin to Dharma (purpose) in Hindu theology and therefore is the only law which one must abide by. This can be seen as a self-established destiny within the flesh. Thus, during each incarnation, the ultimate agenda is for a soul to accomplish its own True Will, whatever it is to be—from a serial killer to a Catholic saint, whether it is aligned with the ordinary concepts of morality or not. Within Thelema, any action in accordance with one's True Will is considered good, and not following one's True Will is ultimately wrong. One well-known, Thelemic quote is *"Thou hast no right but to do as thy will."*

The central concept of Thelema, *"Do what thou will, is the whole of the Law,"* was made famous by Crowley. This is not an excuse to run rampant and do destructive and criminal activities; one must get in touch with their High Guardian Angel (the Dragon) in order to discover their True Will. This fits very well with cycles of the Dragon within the Strigoi Vii Inner Mysteries and the ultimate measure of a Vampyre's potential and purpose of furthering Zhep'r. Those who do not follow their true Will as Vampyres ultimately become iconoclasts to Their own nature, and so only end up facing the Second Death.

Satanism

Anton Szandor LaVey shaved his head on the 30th of May 1966 and declared a new Satanic Age; three years later he published *The Satanic Bible* with Avon Books. This, along with Wicca and the works of Aleister Crowley, laid the foundation for opening up the esoteric world. Many of the LaVeyan principles are strongly common to the Vampyres of the Strigoi Vii tribe because they are just outright common sense. However, it is important to realize that LaVeyan Satanists share much agreement with the perspective of the Dayside Vampyre perspective.

Vodou

by Frater Ash

Very few subjects have captured the imaginations, hearts, and fear of modern culture like that of vampires and Vodou (anglicized as voodoo). The mere mention of either word is usually guaranteed to evoke thoughts of power, mystery, and the unknown. Mystery and the unknown characterize both of them quite well because although both have been depicted a countless times in popular culture and researched by experts, very little is known about the reality of either one outside of the initiated circle and dedicated practitioners. There are many differences that set the religion of Vodou apart from the tradition of the living Vampyre as practiced by the Strigoi Vii. However, if one is looking for a place where the two paths meet at a spiritual crossroads, it would be the roles that Ancestry plays in both traditions. In Vodou ancestral veneration is a cornerstone of the practice. The spirits of one's ancestors are instrumental to the spiritual development of the initiate and bestow important lessons and gnosis that could not be learned elsewhere. The Vodou practitioner will erect an altar and leave offerings like food, spirits (alcohol), tobacco, and other items favored by the spirits to honor those that came before them in return for their knowledge and empowerment.

One would find that a comparative practice in the Strigoi Vii and the Communion Ritual for the SV initiate connecting with the ancestral spirits of the current of Elorath, also known as Strigoi Morte (SM), is integral to their Xeper or spiritual empowerment. Through interaction with the SM one also gains gnosis and a unique kind of empowerment in the form of Ambrosia, or refined energy. The Vampyre Strigoi Vii practitioner also makes offerings in honor of the ancestral spirits in the form of Pranic energy, which is properly directed through the Communion Ritual. During this interaction, the initiate experiences the Elorathian current and receives insight into the nature of immortality while gaining further empowerment of their individual Zhep'r.

Vodou and the Strigoi Vii are both living traditions empowered by distinct spiritual Currents that follow an aeonic flow. The initiates of both paths become immersed in those energies and start to resonate with them on a subtle level. Thus one can be of any nationality and of any ethnic background and still practice Vodou and learn from the ancestors. The same holds true for the Strigoi Vii. By working with the Current of Elorath, one becomes "of the blood" on a subtle level that creates a bond as strong as physical relation and lineage. Many feel "called" to these individual traditions by a pull in Their spirit that They cannot explain. It can be that the spark and connection has always been there; blood calls to blood. If one is already a practitioner of a Vodou path and felt a draw to the way of the Living Vampire, They would do well to start with Their ancestors. Seeking their knowledge, They may just find Themselves communing with a Strigoi Morte that has been there the entire time waiting for Them to answer the call of the Blood.

CHAPTER 3
SOLITARY RITES

Vampyre Magick by nature is a solitary path, one which is based upon individual results and goals. Agreement is where we find power.

—Magister Maelle

Most Vampyre rituals, especially the Communion Rites of the Strigoi Vii, are solitary rites and, unlike Family Rites, such rituals are done by the individual alone and to their own gratification and validation.

Sobriquet-changing Rite

There may be times when the Strigoi Vii initiate feels that they have outgrown or evolved beyond their Sobriquet and wish to adopt a new one. This decision should not be taken lightly but with great care, as one would give thought to getting a tattoo that symbolizes their deepest and most sincere aspects of Self.

Of course, this rite should be communicated directly with the admins of the StrigoiVii.org forums for initiates who wish to formally change their name. This should not be done frequently and requires a long time of meditation. The best time to change a Sobriquet is during an Ascension Rite or within the Sacred Communion, especially within the Outer Mysteries, but it can be done independently with the following incantation:

Ancients, Ancestors, Sorors, and Fraters, Hear my Call! I have evolved, I have changed, and I have felt Zhep'r. With this, I adopt a new Sobriquet, from this time from now I shall be known as [new sobriquet]. Know me by this name from this moment and henceforth.

Awakening of the Vampyre Spirit

The Awakening of the Vampyre Spirit is a ritual in which one touches the outer elements of the Current of Elorath. Evoking the egregore itself in its full form is highly dangerous and not recommended by anyone but Magisters. This ritual is the outer significance of invoking and simultaneously evoking the Vampyre Spirit within the initiate. Such a ritual can be done by Black Swans and Strigoi Vii who wish to reaffirm Their place with the Black Veils, as well.

Here is an example incantation you can employ on your own:

Ancient Ones, Sorors, Fraters, Ancestors, Hear me now! I am open in spirit and mind, body, and soul. Yet within this mirror, as I look to you, I look toward myself. Dragon, come forth, Ride the Current, Awaken yourself within me, for you are me and I am you. Let the virtues and veils awaken within me the noble blood of which I am and honor the Black Veils. HAIL ELORATH. Rise, Awaken, release your coils within me. Zhep'r.

The Dayside Charge

When we arise in the morning and perform the Sarjaah Rite, found in *The Strigoi Vii Codex Book II: Liber Calmae "Coming Forth by Night,"* We encounter the sun. The shift from the Nightside to the Dayside is the contrasting world of Twilight when both experiences and perspectives interact. The Dayside Charge is empowerment and deals with materialism, health, personal goals, and agendas. It is a complement to the Nightside Charge and a reaffirmation of the Dayside perspectives of the Vampyre. The Dayside Charge is best done in the morning when the day begins.

Ancients, Ancestors, Sorors, and Fraters,
Hear my Call, the Roar of My Dragon.
Today I affirm my Quest for material Mastery within the Dayside
and the steps of Zhep'r I have taken to this point.
I shall not fall from my path, nor shall distractions come to me,
be it love, war, or passion.
I continue to secure and reaffirm my Dayside this morning
through furthering my enterprising spirit, personal nobility, and cor-
poreal Immortality.
Through my Will I know I am reborn and revitalized to master
this world.
I shall Rise, Ride my Dragon, and dance for eternity within the Day.
Hail, Elorath!

After speaking these words, you should meditate on the goals for the day and future.

The Nightside Charge

The Nightside Charge is akin to the Dayside Charge; entering the night manifests and empowers your Nightside skills and talents, whilst revisiting lost ideas and techniques which one has not focused upon recently. Pick one focus technique each time you Enter the Night and focus on Amplification that skill as an exercise and practice it. This can be chakra work, sealing, grounding, centering, an application of the Art of Gathering Energy, a Communion you haven't done in a while, or one you need to experience more results with.

Here is an example of a Nightside Charge.

Ancients, Ancestors, Sorors, and Fraters, Hear my Call, the Roar of My
Dragon. Today I affirm my Quest for Twilight within the Nightside and
the steps of Zhep'r I have taken to this point. I shall not fall from my
path, nor shall dis- tractions come to me, be it love, war, or passion. I

continue to secure and reaffirm my Nightside and spiritual Immortality through the continued practice of Vampyrism and Communion. I Shall Rise, Ride my Dragon, and dance for eternity within the Night. Hail, Elorath!

Entering the Twilight (The Twilight Charge)

This ritual, meditation, and exercise focus on strengthening your balance between Dayside and Nightside workings. The Twilight Charge hymn will lead you into the focus of a technique in which you must be able to manifest aspects of both Dayside and Nightside. An example of this is putting aside your belief and then going right into a Communion Rite. This ceremony should happen during the hours of Twilight, preferably in the morning when the world is fresh and new. Begin with a grounding technique and then center yourself. Open oneself to the time between worlds and watch the sunrise. The incantation below can either be whispered or thought in your mind; then begin the Dragon's Throning technique. Here is an example, which you can tailor to your own needs, or create your own as you see fit:

Ancients, Ancestors, Sorors, and Fraters, Hear my Call, the Roar of My Dragon. Today I affirm my Quest for Twilight and the steps of Zhep'r I have taken to this point. I shall not fall from my path, nor shall distractions come to me, be it love, war, or passion. I continue to secure and reaffirm my Dayside through material Mastery. I continue to secure my Nightside in the daily practice of Our Mysteries. I Shall Rise, Ride my Dragon, and dance for eternity within Twilight. Hail, Elorath!

CHAPTER 4
RITES OF THE VAMPYRE SABBATHS

*It is my Will to inform the World of certain facts within my knowledge.
I, therefore, take "magical weapons," pen, ink, and paper. The
composition and distribution of this book is thus an act of Magick by
which I cause Changes to take place in conformity with my Will.*

—Aleister Crowley

As defined in the Liber Zhep'r, the major Vampyre Sabbaths are celebrated throughout the Family according to the Strigoi Vii Tradition. They are intended to be celebrated in chorus with the rest of the Family to raise collective energies and to be simultaneously a personal and private affair. Each of these festivals/sabbaths has a specific purpose and meaning, as well as a corresponding set of rituals.

Those who are geographically solitary and who are not adept in astral travel are encouraged to participate in these festivals in person if possible or simply by celebrating them in a solitary matter. Those adept in Flight are likewise encouraged to participate in group Communion followed by astral projection. Or they should join the grand chorus in the astral.

The following are simply templates and presented in solitary and group workings. Remember a Magister, Priest/ess or an Adeptus should be present when working in group rituals.

Celebration of the Samhain, October 30–November 1

This is the grandest of all Vampyre Sabbaths; it lasts three entire days and is celebrated on Samhain Eve, Halloween, Samhain, and the Day of the Dead. Since this is the equivalent of a Vampyre New Year, many celebrations take place, but traditionally, a Vampire Ball, such as the Endless Night in New Orleans where many mundanes are invited, takes place on or around All Hallows Eve.

During these nights unawakened mortals are touched by a variety of emotions and traditions. These nights, when the walls between worlds are thinnest, it is easy to cross the Veils between various layers of reality. In Latin countries the Day of the Dead is celebrated, during which families remember their ancestors, whilst in North America, particularly in Canada and the United States, Halloween is celebrated with millions going out in costume.

This is the perfect opportunity for a harvest and hunt; the Vampyre has more freedom these evenings to be open about who and what They are because humans are so distracted and simultaneously "in the mood." Aside from the openness and freedom of the Vampyre being able to hunt, these are the nights when it is permitted to perform the Sanguine Mass with mortal-minded guests who would be receptive to the ceremony.

For those who are geographically challenged and cannot attend the grander celebrations or choose not to, the Sanguine Mass may also be performed on a solitary level with the celebrant if they have mastered such skills to perform Flight (as defined in *Coming Forth by Twilight*). Some Vampyres choose to celebrate only the hunt this evening with their chosen sorors and fraters.

Traditionally, the time after these events is a time of reflection and solitude for the individual Strigoi Vii, and it is not uncommon to take a few days after the high energy to perform meditations and sealings of their energy.

A typical Sanguine Mass is held on this night, but the invocations and purpose of the ritual are focused to reflect the specific festival.

The Samhain Hymn/Charge
Let the gates between worlds swing wide open and merge into one.
This Eve, I walk on the fringe of dimensions, as the Veil between worlds
is Thinned.
Let mortal minds witness Our Open Rule with love and loyalty.
The spectrum of Dayside and Nightside are in equilibrium, this night
we Welcome the Twilight.
Masques on and then off, Raise Our Chalices in celebration and dance
in the Light of Day and the Shadows into the Night.
Behold the Vampyre Current of Elorath, Zhep'r.
For tonight the Mortals are the ones wearing the Masque.

The Nightside Mass

Yule/Winter Solstice, December 21 or 22 in the Northern Hemisphere or June 20 or 21 in the Southern Hemisphere

As many Vampyres prepare for the celebrations of Their mortal mundane family's religious holidays such as Christmas, Yule, Ramadan, and Hanukah, the Northern Vampyres are secretly plotting to celebrate Their Longest Night, the time when They are making Their most and deepest Communions into the Current. Here, small groups of Strigoi Vii around the world gather for a grand convergence within the astral layer of reality to perform Communion or in solitary to reflect on Their Nightsides and the spiritual bonds between members of the Family, which is the Current.

The offering this night in Communion is toward the Current directly and not toward the Strigoi Morte. Traditionally, at the stroke of midnight on the night of Yule, the Vampyres join in a Sabbath in the astral, to dance and meet in celebration of Their beloved Current.

For the month before the Nightside Festival, the Vampyre is focusing on Their Nightside skills, performing meditations and energy work to further Their own personal agendas of individual evolution. Communion should be made at least every night for twelve nights, and gather great amounts of Lifeforce before the Nightside Festival finally arrives.

The celebrants, in groups, if possible, or on a solitary level, perform

Sanguine Mass to the point of the Offering. Then at midnight, once safely and comfortably at the climax of the most sacred ritual of the Vampyres, the Meeting begins. This Meeting is to invoke the Current of Elorath into Themselves or, for those who have mastery, the technique of Flight, meet in the astral. Here awareness of the Current is in agreement.

Once the mass communion throughout the world is completed, Strigoi Vii then moves off to meet with the mundane families or to revel in Their empowerment of Our own collective spirit.

The Nightside Festival Hymn/Charge
Ancient spirits and Living Vampires from around the world, we stand together as a chorus this night. Hear my Calls and hails throughout the layers of reality!
I stand here in celebration of Our Ancient Blood, a living fire of Dragons united in celebration.
Let my Dragon ROAR and be heard, the blood be set ablaze, and my Dreams come forth from fantasy to reality.
I awaken within the Dream of my own making, I dance to the drums of my own creation.
Here my Ancients, Sorors, and Fraters let Us evolve and welcome the New Season of Our Own Blood, Our Current, Our Being.

The Crimson Mass

Anti-Valentine's Day, February 14

This celebration is of the existence of Love, a representation of these characteristics of Love that bond the Family and fuel the Current. Unlike many mortals who loathe Valentine's Day celebrations, the Vampyre does the opposite; it is a time of reflection and evolution.

On the personal side, We honor those We have loved, will love, or currently love, both Vampyre and mortal, and reflect on how they have contributed personally to Our individual evolution. For the Vampyre, love is a bond and an energy exchange on a level that is truly intense. Those We have loved are Our teachers and donors, friends and foes whom We have fallen out of positive relationships with. Love assists in defining each individual, and We come to realize this reality and focus and reflect on this.

Love is eternal for the Vampyre because we are timeless beings and the only moment which exists for the Vampyre is the here and now. Each time we have loved comes into a central focus within the Crimson Mass, as each experience of love is different, be it romantic, family, or fraternal.

To celebrate this, we take time a few days before Valentine's Day and perform a Sanguine Mass in solitary confines. On Our own personal altars, We write a short poem for each love in Our life, be it now or during another time. We recall and give thanks for the opportunity to love and light a candle to reflect on each experience.

Lovers whom We are currently with who are open to Our traditions or are initiated often perform the Temple of Flesh Rite or a similar ritual during Sanguine Mass to amplify and honor the love which comes between those who are in love.

During the actual night of Valentine's Day, celebrating with Our mortal lovers is the common mortal traditional way, or if We are single and solitary, We go out and harvest the energies which are radiated by the many lovers out in the world.

The Crimson Hymn/Charge
My Loves,
Attraction, passion, pleasure.
Pain, conflict, discord.
These are the realities of LOVE.
Let me not fear them but evolve from them.
I raise this chalice to celebrate my loves, past, present, and future. For I am who I am today by Our choices, Our Affairs.
Let the Crimson Ties be never forgotten, for love is never the same in time
and in eternity there is no time.
Thank you, my loves.
Your memories are eternal with me.

Walpurgis / Beltaine - Night of Fire, A Celebration of the Dragon Festival

Night of April 30–May 1

Throughout history, predominantly in Europe, this event takes place on the night of April 30 or the first of May. Here within Ourselves, we focus on the Fire of Our Dragons, the Fire which we have burned within our Vampyric souls.

The night of the Dragon Festival excellently falls upon the Celtic festival Beltane, which celebrated the coming of a good growing season and was marked by the lighting of fires in celebration of renewal and rebirth. The very word Beltane means "bright fire" in Old Irish.

In Germanic mythology, Walpurgis Night is when witches gather on the Brocken mountain to hold celebrations with their gods. This is the tallest of the mountains in central northern Germany. Thus, in these lands, many northern European tribes lit bonfires to keep the demons and evil spirits at bay and celebrate the coming of spring, similar to the Beltane celebrations. For the Strigoi Vii this fire represents purification and rebirth, the relation to the symbol of the Dragon.

> The Dragon's Hymn/Charge
> *Oh Great Ancient Serpent. Hear Me!*
> *I call to you, my Dragon.*
> *Rise, RISE, RISE within the Coils of my Eternity.*
> *I summon you the nameless and unseen one*
> *The core of my primal and Immortal Self!*
> *For I am you and you are me.*
> *My life is the expression of your presence.*
> *I am your breath, I am your fire!*
> *I am the perception from your Throne.*
> *My eyes are your eyes.*
> *We are one and Eternal.*
> *As you take your next Breath, I am renewed and Reborn!*
> *Rise, RISE, my Dragon Within.*
> *Hail, Elorath!*

The Dayside Festival Ritual

Summer Solstice, June 21

When We celebrate the Dayside, We focus on the materialistic world of the five senses, Our pragmatic perspective on reality, and the furthering of Our corporeal lives. The Long Day ritual involves a Sanguine Mass where a sigil is burned. Burning a sigil We have prepared months in advance focuses on our Dayside tasks and goals.

> The Dayside Festival Hymn/Charge
> *I stand at the Gates of Day looking to you, my Dragon.*
> *Here I focus on the world materialistic.*
> *Through the Five senses of the Corporeal Realm*
> *We Rise. Rise, RISE, RISE*
> *within the Coils my visions and desires.*
> *Today we affirm our commitment to this corporeal world.*
> *To find our strength in an enterprising spirit.*
> *Live with pleasure, honor, and personal nobility.*
> *I am your breath, I am your fire!*
> *I am the perception from your Throne.*
> *Rise, RISE, for my Dragon's Will Commands it.*
> *Hail ELORATH!*

The Wild Hunt: Celebrating the Bast Festival

This ritual celebrates the night of the wild hunt, where we revel in Our primal natures and forget Our civilized conditionings. This usually takes place in August in the time during the months of summer in the Northern Hemisphere. For those who practice lycanthropy, this is a powerful time to indulge in shapeshifting as the energies of the night are very high.

A woodlands setting or a park late at night is traditionally the location of the Bast Mass. This, like other rituals, should be secluded from the mundane, and only those initiated or Awakened should participate. A bonfire, mead, and food are great tools for the celebratory element of the event.

The Bast Mass is unlike any other Strigoi Vii ritual and involves some daring and courage. The "Wild Hunt" takes place, where members prepare masks and body paints. Each participant should create two masks, one representing noble predators such as the wolf, bear, great cat, shark, hawk, eagle, etc., and one representing the prey animals such as deer, mouse, fish, elk, birds, etc. The presiding priest or deacon of the ceremony should be dressed, of course, in ritual attire.

For attire during the ritual Nightklad dress is highly suggested, of course with body paint and primal elements such as tails, claws, and other details representing the lower animals. This allows celebrants to better enter the spirit of the ceremony and take on the roles they are going to assume.

A Sanguine Mass should commence the ceremonies until the Recoiling. Once this has been established, the core of the ritual shall begin. Members line up in a line, and with the flip of an ancient coin, the priest or deacon will say "predator" and "prey" down the line to each celebrant. This divides the groups into two, and the prey takes on their masks and runs into the night to hide. Then the first round of the Bast Mass begins, and the predators run around the bonfire screaming, howling, and invoking their chosen predatory totems.

Here the skills of shapeshifting come in well. If there are enough celebrants, a drum circle and chanting can be started by a third group to get into the mood.

Once the trance begins and the shapeshifting of the soul invokes the totem spirits, the priest or deacon releases the wolf pack of predatory animals into the night to find their prey.

What is excellent about this exercise is the preparation in advance, creation of the masks, and research into each totem, which will give the celebrants meditative time to reflect on their primal natures.

The first round of the hunt lasts until all the prey are captured (be as gentle or as rough as you like as long as it is done safely) and returned to the bonfire for the feasting. Once this has been completed, the celebrants shift their roles, the prey becomes the predators, and the second round of the Wild Hunt begins. As the night goes on, the roles may be switched as many times as the celebrants have energy for. Upon the completion of the hunt, the Sanguine Mass is completed, and the priests and celebrants enjoy a feast of food and drink.

This ritual can be done alone on a solitary level, in which the celebrant prepares their mask and identity and goes far into the wilderness or within their own home. They practice the arts of lycanthropy and attune themselves to the totem that best fits them. Two celebrants can also perform this ritual with one taking the role of the predator and the other the prey in a secret and forbidden place.

The Wild Hunt Hymn/Charge
(Vampyre Howl)
Tonight is where I hear the call of the Hunt,
The Wild Hunt.
I summon forth the predator in my soul.
Claw, tooth, eye, quill, and talon,
Tonight I am one with the spirit of the prey.
For I am the apex, the master of all.
(Vampyre Howl)
Hail Elorath!

CHAPTER 5
SHAPESHIFTING

At night, the eyes of wolves shine like candle flames, yellowish, reddish, but that is because the pupils of their eyes fatten on darkness and catch the light from your lantern to flash it back to you—red for a danger; if a wolf's eyes reflect only moonlight, then they gleam a cold and unnatural green, a mineral, a piercing color. If the benighted traveler spies those luminous, terrible sequins stitched suddenly on the black thickets, then he knows he must run. Fear and flee the wolf; for, worst of all, the wolf may be more than he seems.

—Angela Carter, *The Company of Wolves*

Vampire legends and myths speak of beings who can shape-shift into felines, serpents, jackals, rats, bats, and of course, wolves. As with so many vampire legends, there is a grain of truth within these tales. The Vampyre can ride these legends, yet know the Truth of their nature and thus revel in Their potential as shape-shifters within the subtle realms of reality.

Please note that shape-shifting is an advanced technique and requires a trained, skilled, and talented individual who has mastered many of the techniques required, so it is best that Vampyre Adeptus practice this form of energy manipulation.

Lycanthropy and therianopy are words that refer to the process of a human being shape-changing to the form of an animal. Lycanthropy specifically refers to shape-shifting into a wolf, and comes from the Greek word for wolf (lykos) and man (anthropos). The archetype of the werewolf who shifts form with the cycles of the full moon is an important symbol to many Vampyres working within the Outer Mysteries. Vampires and werewolves have long been associated with each other in legend and literature. For example, in Bram Stoker's novel Dracula, the vampire count takes the form of a wolf upon numerous occasions. Even contemporary popular culture associates vampires with werewolves, albeit often as enemies, as in the world of Vampire: the Masquerade and the Underworld movies. However, in folklore werewolves are traditionally the servants of vampires, such as in the television show True Blood. For many mortals, the wolf is a primordial predator and symbol of fear, so the association of vampires and wolves is another aspect of our Glamour.

There are many examples of shape-shifting in legends, myths, and religions throughout history. Notable examples from ancient and classical times include the cursed King Lycos in Ancient Greece, the Hengeyoki of Japan, and the Russian shape-shifting magicians called zagovori. Many believed the ferocious Berserker Viking warriors had the ability to transform themselves into bears so as to be even fiercer fighters, and numerous Native American tribes closely identified with various totem animals. One element nearly all the legends have in common is that when the individual shape-shifted into an animal, they gained extra powers of strength, perception, or movement. Within this chapter, we will explore the reality of Vampyre Lycanthropy and shape-shifting, and how it can be used within the Strigoi Vii Mysteries as a tool of power.

Many think of werewolves as opposed to vampires in some eternal war as detailed in Vampire: the Masquerade games and the Underworld films. In reality, this is just a role-playing and Hollywood concept and not the case with the essence of LivingVampyrism. Those Vampyres who embrace shape-shifting, especially with the totem of the wolf, are not pack animals, as one might think; They are highly independent, loyal, and primal individuals who are touched by the Wolf Spirit. Some human magicians, shamans, esoteric traditions, and mystics have learned certain techniques of shape-shifting. However, the mortal-minded perception of shape-shifting is more akin to a spell or curse, so numerous legends abound about the "curse" of the werewolf, or the various beliefs about how one "becomes" a werewolf (these range from drinking water in which the full moon is reflected to being bitten by another werewolf). However, the Vampyre fully embraces this discipline as an elegant and natural form of energy manipulation. Once an individual Vampyre has gained familiarity with the astral energies of reality, They are able to begin preliminary shape-shifting.

However, a common misconception about shape-shifting, which is borne out by many of the legends, is that it occurs primarily on a corporeal level. The reality is that shape-shifting is a form of astral and etheric projection. Shape-shifting begins with conscious and directed visualization of the desired astral pattern. With the necessary force of Will and application of Lifeforce, the Adeptus Vampyre can shape Their subtle body into the form They choose and, through the connection the totem spirit of that beast, can adopt many of its characteristics. In principle, the astral manipulation creates ripples, or echoes, in the etheric and corporeal planes, so theoretically the corporeal shape could shift as a result of astral manipulation. In reality, subtle energies are much more flexible than corporeal matter. A literally daunting effort of Will and magick is needed to shape-shift corporeally in this manner, which is virtually impossible within the laws of physics.

TOTEMS

In Native American lore, totems are animal spirit forms to which a specific Strigoi Vii may be attuned. Not all Strigoi Vii will feel attunement with a specific animal, but those who do will find that animal's form easiest to assume during shape-shifting. Many Strigoi Vii find Themselves attuned to whichever animal was Their favorite during childhood, or the animal is Their favorite type of pet. Wolves are obviously common totems amongst Strigoi Vii. The members of the Family who claim the wolf as Their totem are known amongst the Strigoi Vii as Cainus Lupus. However, there are many more totems and favored shapes.

It is important to note that, with practice and skill, the Strigoi Vii can shape-shift into any animal or form They choose. Totems represent animals with which an Adeptus Strigoi Vii has a special affinity, and which are attuned to their Dharma. As a similar example, although any Strigoi Vii can train Themselves in any of the three Trinity Pulses of the Current, many Vampyres, members of the Priesthood, will find Themselves naturally and innately drawn to one of the three roads as one would fall in love with another individual. Just as with the Trinity Pulses of the Current, some Strigoi Vii may not have a personal totem, and some rare Strigoi Vii has more than one. However, a greater percentage of Strigoi Vii associate with a totem animal than do those who are formally initiated into one of the Trinity Currents of Elorath of Kitra, Mradu or Ramkht.

Once a Strigoi Vii has determined Their totem animal, either through intuition, meditation, or the Rite of Totems, the first step is to familiarize themselves with that animal. If the animal is a domestic pet such as a cat or a dog, the Strigoi Vii should attempt to carefully observe and interact with that animal. If the totem is a more "wild" animal such as a lion, monkey, or eagle, the Strigoi Vii Adeptus should make every attempt to safely observe that animal in its natural habitat or at least within a zoo, and personally research the animal's habitats and behaviors. Many excellent nature videos are available that may aid in the process.

The Strigoi Vii can then begin to assume their totem's form in the astral realm through meditation. During lucid dreams, or astral Flight, the Strigoi Vii should visualize Their astral Self as, not a humanoid double, but their totem animal. Or they should consciously change into any animal they desire, with the totem usually being the easiest form to take. Perhaps the best way to begin this process is by deliberately shifting one's shape during lucid dreaming. Instead of journeying through the dream as yourself, concentrate, and shape that self into animal form. The Vampyre Adeptus who has practiced lucid dreaming already has experience shaping the dream around them; now it should be possible to shape the self within the dream. Once the "transformation" is complete, the Strigoi Vii can perceive, through the Dreamworld, the five senses of this form, such as the form of a wolf running swiftly through a forest or a majestic hawk soaring through the air.

The next step is to shape-shift during astral Flight. Many Vampyres find this process is facilitated by visualizing, instead of an astral double, an "astral totem," as they begin their Flight. Once you have successfully shape-shifted into your astral totem, you will be able to interact with the astral realm in this form and with all the skills and powers of the totem animal. Astral shape-shifting provides an entirely different experience of and perspective on the astral plane!

The process for astral shape-shifting into other animal forms is the same as for shape-shifting into one's totem animal. However, most Strigoi Vii find it, initially, much harder to shape-shift into animals other than their totem animal. That is why we recommend attempting to discover and shape-shift into your totem animal first.

Ritual: Rite of the Cainus Lupus

This ritual begins in the astral realm and is best done on the night of a full moon, due to the linkage of werewolves and the full moon in the collective unconscious. In this ritual, the Strigoi Vii Vampyre embraces and draws upon the primal nature of the Wolf Totem.

The first step is visualization. The Strigoi Vii will, of course, have prepared beforehand, observing and studying wolves as described earlier. In a secluded place, preferably a rural outdoor location, the Vampyre Adeptus begins by visualizing the image of the wolf as clearly as possible.

Once the Adeptus has fixed upon the Wolf Totem, They should begin drawing and accepting the wolf into Themselves. Some visualizations include howling like a wolf, dancing wildly, dropping to all fours, growling, and performing whichever actions bring Them closer to the Wolf Totem. The Vampyre Adeptus should attempt to lose themselves in the primal spirit of the Wolf and suspend disbelief so that true astral and spiritual shape-shifting can take place.

If available, a drum circle may help the Adeptus shift from the corporeal human mentality to the primal animal state. There are also many recordings of wolf calls and howls available, which may serve as useful triggers, especially if this rite must be performed indoors. If possible, it is also empowering to perform this rite wearing a wolf mask, and Nightklad or clad only inappropriate body paint. Some similar shamanistic ceremonies called for the celebrant to wear a wolf pelt to further the identification with the animal. Many species of wolves are currently considered endangered, so this technique should only be employed if the Vampyre is absolutely sure the pelt has been obtained legally and ethically.

Summation

Once the initiate has fully mastered shape-shifting, They have gained the potential to Ascend to become an Adeptus in the Vampyres Mysteries. From the Outer perspective, shape-shifting takes place primarily in the astral realm. Shape-shifting is an advanced skill that, like Flight, takes time and practice to master. If the Vampyre does not achieve success at first, They should persevere, remembering that shape-shifting is a natural part of the Strigoi Vii. For the Strigoi Vii, shape-shifting is a powerful tool of personal evolution and spiritual transformation and an important step upon the journey of Zhep'r.

CHAPTER 6
SEX MAGICK

Our Order possesses the key which opens up all Masonic and Hermetic secrets, namely, the teachings of sexual magic, and this teaching explains, without exception, all the secrets of Nature, all the symbolism of Freemasonry, and all systems of religion.

—Jubilaeums-Ausgabe Der Oriflamme (1912)

S ex magick is the mastery of sexual Lifeforce energies to fuel elements of a specific working. This can be done as visualizations alone or copulations of two or more individuals. We think of the Witch's Sabbat with an orgy in reverence to Satan or demonic powers, but in its most pure form, even abstinence from sexual activity can be considered sex magick. Whatever the practice, the energies released and/or raised are intended to focus on a specific purpose or goal.

Many occultists had different applications on sexual magicks. Aleister Crowley uses orgasm as a tool of release and focuses in his religion of Thelema. He stated that all violence in the world was a result of repressing sexual behavior. This is particularly interesting because he lived and practiced his magick during the Victorian Era. Whilst others, such as Samuel

Aun Weor, proclaim avoiding orgasm as much as possible followed by an intense act of sexual release to focus the energies.

Sexual energies are an extremely potent form of energy; when focused they can achieve corporeal health and powerful results. During orgasm the practitioners achieve a heightened sense of transcendence over normal reality.

Hierodule or temple prostitutes (a term not popular due to mod- ern connotations) performed sexual magicks in the ancient days. There are legends of hierodule in the temples of Ishtar and even Aphrodite. A clear example of sacred prostitution is seen in the Torah, which has two different words for prostitute: zonah (זנה) and kedeshah. The word "zonah" simply meant an ordinary prostitute or loose woman; but the word "kedeshah" literally means "consecrated female," from the Semitic root q-d-sh (קדש) meaning "holy" or "set apart." What is important to note is that these historical references do not fully confirm the concept of sexual magick within religious bodies but show that these cultures considered the thought of sexuality and freedom of such.

Vampire legends and literature seriously delve into the concept of sexuality amongst the Undead. The succubus and incubus are prime examples of this. The Vampyre, being a libertine in the truest sense, personally rises above the mortal limitations of sexuality, especially as one gains more and more Zhep'r and enjoys the freedom of the astral. Who knows? The legends of the incubus and succubus may be truly the Whisperers and advanced Living Vampires practicing the Art of Gathering Energy.

Many more conservative elder Vampyres consider the sexual bounds of human society to be a form of sex magick perpetuated by the Ancestors. By focusing their energies inward toward heterosexual relationships, the human population exploded and energies focused, and this meant a more bountiful harvest of Lifeforce for Them.

For the Vampyre, especially the Adeptus may enjoy freedom from sexual bondage, or at least an understanding of it, is why so many Strigoi Vii are drawn to (or at least open-minded to) homosexuality, libertine activities, and BDSM. For some of us, We do not even consider some acts to be ones which are libertine or even fetishistic; they are simply instinctual desires and acts we do not wish to put labels on. Freedom from Judeo-Christian thought patterns is a point of Zhep'r and a freedom of the Self. However, this does not necessarily mean all Strigoi Vii partake in these activities, it is just that we are not judgmental toward others for their choice of behavior as long as it respects free will.

Empowering the feminine, or the submissive, roles, which are traditionally considered to be passive, is a form of empowerment for the Vampyre. Many Vampyre Gents who are worship the Vampyre Witch and in return they are worshipped.

Invokation of the Dragon Goddess
Ritual by Magister Maelle

This Invokation is, at its core, a practice of sex magick, communion, and Vampyrism, and the standard version is to be performed with two partners, one male and one female, whilst this ritual deals with the feminine elements of the Currents of Elorath. The male partner is to act as the priest and together they invoke the Goddess within.

The priestess should be naked during the ritual and have the goal of invoking the Current, with divine feminine glyph (usually a kitra glyph) below her navel on the phallus chakra. The priest is to invoke the masculine within the Current and put the divine masculine in the same location as an offering. Both should put the sigil of Elorath on their foreheads above their third eye. This can be done with eyeliner or any form of makeup.

The temple should be completely filled with incense (i.e., opium or musk) and the altar should be prepared where the sexual communion is to take place. Of course, the room should be filled with red and black candles to represent the blood of the Current and darkness, respectively.

The ritual begins with the priestess lying on the altar chanting *"la, la, Kitra, Lilith, Hel, Kali, Isis, Sekmet, Mary, Aset."* Then the priest recites the incantations, and the priestess should focus on a silent communion and Amplification the divine feminine and making a deep offering of lifeforce to the Strigoi Morte. She should envision the goddess in all her attributes, where the consciousness of the priestess and the goddess become one. Once communion has been initiated, the priestess should arouse her Dragon through the Kundalini serpent visualization, which is a snake coiled at the bottom of the spine rising up and coming out of her third eye chakra. The goal is to inflame herself with the primal lust of the Dragon and become embodied by the Goddess energies of the Vampyre Witch Queen Within.

The Priest:
Ancient ones come and feast,
Divine Goddesses of the Current,
Kitra, crux of all that is feminine, powerful, and divine.
I summon you to this temple, a temple of flesh!
Possess the body of our priestess,
join us in this ecstasy and union!
I offer myself, as your vessel,
your sacrifice on the altar of pleasure!
Through love and loyalty, Blood and Fire!
Reveal yourself to me.
Let me taste your forbidden knowledge,
Let me gain wisdoms of an ancient time.
Open your womb of Blood.
Come to me my goddess, let us dance in eternity!
Followed by chanting in ecstasy: *Hail Elorath!*

At this point the priestess is writhing on the altar, masturbating but not reaching climax. When she feels the inspiration, she shall rise and begin her part of the ritual and continue the chanting.

The Priestess
I am here to welcome the goddess into me,
Kitra I am you and you are me!
I am the catalyst of transformation, from flesh to spirit!
Within me is the womb of all Life and creation!
Drink from my cup of extract!
Taste my insatiable lust!
I am here to be purified of all mortal consequence
through love and passion!
I am the key to the garden of delights!
I am the vessel that brings death back into life!
Delve into my dissolving embrace,
and rise in the communion of the Goddess Within.
Hail Elorath! Hail Kitra!

Once the incantations are complete, she begins arousing the priest and when he has been completely filled with lust, she mounts him. The congress begins and she is now the embodiment of all primal feminine lust.

During the congress, the offering should be released and continue through orgasm jointly if possible, for the most powerful Gift. Both participants can growl, howl, scream, and hail the currents, and should be completely open to all Strigoi Morte who come to the feast. Allow the most primal and dark visions of sexuality to be brought to the forefront of the mind and acted out if possible.

Once the offering is complete, continue and the Recoiling; once complete, both participants shall drink from the chalice and receive the sacraments of the Blood, which is charged with Ambrosia. A banishing is highly suggested after the ritual is complete in the summation.

Opening the Gates of the Throne
A solitary ritual by Aziza Rii

The ritual involves working with sexual energy to clear/open energy centers/chakras up to the Crown chakra, which is akin to an energy ladder, which one can "climb" to one's Throne, to hear the voice of their own Dragon, or Higher Self.

Clear your mind. Start by igniting the spark of lust; concentrate on it. Growing the energy in your sacral chakra until the feeling of tension arises and wishes to be released. Do not release it by any physical means.

Magnetize your hands by rubbing palms to each other in quick motions, until you start to feel pins or tension in your palms or any familiar sensations signifying your palms are charged. By Will, form this charged energy to be magnetized. Let the energy in your sacral center rise and grow, by concentrating on your object or idea of lust.

It is better to visualize it since you'll need visualization to get effective results; it is also better to use your mind for concentration on the arousal of this energy. Closed eyes, and a focused mind, will clear your path of disruptions.

When you begin to feel a pleasant burning sensation, start to move your hands in front of your body from the lower chakra to the upper crown chakra, center by center. The movements should be as if you are caressing the energy body with hands (which are at this point magnetized and should be concentrated to attach energy from the abdomen, raising it up).

Move energy to the upper body realms. Keep in mind that you should avoid touching your body with your hands or with any physical object. Rather, keep a focus and feel the sensation of energy covering and rising up your body. This way, the fire energy in your abdomen should release and push stagnation, even blockages, of your subtle body as you move along them all.

As you move up, breathe deeply and rhythmically while raising the energy up to the Crown—one deep breath per one circle of rising. Lead the energy up and return your hands in slow motion half circles around your body to the lower chakra with exhalation.

The session gains its goals when you start to feel something like a crowning sensation around the crown chakra. The sensation may vary and be subjective. I find it to be cooling, but one should feel as if the head is "crowned" or "opened," or "released."

From this point on, as you open your eyes, your perspective should be changed, because you're watching, seeing, and realizing the reality from another, now fresh, perspective. This is what I call the gates of Throne opened. The Throne is unleashed for you to ride with your Dragon and merge It into your conscious awareness.

As a Vampyre, you might like to engage in collecting Lifeforce from a particular main energy center while you feed, and work the same episode session from the center you concentrated Lifeforce around. You might either like to engage astral feeding as Incubus or Succubus by collecting energy to the sacral center, then working to the point of opening the Gates directly while performing the feeding.

Because this ritual is solitary, you contact the essence of your primal/pure core and ignite the energy to center. Using an object of lust is more effective, spontaneous, and easy flowing, and it can produce basic desired results for this particular private session.

CHAPTER 7
BLOOD & ROSES
HANDFASTING RITES

Love is a living and breathing spirit between two or more people, often culturally expressed in the rituals and ceremonies of marriage. When that love changes, dies or evolves, there are few options for humans. Vampyre culture seeking immortality realizes such agreements must be renewed over time; thus, our marriage rituals reflect our freedom that people change and evolve.

—Magister Maelle

As mentioned in William Shakespeare's Cymbeline, handfasting is an alternative Christian style of European wedding. This Black Veils & Strigoi Vii Vampyre Wedding Rite, known as Blood and Roses, is in fact very similar to this tradition. Like most wedding traditions there is an exchange of "rings," often on three levels. Each ring represents a deepening of the marriage and reflects on the relationship. Blood & Roses handfastings have some interesting traits compared to modern traditional marriages and are in agreement with the reborn practices of many neo-pagan traditions. The

Blood and Roses ceremony can be a civil and or spiritual commitment, and it traditionally goes in three levels, each known as "Rings." The First Ring is a year and a day engagement; the Second Ring is for a period of seven to thirteen years, or "as long as the love lasts"; and the Third Ring is for all eternity.

What is important to note is that Strigoi Vii is encouraged to have more than one ceremony in order to accommodate Nightside and that of their Dayside. The first ceremony, the "Dayside Wedding," is a typical wedding of the religion of the mortal family and is especially important when only one member of the couple is of the Blood. Such Dayside Weddings are often traditional weddings depending on the customs of the individual and their families. This allows for no pressure and for the Strigoi Vii to honor their mortal friends and family, and to further promote the Glamour.

The second, "Nightside," wedding is usually done separately from the mundane world, in a private Quorum in the presence of a Magister. This ceremony, of course, can be witnessed by Black Swans or those of polarizing Traditions. Most importantly, this form of marriage is traditionally presided over by the couple themselves, who determine their own vows. A Magister or Priest/ess may preside over the ceremony, but their focus is solely on observation and leading elements of the Sanguine Mass. Couples may, of course, opt to perform the First Rings as an engagement completely on their own, without a Magister present, just as lovers are welcomed to perform group Communion without a Magister or Priest/ess present.

The Three Levels of Handfasting

Within Strigoi Vii, there are three levels of marriage, each leading into the next. The three levels are akin to normal levels of developing relationships in many cultures. What makes Strigoi Vii unique is the third level of marriage, the Third Ring, which is an eternal sealing for both souls and outlasts the death of either partner. The Second Ring only lasts whilst both individuals are incarnated and are broken by the First Death of one partner. Of course, these wedding traditions are not wise to have with white swans or mundanes and are only specifically for Black Veil Vampyres, Strigoi Vii, and Black Swans. What is important to point out is that these forms of marriage are only representations of what truly is there.

First Rings (Engagement)

The First Ring level is equivalent to an engagement and allows members of the marriage to test their relationship and compatibility in an official and ceremonial format. The First Ring traditionally lasts for a year and a day. It can either be renewed, allowed to expire, or the members of the agreement can move to the Second Rings.

Second Rings (Wedding)

The Second Ring is a formal marriage, and these vows traditionally last seven years. This limited scope acknowledges that individuals evolve and change throughout their own personal development. The exchange of the Second Rings often takes place when a civil marriage will coincide with the official marriage. Like the First Ring, the members can allow it to expire, renew the Second Ring, or move to the Third Rings.

Third Rings (Eternal Sealing)

The Third Ring is the most intimate commitment and is equivalent to a renewing of vows and bonds between the lovers' souls on an eternal basis, beyond the First Death. This is the highest of all Vampyre commitment rituals and cannot be broken. The individuals will be bound permanently and almost nothing can break this bond. The Third Ring should only be done when individuals are absolutely sure of themselves, and it is wise to wait after renewals of the Second Ring. Often this is done as a renewal of vows when the two know they are soul mates.

The Breaking of the Rings

The Breaking of the Rings is equivalent to a Vampyre divorce and can be done for either of the first two levels of marriage. This can be done with both individuals present and usually takes place before the expiration of the commitment of a handfasting.

Self-Marriage

Self-marriage is a common tradition amongst Vampyres who are highly individualistic and consciously choose not to have a lifemate. This usually is when the individual performs a Sanguine Mass alone or in a group and then makes their vows in a mirror alone or with a Priest/ess and Magister present.

CHAPTER 8

VAMPYRIC HEALING

The Art of Gathering Energy, when done properly, is the responsible and ethical feeding of human Lifeforce, removing negative and stagnant blockages of energy within the human subtle body. It thus has a beneficial side effect of healing.

—Magister Maelle,
Grande Master of the Ordo Strigoi Vii

Vampyres as healers was covered in previous books of The Strigoi Vii Codex, and we know this comes from the reality of the nature of the Current and from direct interaction and manipulation of subtle energies. Long demonized due to misunderstanding by the mortal world, the Strigoi Vii, as a spiritual being, is thought to only fill the role of a predator; in fact, the Vampyre serves a similar but more evolved purpose in the hierarchy of nature. Subtle skills of healing come naturally to many Strigoi Vii, and the practice of the Taoist healing Qi Gong and Reiki is very common amongst the Family.

Simply by practicing the Art of Gathering Energy, we remove stagnant energies and facilitate the flow of Lifeforce in our donors. In this chapter, we will explore the various modes and techniques of intentional Vampyre Healing, with one example of healing from each of the Pulses of the Currents of Elorath. We will describe how they interact with each other and how to apply with full intent the concept of subtle Healing.

First and foremost, the health and strength, mind and spirit of the individual is the most powerful tool in healing. Placebos have proven to work well, and we have all heard stories of cancer immediately disappearing from a person otherwise doomed to death. The mind and spirit are tied together and reflected in the corporeal body. Unlike Western medical practices, which focus solely on the corporeal body and aim to destroy the symptoms, not the actual ailment, Vampyre Healing thinks globally and seeks to balance the healing of the mind, body, and spirit through healing on the levels of the corporeal, ethereal, astral, and beyond.

An understanding and mastery of one's subtle body and Lifeforce flows are, of course, the prelude before practicing any form of Vampyric healing. The more skilled the Vampyre is at cycling, meditation, grounding, breath work, the geography of the subtle body, and the Art of Gathering Energy, the more prepared the practitioner is to develop Their skills as a healer. One word of warning, subtle healing is not corporeal healing, and this should only be done by a licensed and trained medical care professional. Never will subtle healing techniques, which focus on the ethereal and astral layers of the body, completely replace physical healing, so it is wise and advisable for all Vampyres to train in first aid and CPR.

Not all Vampyres practice healing because they are focused on their own personal Zhep'r, materialistic pursuits, enlightenment, and personal evolution. Those who focus on such techniques truly are in love with the process of furthering and facilitating life and care for those around them.

The Basics

When we think of healing, we think of working on others, but many of these techniques can be done to yourself. The reason we start with learning the facets of healing at the level of Priest/ess is that not only does it require specific skills to be learned beforehand, it also demands a strong sense of energy and the ability to manage it. What you do not want to do is use your own harvested Lifeforce to sacrifice to your subject unless they are in great need. Remember we are focusing on the ethereal body; the astral is much harder to damage because it is so fluid and less dense; this could be equated to trying to damage water or vapor.

Energy healing traditions such as Reiki do not use the energy of the practitioner; rather, they channel and become the universal energies, which have an unlimited source. Without attunement and proper initiation into Reiki (which comes easily to many Vampyres), it is essential not to try to draw upon such energies, or you will often just use your own and become drained and weak. What the Vampyre wants to do is cycle the energy and allow the subject to heal themselves. Whatever purpose of healing you are working on, it is essential at first to read the subject and find out what requires the most attention. This can be done by closing your eyes and simply scanning the etheric body with your hands or touching the back and sending your tendrils over and into their body, letting your senses guide you to what needs the most attention. Be careful to ask permission beforehand and explain exactly what you are doing so there is full consent.

Etheric Wounds

Etheric wounds can be caused by psychic attacks, attachments from subtle entities, and excessive practice of the Art of Gathering Energy. Healing etheric wounds is different from basic healing in that it is important to know exactly what the ailment is and what caused it. Whether you are attempting to remove an attachment or repair damage from psychic attack or a subtle wound, the first step is to diagnose the actual problem and perform a simple reading of the subject. This will determine what needs to be repaired and help you formulate a proper approach to perform the healing. Like an attunement, it is important to prepare a sacred space with a high frequency of energy and proper shields and environment. Such sacred places are as important as any doctor's office.

The more complex the operation, the more secure the sacred space should be. Use many of the same procedures as in the attunement technique to prepare the sanctum. Of course, be grounded and centered and warm up beforehand. Your patient must work with you and be involved in the healing, so consistent communication is essential. The process of healing the wounds should include an awareness of vulnerabilities and potential energy loss.

The Strigoi Vii, like most vampyric beings, have subtle tendrils in their etheric bodies, which can be used as tools akin to a surgeon's knife and needle. These come in extremely handy when cauterizing wounds, sewing subtle wounds, and cutting the etheric body. Perception and, of course, a strong awareness of the etheric are required to truly apply these techniques. Visualization seriously helps with subtle surgery and, in most cases, is required to perform the most complex tasks.

The Trinity Pulses

The Trinity Currents each have different advantages in specific types of healing, as do their attunements. Kitra is most excellent at attunements, which are cleansings to promote flows of energy and remove stagnant energies throughout the subtle body. Mradu are known for their ability to ground, shield, and center individuals. Finally, Ramkht are known to be of most advantage when it comes to removing subtle entities and are known for skill at what we will call "exorcism." Of course, all Strigoi Vii are capable of working with these techniques; it just happens that the frequency of each Current and their interactions with energy usually give an advantage for a specific type of healing.

Attunements (Pulse of Kitra)

These are a form of cleansing which is highly important when there are negative or unhealthy energies within the individual. Such a working can also be used to create and promote a healthy flow of energies within the subtle body such as unblocking clogged chakras and meridians.

Skill with cycling energy within the practitioner's subtle body is essential to learning how to perform an attunement. The Kitra, since they cycle energy on such a high frequency, can best apply this technique with little effort. However, this can be done with tools such as Florida Water, incense, and even salt. One great thing about attunements is that they can be combined with massage or even tantric workings.

Performing an attunement on another does not require physical contact, but it does require the connection of the two etheric bodies. Therefore, it is essential to either touch the subject if they are comfortable with that, or for you to place your hands just a few centimeters above their skin. Of course, it is best to be grounded and centered before working directly and deeply in an individual's subtle body. Performing a banishing before and after in the area where the attunement takes place can also be of great help. Attunements can either be performed with your subject sitting or lying down on a table, bed, or massage table. This will vary depending on the places of the subtle body you wish to affect and the type of attunement you wish to perform.

Once the area has been established for the attunement, it is important to create a phylactery in which to deposit any excess or negative energies taken from the patient. This should be cleansed as a surgeon would a disposal bin after corporeal surgery. Keep in mind to never take any of these energies into yourself because, like bacteria, they can bring afflictions to you as well.

Once you are prepared and the subject is comfortable, the next step is to begin to build up energy in your hands in a similar fashion as the energy ball, not as an evocation but rather as an invocation within your palms. This charge can be combined with physically rubbing your hands together to warm them up. Once this is done, have your subject breathe slowly in through their mouth and out through their nose to create a subconscious cycling within their subtle body. Now with everything prepared, it is time to sync up with the energy of your subject. To do this, you must simply have your hands close enough to have your aura fields overlap and use your etheric tendrils to extend into the subtle body of your patient. The hands should have the fingers closed and angled in a cup-like position for some portions of the attunement, especially when removing blockages. They should be held palms straight and flat when pushing energies off the body.

Start with a warm-up and cycling of the energy within the subject to loosen any stagnant energies and work down their body pulling their energy into your hands. This is basically creating a subtle link but not a deep connection unless you wish to do an advanced attunement. Your goal is to do the cycling, grounding, and centering combination to pre- pare for the more complex portions of the procedure.

Second, begin with the Crown chakra and extend your tendrils into the patient's chakra. You may feel tension with blotches and stagnant energy throughout the body. With your tendrils begin to break up this energy and pull it out of the body and place it in your phylactery. These blotches are actually energy blockages in the subtle body akin to plaque in the arteries of the corporeal body. Simply visualize pulling the energies up and into your hands; the use of a sun ball technique is powerful. This is like using a laser to do surgery. Imagine a ball of fire, which is made from Lifeforce forming in any area where you feel resistance. As the blotches and blocks are broken up, you remove them with your hands like a magnet pulling on metal. This visualization organizes your energy into a format to collect the negative energies. It is wise to use a cycling motion in the little balls of energy to magnetize the energy toward them so that it can be collected in these "sun balls." Of course, there are other forms of visualization that can be employed, like small black holes or vaporous balls of black smoke. Experiment and discover which works best for you. Whatever the case, make sure your visualizations are as simple as possible and do not complicate your work. Your goal is to make energy cycle and flow and remove the negative energies.

Simply repeat with each chakra until you are done, leaving the Solar Plexus for last because it requires special attention and care. When it is approached, it is best never to physically touch this special area if you are making corporeal contact. Focus on the Solar Plexus with the longest duration of time. Be absolutely careful because this affects the rest of the subtle body.

Once the chakras are taken care of, move to the limbs, and as the initial cleansing, begin to use your hands like a broom and push all the energy out through the hands and feet. Focus on the joints as you did with the chakras first, especially the shoulders where the most tension is often centered. These should be dramatic and quick strokes with the use of breath and often the word *ashe*, which refers to life in Santeria. Once the limbs are cleansed, move onto the head and finally the torso, repeating once more the limbs to remove any energies which were pushed from the torso. Remember if you sense additional points on the subtle body which do not have a corresponding corporeal component, take care to read them before making any attunements so as to find their structure of meridians. These are especially common on Magisters and other types of Awakened beings besides Vampyres.

Now that you have actually completed the core work on your subject, it is time to make the break and separate your energies. Step away and visualize your tendrils retracting; shake off any energies that may have stuck to you and perform a cleansing on yourself or have an assistant do so. One great tool to have is Florida Water, which can be used to "sterilize" and cleanse yourself after the attunement. Take a few moments to ground and center yourself to regain a clean separation of energies.

For a few hours or even up to a day after you have finished, the recipient of attunement may feel a strong sensitivity to subtle energies. After a massage, chiropractic technique, or corporeal body cleansing, they should not move quickly; they should relax and allow themselves to get used to the rush of energy. The main benefit of attunement is that the body will respond to a healthier flow of energy and be happier. Of course, it is fine to convert the frequencies of the negative energies afterward and consume the Lifeforce for yourself. Performing attunements on mortals and other Awakened beings is a great and honorable way to practice the Art of Gathering Energy.

Exorcism (Pulse of Ramkht)

Exorcism is the providence of the Ramkht and is most often considered akin to the same term as defined by the Catholic Church. Possession happens more often than one can think, and most of the time is not a powerful being, but a mindless subtle entity. These entities make attachments to the etheric body, usually for parasitic purposes to feed on the Lifeforce of the target. Examples of the most common type of these beings, which must be removed, include parasites, revenants, and lost servitors. Such entities can be drains on the victim, and the loss of energy can affect their mental, physical, and subtle health. Removing them will return the individual to their normal state of energy flow and there will not be a drain.

Rarely are these creatures more intelligent than an animal and thus they are not malicious in their intent, only bent on survival and driven by instinct. One type of these more basic beings that can somewhat be reasoned with are revenants, who are spirits of humans who have become vampiric due to being psychic vampires in life or who have manifested these tendencies after death. Do not confuse revenants with Strigoi Morte; they are stuck and driven on instinct for feeding on Lifeforce. These beings are usually mindless or completely lost and caught between the First and Second Deaths. Due to their lost or mindless state, they have no conception of their past lives and are akin to zombies of myth but are, in fact, just subtle entities.

Most of the time it is not hard to remove the entity; simply showering or directing forceful or unpleasant subtle energy will convince it to leave. Other times they can be distracted with another source of food or even a simple request or etheric slap. However, most times they must be forcefully removed, and this involves using the subtle forces of energy and the tendrils of the Vampyre.

For the best application of removing an attachment, it is important to have the patient relax. Most attachments are from tendrils of the subtle being making links into the subtle body of their host. These must be cut and cauterized in order to not cause damage to the subtle body of the patient. Strigoi Vii who are advanced in ascensions usually can remove most entities on their own, but humans and others who are only slightly Awakened do not have the ability to remove such entities on their own. Most advanced Strigoi Vii will simply convert the entity into a compatible type of energy and consume it as pure Lifeforce. Simply subtle parasites often will be latched on like a tick, with the tendrils and links functioning as the "fangs," which are buried into the subtle body. They can either be suffocated by a shield of Lifeforce or the tendrils and links can be cut by those of the Vampyre. In this case, the entity must be removed, then bonded or banished so that it does not cause harm to the patient or another in the vicinity. This is done by perceiving the subtle entity, locating the connections to the patient, and simply grabbing it like an energy ball and, using the subtle tendrils like a knife, cutting and removing it. Advanced Strigoi Vii can simply touch the entity and absorb it by changing the frequency through the application of their Will.

What is most important in performing this form of removal of such entities is to make sure that the wound is sealed. This is mostly done by the subject, by visualizing as you would any wound and directing Lifeforce to the wound. If the patient is not awakened or not experienced with self-maintenance, the wound must be sealed as described in subtle surgery. Be cautious to sever all of the links attached from the entity to the patient and to remove the energies of the entity, because the pieces of their tendrils may be left in the subtle body and cause a leakage of energy or a wound that continues to affect the subject.

Most advanced beings may be stronger than the Strigoi Vii performing the exorcism, so teamwork may be required to accomplish the exorcism.

More advanced beings may require complex rituals to raise enough energy to release the being. These are often conducted by advanced Strigoi Vii, assistance from other Awakened, a group of Strigoi Vii, or even a request from the Strigoi Morte. This is like a traditional surgery by a group of doctors and nurses performing surgery. The advanced rituals and techniques are kept within the higher mysteries of the Family and are not intended to be released publicly. Ramkht, when performing the more advanced forms of exorcism, may benefit from having a Mradu and a Kitra present to assist in their workings. This will give them an extra grounding from the Mradu and the profound flow of energy from Kitra. With their support, combating and removing a subtle entity becomes much more effective.

If a Strigoi Morte is in possession of a mortal by "skin riding," it is only polite to communicate with them and ask their intentions. It is not wise to ask them to leave because there may be an agenda on a higher level than the Strigoi Vii is privy to, and it may be in the service of promoting the Zhep'r of the Family.

Augmentation (Pulse of Mradu)

Augmentation is the providence of the Mradu Current and is the equivalent of physical therapy or a personal trainer for the corporeal body. Augmentation strengthens the subtle body. This involves a combination of grounding and centering techniques, which the Mradu works upon within the subtle body of the recipient. In order to perform such techniques, the Mradu, of course, must first be fully energized and grounded. They must then sync up with the patient and bring the patient's energy into the same frequency as their own. An augmentation must take place on what the patient will require most aid with. Augmentation Therapy is training a patient's energy to become stronger and help create more powerful shields and centering techniques.

Augmentation for shielding is important if the patient's shields are naturally weak. The practitioner basically can create a protective bubble around the patient and feed Lifeforce into their weaker shields, basically layering a piece of etheric energy around the patient like a cast or armor. This will fade over time, but if the subject is wounded or has to heal from some wounds, this is an excellent tool to have temporary protection in order for the subtle body to heal on its own. The Vampyre forms the protective bubble around the patient by extending their etheric body around the subject's subtle body. Visualization is often used to guide this maneuver, and with the breath, the practitioner guides the energy like a force of light around the subject while forming links between the subtle bodies of both. As the shield becomes stronger, the subtle body of the patient will join in shape with the practitioner, very much like a mold.

The second technique, known as *Raising Vibrations*, would be to focus energy into the patient and sync up with them to bring the patient into vibration with the practitioner. This is done in a way similar to an Attunement, but the focus is on the frequency of the individual's subtle body and then allowing a little Lifeforce to flow into the patient to stimulate the flow of energy. As the injection works, the patient's energy signature will begin to vibrate and emulate the frequency of the healer. The patient should remain lying down or sit comfortably and let the practitioner in by welcoming their energy and lowering any shields they may have up.

The Centering Augmentation technique is of great importance to the Vampyre healer and allows the patient to also learn from the experience. Many times this technique will allow the patient to be more receptive to other forms of healing because their subtle body is more open. Preparing the patient is important, allowing the individual to relax first. An attunement is definitely of huge benefit when using this technique. Like the shielding sync technique, the individual should lie down or sit in a comfortable position.

First, the healer creates a powerful energy ball, which is grounded and centered. The healer then charges it in their hands to a strong point of heat. The healer then syncs up with the patient's subtle body through touch or interacting directly with the subtle body. Followed by this, the ball is injected into the solar plexus of the patient, allowing it to be much like an egg. The healer then brings the breathing of the patient and himself into sync and repetition. As they breathe in and out, the energy ball will grow within the subject and expand and contract to center the individual. This will also aid in centering.

The Grounding Augmentation is done almost like the self-grounding technique. It is most important that augmentation be done as an invocation or evocation. The invocation is when the healer actually places a small portion of their energy into the patient. The evocation is when they simply interact on a subtle level to help train the patient's body to mimic and attune itself to as close a frequency as possible to the healer. With this in mind, a healer must be on a stronger frequency than the patient.

Summation

Listed here are only a few of the most general and basic concepts of Vampyre Healing. The nature of Our healing may not be welcomed by most who are unclear who you are and what you are doing. For some mortals, it is not necessary to tell them what you are; just that you are an energy worker or psychic is enough for them to be open-minded. Sometimes the Art of Gathering Energy will happen naturally. The patient and the healer, the Vampyre, should not be concerned about this because the patient is always interacting with energy. What must be of concern most of all is if the patient begins a one-way draw toward the Vampyre. This can happen in many cases, both intentional and unintentional, such as with psychic vampires. Those of the Current will obviously be more receptive to those who are not of the Family. This is simply caused by the difference of frequencies, but the Strigoi Vii are at an advantage because They are more sensitive to energy work than the average mortal.

CHAPTER 9

ENERGETIC AMPLIFICATION

During the seventh year (I would be fourteen), the two old people led me blindfolded to the mountains of the white tigers. They held me by either elbow and shouted in my ears, "Run. Run. Run." I ran and, not stepping off a cliff at the edge of my toes and not hitting my forehead against a wall, ran faster. A wind buoyed me up over the roots, the rocks, the little hills. We reached the tiger place in no time—a mountain peak three feet from the sky.

—Maxine Hong Kingston,
The Woman Warrior

A mplification is a Vampyric manipulation technique of flowing Lifeforce to various parts of the subtle body, which in turn charges and enhances the corporeal body. This can be used for healing the corporeal of wounds and illness as well as enhancing speed, reflexes, and strength. However, Amplification burns stored Lifeforce rapidly, and if it is not used properly it can result in damage to the corporeal and subtle bodies.

Vampire Myths

Mythical vampires possess superhuman qualities such as enhanced senses, increased strength, and rapid healing, as well as complete mastery over their corporeal bodies. However, such tales are not limited to vampire mythology; even within the mortal world, there are numerous stories of humans temporarily exceeding their normal limitations. Consider, for example, the ubiquitous stories of parents lifting cars off their trapped children after a wreck. There are seemingly endless accounts of people somehow surviving otherwise fatal accidents or situations, such as crime victims who muster the unsuspected strength to fight off their attackers or adventurers who manage to survive under extremes of temperature or privation. Various human cultures have ascribed superhuman powers to dedicants of various mystic paths, from the Yogis of the East to the medicine men of the Native Americans. On a very mundane level, the children's game of *"light as a feather, stiff as a board"* assumes the possibility of mastering the corporeal realm with an application of Will. Such mastery is reflected within the Vampyre reality as Amplification.

The Dayside reality of Amplification is that with a focus of Will both mortals and Living Vampyres can push their physical bodies beyond normal human limits, temporarily overcoming ordinary corporeal restrictions. The human body is an amazing machine! As any mechanical engineer knows, machines, such as cars or computers, can be supercharged in order to achieve enhanced performance. However, such states usually cannot be maintained permanently and will damage the device if sustained over long periods of time. The analogy extends to the human body. People who are reputed to have lifted cars or other heavy objects off trapped victims were acting under the conditions of panic and the associated biological reactions, such as the release of large amounts of adrenaline. Anyone who tried to lift a car on a regular basis would quite seriously injure themselves, even to the point of death!

However, like a machine, the human body can be tuned to its optimum performance and occasionally supercharged when necessary. Just as humans only use a small fraction of their brain capacity, most mortal-minded only access a correspondingly small portion of their corporeal physical capacity. There are notable exceptions, such as Olympic athletes who break world records or the magician and stuntman David Blaine, who, in one of his performances, remained under water for over seventeen minutes. Skilled practitioners of martial arts like karate and Qi Gong are capable of performing feats that would be superhuman from the perspective of the average untrained person. Even more mundane stunts, such as walking on hot coals, are examples of the Amplification of Will over the corporeal body.

Of course, not everyone is physically capable of reaching the same levels of corporeal mastery as a professional athlete or martial artist. However, from the Strigoi Vii perspective, We should all strive to Amplify our full corporeal potential. This includes not only keeping Our corporeal bodies in as good shape as possible, but also remaining aware of and receptive to emerging technologies of transhumanism such as genetic engineering, nanotechnology, and cybernetic implants. We Strigoi Vii have an enormous advantage over most mortal-minded that allows us to more easily corporeally amplify Our full potential. We are able to apply our Will in a focused manner of which humans are simply not capable. As you grow in evolution of Zhep'r, you will find it increasingly easy to Manifest your Will over your corporeal body.

From the Strigoi Vii perspective, Amplification has a Nightside aspect, because when We amplify, We deliberately concentrate Lifeforce and direct it by Our Will to achieve the desired results. These results may Manifest on the corporeal, Etheric, astral, or other planes. Obviously, for the Strigoi Vii Adeptus, amplification is most limited on the corporeal plane because that plane has the greatest number of restrictions from the Morrah perspective. It is always important for the Strigoi Vii Adeptus to be aware of corporeal limitations so as not to injure their physical body. A Strigoi Vii of very slight build would suffer greatly from attempting to Manifest the same corporeal strength as a Strigoi Vii who regularly lifts weights. For this reason, Corporeal amplification should be supported by associated physical training and preparation.

With these cautions in mind, amplification will be most efficient when accompanied by a rational suspension of disbelief. The mortal-minded tendency is to sabotage oneself by devaluing or disbelieving the extent of one's abilities. The Strigoi Vii knows not only that harvested Lifeforce and application of Will can extend Their natural capacity, but also that Their natural capacity is far greater than that suspected by the mortal-minded.

Once the Strigoi Vii has gathered large amounts of Lifeforce and centered their energies and attentions to the desired amplification, They commence the process of Amplification by beginning to bring their gathered Lifeforce and own reserves of vital energy into focus around their solar plexus. Visualization and sincere intent are extremely important here, especially for individuals who are attempting this for the first time. Verbalizations are also contributing factors to those new to amplification. Often the Strigoi Vii will employ an incantation or mantra to focus the Will and empower the amplification.

After the Strigoi Vii has attained a state of strong focus, they should hold in the energy by utilizing breathing techniques. Before releasing the energy into the amplification, the Strigoi Vii must concentrate on the exact form of the amplification. For example, if the Strigoi Vii wishes to amplify increased physical speed, They should imagine the collected energy and Will flowing through their muscles and tendons, increasing their heart rate. They should strongly envision themselves moving like a blur through the corporeal world. To Manifest great physical strength, the Strigoi Vii should visualize their muscles firm as iron and their whole body stable and centered. Only then should the energy be released to fuel the amplification. It is important to realize that the amplification takes place on multiple levels; the ethereal and astral bodies must also be empowered and directed to support the corporeal body beyond its ordinary limits. Thus, amplification is a technique of the Twilight because all levels of the body must harmonize and become one in order to successfully amplify.

The applications of Amplification are virtually unlimited. Along with increasing one's strength and speed, Amplification can also be used to enhance one's corporeal senses.

Amplification is a skill that requires dedicated practice. Like astral Flight, the Strigoi Vii Adeptus may not achieve results at first and may have to make many attempts before accomplishing a successful manifestation of amplification.

Amplification requires a solid foundation in energy work and a strong underpinning of Zhep'r. The Morrah who is experiencing severe difficulty in amplification may want to review the techniques and practices detailed in earlier sections of The Strigoi Vii Codex before continuing with this practice. Eventually, amplification will come naturally, and the Strigoi Vii will be able to manifest increasingly stronger. Some of the Inner Mysteries of the Strigoi Vii include Manifestations such as curing disease and retarding aging; however, these are Secrets of Clavicula Sangraal and shall not be spoken of further here.

Up to this point, we have primarily discussed amplification in the corporeal world. It is essential to practice amplification; this Adeptus skill takes all of your previous energy work and training plus Zhep'r to fully realize. One cannot just suddenly Amplify energy through the Nightside because learning to gather and direct energy is essential with these techniques. Nor will Nightside Amplification work alone without the direction of Will in the Dayside. Such foundations require balance, discipline, and long practice. Eventually, amplification will come naturally, and this one can build on, furthering Zhep'r and resulting in what could be considered superhuman feats. It is best not to perform amplification in front of mortals, except as parlor tricks for your own vampyric entertainment. This can damage their belief structures and cause mental trauma.

Amplification can also be used to increase the corporeal senses, and this requires also gathering into the astral senses and awakening the subtle body. *"Seeing with Five Eyes is better than None,"* a Vampyre said once. Combining and enhancing the subtle senses as well as the corporeal is essential for amplification most efficiently. Often, one sense will need to be focused upon.

Nightside Amplification

Nightside amplification can also be used to supplement Vampyric Self-Healing. This is mainly done through focusing energy into a specific area of the body, such as a limb, organ, muscle or wound for more rapid healing of tissues. Illnesses can also be reduced through amplification of specific defense mechanisms in the body such as the immune system. What is important to note is that when you perform Amplification for self-healing, the illness may seem to increase quickly, but the recovery time is seriously reduced. Never rely on Amplification alone for healing; including mental, spiritual, and corporeal medicines to make a cocktail of workings. Take what is best of each for the most efficient results.

Sex can also be increased with amplification in the same way as any other corporeal application of this technique. Stimulating sexual organs can also increase blood flow to those essential portions of the body. Directing energy into endurance and speed can also increase pleasure for all partners involved. Try it with your lover(s) and see how it works out. Remember always that Nightside amplification is like an adrenaline rush; once it is over, the corporeal body may ignore pain or damage. Taking care and baby steps are important to avoid such damage. Nightside amplification, depending on how far you go, also requires more and more energy. A healthy, disciplined, and well-trained Vampyre who has achieved a high level of Zhep'r and storing energy will be much more efficient. So be forewarned and practice, practice, practice.

Within the three Pulses of the Current, each of the three has special relationships with amplification. Ramkht is often in the most need of this since they usually are developing their own astral skills more, so it can be seen as a supplement for their common lack of physical development. However, increasing their senses is most often their most skilled area. For the Mradu, amplification is almost second nature, since mastering amplification techniques is basically a part of the Mradu Pulse. Mradu are best at increasing strength and endurance through Amplification. In the end, Kitra usually is most adept at amplification due to increased sexuality and agility.

Within the Twilight perspective, amplification during Flight can be extremely empowering. Once OBE is genuinely achieved, the Living Vampyre can look back to the corporeal world through the mirror of the ethereal and manipulate physical objects. Of course, this is the most difficult technique to master and requires enormous reserves of Lifeforce, which require the highest vibrational levels to perform properly. The result of this, if perceived by a mortal, would be traditional poltergeist activities or objects levitating and moving without any source.

Learning to first amplify in the astral is essential because that level of the subtle reality is less dense and more vaporous. Once the amplification and moving of objects and control of the astral body are achieved, it is essential to work backward to the Ethereal and finally out into the astral. Only a small number of Strigoi Morte can amplify into the corporeal, and even fewer Strigoi Vii have been able to achieve this with great success.

An example of Twilight Amplification into the corporeal from a disembodied state can be seen in the 1990 movie *Ghost*. Here, the main character Sam cannot touch anything in the physical until he gets enough energy into his gut during an emotional encounter to affect the corporeal by knocking over a picture frame. Then, after meeting another ghost in the subway who can amplify in short bursts by smashing windows and knocking people over, he goes back to this other ghost and learns how to amplify energy into the corporeal. In summation, amplification is a combination of Will, discipline, skill, and directing energies.

CHAPTER 10
SERVITORS

"It is good thus to try in our imagination to give any form some advantage over another. Probably in no single instance should we know what to do, so as to succeed. It will convince us of our ignorance on the mutual relations of all organic beings; a conviction as necessary, as it seems to be difficult to acquire. All that we can do, is to keep steadily in mind that each organic being is striving to increase at a geometrical ratio; that each at some period of its life, during some season of the year, during each generation or at intervals, has to struggle for life, and to suffer great destruction. When we reflect on this struggle, we may console ourselves with the full belief, that the war of nature is not incessant, that no fear is felt, that death is generally prompt, and that the vigorous, the healthy, and the happy survive and multiply."

—Charles Darwin,
The Origin of Species

S ervitors are artificial thoughforms and elementals created by a magician, mystic, sorcerer, or Vampyre Adeptus that are programmed or attuned to a specific purpose and goal. For centuries humanity has created servitors through pure intent or simply by action. Some mortal magicians chanted or visualized specific energy or purpose until there was adequate energy for the elemental to manifest. Servitors may be added to items to create magickal weapons, sigils, technological wonders (such as robots or even computers), or even words.

Other forms of servitors include the golem in Jewish folklore of the Czech Republic or the Homunculus of alchemy. These corporeal representations are charged with the spirit of intent and desire, energy manifested and infused into an object. Yet some servitors have no corporeal counterpart and remain in the astral as simply an idea for force. Much to the surprise of the Immortal, many humans create servitors and do not even realize what they have done. For the Awakened being, it is important to master this technique.

Strigoi Vii has Their own process of creating servitors, which is attuned specifically to and born from the very essence of Our Current. This system of management and creation can be compared to the servitors of mortal mystics or other Awakened beings. Yet they cannot be controlled by anyone who is not attuned to or born from the Current. If they are not maintained, most servitors are dependent on the Lifeforce of either the host or another individual for whom they are created or one they feed on in a format similar to psychic vampirism. For best results, Vampyre servitors require the skill of creating and charging Vampyre Sigils, thus perfectly suited as a core skill for the Priest/ess. The creation, maintenance, and evolution of servitors is something that is done with a cocktail of Will, intent, Lifeforce or the "Blood of the Vampyre," and a touch of Ambrosia. Servitors can be used for benevolent or malefic purposes, depending on the intent they are programmed with. What must be known first and foremost in dealing with Strigoi Vii servitors is that if they are imbued with Ambrosia, they are attuned and effectively a part of the Current of Elorath.

This results in the reality that they will always go in the interests of Elorath first, before all else and any other programming. Humans and other Awakened beings can create as many servitors as they wish; however, the difference lies in the fact that a Strigoi Vii has the Vampyre Current of Elorath going through them, so any servitor created with their spirit is automatically attuned to the Current, even more so after the proper initiations. If a servitor is created to harm a member of the Family, it will simply not work, or if it is used directly to oppose the Family, the servitor may, instead of following its programmed task, turn on its creator. Thus, a Strigoi Vii servitor will never cause harm or attack another Strigoi Vii, no matter how strong the programming.

More advanced and successful servitors can survive the creator if they pass into the Second Death or can be bound to a human or animal effectively possessing them and creating a "familiar," giving that individual the purpose, tasks, and skills of the servitor. These entities become servants of the Will of Elorath and often come into their own, evolving into entirely different entities than originally conceived.

Creating a Servitor

For the purposes of this chapter, we will begin with the creation of a Minor Servitor, which is the simplest form of servitor. Higher Servitors are far more complex and require months if not years to give birth to, with many even evolving for centuries unless dispersed, destroyed, or extinguished. Some eventually even evolve into egregores or god- forms as they have in the past, moving on to other stories and fostering entirely different movements than one can imagine. Some Magisters of the Strigoi Vii theorize this is how Elorath manifested an egregore, but that is not the purpose of our discussion here.

The creation of Minor Servitors first involves the creation of a simple sigil and imbuing it with intent and purpose. This should be like any basic sigil and will serve as the "skeleton" of the entity. This skeleton sigil is pictorial as Austin Spare, the "father of Sigil magick," called it. These entities for the newer creator should be simple and have a specific purpose. As the Vampyre develops Their skill in creating servitors, the entities that are created can become more and more complex and intricate. This is why such a creation as a Vampyre Servitor must be undertaken with careful planning.

Once the skeleton is created, it is wise to begin to fill the servitor's flesh with life. This is done with feeding the sigil Lifeforce and Ambrosia. This can take a period of time depending on the complexity of the entity, its purpose, and the goals intended. One should be able to create a simple servitor in a few days. Once the initial ceremony of creating the skeleton sigil has been completed, which should only take less than an hour, it must be fleshed out. This is as simple as concentrating on the sigil and, as in the Offering in Communion, feeding it Lifeforce. Eventually, the entity will begin to take form, and through results, you will see it at work. Remember, it is essential that the servitor be maintained, fed, and if it gets out of control, destroyed.

Maintaining a Servitor

Maintaining a servitor is very important because, as vampiric entities, they cannot survive without infusions of Lifeforce from other entities; they cannot generate any on their own. They can either be dependent on the energies of their creator or feed from the Lifeforce of a target's energies or randomly go out and feed. This can be dangerous because a servitor who is not maintained can be a drain on anyone it encounters unless it lies dormant or is destroyed.

Another and greater concern for maintaining a servitor is how We treat them. Like any of the less evolved animals, such as dogs and cats, if you treat them well and give them attention, they will in most cases respond in kind. However, due to Our limited view of the universe and closeness to human perceptions, which is much more linear and hierarchical, they often will gain their own sentience and will, thus turning on their masters. This is often called the Frankenstein syndrome in esoteric circles.

We must see Vampyre Servitors as forms of energy; and energy, when woven together for a specific purpose such as life, evolves on its own. Thus, it is most advantageous and wise to see our servitors as living beings, who have the potential to evolve beyond their original programming. We have seen this in countless science fiction and horror stories, from Frankenstein to 2001: A Space Odyssey. These entities start with the cocktail of their own personality; instincts, Will, and Karma, however, will evolve on their own over time and are in effect a magickal childe of sorts and must be cared for as such. Many times servitors will evolve beyond their initial programming and become their own entities if not destroyed, bound, made appropriately, or controlled properly.

Binding a Servitor

Binding a servitor involves the advanced and complex ability to create a subtle prison for entities and beings through the sheer Will of the Vampyre.

This is an extremely important portion of managing Servitors. Binding can be to a specific location or item either in the corporeal or in the subtle realities. Binding is very different from banishing; it requires a strong intention and a high investment of Lifeforce and Will for more powerful entities. Lower entities such as subtle parasites can easily be bound, while beings with self-awareness and free will are much more difficult. Corporeal components of the ritual can be used but are not necessary if the Vampyre has enough focus and skill in the more subtle realms, especially with visualization.

At the core of this technique is accepting the reality that binding is completely a force of Will, is very aggressive, and is all about the control of one being over another. Most effective bindings work for the weakest of subtle energies such as etheric parasites. These can be bound in a phylactery, which is a physical container that has been charged and named with corresponding etheric and astral equivalents. The danger in binding is that, for whatever reason, if the entity gets loose and understands the concept of resentment, it can become hostile like a zoo animal escaping from a cage. So, it is wise not to try to bind an entity that has a stronger will than your own, or it will possibly seek revenge, possibly even attempting to place a bind on you.

Since binding requires tremendous focus and large amounts of energy, sigils are excellent tools. This can be used as a "seal" for the phylactery or magickal prison created or as an anchor to a specific place.

Most effectively, binding is usefully placed on opposing entities, individuals, or those who are consistent threats. For example, binding an enemy who is hostile to you can be done with a poppet (a doll). This physical representation should be imbued with harvested Lifeforce from the named and as a multilayered physical, ethereal, and astral representation. Then through ritual, beginning with ceremonial techniques in the corporeal, you can echo out the actions to the individual and seal it with a sigil. This should prevent them from specific actions, especially if they are hostile to you or others you choose to name in the sigil.

Subtle entities should simply be bound to a sigil or a phylactery, and this should only be done if they cannot be destroyed or repulsed permanently. For example, subtle parasites and discarded servitors are prime examples of subtle beings who should be bound. More advanced subtle entities will require many more resources and, at times, call for more than one Vampyre to perform the working to raise enough Lifeforce and Will to effectively force the binding.

What is important to note is that bindings are only used as a last resort and not something to be taken lightly. This is especially due to the fact that they must be maintained and watched over. Even the most powerful bindings only last for a period of time and eventually weaken and break down. Entities with strong wills who are aware of what is going on will seek to always escape their bindings and, as mentioned before, will seek out their imprisoner and exact revenge.

Bindings can also be beneficial; for example, binding a servitor to a talisman or magickal tool can give it more life and empower the item. Especially if the servitor is designed to be willing to do so and has a purpose. Such items, even after their corporeal component has been destroyed, can be carried after the First Death. This is why so many ancient cultures bury items with their dead. These talismans and consecrated tools can be of great value to the Strigoi Vii, other Awakened beings, or for beloved Black Swans. Some can even be used as gifts and protective or motivational tools. Such items are often called magickal items and can include chalices, talismans, amulets, clothing, canes, hats, boxes, or containers. The servitor bound to the item gives it life and name.

CHAPTER 11
VAMPYRE MAGICKAL FETISHES

"There are two types of fetishes for Vampyres: magickal fetishes and sensual fetishes. Do not confuse the two."

—Master Maelle,
Grand Magister of the Ordo Strigoi Vii

Vampyre fetishes are not what one might think of as a "sexual fetish"; these fetishes are actually similar to "magickal fetishes," which are corporeal objects that are infused with magickal energies or the Vampyre Current or properties such as talismans, amulets, rods, books, staves, chalices, bells, or weapons.

The concept of fetishism in a spiritual sense was originally used by the Portuguese to refer to objects of religious cults in West Africa. Similar concepts also manifested in almost every religion in the world with such examples as in Ancient Egypt of talismans and amulets, the Holy Cross in Christianity, and poppets in Vodou. Ingredients, or elements, of a fetish can include blood, bone, claws, feathers, gemstones, water, plants, wood, skin, and hair.

What is most important to realize is that these tools for the Vampyre Magician are not just symbols and focuses, particularly on the Dayside perspective. In the Nightside, they function as a carrier that works within the Web of Wyrd to weave and transfer energies. From the Twilight perspective, unlike normal ritual items used by ritual magick and in witchcraft, these are infused with the Current of Elorath, making them specifically useful in Vampyre Magick. They not only are used to direct Will and energy manipulation, but also to direct the Current itself, and so they are a powerful focus and possess symbolic values. Most fetishes are made of materials that amplify energy and are easily able to generate many links of energy.

Fetishes are usually simply made by an individual using the object repeatedly, and thus many links will be made between the user and the object. However, a fetish consecrated and attuned can hold more links and thus can be infused with greater qualities and charged to a higher level. A properly attuned Vampyre Fetish is infused with three levels of energy, including Lifeforce, the energy of the Current, and that of its user. Of course, knowing how to use the item is very important, and those initiated into Strigoi Vii will find greater use from Vampyre Fetishes than someone who is not.

Fetishes that were made of materials, which were once alive, such as wood or bones, will be able to more easily have doubles created in the subtle reality. However, certain minerals, such as iron or silver, are of particular use to a Vampyre and can be used to create items such as ar'thanas which have a stronger astral counterpart.

Consecrating and attuning a Vampyre Fetish will amplify the links the item can immediately possess and how much energy it can channel. For best results, it is beneficial to consecrate and attune an object with a specific individual Vampyre using it; thus, it becomes a sacred item of that individual. Some items can eventually even become a sacred relic within the Family. Such an item usually continues to be connected to the user if they ascend and the corporeal object is tied as a relic and bound to that user even if they Rise to become Undead. Thus, a fetish created for a specific Vampyre will often have the Radiance, or signature, of its bearer within it.

If a fetish is corporeally destroyed, its essence is not necessarily destroyed in the subtle layers of reality. Such energies can be bound to a new item of similar shape through various rituals and energy manipulations.

Psychologically, attunement and consecration of a fetish work to help establish a bond with a specific item, in the end, these are only magickal tools. Like the corporeal body having a double, so do magickal tools; thus, they will be able to be carried forth into the subtle reality. Following are several examples of fetishes used within the Strigoi Vii.

Magickal Weapons & Consecrations

These objects are used in many other systems of magick, including protection, directing energy, binding, cutting subtle energies, and as a symbol of power. Most Strigoi Vii have an ar'thana (known as athame in most mystical systems), which is a black-hilted magickal knife used for ritual and symbolic drawing and for directing Lifeforce. Many Vampyres, most notably Mradu and Vampyre Gentleman, always carry Their own consecrated ar'thana with Them for ritual use, utility, and even to cut Their own food in restaurants. The more They interact with and use their blade, the more attuned it is to Them, as more links are forged.

The Ar'thana Consecration & Blade Blessing

See Black Veil Arthana

This consecration will attune a specific blade to its user. This is often done during a Sanguine Mass, in which the Undead are called forth to offer Their additional blessings and infuse the Current within the item. Psychologically and for energetic purposes, it is wise to cleanse the item of any energies before the ritual is begun so that it is spiritually neutral unless the blade was specifically made for the user. This can be done with salt, incense, or liquids such as Florida Water.

Once the blade has been cleansed, it is time to begin the Communion. In the Invokation, state your intentions to consecrate and attune a new fetish. After your Offering, attune the blade by holding it above the altar to the west or leave it on the altar and push what remaining energies you have into it. Then upon the Recoiling, a part of the Ambrosia from the Strigoi Morte will enter into the blade. This will charge the item. Of course, naming the blade will be a powerful focal point for the item. Another example of consecration might be:

Oh Ancient Ones,
I come forth this night to attune and consecrate a new Ar'thana.
Hear me! For this is a fetish in honor of the Family & Current
and for the Great Work we together Pursue!
Together we will forge this item into the astral.
Let this blade be the symbol of directing
Our Blood, Our Source, Our Current, and Our Immortality.
Hail Elorath!

Once consecrated, the blade will then be attuned with the radiance of the intended Vampyre it is for.

Wands
See Black Veil Wands
Unlike the blade, wands are used for directing Will and most often are made of wood or, for more precise uses, specific materials and crystals.

Grimoires
See Black Veil Grimoires
Also known as Magickal Journals, grimoires are covered in Coming Forth by Day as an important tool for ascension. Also included is a consecration of a grimoire.

Amulets & Talismans
See Black Veil Amulets & Talismans
These objects are often worn as jewelry, particularly necklaces or bracelets; they function with magickal properties such as to bring luck, benefits, or protection to the wearer. Talismans are usually made from organic materials and amulets from minerals or metals. They are often infused and bound with a servitor and thus manifest an identity and personality of their own. They can be made with preprogrammed intentions and are often attuned to and created for a specific individual.

APPENDIX I: ABOUT THE AUTHOR

Photo by Chad Michael Ward

Father Sebastiaan is one of the central personalities of the Vampyre Culture and community (VC) worldwide. He entered the subculture in 1992 and is best known as the Endless Night Vampire Ball Impresario, author of several books including BLACK VEILS "Master Vampyre Edition" and 'Founding Father' of the Sabretooth Clan, Magus in the Ordo Strigoi Vii (OSV) and countless organizations and businesses. He is an avid student of chaos magick, lover of roleplaying games, student of the paranormal, an expert on Vampyre Culture, fascinated by ancient cultures, and devoted to exploring art, music, tradition and history.

Over the three decades in the VC, Father has appeared on a multitude of television programs and networks including Travel Channel's *Ghost Adventures*, A&E, CNN, Discovery Channel, History Channel, National Geographic, USA Up All Night, and MTV's *Oddville*. He was also featured as a central character in the French documentary and book *Vampyres: Reality Is Stranger Than Fiction* by Laurent Courau, as well as Katherine Ramsland, Anne Rice biographer's, book *Piercing the Darkness; Undercover with Vampires in America Today*. In print media he and his projects have had feature articles in *Revolver Magazine, Rolling Stone, Cosmopolitan, The New York Times, The Financial Times, InStyle Magazine, Glamour, Skin Two*, and *Time Out New York*.

Sebastiaan was born in San Diego California, the New York metropolitan area and has lived in Amsterdam, Philadelphia, Los Angeles, Paris, Dubai and Berlin. He now is pursuing his writing career as a gypsy somewhere in the world ona Vampire Adventure.

For more information on Father and his projects please visit

www.fathersebastiaan.com

www.facebook.com/fathersebastiaan

www.instagram.com/fathersebastiaan

www.twitter.com/fatherseb

APPENDIX II: WORKS CITED

The various literary works listed in "Further Reading," following this section, are also all highly recommended reading for Strigoi Vii. You should seek to build a solid foundation in all fields of thought influenced by Our Current, be they poetical, literary, philosophical, psychological, or any other.

Aiken, Conrad. The Jig of Forslin in The Divine Pilgrim. Athens: The University of Georgia Press, 1916, 1949; 39–102.

———. "Preludes for Memnon," Selected Poems. New York: Oxford University Press, 1961, 2003.

The Bible, King James Version.

Blake, William. "All Religions Are One." In The Complete Poetry and Prose of William Blake, David V. Erdman (ed.). Garden City, NY: Anchor Books, 1982; 1–2.

———. "Augeries of Innocence." In The Complete Poetry and Prose of William Blake, David V. Erdman (ed.). Garden City, NY: Anchor Books, 1982; 490–492.

———. "The Four Zoas." In The Complete Poetry and Prose of William Blake, David V. Erdman (ed.). Garden City, NY: Anchor Books, 1982; 300–407.

———. "The Marriage of Heaven and Hell." In The Complete Poetry and Prose of William Blake, David V. Erdman (ed.). Garden City, NY: Anchor Books, 1982; 33–44.

Budge, E. A. Wallace (ed. and trans.). The Egyptian Book of the Dead (The Papyrus of Ani). Brooklyn: A&B Book Publishers, 1994.

Chaucer, Geoffrey. "The Franklin's Tale," The Canterbury Tales. In The Riverside Chaucer, 3rd Edition, Larry D. Benson (ed.). Boston: Houghton Mifflin Company, 1987.

Coleridge, Samuel Taylor. "Christabel." In The Standard Book of British and American Verse, Nella Braddy Henney (ed.). Garden City, NY: Garden City Publishing Company, 1932; 301–319.

Crowley, Aleister. Magick in Theory and Practice. New York: Dover Publications, 1976.

Fitzgerald, Edward. "The Rubaiyat of Omar Khayyam." In *The Standard Book of British and American Verse,* Nella Braddy Henney (ed.). Gar- den City, NY: Garden City Publishing Company, 1932; 438–455.

Gaiman, Neil. "Desire," *The Sandman: Endless Nights.* New York: Vertigo/DC Comics, 2003; 37–56.

H. D. "The Walls Do Not Fall," *Trilogy.* New York: New Directions, 1998; 1–60.

Hesse, Hermann. (Michael Roloff and Michael Lebeck, trans.) *Demian.*

New York: Bantam Books, 1925, 1969.———(Hilda Rosner, trans.). *Siddhartha.* New York: Bantam Books, 1951, 1971.———. (Basil Creighton and Joseph Mileck, trans.) *Steppenwolf.* New York: Bantam Books, 1927, 1963.

King, Dr. Martin Luther. (Marlene Clark, ed.) "Letter from Birming- ham City Jail," *Juxtapositions,* 1st Edition. Boston: Pearson Custom Publishing, 2004, 2005; 95–111.

Lee, Stan. *Amazing Fantasy,* no. 15. New York: Marvel Comics, August 1962.

Le Fanu, Joseph Sheridan. *Carmilla.* In *Vamps,* Martin H. Greenberg and Charles G. Waugh (eds.). New York: BP Books, 1987; 322–420.

Longfellow, Henry Wadsworth. "Hymn to the Night." In *The Standard Book of British and American Verse,* Nella Braddy Herney (ed.). Gar- den City, NY: Garden City Publishing Company, 1932; 432–433.

Lovecraft, H. P. "The Descendent," *The Dream Cycle of H.P. Lovecraft: Dreams of Terror and Death.* New York: Ballantine Books, 1943, 1995; 5–8.

————."The Nameless City," *The Dream Cycle of H.P. Lovecraft: Dreams of Terror and Death*. New York: Ballantine Books, 1943, 1995; 55–65.

Milton, John. "Areopagitica," *Selected Essays of Education, Areopagitica, the Commonwealth*. New York: Kessinger Publishing, 2005; 31–141.

Muller, Max (trans.). Chandogya Upanishad. *sacredscripts/hinduism/upanishads/chandogya.asp*

Nietzsche, Friedrich. *Thus Spake Zarathustra*. In *The Portable Nietzsche*, Walter Kaufmann (ed. and trans.). New York: Penguin Books, 1954, 1976; 112–439.

Nin, Anaïs. *Henry and June: From a Journal of Love*. San Diego: Harcourt, 1966, 1989.

Plato. (Benjamin Jowett, trans.) *The Republic,* vols. 1–3. Buffalo, NY: Prometheus Books, 1986.

Poe, Edgar Allan. "Ligeia," *The Complete Tales and Poems of Edgar Allan Poe*. New York: Vintage Books, 1975; 654–666.

Pope, Alexander. *An Essay on Man in Four Epistles to Henry St. John, Lord Bolingbroke*. West Brookfield: C. A. Mirick & Co., 1843.

Pound, Ezra. (J. P Sullivan, ed.) "Mediaevalism and Mediaevalism (Guido Cavalcanti)," *Ezra Pound: A Critical Anthology*. Harmonds- worth: Penguin Books, 1970; 98–99.

Rand, Ayn. *Anthem*. NewYork: New American Library, 1946.

Rice, Anne. *Interview with theVampire*. NewYork: Knopf, 1976, 1989. Shakespeare, William. *Hamlet*. In *The*

Complete Works of William Shakespeare, William George Clark and William Aldis Wright (eds.). New York: Grosset & Dunlap Publishers, 1911; 1007–1052. ————. "Sonnet 116." In *The Complete Works of William Shakespeare,* William George Clark and William Aldis Wright (eds.). NewYork: Grosset & Dunlap Publishers, 1911; 1302.

Stoker, Bram. *Dracula*. NewYork: Bantam Books, 1981.

Tennyson, Alfred, Lord. "In Memoriam," *Tennyson's Poetical Works (Illustrated)*. Boston: Houghton Mifflin/Riverside Press, 1899; 217–259.
Whitman, Walt. "Song of Myself." In *The Oxford Book of American Verse.*

F. O. Matthiessen (ed.). New York: Oxford University Press, 1950, 1957; 279–253.

Wordsworth, William. "Lines Composed a Few Miles above Tintern Abbey." In *The Longman Anthology of British Literature,* vol. 2, David Damrosch (ed.). New York: Longman, 1999; 328–331.

APPENDIX III: FURTHER READING

AUTHORS NOTE: Here are books suggested by myself, which further expand Zhep'r (understanding) upon the words of power in this book. It is wise to read these books as they are the supporting and source material for this book.

Foundations for Seekers

Black Veils: Master 888 Edition by Father Sebastiaan

The Power of Myth by Joseph Campbell

The Vampire Chronicles by Anne Rice

Vampire: The Masquerade by White Wolf Publishing

Piercing the Darkness by Katherine Ramsland

Vampires Among Us by Rosemary Ellen Guiley

Vampires: The Occult Truth by Konstantinos

The Satanic Bible by Anton LaVey

The Satanic Witch by Anton LaVey

Vampires & Vampirism by Montague Summers

Montague Summers

Jahira – Coming forth by Day

The Book of Dayside Mastery by Temple of the Vampire

The Art of Seduction by Robert Greene

Mastery by Robert Greene

The Rules of the Game by Neil Strauss

The 50th Law by Robert Greene and 50 Cent

The 48 Laws of Power by Robert Greene

The 33 Strategies of War by Robert Greene

Your Beauty Mark: The Ultimate Guide to Eccentric Glamour by Dita von Teese

Psychic Self Defense by Dion Fortune

The Art of War by Sun Tzu

Beyond Good and Evil by Friedrich Nietzsche

Thus Spoke Zarathustra by Friedrich Nietzsche

How to Win Friends and Influence People by Dale Carnegie

Calmae – Coming forth by Night

Energy Work of the Vampyre by Donn Webb

The Vampire Bible by Temple of the Vampire

The Psychic Vampire Codex by Michelle Belanger

Lords of the Left-Hand Path by Stephen E. Flowers, Ph.D.

Liber Null & Psychonaut by Peter J. Caroll

The New Encyclopedia of the Occult by John Michael Greer

MONSTERS by John Michael Greer

Vampires Way to Psychic Self Defense by John Krieter

The Grimoire of Deharan Magick: Kaimana (2005) by Storm Constantine

Morrah – Coming forth by Twilight

The Vampire Predator Bible by Temple of the Vampire

The Vampire Priesthood Bible by Temple of the Vampire

Out of Body Experiences; Quickly and Naturally By: John Kreiter The Way of the Projectionist By: John Kreiter

The Way of the Death Defier By: John Kreiter

The Phase; A practical guidebook for lucid dreaming and out of body travel By: Micheal Raduga

NLP; The Essential Guide to neuro-linguistic programming By: Tom Hoobyar and Tom Dotz with Susan Sanders

APPENDIX IV: LEXICON

Here we present the simplified Strigoi Vii Lexicon. There are notes next to many of the terms. A superscript 1 denotes words specific to the Strigoi Vii "Elorathian" language. A superscript 2 denotes words that originate from other historic or esoteric sources, but which have been modified for SV use. A superscript 3 marks a word that is used by other groups and systems, such as Traditions or occult traditions, but with a different meaning from how it is used by Strigoi Vii.

The terms here are specifically related to the Outer Mysteries, particularly those teachings found within *the Strigoi Vii Codex*.

There are two levels of terminology in this Lexicon: informal and formal. For example, *Mradu* is the formal of "warrior": *Jahira* is formal for an Initiate who has Come forth by Day. The Outer Mysteries present the informal terms first, whilst in the Inner Mysteries the formal is primarily used.

Please note that all words specific to the formal "Strigoi Vii language" are gender neutral, so their English equivalents are sometimes defaulted to male or female at random. For example, a Jahira is just a Jahira; there is no gender. However, sometimes they may be referred to as a Magistra, and sometimes as a priestess, unless they are used to refer to a specific individual.

Special thanks go out to Lilith Madleh, Lucian, Meijin and Maelle for their assistance with this Lexicon.

Abani[1] /aban'nie/—the formal term for being of a certain Halo or legacy.

Ex: Gryphyn abani Gotham Halo.

Abbon[1] /ab'bon/—The formal term for an ally and friend of the Strigoi Vii Family from another Legacy.

Adeptus[2]—the informal term for Morrah.

Adra[1] /od'dra/—the formal term for a mentor or teacher of the Strigoi Vii Mysteries. Adra usually are Magisters or Morrah, but never teach above their level of initiation; for example a Calmae should never teach Morrah teachings.

Aeonic Words[2] –Are Words that support and enhance the overall mindset, belief structures and perpetuation of ideas that define an Aeon. An Aeonic Word typically has a very specific meaning and encapsulates, or titles, a significant supporting teaching that furthers the development of individuals within the Aeon.

Aeons[2] –This term denotes a time period or periods that is notable for a specific type of mindset and energy that affects the actions and belief structures of a large number of individuals. This term originated in Gnosticism. For the Strigoi Vii, our Aeon of Elorath is known as a definitive emanation that came forth from Elorath into the world.

Albion Halo[3]—The first Halo of the United Kingdom, centered in London.

Altar—A physical table in a Sanctum that is used as the center point in ritual.

Ambrosia - The divine and Immortal subtle Blood of the Strigoi Morte, which is exchanged in Communion for Lifeforce. Other similar words in history include *ambrosia, numina,* and *somna.* It is also referred to as the Philosopher's Stone. *See Sorrra.*

Ambient—Excess energy "evaporated" from the subtle body that "radiates" into the surrounding area. This can be tapped as a basic form of Vampyrism.

Ancestors[2]—an informal term for the Strigoi Morte.

Ancients[2]—an informal term for the Elder gods; these are not Strigoi Morte.

Angael Halo[3]—Los Angeles metro area Halo. Includes most of Southern California.

Art of Gathering Energy[3]—The process of harvesting Lifeforce (life-force) radi ated by the human subtle body.

Ardetha[1]—the formal term for Made Vampyres through magick and ritual.

Ar'thana[1] /ar'tana/—The Vampyre term for an athame, a double- bladed, black-handled ritual knife.

Asarai[1] /ass'r'aye/—The formal term for traditional psychic vampires; parasitic mortal-minded or mundanes who have an energy deficiency and must feed from Pranic and emotional energy.

Ascension[3]—The informal term for an Initiation and recognition of completing one Ordeal by coming into being and understanding the teachings of a specific Aeonic Word.

Ascension Festival[3]—The "Vampyre birthday" of a Strigoi Vii Initiate, marking when they took their first steps to Zhep'r. Celebration of this festival is of the individual Initiate's choosing.

Astral Body—The aspect of the Self that exists on the Astral plane.

Astral Plane—The deepest of the outer layers of the subtle planes, where dreams, emotions, and spirits exist.

Astral Projection—Pushing the consciousness into the Astral plane, out of and away from the Corporeal body. Also known as out-of- body experiences or OBE.

Awakening—To come into awareness of one's Vampyre nature and abilities. This is the beginning of the process Strigoi Vii call Zhep'r.

Azralim[1] /azz'rael'im/—The Strigoi Vii formal term "old-school vamps" of Gotham Halo before 1995.

Bast Festival[3]—Lammas, in August, celebrates the primal nature of Our Selves. The Hunt of Bast is enacted during this festival.

Beacon—The Kheprian and psychic vampire term for the equivalent of Radiance.

Becoming—To experience Zhep'r and achieve your potential as a Strigoi Vii.

Bellah[1] /bell'laah/—An old-school formal term for a Prospectii.

Black Flame[2]—The potential within an individual to achieve Zhep'r.

Black Swan[3]—A lover, friend, ally, or donor of a Strigoi Vii who is mortal-minded but supportive and accepting of Strigoi Vii. This term was originally coined by Father Sebastiaan at Long Black Veil in spring 1997.

Black Veils[3]— small words of power which are inspirations and knowledge for Vampyres on a wide range of subjects.

Blood, The[2]—(capital B). The metaphorical term for Lifeforce and the Current of Elorath. *See also* Sanguine.

Blood and Roses[3]—A Strigoi Vii term for a handfasting or wedding ceremony.

Born Vampyres—Individuals who were born awakened to the Vampyre Current. The formal term for this is *Quissain*.

Calling, The[2]—An un-Initiated potential's drive to explore the Mysteries.

Calling—Use of techniques and energy manipulations to pull on links to summon an individual.

Calmae[1] /kal'may/—Understanding of this supporting Aeonic Word reflects a Strigoi Vii Initiate who has Come forth by Night; a Strigoi Vii Soror or Frater.

Carroll, Peter J.—The founder of Chaos Magick and co-founder of the Illuminates of Thanateros (IOT).

Caste—The Kheprian equivalent of Strigoi Vii Pulses, composed of priest (Ramkht), councilor (Kitra), and warrior (Mradu). This term was once used amongst the Strigoi Vii; however, it is now simply called Currents within the Strigoi Vii paradigm.

Centering—An energy work technique in which one moves to the core of the Self and pulls energy into their core; similar but different from grounding.

Chakras—Seven recognized energy centers within the subtle body. Each has a different function.

Chaos—Change, breaking of old ways and energies, and rebirth to new. The Strigoi Vii embraces chaos, an essential aspect of Zhep'r.

Chaos Magick—Originated in the 1970s by Peter J. Carroll, mix ing Discordianism, Thelema, Tantra, Taoism, and Sex Magick. The Chaos Magician is without a fixed paradigm, as they can shift spiritual/reli-gious traditions and systems of magick as one would change clothes.

Coming Forth by Day[2]—the Jahira Ordeal, which is a process of under-standing the Corporeal and material world through the Seven Dayside Principles.

Coming Forth by Night[3]—The Calmae Ordeal leading to an elementary understanding and Gnosis of the Nightside of Strigoi Vii theology and the Ethereal plane of existence.

Coming Forth by Twilight[3]—The Morrah Ordeal leading to an elementary understanding and Gnosis of the Twilight of Strigoi Vii theology and the Astral plane of existence. The Morrah is an adeptus and completed graduation as a fully mature Vampyre.

Coming out of the Coffin—Openly admitting to friends and family that you are a Vampyre. This humorous term originated at Long Black Veil in fall 1997, because MOTHER, the club hosting the event, was a gay club.

Communion[2]—The circuit and exchange of energies in ritual between a Strigoi Vii and the Strigoi Morte. This term is inspired by the Temple of the Vampire concept of Communion.

Conclave—An international meeting of Strigoi Vii.

Corporeal Plane—The physical/tangible world experienced through the five senses.

Councilor—The informal term for an individual ordained into the Kitra Current. This term comes from the Kheprian Order.

Courtly Garb—Clothing with imbedded Strigoi Vii symbolism for use in formal gatherings, masque balls, and special occasions. Often, courtly garb is historic or theatrical in nature.

Crimson Festival[3]—February 14, Valentine's Day. The Crimson Festival celebrates loves past, present, and future.

Crowley, Aleister—"The Great Beast," occult writer, and magus. He inspired much of the occult literature and practice of the twentieth and twenty-first centuries.

Crown Chakra (AK)[1]—The divine chakra, residence of the Dragon, the seat of the Immortal Self, wisdom, will, and balance.

Cult of One[2]—Refers to the individual being their own leader and adhering to their own validated perceptions through experience. One of the Seven Dayside Prinicples.

Current, The[3]—The spiritual "Blood" of the Family.

Current of Elorath[1]—*See* The Current.

Cycling—A technique of energy work in which the Vampyre flows energy through Their body. This aids in sealing and self-cleansing.

Dark Moon—The time of the month when the moon is not visible from Earth. Also known a the New Moon, it is a time of power for the Strigoi Vii.

Dayside[2]—The physical world of the five senses, the physical Corporeal reality of how a Strigoi Vii interacts within the mundane world.

Dayside Festival[3]—Summer solstice, celebrates the Dayside. The Dayside Festival falls on June 20 or 21 in the Northern Hemi sphere, December 20 or 21 in the Southern.

Deep Gathering —A form of the Art of Vampyrism in which the Vampyre penetrates deeply into the subtle body of their donor. If done forcefully or too often, it can cause wounds or permanent damageto the donor's subtle body.

Dragon[2]—The Strigoi Vii term for the higher Self—a symbol of power, fire, mystery, and magick.

Dragon Festival[3]—May Eve/the pagan Beltane, celebrates the higher Self, the Dragon.

Edorsia[1] /ed'or'see'yah/—Regression in Zhep'r caused by ego inflation.

Egregore—A self-aware created spiritual elemental made up of common will, karma, dreams, and agreement.

Elder—An individual who has been active in the Vampyre culture for more than 5 years. However each clan/order/velvet has their own definitions and requirement's for becoming an elder.

Elorath[1] /elle'or'ath/— this Aeonic Word reflects an egregore of the OSV, Sabretooth Clan and Vampyre age of openness to the mundane world.

Endless Night—The annual gathering of the Vampyre and vampires tribes in New Orleans on Halloween and during the Twilight Festival.

Ethereal/Etheric Body—The most solid part of the subtle body, where Lifeforce, auras, and chakras reside.

Ethereal/Etheric Plane—The substructure of reality and Lifeforce (Lifeforce, *Chi, Ki,* etc.). The Ethereal plan is located above the Corporeal and below the Astral. The Ethereal plane can be considered analogous to liquid water, whilst the Corporeal is akin to ice and the Astral to vapor.

Ethical Psychic Vampire—Individuals with an energy deficiency (such as a damaged subtle body) who are aware of and seek to manage their condition ethically through consuming human Lifeforce.

Evokation—Refers to invitations to spirits and entities that are ex- ternal to the summoner.

Excommunication—*See* Sin Nomine.

Ezerix[1] /ezz'are'ix/—The formal term for a metaphysical tattoo of a symbol, sigil or glyph imprinted on the subtle body.

Familiars—Animals that carry the Current of Elorath within their Pranic bodies. They are excellent companions for the Strigoi Vii and can be beneficial in magickal workings.

Family Dentist—*See* Fangsmith. This name for a fangsmith was coined by Lady Vi Johnston of the House of Lilith.

Fangsmith[3]—A specialist craftsperson of custom-made theatrical fangs. This term was coined by the Fangsmith Maven.

Fifth Principle of the Strigoi Vii—The Principle of Secrets. "What happens amongst Vampyres, stays amongst the Vampyres."

Filtering—The ability to filter out negative or harmful subtle energies when gathering or doing energy work.

First Death—The death of the physical/Corporeal body.

First Principle of the Strigoi Vii—Law. Stay within mundane law.

Flight—Astral projection, OBE (out of body exp riences).

Fourth Principle of the Strigoi Vii—the Quest. Find potentials for the Vampyre Current and guide them to the Family.

Gaja[1] /ga'jah/—The formal term for "wannabe" vamps who some- times are immaturely obsessed with and/or contemptuous of Vampyres and Strigoi Vii.

Garb[2]—Attire worn by a Strigoi Vii to enhance the Glamour or for symbolic reasons. This can include courtly garb for formal gatherings, temple garb for Quabal and ritual, and mundane garb for Dayside life.

Glamour[3]—The use of social dynamics, NLP, body language, aesthet- ics, scent, etc., to maneuver through the mundane world. The Outer Glamour is the use of the vampire archetype, often by newer Strigoi Vii Initiates and Ronin.

Grounding—A technique of energy work in which the individual pushes energy out into the ground and finds a sense of calm and stability.

Gnosis—1. To accept and validate spiritual knowledge for oneself. 2. A state of being in meditation.

Gotham Halo[3]—The Strigoi Vii term for the Halo of the New York City metropolitan area.

Grimoire[2]—A personal magickal and spiritual journal used by a SV.

Halo[2]—A designation for a geographic area, such as a large city. *Halo* refers to the large amounts of ambrosia from communion rites and ambient human Lifeforce in these areas due to the large and active population.

Heart Chakra (SA[1])—Emotions, balance of ego, self-love, and self- acceptance.

Hermetic Magick—The most influential form of Western magick, which was inspired by the meeting of Greek and Egyptian systems.

Hyle /high'el/—The Gnostic term for mortal-minded humans, used by the Strigoi Vii to refer to mundanes.

Initiate—An individual who formally Initiates into the Strigoi Vii system of Ordeals and achieves a degree. This can also refer to an individual who has Come forth by Day through understanding of the word Jahira.

Inner Mysteries— Those Initiated to the Inner Mysteries, Magisters, and practitioners of *Clavicula Sangraal* Sorcery and the *Labyrinth of Kaladra*.

Invokation—To summon an entity (spirit, ancient, Ancestor) to possess the subtle body of the summoner.

Ipsissimus—The highest level of Magister Initiation, the Ipsissimus cannot be measured in Ordeals or Initiations. They have spoken an Aeonic Word and it has evolved beyond them causing an impact to the universe.

Jahira[1] /jah'here'ah/—A Strigoi Vii Initiate who has Come forth by Day, I°.

Ka – the Egyptian equivalent of the soul.

Keepers[3]— An of honor guard to Sanctums and guiding the Current.

Kharrus[1] /car'rus/— Ordained Vampyre Priest/sses. Known as the "Chorus of Elorath," these are individuals who exhibit the traits of one of the three Trinity Pulses of Kitra, Mradu, or Ramkht. They are able to preside over the Seven Sacraments and lead group rituals.

Khaskt[1] /kask/—The Strigoi Vii equivalent of negative karma for opposing the Black Veil or the Current.

Klavasi[1]—The formal term for Latent Vampyres. They must be approached respectfully and carefully.

Khem—"The Black Land," a name for Ancient Egypt due to the black soil deposited around the Nile.

Khemetic—A system of Ancient Egyptian magick and religion.

Kheprian— a tradition of psychic vampires from Ohio based on Egyptian theology.

Kitra[1] /Keet'trah/— Word of power / Aeonic word which related to the Junging archetype of the lovers. The formal term for weavers and councilors of the Trinity Current of Elorath. In Hebrew, this means "crowned one."

Knight—A Strigoi Vii who adheres to courtly ideals.

Krere[1]—A formal term for renegade Vampyres who have tasted Zhep'r yet still identify more as a mortal-minded than Immortal-minded.

Latent—An individual who has the Current within their spirit yet does not Awaken until a trigger occurs, such as being fed on, being exposed to the Quest, or a traumatic event takes place. The formal of Latent Vampyre is *Klavasi*.

Legacy[3]—A tradition of vampirism/Vampyrism. *See traditions*.

Legacy Ankh[3]—The sigil of the Black Veils, a bladed ankh created by Master Metal Manipulator D'Drennan in 1996. Originally the Sabretooth Coven Ankh.

Life-force – the vital energy which is life. Also known as Ki, Chi, Mana and Lifeforce.

Links—Connections between Ethereal subtle bodies, often rein- forced over intimate or prolonged contact between two individuals or objects.

Lutetia Halo[1]—The Strigoi Vii Halo of Paris, France. The name comes from the most ancient name of the first settlement where Paris currently stands.

Lycanthropy—The ability/skill to shape-shift the subtle body into a wolf.

Made Vampyre—A concept in which an individual who is not a member of the Family is given the potential of Awakening through a ritual only known to select Magisters. This is known as the "Kiss of Elorath."

Magick—The application of the will over the layers of reality. This spelling was coined by Aleister Crowley to differentiate from stage magic.

Magister/Magistra[2]—An Initiate of the Strigoi Vii Inner Mysteries.

Mentor—To teach another; not a title but an action. *See also* Adra.

Meridians—Energy lines in the Ethereal body, the equivalent of subtle veins and arteries.

Moot[2]—An informal gathering of Strigoi Vii for dinner, cocktails, celebration, or socialization.

Morrah[2]/moor'roy/—The supporting aeonic word and a formal term for a Vampyre Adeptus who has Come forth by Twilight. Means living vampire in Romanian mythology.

Mortal—A mundane, the mundane realm. *See also* Hyle *and* Mortal-Minded.

Mortal-Minded[3]—Individuals who have not Awakened to the po tential of eternity. They are sometimes referred to as *mortals*.

Magus/Maga – within Strigoi Vii this is the term for Magister who has spoken an Aeonic Word or supporting Aeonic Word such as Elorath, Kitra, Mradu, Ramkht, Jahira, Calmae, Mora and Kharrus. This originated with Michael Aquino founder of the Temple of Set when he spoke the word Xeper.

Mradu[1] /mrad'oo/—The Aeonic word for the guardian or warrior aspect of the Current of Elorath.

Mundane[2] or "Danes"—Inhabitants of the normal world, generally un-Awakened to the world beyond the five senses and the subtle real ity. This term was used in the early days of the Sanguinarium and was used by the Renaissance faire "Rennies" to refer to normal people.

Mundane Garb—Clothing for use within the mundane world. Aesthetically chosen according to the situation to subtly enhance the Glamour.

Nietzsche, Friedrich—A German philosopher and Social Darwin- ist who wrote *Thus Spake Zarathustra, Beyond Good and Evil,* and *The Birth of Tragedy.*

Nightside—Focused on the Ethereal plane, this is the subtle, magickal, and spiritual world beyond the Corporeal plane.

Nightside Festival[3]—Winter solstice, celebrates the Nightside. The Long Night Festival falls on December 20 or 21 in the North- ern Hemisphere, June 20 or 21 in the Southern.

Noir Haven[3]—A Vampyrei–run event, usually gothic, fetish, or steam-punk, with a dress code and back room for members of the Family.

Offering—The offering of Lifeforce to the Strigoi Morte in Communion, a most sacred Strigoi Vii act.

Ordeals[2]—Rites of passage within the Strigoi Vii Mysteries to understand the meaning of the words Jahira, Calmae, Morrah, etc.

Ordo Strigoi Vii (OSV)— an invitation- only Initiatory order of Strigoi Vii who set forth a prime example for the Family through actions and deeds. Founded by Father Sebastiaan and Maelle in Amsterdam in 2002.

Outer Circles—Those Initiated to the levels of Prospectii, Jahira, Calmae, and Morrah, including Ronin and Black Swans.

Outer Mysteries—The open secrets published in the *Sanguinomicon and the Mysteries of Prospectii, Jahira, Calmae and Morrah.*

Paradigm—A school of mortal thought, most often a spiritual or religious preference of the individual Strigoi Vii. Examples include Dark Pagan, Chaos, Lilith, Discordian, etc.

Paradigm Shift—The ability for an individual to shift perceptions from one set of beliefs to another.

Posthumanism—*See* Transhumanism.

Lifeforce—The subtle energies, which are vital Lifeforce (*Chi, Ki,* etc.), on the Ethereal plane.

Priest/ess—The informal term for an individual ordained into the Priesthood of Elorath. *See Kharrus.*

Primus[3]—The official title of the founder of the Sanguinarium, Sabretooth Clan and who is also the first Keeper of Elorath.

Principles—The five core ethics of the Strigoi Vii.

Prospectii[3]—A prospective or Seeker who has formally displayed a serious personal interest in Strigoi Vii. This is also known as a Vampyre dedicant.

Prospectus—The prelude book of the *Strigoi Vii Codex,* containing the elementary mysteries of Strigoi Vii.

Psychic Vampire—For traditional, *see* Asarai; for converse, *see* Ethi cal Psychic Vampire.

Pulses—The term for the three aspects and supporting Aeonic Words of the Current of Elorath including Mradu, Kitra, and Ramkht.

Quest of Family[3]—The search for others of our kind to let them know we exist and to provide subtle invitations without force and with respect for free will.

Quissain[1]—the formal term for a Born Vampyre.

Quabal[3]—A private, face-to-face gathering of Strigoi Vii Initiates for ritual, usually held in conjunction with a Moot. This term means "select group" in specific esoteric circles.

Radiance[3]—The energy signature of those who are of the Vampyre Current, a beacon.

Ramkht[1] /rohm'ket/—The formal term for the inspirational and magician pulse of the Current of Elorath. Very similar to Carl Jungs archetype of the Magician.

Recoiling[2]—The receiving of Ambrosia in Communion from the Strigoi Morte.

Regalia— Magicakal tools used within a ritual, such as ar'thana, masks, and rods.

Renegades—The informal term for Krere.

Ronin[2]—An individual who is of the Vampyre Current yet does not use formal Initiations or Ordeals.

Root (NE)[1]—The chakra focused on grounding of the Self, the Elorathian aspect of Mradu.

Sacral (AE)[1]—The chakra associated with the Elorathian aspect of Kitra, the weaver of life, self-gratification, sexuality, and instincts.

Sanctum[2]—A sacred space for the Strigoi Vii to escape the "noise" of the mundane world.

Sanguinarian—A vampire who believes they must drink blood to survive. Not to be confused with a member of the Sanguinarium.

Sanguinarium[2]—The international movement of the Vampyre Culture & Current that came from the Legacy and revelation of the Aeon of Elorath. Not in general use today.

Sanguine[3]—1) Refers to being of the Family, the Current of Elorath; 2) short for a blood-dinking vamp in the online vampire community.

Sanguine Mass—A formalized and ceremonial Communion ritual.

Sanguinomicon[1]—The core texts of the Strigoi Vii Outer Mysteries, also known as the Strigoi Vii Codex.

Sealing—The energy technique of digesting gathered Lifeforce, often combined with cycling.

Second Death—The death of the Ethereal body and release of the KA.

Second Principle of the Strigoi Vii—Responsibility. Strigoi Vii is for adults only, no minors under the age of majority (eighteen in the United States).

Shielding—The ability to block energy or subtle attacks.

Signature—The subtle energetic fingerprint or sense of an individual. Similar to the *Radiance.*

Sin Nomine—To be excommunicated, stripped of name.

Sobriquet[2] /sob'ree'kay/—A specific chosen name to be used within Vampyre Culture, separate from a mundane name and the equivalent of a "call sign" for a pilot and a "magickal motto" in the Hermetic Order of the Golden Dawn.

Solar Plexus (TA)[1]—The chakra that is the center of the Self, the core, the seat of the Dark Flame and Self-empowerment.

Somnisium—Taking a break from being active in the Vampyre Culture and/or vamp community, a sabbatical. This term was coined by Daemonox.

Sorrra[1] /sore'rah/— the old guard term for Ambrosia.

Strigoi Morte[2] /strig'oy mort'a/—Our Ancestors; often called undead, as they have defeated the Second Death and achieved Im mortality. Also known as the Ascended Masters.

Strigoi Vii[2]/strig'oy vee/—The plural translation from Romanian for "living vampire witch," the namesake of the Strigoi Vii Myster ies, teachings, and tradition.

Strigoi Viu—The singular of Strigoi Vii.

Strix—An undead vampiric shrieking bird in Romanian mythology.

Subtle Body—The Ethereal and Astral aspects of the physical body beyond the Corporeal. Also known as the Aetheric Body.

Swan[3]—Short term for a Black Swan. This term originated within the Sanguinarium.

Sympathetic Vampire—A temporary condition of traditional psychic vampirism in which a mundane has been fed on so deeply that their subtle body instinctively engages in an act of vampirism to replenish its depleted Lifeforce.

Synod[2] /sin'odd/—The spiritual and administrative body of the Ordo Strigoi Vii and the architects of the Sanguinarium and keepers of Black Veils.

Temple Garb—Clothing such as robes, masks, and paraphernalia used in ritual, Sanctums, and Quabal.

Tactile—The Art of Gathering Energy as performed through touch.

Techniques—energy manipulations such as shielding, filtering, sealing, cycling, etc.

Tendrils—Cords and links of subtle energy that extend from the Ethereal body. These can be used to tap, gather and absorb energy. Akin to hairs on an arm and are energetic fangs.

Third Principle of the Strigoi Vii —Blood. Advanced Strigoi Vii do not need consume physical blood for the purposes of the Art of Gathering Energy.

Thirst—The "Need" or "hunger" for Lifeforce, which results from Zhep'r and the enhanced frequency of the subtle body.

Throat Chakra (AY)[1]—Power, voice of telepathy, self-expression, voice, and creativity.

Throne Chakra (AH)[1]—The seat of perception and the sixth sense, which sees into the subtle reality. The main chakra of the Ramkht.

Throning[3]—A Calmae exercise of "nothingness," experiencing the Dragon and eternity. This is a Strigoi Vii–specific term.

Thrumanti Halo[2]/through'mant'ee/—The Halo comprising the area of Germany around Essen, Cologne, and Dortmund. Term coined by Ventear.

Tiamantis[1] /tee'a'mont'iss/—The Strigoi Vii term for the Temple of the Vampire, their philosophies, and traditions.

Traditional Psychic Vampire[3]—*See* Asarai. Specifically used within Strigoi Vii and Black Veils.

Traditions – Are paths of esoteric Vampyre/Vampirism such as *Strigoi Vii*, *Tiamantis* (Temple of the Vampire), *Setian Vampyrism* (Order of the Vampyre / Temple of Set), *Aestian* (Kemetic Order of Aset Ka), *Kheprianism* (House Kheperu), *Path of Lylyth*, etc. *See also Legacies.* Some of the names here are the Strigoi Vii names for these traditions.

Traditionalist Strigoi Vii[3]—An Initiate or Ronin who has validated the Strigoi Vii Mysteries almost identically to the ones described in the *Strigoi Vii Codex /Sanguinomicon.*

Transhumanism—Also called posthumanism; to seek conscious personal evolution through science, technology, philosophy, and medicine..

Trinity, The[3]—The term for the three aspects & pulses of the Current of Elorath including Mradu, Kitra, and Ramkht. These are supporting Aeonic Words. *See Pulses.*

Twilight[3]—A balance and equilibrium of the Nightside and Dayside, which Strigoi Vii strive to achieve. This term came from the Temple of the Vampire.

Turning – the point in a Strigoi Vii's life which is a catalyst of their awakening. The Adra is the individual who facilitated the turning point.

Unconscious Vampirism - when an individual has not yet Awakened and is usually unrefined in the skills of the Art of Vampyrism or from a psychic vampire.

Undead—An informal and little-used term within the Ordo Strigoi Vii to refer to the Strigoi Morte, as they are between the First and Second Deaths.

Vampire—The newer spelling of *vampyre*, used primarily in the online vampire community (OVC). Traditionally within Strigoi Vii, this term usually refers to mythical and Hollywood vamps like Dracula and Lestat.

Vampyre—The older eighteenth-and nineteenth-century spelling of *vampire*, used primarily by the Strigoi Vii.

Vampyre Monk - is an ordeal of solitude for internal work and reflection away from the Vampyre Community and the Order. "Socialization is limited and they are silent, often watching from time to time and working on their Zhep'r. See Somisium.

Visual Gathering —The Art of harvesting lifeforce via sight or eye contact.

Warrior—The informal term for an Initiate of the Mradu Pulse of the Current.

Weaver—A primary and informal term for an Initiate of the Kitra Current.

Whisperer[3]—Another term for a Strigoi Morte.

Witch[2]—The informal term for a female Strigoi Vii, not always used.

Xeper—In the terminology of the Temple of Set, this means to "come into being"; it is their equivalent of the Strigoi Vii term *Zhep'r*.

Zadyrere[1]—The formal term for the Outer Mysteries.

Zhep'r[1] /zep'fher/—The SV spelling of *Kheper*, which means to evolve, transform, and become.

APPENDIX V: VAMPYRE ALPHABET

ELORATHIAN ALPHABET

(C) Sanguinarium.net by Aziza Rii

FINIS

Milton Keynes UK
Ingram Content Group UK Ltd.
UKHW052045140824
446844UK00018B/998